THE
Story of Civil Liberty in the United States

By LEON WHIPPLE

GREENWOOD PRESS, PUBLISHERS
WESTPORT, CONNECTICUT

Originally published in 1927
by Vanguard Press, Inc., New York

Reprinted 1970 by
Negro Universities Press
A Division of Greenwood Press, Inc.
Westport, Connecticut

SBN 8371-2198-1

Printed in United States of America

To Albert DeSilver

*A champion of civil liberty, who gave joyously and gen-
erously of his time, money and legal training to
all whose rights were attacked in time
of war and industrial
conflict*

FOREWORD

THIS book was born out of war and ignorance. During the War and post-War years in the United States (1917-1921), the phenomena of conscription and the punishment of conscientious objectors, of the postal censorship, of new laws that sent economic or social radicals to jail for twenty years or more, of the "deportation delirium" challenged liberal-minded men to a new study of the meaning of civil liberty. Their ignorance made them believe that they had only to turn to American history to prove to the prosecuting agents and courts that they were violating our most sacred traditions. They sought the noble precedents of the past with which to confound the present intolerances. They did not know much about liberty or its preservation for they had indolently taken liberty for granted.

But they discovered that we had never enjoyed the full and beneficent liberty of which we had boasted. There were as many precedents for intolerance as for liberty. The events of 1917-1921 were not new. They had all happened before. Certain students of liberty, and the American Civil Liberties Union, then commissioned the author to examine the history of civil liberty in this country, and make a record of the cases that might throw light upon their problem. They wanted to know where our ideals and guarantees of liberty had come from; what they actually meant; and how they had been put in practice in the past. The present grim and sometimes bloody story is the result.

The first step clearly was to define American Liberties as they were conceived when the United States came into being. That definition demanded such fulness that it became a separate volume on the origins and meanings of the constitutional guarantees. The reader is referred to this study for the backgrounds of the present case-record. The record extends from 1776 up to 1917 as the cases since the latter date demand special treatment. The present cases are grouped around the struggles of important minorities, arranged in rough historical sequence. Each chapter opens with a brief explanation of the significance of the period, or group. It was intended to compile a mere case-record, without thesis; but this impartial design was ruined by the cases themselves. They set up their own thesis: that whoever has power, economic or political, enjoys liberty.

If the picture seems disheartening, that is because the author has not had room to point out how liberty has advanced, not through the intervention of constitutions, but by progress in education, by extensions of democracy, by the increase of scientific knowledge, by the growth of religious tolerance, by the advances of labor and of women, and by the general diffusion of social tolerance. In spite of fear and greed, a kind of divine sense of fair-play in common men does give the indestructible truth a chance to prevail.

This book was made possible largely through the generosity of Alexander Fleisher and Albert DeSilver, and the criticism and energy of Roger Baldwin. Each of them expended his philosophy, his experience, and his sympathy to help make these pages true and useful. The author acknowledges his debt with joy. He also acknowledges his indebtedness to Dr. Charles A. Beard, Walter Nelles, and Professor Zechariah Chafee, junior, for counsel in matters of law and history. The services and sympathy of the Board and staff of the American Civil Liberties Union, as well as their patience, have been a constant inspiration. The author and all who have helped will be fully rewarded if this book helps men to love truth and to understand how truth grows.

LEON WHIPPLE.

January 20

CONTENTS

CONTENTS

THE STORY OF CIVIL LIBERTY
IN THE UNITED STATES

CHAPTER I

FIRST INTERPRETATIONS

WHOEVER has power has civil liberty. Any one who has studied civil liberty in the history of the United States must remain convinced of this. Even before there *was* a United States the truth was proven.

The Declaration of Independence is evidence of how few liberties our Colonial forefathers enjoyed as long as the English were in power. The whole pre-Revolutionary struggle was for civil liberty, whether the ancient and inherited rights of the English subject, or the more philosophical "natural rights." The Americans held the tyrant up to high heaven for denying these "inalienable possessions of every human being." But the very day the balance of power began to swing to the Colonists, these libertarians promptly began to deny these "inalienable rights" to their late oppressors, now the new minority —the Tories. And forgetting the very rock of their faith, religious liberty, they later persecuted the Quakers, not for back-sliding, but for acting too literally on the words of Jesus.

For example note how freedom of the press followed the shift in power. In 1722 the Crown government of Massachusetts sent James Franklin—Benjamin's brother—to jail, practically for *lèse majesté:* but in 1754 the Colonial assembly was strong enough to imprison one Daniel Fowle, a Boston publisher, upon suspicion that he had printed remarks derogatory to some members of the people's legislature. Ideal free-

dom of the press existed no more under Colony than under
King. The attitude of the pre-Revolutionists toward abstract
liberty has been thus described:

> The last years of the debate over imperial and colonial
> rights were characterized by a non-legal, but very real
> invasion of the rights of freedom of discussion. The radi-
> cal party became utterly intolerant of open defence of
> the policy of the king and Parliament by its conservative
> opponents. Riotous demonstrations, boycotts, mob vio-
> lence, were directed against the authors or supposed
> authors, of articles and pamphlets which were not agree-
> able to the popular taste. . . . All questions of freedom
> or restraint of the press became subordinate to the supreme
> issue of loyalty or disloyalty to one or the other of the
> contending parties.[1]

By 1765 the Sons of Liberty had been formed, and illegal,
though patriotic, violence against the Tories increased. The
contending parties, especially around Boston, reached a kind
of equilibrium in power in which no liberty survived.

> It was hopeless to appeal to the civil or judicial powers,
> and not infrequently conditions were such as to prevent
> action under martial law. And thus the only recourse
> was the popular administration of justice.[2]

Then came the famous Committees of Correspondence and
of Safety. These were by nature revolutionary, therefore outside of constitutional forms, and voluntarily exchanged civil
liberty for what now is called "direct action." Such revolutionary devices are beside the point in this study, but their success had a lasting influence upon our general and instinctive
American notion that, in emergencies, the popular will is
superior to all constitutional forms. Suffice it to recall what
most Americans do not know, that their Revolution, like all
revolutions, showed small respect for the liberty which furnished texts for orators and manifestos.

But by 1776 we began to have established governments in

states now called "American." This is the beginning of our field. Constitutional guarantees of civil liberty began to take form. Yet almost before the ink was dry on the Virginia "Declaration of Rights," New York, Pennsylvania, South Carolina, and the rest began to disregard the lofty phrases. These paper proclamations preached more than their governments could practice. There was, as usual, no real extension of a novel liberty to the other fellow; no tolerance was offered those held to be enemies of the people. Yet this humorous incongruity between pledge and practice seems, happily perhaps, to have escaped emphasis by both cynic and historian.

Almost at once the infant American commonwealths grasped the axioms which in actual fact determine the exercise of civil liberty. These are stated here for their light on subsequent events. First, whoever has power has liberty. Second, the state will and must exert all its power to preserve itself, *as it is*, regardless of scraps of paper about constitutional guarantees. Third, it is just that this righteous preservation of the state be undertaken by the majority with coercion, whether by votes or by direct action. This preservation is of course undertaken by the most interested, adroit, or audacious fraction of the people that can enforce its private designs while pretending to carry out the will of the whole people. Finally, since war presents the moment at which the state seems most to need this rough-and-ready preservation, war is always invoked to suspend the constitutions. There seems small chance for argument that it is better to preserve the state without a constitution than a constitution without a state! The Revolution very quickly taught the American States this code; and so we direct attention to some violations of civil liberty during this period.

CIVIL LIBERTY IN THE AMERICAN REVOLUTION

The Revolution offered, of course, an excuse for not living up to the theoretical liberty of the Bills of Rights. There is always an excuse. War was everywhere, and war is the final proof of the rule that who has power has liberty. The young governments were weak and self-centered, often without settled seats or efficient officers. Revolutions, moreover, leave no place for the niceties of constitutional procedure; more even than other wars they suspend liberty in favor of the glorified mob, and pure fear. But (and this "but" is the residual conundrum of this volume), if the guarantees are no protection in a crisis, then of what good are they at all? We need them only when attacked.

The chief dissenters from the Revolutionary War were the English loyalists, or Tories. In so far as the Tories were enemy aliens who by word or deed were actively helping the British forces, we need not study their sufferings. They had exchanged civil liberty for the laws of war. But there were also many so-called Tories who for sentimental and economic reasons desired to continue allegiance to their mother country, but did at the same time love the Colonies as their "home," the place where they lived and worked. They did not support the war because they believed relations with the Crown could be adjusted peaceably. They were not traitors in any real sense, but according to their own lights worked for the best interests of both England and the Colonies.

To students of liberty they represent a true minority opinion, entitled, before war came, to tolerance and freedom of discussion, and during the war, at least to the humane treatment accorded the misguided. They received neither, nor were they even allowed to remain quietly neutral. The Tory was no longer protected by the English Constitution save where the English troops held the power; and he got scant protection under the guarantees of the new States. He did not recognize these States, and when he did, got little reward for his abasement. The following is an outline of some of the violations of his liberties:—

Events similar to the New England riots occurred elsewhere. On May 10, 1775, a mob drove Myles Cooper, president of King's College, New York City, who had advocated the Tory cause, by tongue and pen, over the College fence, half-dressed, until he was finally smuggled aboard a sloop bound for England. Later, here, the Committee of Safety disarmed all Tories.

Later, everywhere, there was a general scrutiny of loyalty. First, by associations who circulated documents to be signed by those who approved of their American sentiments. Those who refused to sign suffered informal persecution. Next, formal test laws were passed by which persons had to swear loyalty to the new States. The form ran that the juror testified and declared before the everlasting God and the world that the war of the Colonies was just and necessary, that he would not aid and abet the forces of Great Britain, but would betray all plots and conspiracies, that he renounced all allegiance and obedience to George III, and promised faith and true allegiance to his State.

Many undoubted patriots refused to sign on the ground that it was unnecessary and tyrannical, and those who did might rather have been banished since they got no more toleration than before. Quakers, Dunkards, and others were allowed to affirm instead of swearing—a recognition of the rights of conscience that cost nothing. Failure to sign was followed by political, legal, and civil disabilities; by disarming and imprisonment; by special taxation—one of the oddest cures for disloyalty ever tried. The Tory was early deprived of his vote in every State, and prohibited from holding any office of trust or profit. All legal rights to redress were denied—even the rights of a foreigner. He could neither buy land, nor transfer it; was forbidden to travel or trade with the enemy; and could not serve as a juryman in most States.

The professions had to give proofs of loyalty. Lawyers in New York had to secure certificates. In Philadelphia all teachers in colleges of so-called Tory leanings (generally but peaceful Quakers, bent on being neutral) could be prosecuted for doing their duty. Apothecaries suffered exile, but doctors were spared in one of the Carolinas "for the exigencies of the ladies." The baiting of the professions went on merrily since in some places one-half the fine went to the informer. The Tory was a social leper, and it was only by the greatest sacrifice that he kept up any commercial activity.

The freedom of speech was suppressed, the liberty of the press destroyed, the voice of truth silenced, and throughout the Colonies there was established a lawless power. In April, 1775, of the 37 newspapers, 23 were Whig and only seven or eight for the Crown. Connecticut passed a sedition act declaring that whoever wrote or spoke or by any overt act libelled or defamed Congress or an act of the Connecticut general assembly should be brought to trial, and convicted, be fined, imprisoned, or disfranchised. Massachusetts also had such a statute and Virginia. In South Carolina occurred the inevitable jest of all wars: a Loyalist was reprimanded for calling his dog [sometimes it is a baby] by the name, "Tory." Here the Tories could not pray for the success of the King's arms in their regular ritual, nor speak derogatorily of the currency, discourage the people from supporting the Declaration of Independence, or from raising the Continental Army.

Eight of the thirteen States formally banished certain prominent Tories: in others the threat of violence got the same results. In January, 1776, Congress resolved that the majority of the inhabitants of Queen's County, New York, be put out of the protection of the Colonies. All trade and intercourse with them ceased; they were not permitted to travel or to abide in any part of the Confederacy; no attorney could defend them in any action at law. The States interchanged their exiled Tories and Quakers. The "non-importation societies" controlled the economic life.

The game worked both ways: Loyalist generals offered rewards for American Committeemen, and held up the mails and stole valuable letters to be published by Rivington, the royalist publisher, for the edification of Tory refugees in New York. Even before this, however, the Whigs stopped the mails and took out the letters so that Gage complained that by this means the most injurious and inflammatory accounts of Lexington and Concord had been spread throughout the country because only the Whig stories were circulated.

At first the local committees regulated the Tories; then the military power; finally Congress and the State legis-

latures. The Committees had enormous power. In North
Carolina they could commit persons accused of practices inimical to America, that is, the Revolutionary
party, and even restrain persons trying to leave the
Colonies. Virginia granted them the highest executive
power of pardoning.

After the first year, there was no murderous rioting,
but everything was done, though sometimes roughly, as
if with legal sanction. The Americans were not particularly bloody-minded, the written recantation of a Tory
usually cancelled his offences of opinion (though it did
not restore his property). The Committees of Correspondence based their acts upon the idea that the legality
of the acts depended upon the approval of the majority
of the community. They offered their new creed that
the people ruled. The opinion of contemporaries seems
to be that the extraordinary powers thus placed in the
hands of the executives were not abused. The preservation of a fair degree of social order seems to have been due
to the continued stability of local government developed
in America as nowhere else in the world.

> Charles H. Van Tyne, *Loyalists in the
> American Revolution* (condensed).

Here is proof that the Americans were not interested in
abstract liberty, but in the very practical liberty of winning
a war against their exploiting cousins and King. Of the final
tragedy of the exile of the loyalists we must have only pity.
After the peace the Continental Congress could do little; in
some States, like South Carolina, the legislatures reported in
favor of most of the Tories, and their names were struck off
proscription lists. Elsewhere they were treated with inexcusable hatred. The War of 1812 had been fought before
the laws against the Tories had disappeared from the statute-
books.[3]

NO FREEDOM OF CONSCIENCE FOR QUAKERS IN REVOLUTION

The Quakers suffered many violations of liberty during the
Revolution, some because they were loyalist sympathizers,

others because as pacifists they hated all war. Let us note here that the Quaker has always been the supreme champion of civil liberty. He holds that his first duty is to God, and so he refuses to obey the commands of the earthly state against his conscience. At the same time his conscience forbids using force against the state. Since he never takes up arms, he is not easily gotten out of the way as a rebel or conspirator. This peaceful man must therefore usually be punished point-blank for his sincere scruples against war. Such cruelty is hard to justify (especially in a religious nation based on freedom of conscience!) so that the Quaker has ever been a thorn in the side of authority. In the Revolution, the Friends and certain other sects first presented in any important numbers the problem of the conscientious objector to war. And here, as always, his sufferings were aggravated by the ignorant or intentional confusion of his conscientious objections with treason, espionage, and sedition.

> Refusal to join the militia was early regarded as evidence of Tory sympathies. . . . As the struggle grew fiercer, exemption even on religious grounds was denounced. Heavy fines were imposed for non-attendance in arms at the regular muster. Rhode Island gave exemption on oath, but later amended to demand the hiring of a substitute. The dragging out of the disaffected to serve in the militia is attended with every species of violence and depredation.[4]

The Quakers suffered mob violence. They were attacked for refusing to stop work on a Congressional fast-day, or otherwise to mourn or celebrate with America. Quarterly meetings were forbidden "as centers of plotting against the government." Mifflin who signed the Declaration of Independence was hardly safe in his own city.

Fourteen Friends, having been drafted, were forcibly conscripted and taken to the militia encampment where they refused to partake of provisions or handle a musket. They were finally forced to march in military order, had guns tied to their bodies, and had to stand watch. Three others were kept in Laurelton jail for fifteen months. Two were arrested for aiding the Indians and held under ten pounds bail. In 1778, the fines against them amounted to £9,500, and by the war's end totalled £35,000.

There was the quick perception of war-time that the minds of the young must be bent to patriotism, by force, if reason failed. Pennsylvania passed a law that all school teachers must take the test-oath, and upon the refusal of the teachers to obey for conscientious reasons, many Friends' schools were closed. Some were thrown into jail for non-payment of fines, one fine amounting to £100. In Philadelphia all teachers of Tory sympathies might be prosecuted simply for doing their duty.

The process of proscription began, as against loyalists, with social ostracism. Suspected persons were isolated and ignored, neighbors did not speak, and they became outcasts with none daring to give them food and lodging. Next they were quarantined in their own homes. Third, came arrest. Local committees could issue warrants to confine suspects without bail. The final step was imprisonment in reconcentration camps, or banishment. The following is an example:

"THE VIRGINIA EXILES"

When the British threatened Philadelphia, resolutions against disloyalty were passed. Under cover of these resolutions, the Council—the Supreme Executive Council of Pennsylvania—proceeded to arrest 40 persons, more for the purpose of striking terror into British sympathizers than anything else. There was no trial or even hearing. They were merely hurried into confinement, their houses searched, their desks broken open in search for compromising papers and a parole demanded of them. All the evidence secured against the imprisoned Friends was the minutes of a meeting that contained only general advice not to take part in the Revolution .

They refused to give paroles. A writ of habeas corpus was allowed by Chief Justice McKean which the State authorities chose to disregard. They were ordered deported to Virginia, first to Staunton, then Winchester, and compelled to make the trip on foot. Protests to the Council and then to Congress availed nothing; nor did an appeal to the people of Pennsylvania. During the winter made historic by the suffering at Valley Forge, these resolute martyrs suffered in poor quarters with an insufficient supply of clothing in the cold of the Virginia hills. Two died—Thomas Gilpin of lung trouble from exposure, March, 1778, and later, John Hunt.[5]

> Isaac Sharpless, *History of Quaker Government*
> *in Pennsylvania,* II, 153.

Clearly the State constitutions failed to protect Tory or Quaker. Doubtless there were many other violations of civil liberty, for, whatever theory is preached, war in fact *does* suspend the constitution. But no government can be expected to enforce its liberties to protect its enemies, and since in the turmoil of war it is often difficult to discern precisely who is an enemy, the above cases need not be debited too heavily against the American tradition of liberty.[6] But when the war emergency had passed, a dangerous precedent remained. The nature and devices of the Revolution fixed in the popular mind a conception of the *force majeure* acting for its self-conceived "common good." The basis of democracy is here, so also is the basis of mob rule.

VIOLENCE OVER THE CONSTITUTION

The next significant losses of liberty occurred over the very adoption of the Constitution of the United States. Two days after the Continental Congress had submitted the document to the States, the Federalists in the legislature of Pennsylvania moved for a State convention to consider ratification. To prevent a quorum, nineteen anti-Federalists absented themselves from the Hall. This followed:

> The sergeant-at-arms was sent to summon the delinquents but they defied him, and so it was necessary to adjourn until next morning. . . . Soon after breakfast

next morning two of them were visited by a crowd of
men who broke into their lodgings and dragged them off
to the State House, where they were forcibly held down
in their seats, growling and muttering curses. This made
a quorum, and the State Convention was immediately appointed. . . . Sixteen of the men who had seceded from
the assembly issued a manifesto setting forth the ill-
treatment they had received and sounding an alarm
against the dangers of tyranny to which the new Constitution was already exposing them.

> John Fiske, *The Critical Period of*
> *American History,* 311.

Defeat of the Constitution by Pennsylvania at that time
would probably have killed it. There is irony in the notion
that if Pennsylvania had protected the liberty of these two
citizens, the United States might never have existed.

Later when New Hampshire, the necessary ninth State,
ratified, there was a celebration, July 4, 1788, during which
riots broke out. Rhode Island forgot about freedom of assemblage when a mob of a thousand men, some armed, and
led by a judge of the Supreme Court, compelled a Federalist
meeting to strike out all reference to the Constitution.

The free press suffered, too. *Greenleaf's Political Register*
spoke disparagingly of a Constitutional procession in New
York City. In a few nights, news having been received that
the New York Convention had ratified, the mob attacked the
obnoxious printing office, broke the doors and windows and
destroyed the type.[7] Of course, the Federal guarantees had
not been adopted, but the State bills flourished their promises.

CIVIL LIBERTY UNDER THE CONSTITUTION

The Bill of Rights amendments to the Federal Constitution
were proclaimed on December 15, 1791. From then until
1830 at least came a period of interpretation. What did the
liberty guarantees mean? They did not seem particularly
clear to anybody—nor do they yet! They did not mean the

same thing to different factions, and they did not mean the same thing to anyone very long. There were three general views which have persisted roughly ever since. The conservative wanted them interpreted *legally*, along the English tradition, and not adding many new ideas from the Revolution. The people wanted them interpreted *practically*, as they had been evolved and used in the Revolution, first, as the means of freeing themselves from tyranny, second, as the necessary instruments of self-government. The rare libertarian wanted them interpreted *philosophically*, as an ideal of spiritual and intellectual freedom looking toward the future, and now at least roughly expressed in words.

For a decade nationally, and longer in the States, the conservative group, the Federalists, held power, and so by our axiom one party had liberty. They achieved this by a combination of control of the government, especially the courts, with a process of definition of the guarantees. This process must be examined in some detail.

The Federalists were authoritarian at heart, men of property and power, still largely Englishmen psychologically, and torn between a fear of a dictatorship that would limit them as individuals and a hope of a dictatorship that would establish their class in power. They distrusted the unwashed masses, and doubted the wisdom of an absolute democracy. They designed to conduct the government *for* the people, but *by* certain powerful wise men, acting through politcal parties as a king and his cabinet might act. They might deny liberty, but they would deny it in kingly ways . . . for the good of the subject. Such men dared not accept the Constitutions as original and self-sufficient rules, or the liberty guarantees as meaning what they said. The people would have had *too much* liberty—the word "license" always bobs up here—and might interfere with the statecraft of these superior wise men . . . might even put them out of power and profit. The Constitution really did need interpretation so that its novel theories could be applied to the practical problems of government, and so for years, the Federalists, some moved by a noble ambition to found a great state, others moved by selfish desires to remain in power at the expense of their political opponents, sought to establish behind the Constitution some rule to serve as a check or guide.

The interpreters of the Constitution decided that three elements, roughly intermingled, were the background of the instrument. First, some ultimate law of nature on which all constitutional compacts must be founded; second, a sort of basic system of morals arising out of the Christian ethics and the rights of private property; thirdly, and most largely, the common law of England complicated with ideas of the divine rights of governors, and the inevitability of a state church. By referring the liberty guarantees to this vague "higher sanction" the courts could at once decide things according to their own notion of right, justice, good morals, or expediency. The "law of nature" meant in practice "reason and the general principles of right." It arose partly from the abstract social principles in the Bills of Rights themselves; partly because the judges had to decide what was constitutional, and so postulate as a guide for themselves an *unwritten* constitution covering all matters of right and judgment. They sought to deduce a system of just rules from freedom or equality or happiness, as fundamental conceptions.[8] These indefinite things naturally meant what the judge said they meant— whether he was sincere or time-serving. Alexander Hamilton, as usual, clearly states the main contention: "Such is the general tenor of the Constitution that it evidently looks to antecedent law . . . natural law and natural reason applied to the purposes of society. . . . The courts have applied moral law to constitutional principles." This throws overboard the carefully worded protections of the constitutions, and substitutes court-made "moral law." Since there is no standard "moral law" the judge might give it any content dictated by personal bias, religion, political ambitions, or all other complexes of emotion of reasoning needed to justify his will-to-power. It put the whole thing in the air, with the courts of the party in power as the deciding factor,—a place where ever since a large part of civil liberty has remained.

THE CONSTITUTION VERSUS THE COMMON LAW

When appeals to the "law of nature" or the "moral law" seemed far-fetched and dubious, these interpreters of the Constitutions fell back on the Common Law which indeed they claimed as part of the constitutions. There was a steady struggle to keep the new and broad liberties written into the Bills of Rights by the Revolution from being cramped and weakened by the narrow precedents of the older common law.[9] The common law jurisdiction of the United States was precariously established for a time. Robert Worrall was tried in 1798 for attempting to bribe a commissioner of the revenue, the crime not being then provided against by Congressional act. The opinions of the divided Circuit Court of the Pennsylvania district are worth quoting, not because the case concerns civil liberty, but as a light on the entire question:

> *Chase, justice:* Do you mean, Mr. Attorney, to support this indictment solely at common law? If you do . . . the indictment cannot be maintained. . . . The question does not arise about the power of Congress to define and punish crimes . . . but "Whether the courts of the United States can punish a man for any act, before it is declared by a law of the United States to be criminal?" . . . It is attempted to supply the silence of the Constitution and the Statutes by resorting to the common law for a definition and punishment of the offence . . . but in my opinion the United States have no common law; and consequently no indictment can be maintained. . . . The United States did not bring it with them from England; the Constitution does not create it; and no act of Congress has assumed it. . . . Judges cannot remedy politcal imperfections, nor supply any legislative omissions.
>
> *Peters, justice:* Whenever a government has been established I have always supposed that a power to preserve itself was a necessary and inseparable concomitant. . . . The power to punish misdemeanors is originally and strictly a common law power; of which I think the United States

are constitutionally possessed. It might have been exercised by Congress in the form of a legislative act; but it may also in my opinion be enforced in the course of a judicial proceeding.

United States v. Worrall, 2 *Dallas* 384.

The court, after consultation, sentenced the defendant to three months in prison and to pay a fine of $200.[10] It is clear that civil liberty cannot long endure if the court can disregard all constitutional guarantees and invoke as a part of the jurisdiction of the state, whatever common law doctrine may be needed to satisfy the judge's ideas of "right and reason." Yet for years attacks on liberty were made through common law doctrines drawn from English ideas and conditions,—in the States, upon the right of workers to associate together in what came to be called "unions," and in both States and Nation, upon freedom of the press. The labor cases as generally viewed do not involve civil liberty, unless it is as an aspect of freedom of assemblage. But since these trials marked the beginning of the use of the police power to restrict the activities of the workers, and since the issue is still open, a brief note of the facts is pertinent.

THE CONSPIRACY CASES AGAINST STRIKERS

These prosecutions of laborers for striking, between 1806 and 1843, were conducted under the English common law doctrine of a criminal conspiracy. This involved two concepts descended from the Middle Ages: First that a maximum wage may be fixed by law. Statutes providing such wages had existed since Edward III (Statutes 23). Second, that workers may be compelled to labor. This concept of compulsory work had arisen when in 1349, the Black Death had caused a shortage of labor, and had resulted in the first Statute of Laborers. The combination of these ancient ideas produced the rule that a workman can be forced to work and at a prescribed wage,—which shall be the average or standard rate for his sort of work. Therefore when workers refused to work at the standard wage, and "struck" in an effort to force a raise in wages, they were guilty of a criminal conspiracy at common law. This law was repealed in England in 1824.

Six such prosecutions for criminal conspiracy are recorded against the shoemakers of which four were decided against them. One of them they won and the other, the Pittsburgh case of 1814, was "compromised," the shoemakers paying the costs and returning to work at the old wages! These were the first American court cases against organized labor. The testimony showed that the masters partly financed both the New York and Pittsburgh prosecutions. The indictment in the case of Commonwealth v. Pullis at Philadelphia in 1806, shows how liberty was curtailed.[11]

> George Pullis, et al. . . . not being content to work at the usual prices and rates for which they and other workmen and journeymen, in the same art and occupation were used to work. . . . But contriving and intending unjustly and oppressively to increase and augment the prices usually paid them . . . and unjustly to procure great sums of money for their work . . . did combine, conspire, confederate, and unlawfully agree together that they would not work but at certain large prices and rates . . . more than the prices which had been and were then used to be paid . . . to the damage, injury and prejudice of the masters employing them . . . and of the citizens of the commonwealth generally, and to the great damage and prejudice of other artificers in the said occupation. . . .
> . . . That the said George Pullis, et al. did combine . . . that each and every one of them should and would endeavor to prevent by threats, menaces, and other unlawful means, other artificers, et cetera, from working at the said art, but at certain large prices . . . which they then and there fixed and insisted on being paid for their future work. . . .
> . . . That they unlawfully designing and intending to form and unite themselves into a club and combination and to make and ordain unlawful and arbitrary by-laws,

rules, and orders amongst themselves, and thereby to govern themselves and other artificers . . . and unlawfully and unjustly to exact great sums of money by means thereof, did unlawfully assemble and meet together and unjustly and corruptly conspire . . . that none of them after the first day of November would work for any master or person whatever, who should employ any artificer, etc. . . . or other person who should thereafter infringe or break any or either of the said unlawful rules . . . and that they would by threats and menaces and other injuries prevent any other workmen for working for such a master, and they refused to work at the usual prices, and still do. . . .

The charge of the Recorder, Levy, and the verdict of the jury are thus given:

It (the Common Law) says there may be cases in which what one may do without offence, many combined may not do with impunity. . . . If the purpose to be obtained, be an object of individual interest, it may fairly be attempted by an individual. . . . Many are prohibited from combining for the attainment of it. . . . A combination of workmen may be considered in a two-fold point of view: one is to benefit themselves, and the other is to injure those who do not join their society. The rule of the law condemns both. . . .

The reporter took the verdict down in these words: We find the defendants guilty of a combination to raise their wages. . . . And the court fined the defendants eight dollars each with costs of the suit, and to stand committed until paid.

John R. Commons, *Documentary History of American Industrial Society*, III, 61, 231.

Mayor De Witt Clinton thus stated the doctrine on passing sentence upon the New York cordwainers:

No alteration having been made by our Constitution or laws, the common law of England . . . must be deemed to be applicable and by that law the principles

already stated seemed to be well established. . . . Whatever might be the motives of the defendants or their objects, the means thus employed were arbitrary and unlawful. . . . That they had equal rights with all other
members of the community was undoubted, and they also
had the right to meet and regulate their concerns,
and to ask for wages, and to work or refuse; but that the
means they used were of a nature too arbitrary and
coercive, and which went to deprive their fellow-citizens
of rights as precious as any they contended for. . . .
They were each fined one dollars and costs.[12]

This denial of what has since been called the "right of
association" on the ground that the association was an unlawful conspiracy has continued down to date. It is true that in
1842, in the case of Commonwealth v. Hunt, the Supreme
Judicial Court of Massachuetts did justify the right of workingmen to combine to secure better wages; but the decision
was not complete and final. In modern days the injunction is
used to forbid workers to carry on a strike on the ground that
their conspiracy will result in violations of laws. It is not
based on the medieval statutes of compulsory labor and wage
fixing, but the effect is the same.[13]

THE COMMON LAW AND FREEDOM OF THE PRESS

The second use of English common law doctrines was
against freedom of the press. The doctrines deserve statement,
both for their interest and for their influence on all later
efforts to muzzle the press.

Censorship of the press by authority had ended in England
in 1694, and in America about 1721. Later Blackstone had
defined freedom of the press as the absence of all such previous
restraints on publication. The government, still seeking a
means of controlling printing, turned to prosecutions after
publication, for "seditious libel." What is seditious libel?

In England, seditious libel was to publish orally or
otherwise any word or document with an intention to

bring into hatred or contempt or to excite disaffection against the king and the government and the Constitution of the United Kingdom as by law established, or either House of Parliament or the administration of justice, or to excite British subjects to attempt otherwise than by lawful means the alteration of any matter in Church or State by law established, or to promote feelings of ill-will or hostility between different classes.[14]

Here is clearly a vast and terrible power which those in authority may use to punish almost any opinion which they disapprove. Moreover, the silence induced by a fear of prosecution under such a blanket charter is in itself a potent censorship.

The English doctrine was based on the divine nature of the King and his government. They were superior to the people and so immune from criticism. It was further supported in the dual character of the King as head of the Church as well as of the monarchy. It was therefore possible to prosecute a reflection on the government either as seditious libel or as seditious blasphemy, according as you chose to view the King as the temporal or as the spiritual ruler. Moreover,

There was no need to prove any intention on the part of the defendant to produce disaffection or excite insurrection. It was enough if he intended to publish the blame, because it was unlawful for him merely to find fault with his masters and betters.[16]

In short the people had no right whatever to criticize their government, especially if their words had a bad *tendency*—and "tendency" was to be defined by the government itself.

The enforcement of such a doctrine in the United States would seem impossible and ridiculous. The people *were* the government. There was no divinely anointed king, no state church. The constitutions and government were their own creation to be changed at will. There were supposed to be no classes between which hostility could be excited. Public officers were public servants who by offering themselves for

office invited the public to discuss their merits or demerits
And finally, special guarantee of freedom of speech and of
the press had been demanded and included in the Constitution,
'nd surely this meant more than the mere prohibition of a
.ensorship—which had been abolished in both countries nearly
a century before. To the popular mind, indeed, the guarantee
meant unlimited right of discussion of all public matters.

Despite all this, repeated efforts were made by both Federalists and Republicans to punish their political opponents by
invoking this common law doctrine of seditious libel. There
was even an attempt to revive "seditious blasphemy" to punish
hostile comment on politcal personages. The president was
to be divinely immune like the King.

On of the first tests of the free press clauses was the trial
of Edmund Freeman in Massachusetts, 1791. The decision
in affect simply reaffirmed that the Constitutional guarantees
meant nothing but a declaration of the law as it had been
established for sixty years, with an added prohibibtion of any
possible re-establishment of the censorship.[16]

Republicans were prosecuted too at common law:

> Benjamin F. Bache, editor of the "Aurora," was arrested
> in Philadelphia on June 26, 1798, for "sundry publications
> and republications" of an earlier date which were alleged
> to be libels upon the Executive Department of the United
> States government. . . . Two irreverent citizens of Tren-
> ton were punished for some light remark in regard to
> President Adams, and Anthony Haswell, editor of the
> leading Republican paper of Vermont, for publication of
> an advertisement of a lottery for raising the amount of
> Matthew Lyon's fine.
>
> Frank Maloy Anderson, *Enforcement of the*
> *Alien and Sedition Laws.*

Federalists also suffered. Richard Hildreth in his history
of the United States, (V, 392) says:

> The sickness of Judge Patterson, by leaving Pierpont
> Edwards to sit as sole judge in the Circuit Court of

Connecticut, gave occasion for some remarkable proceedings. Under his instructions, a grand jury, specially selected by the Democratic marshall, found a bill of indictment against Tappan Reeve, one of the judges of the Superior Court of Connecticut, for writing, and against the publisher of the Litchfield paper for printing, an alleged libel against Jefferson. A young candidate for the ministry was also indicted, charged with having spoken disrespectfully of the President in a Thanksgiving sermon. Being arrested thereon, and carried to New Haven, where he had no acquaintances, he was obliged to lie a week in jail before he could obtain bail.

THE ALIEN AND SEDITION ACTS

These common law prosecutions against free speech and free press were not satisfactory because such grave doubt existed as to the common law jurisdiction of the United States. The Federalists therefore induced Congress to make seditious libel a crime. The resulting Sedition Act, with the accompanying Alien and Naturalization Acts, marks the first use by the United States of the emergency of war to pass laws limiting constitutional liberty. No war in reality exisited, though diplomatic relations with France had been broken, and a few "foreign agitators" were abroad in the land.

The laws were political weapons. They were never invoked against alien enemies, or possible traitors, but solely against editors and public men whom the Federalists under President John Adams desired to silence or deport in order to suppress political opposition.

In a word the primary purpose of the acts was to advance the interests of the party in power by restraining the freedom of speech and of the press while enlarging at the same time the scope of the federal judiciary through an implied recognition of its common law criminal jurisdiction.[17]

A later President, Woodrow Wilson, wrote:

The sedition act cut perilously near the root of freedom of speech and of the press. There was no telling where

such exercises of power would stop. Their only limitation and safe-guards lay in the temper and good sense of
the President and the Attorney-General.[18]

THE SEDITION ACT

This act passed the House, 44 to 41, on July 10, 1798.
The Senate finally passed it July 12, and President Adams
approved it July 14. It was to run until March 3, 1801.
Section 1 provided punishment for conspiracies against measures of the government, or to intimidate officers of the government. The important part ran:

> Section 2 . . . That if any person shall write, print,
> utter or publish, or shall cause or procure to be written,
> printed, uttered, or published, or shall knowingly and
> willingly assist or aid in writing, etc. . . . any false,
> scandalous, and malicious writings against the government
> of the United States, or either House of the Congress
> . . . or the President, with intent to defame the said
> government, (etc.) . . . or to bring them into contempt
> or disrepute; or to excite against them . . . the hatred of
> the good people of the United States, or to stir up sedi-
> tion in the United States, or to excite any unlawful com-
> bination therein for opposing or resisting any law . . .
> or any act of the President of the United States done in
> pursuance of any such law, or of the powers vested in him
> by the Constitution . . . or to resist, oppose, or defeat
> any such law or act, or to aid, encourage, or abet any
> hostile designs of any foreign nation, against the United
> States, their people, or government, then such person,
> being thereof convicted before any court in the United
> States having jurisdiction thereof, shall be punished by a
> fine not exceeding two thousand dollars, and by imprison-
> ment not exceeding two years.
> Section 3 . . . That if any person shall be prosecuted
> under this act, for the writing or publishing of any libel
> aforesaid, it shall be lawful for the defendant . . . to
> give in evidence in his defence, the truth of the matter
> contained in the publication charged as a libel. And the

jury shall have a right to determine the law and the fact, under the direction of the court, as in other cases.

United States Statutes at Large, I, 596.

This practically barred comment on the Federalist government, since it was easy for a prejudiced judge to charge a jury that any criticism was "malicious, scandalous, and likely to bring the government into disrepute." An editor could not know in advance from the vague general terms of the law what was "scandalous" or "malicious." Before considering the defects, let us note the companion measure.

THE ALIEN ACT

This provided a means of deporting from the United States opponents of the Administration, especially certain editors of English birth. It applied to *all* aliens, not to enemy aliens. Another statute made special provision for the restraint or deportation of enemy males. (*United States Statutes at Large*, I, 577.) Still another provided for the registration of the entrance of aliens, and extended the residence period for naturalization to fourteen years. The Alien Act proper applied sweepingly to *any* alien against whom the President issued an order . . . and was effective without trial of any sort. All that was needed was the executive ukase. It passed the House 46 to 40 and the Senate concurred. It was approved June 25, 1798.

Section 1 . . . That, it shall be lawful for the President of the United States at any time during the continuance of this act, to *order* all such *aliens* as he shall judge dangerous to the peace and safety of the United States, or shall have reasonable grounds to suspect are concerned in any treasonable or secret machinations against the government thereof, to depart out of the territory of the United States, within such time as shall be expressed in such order. . . . In case any alien . . . shall be found at large . . . after the time limited for his departure, and not having obtained a license from the

President . . . every such alien shall, on conviction, be imprisoned . . . not exceeding three years, and shall never after be admitted to become a citizen of the United States, *provided always* . . . that if any alien so ordered to depart shall prove to the satisfaction of the President, by evidence to be taken before such persons as the President shall direct . . . that no injury or danger to the United States will arise from suffering such an alien to reside therein the President may grant a license . . . to remain within the United States for such time as he shall judge proper, and at such place as he may designate.

United States Statutes at Large, I, 570.

This act was to continue for two years from its passage. It gave the President kingly powers, and has been the inspiration and prototype of all subsequent legislation to exclude or deport from the United States aliens whose political beliefs or social philosophy were not approved by existing authority.

PROSECUTIONS UNDER THESE ACTS

Actual prosecutions under these measures were few. Immediate popular clamor against them made enforcement difficult, so convictions were secured chiefly through the bias and power of the judges. The facts were gathered by Frank Maloy Anderson.

John Adams, writing to Jefferson in 1813, asserted that he had not applied the Alien law in a single instance. This statement was . . . at least technically correct. Yet it should not be supposed that the alien law was entirely devoid of effect nor that the administration refrained entirely and on principle from using it. There are indications, if not proofs, that a considerable number of aliens, anticipating the enforcement of the law, left the country. In at least one instance . . . John D. Burke (an Irishman) . . . the administration made use of the alien law in connection with a prosecution for sedition to drive from the country, as it supposed, an obnoxious alien. In still another instance, that of General Victor Collet, the administration decided to expel him, and it would seem failed to do so only because of his opportune departure from the United States.

SEDITION ACT PROSECUTIONS

There is no evidence to show that President Adams ever personally interested himself in the enforcement of either law. But Pickering, his Secretary of State, the Federal Judges, quite generally, especially Justice Chase, and the Federal district attorneys and marshals were by no means inattentive to the enforcement of the sedition act. . . . As a result of what may be characterized as a fairly systematic effort to enforce the sedition law, proceedings were begun or attempted against one or more persons, in each of the States except New Hampshire and Rhode Island . . . and in the far South and West. . . . There appear to have been about 24 or 25 persons arrested. At least 15 and probably several more, were indicted. Only 10, or possibly 11, cases came to trial. In 10 the accused were pronounced guilty. The eleventh case may have been an acquittal, but the report of it is entirely unconfirmed.

They may be said to fall into four classes. The first includes the proceedings aimed at the leading Republican newspapers . . . the "Aurora" (Philadelphia), the "Examiner" (Richmond), the "Argus" (New York), and the "Independent Chronicle" (Boston). . . . All four were attacked through their proprietors, editors, or chief writers, and that the "Aurora," the ablest, boldest, and most influential, was repeatedly attacked, was probably in a large measure responsible for the belief among the Republicans that a real effort was being made to silence the Republican press.

The second class consists of proceedings aimed at minor Republican papers . . . at least four cases. . . . A third class was of cases not primarily against the press, but against individuals of considerable national or local importance. . . . The fourth class consists of cases against insignificant persons whose acts it is hard to believe could have been of any serious import.

Frank Maloy Anderson, The Enforcement of the
Alien and Sedition Laws.[19]

Several of these cases were dramatic. Matthew Lyon's was perhaps most notable. He was a member of Congress and was called "Scourge of Aristocracy." He suffered both fine and imprisonment, and his residence was sold by lottery to pay the fine. He refused to sign an appeal for his own pardon. The popular attitude is shown in the fact that Lyon was promptly re-elected to Congress. When the final reversal of the movement came years later, his fine was refunded by the United States (July 4, 1840). Thomas Cooper's fine was also refunded (July 29, 1850).

Anthony Haswell and James Thompson Callender, both editors, were tried. Callender's trial took place before Judge Samuel Chase at Richmond, Virginia. The prejudice of this Federalist judge forced Callender's counsel to withdraw from the courtroom, while Chase's charge to the jury was a model of partisan pleading. In Massachusetts, Thomas Adams was arraigned in the Federal Court, October, 1798, and his son Abijah was punished for libellous and seditious publications. This decision sanctioned punishment for a libel against an officer of the government in his official capacity.[20]

Frank Maloy Anderson says of the cases:

> Charges of unfairness were numerous. They turned chiefly upon the alleged packing of juries, the construction of the law by the courts, and the general deportment of the judges at the trials. It is evident from some of the replies made to the judges' charges by the grand juries . . . that they were composed preponderantly, if not exclusively, of Federalists. . . . In the trial juries, some could scarcely be called impartial. . . .
> Charges of unfair construction of the law by the courts had to do chiefly with two matters: (1) the question of the constitutionality of the sedition law; (2) the construction to be placed upon the provision permitting the truth of the alleged libel to be offered as valid defense. Upon the first . . . although they did not altogether refuse to permit discussion on that point, the reports of the trials make it abundantly clear that their

minds were made up and that practically no consideration was given to the arguments against the constitutionality of the law. The value of the provision with regard to the truth depended upon the construction put upon it by the courts. By refusing to distinguish between fact and opinion and by requiring that every item in every allegation should be fully proved the courts would deprive the provision of all value as protection for the accused.

"A WANDERING APOSTLE OF SEDITION"

The greatest sufferer under the Sedition Act was as usual a labor agitator, described as "a wandering apostle of sedition." His punishment shows the constant tendency of the courts to apply such statutes with especial severity to discontented members of the laboring class. Anderson says here:

In October, 1798, there was erected at Dedham, Mass., a liberty pole with the inspiration—"No Stamp Act, No Sedition, No Alien Bills, No Land Tax; downfall to the Tyrants of America, peace and retirement to the President, long live the Vice-President and the Minority; may moral virtue be the basis of Civil government." Some of the citizens arrested Benjamin Fairbanks who had taken a hand in the erection of the pole, which had been brought about by one David Brown . . . the "wandering apostle of sedition". . . .

In March, Brown was arrested, and a number of manuscripts found on him, which, with the liberty pole, became the basis of the sedition charge. . . . During the two preceding years (by his own statement at the trial at which he pleaded guilty) he had been engaged in preaching and writing politics. . . . Judge Chase after examining several witnesses, "that the degree of his guilt might be ascertained," sentenced him to pay a fine of $400 and to go to prison for 18 months . . . a sentence more severe than that against any other person convicted under the sedition law. Brown actually remained in prison fully two years (serving his fine) and was altogether the most grievous sufferer from the law.

. . . The conclusion is that the exceptional severity against Brown was due to a fear of the possible effect of his political activity.

Some of the apparently harmless platitudes which drew upon their author so severe a punishment sound much like the sentiments of a modern soap-boxer:

> They have sold the lands by fraud and without any power derived from the people to justify them in their conduct. . . . Here is one thousand out of five million that receive all the benefit of public property. . . . Indeed all our administration is as fast approaching to Lords and Commons as possible. . . . There always has been an actual struggle between the laboring part of the community and those lazy rascals that have invented every means that the Devil has put into their hands to destroy the laboring part of the community. . . . I never knew a government supported long after the confidence of the people was lost, for the people are the government. . . .

The words of this obscure philosopher and prophet did not have to wait long for fulfilment. The strong oppositon to these laws which had existed since their passage expressed itself decisively in the defeat of the Federalists at the polls in 1800 and the election of Jefferson as President. The Federalists never regained power. Jefferson on assuming office at once pardoned all persons convicted under these laws.[21] He states his view in a letter to Mrs. Adams, July 22, 1804:

> But I discharge every person under punishment or prosecution under the Sedition Law, because I considered, and now consider, that law to be a nullity as absolute and palpable as if Congress had ordered us to fall down and worship a golden image. It was accordingly done in every instance, without asking what the offenders had done, or against whom they had offended, but whether the pains they were suffering were inflicted under the pretended sedition law.
>
> Thomas Jefferson, *Correspondence* IV. 23.

Meanwhile the acts themselves had lapsed by limitation in spite of efforts at their continuance. The many petitions praying for their repeal were referred to a special committee whose report favoring repeal was accepted without action, 52 to 48, on February 25, 1799, when the Federalists by noise and confusion prevented debate.[22]   January 23, 1800 a second effort at repeal was defeated with the help of the Republicans themselves, as the repeal involved allowing the vicious doctrine of common law offenses against the United States to be established. February 21, 1801, "a bill was brought in by the vote of the speaker, for continuing the law in force. . . . This would seem to prove that its friends had been influenced by other motives than a mere desire to silence their opponents. . . . This bill failed on its third reading by a considerable majority."[23]

So ended our first national drama around the principle that those who have power have liberty.

CAN A CITIZEN LIBEL HIS OWN GOVERNMENT?

The constitutionality of the Sedition Act was never passed on by the Supreme Court. The Federalists' argument in its favor was summed up in the "Report of the Committee on Petitions Complaining of the Sedition Act." (February 21, 1799.) This interprets the First Amendment as a restatement of the old Blackstone dictum about the prohibition of censorships, and as merely declaratory of the Common Law to make it more generally known and easily understood. Liberty of the press had never meant the right to the mischievous publication of false, scandalous, and malicious writings against the government. It was argued that while Congress was forbidden to pass any law respecting an establishment of religion, it was only forbidden to pass one that actually *abridged* the freedom of the press. Finally it was argued:—

A law to punish false, scandalous, and malicious writings against the government with the intent to stir up sedition is a law necessary for carrying into effect the

power vested by the Constitution in the government of
the United States . . . because the direct tendency of
such writings is to obstruct the acts of the government,
by exciting opposition to them, to endanger its existence
by rendering it odious and contemptible in the eyes of
the people, and to produce seditious combinations against
the laws, the power to punish which has never been questioned because it would be manifestly absurd to punish
sedition and yet to be void of the power to prevent it by
punishing those acts which plainly and necessarily lead
to it.

This unwritten right to preserve the government is the basis
of all such defences of sedition laws.

Arguments against the constitutionality of the act include
the Virginia Resolutions, by Jefferson, and the Kentucky
Resolutions by Madison.   They declared Congress had no
power over the press.

The people retain to themselves the right of judging
how far the licentiousness of speech and of the press may
be abridged without lessening their useful freedom, and
how far those abuses which cannot be separated from their
use should be tolerated rather than the use be destroyed.
. . . The First Amendment guards in the same sentence
and under the same words the freedom of religion, of
speech and of the press, insomuch that whatever violates
either throws down the sanctuary which covers the others,
and libels, falsehoods, and defamation equally with heresy
and false religion are withheld from the cognizance of
the Federal tribunals.[24]

The Alien Act was likewise claimed to be unconstitutional
in that it deprived a man of liberty without due process of
law, denied a jury trial to the accused in a criminal case, and
transferred the judicial power from the courts to the President,
contrary to the Constitution.   The other States to whom the
Resolutions were submitted refused to act with Virginia and
Kentucky to nullify the laws.   The answer to the Federalists
is perhaps best stated thus:

To those who ask if the federal government be destitute of every authority for restraining the licentiousness of the press and for shielding it against the libellous attacks which may be made upon those who administer it, the reply given was that the Constitution alone can answer that question . . . that no such power being expressly given and such power being expressly forbidden by a declaratory amendment . . . the answer must be that the Federal government is destitute of all such authority. . . . There is no common law. . . . And therefore that government has no power . . . to assume the right of punishing any action because it is punishable in England, or may be punishable in any or all of the States.[25]

We may conclude that the Federalists in power believed in shutting the mouths of their opponents, while Mr. Tucker's party, out of power, believed in the utmost freedom of speech to throw out the party in power. Practically, the people decided the issue at the polls by voting the Federalists out.[26]

STATE SEDITION LAWS

The states have also had their sedition acts. We noted one in Connecticut during the Revolution. (*Supra*, page 6.) New Jersey and other states passed such laws during the first decades of the Union. Tennessee in 1817, passed the following:

Whoever shall be guilty of uttering seditious words or speeches, spreading abroad false news, writing or dispersing scurrilous libels against the state or general government, distributing or obstructing any lawful officer in executing his office, or of instigating others to cabal and meet together, to contrive, invent, suggest, or incite rebellious conspiracies, riots, or any manner of unlawful feud or differences, thereby to stir the people up maliciously to contrive the ruin and destruction of the peace, safety, and order of the Government, or shall knowingly conceal such evil practices, shall be punished by fine and imprisonment at the discretion of the court and jury trying the case, and may be compelled to give good and sufficient security for his or her good behavior during the courts' pleasure, and shall be incapable of bearing any office of honor, trust, or profit in the State government for the space of three years. It shall be the duty of the judge to give this section in charge to the grand jury, and no prosecutor shall be required to an indictment under this section.

Acts of 1865, Chapter 15, section 6663 in
Thompson's Shannon's Code.

The history of this is a good example of how liberty shifts with power, and how sedition laws become the tools of tyranny. This act was repealed in 1859, probably to permit the unbridled discussion of slavery, but it was re-enacted by the carpet-bag State government in 1865, as an instrument by which they might gag the people of the State that had first passed it, and so prevent them even from discussing the conditions of "Reconstruction" which they were then enduring.

This discussion of the losses of liberty through sedition prosecutions should be supplemented by two cases that enlarged American liberty, first by denial of the possibility of treason by words alone; second by denial that there was a common law of the United States.

"NO VERBAL TREASON"

The notion that criticism of the form of government, without actual incitement to rebellion, could be a crime was knocked in the head for nearly a hundred years by the judge and jury in a Pennsylvania case in 1805. On April 23, 1803, at Philadelphia, Joseph Dennie wrote and published this criticism of democracy:

A democracy is scarcely tolerable at any period of history. Its omens are always sinister and its power unpropitious. . . . It is on trial here, and its issue will be war, desolation, an anarchy. No wise man but discerns its imperfections; no good man but shudders at its mysteries; no honest man but proclaims its frauds; and no brave man but draws his sword against its force. The

institution of a scheme of polity so radically contemptible
and vicious is a memorable example of what the villainy
of some men can devise. . . .

For this and similar academic rhetoric Dennie was indicted
as a "factious and seditious person" who was "maliciously
doing" the following terrible things:

> intending to bring into contempt and hatred the
> independence of the United States, the constitution of
> this commonwealth . . . to excite popular discontent
> and dissatisfaction against the scheme of polity . . .
> upon trial in the said United States . . . to condemn
> the principles of the revolution, and revile, depreciate
> and scandalize the characters of the revolutionary patriots
> and statesmen, to endanger, subvert, and totally destroy
> the republican constitutions and free governments of
> the United States, to involve the United States in civil
> war, desolation, and anarchy, and to procure by art and
> force, a radical change and alteration in the principles
> and forms of the said United States and this common-
> wealth. . . .

This list of disasters to follow the above essay shows that
then, as now, the states prosecutors could wield a wicked
pen. Even the pinch-beck rhetoric is found in our modern
indictments. The wisdom of the judge and jury are not
always imitated.

> *Charge of the judge:* Thus it is evident that legislative
> acts, or any branch of the government, are open to public
> discussion; and every citizen may fully speak, write or
> print on any subject, but is accountable for the abuse
> of that privilege. . . It is no infraction of the law to
> publish temperate investigations of the nature and form
> of government. . . . The enlightened advocates of repre-
> sentative government pride themselves in the reflection
> that the more deeply their system is examined, the more
> fully will the judgments of honest men be satisfied that
> it is the most conducive to the safety and happiness of
> a free people. . . . It is true it may not be easy in every

instance to draw the exact distinguishing line. To the jury it belongs peculiarly to decide on the intent and object of the writing . . . leaning to the favorable side where the criminal intent is not clearly and evidently ascertained. . . . If the publication was honestly meant to inform the public mind, and warn them against the supposed dangers in society, though the subject may have been treated erroneously . . . the jury should acquit the defendant.

Verdict: Not guilty.[27]

Respublica versus Dennie, Yeates' Reports, IV, 267.

NO COMMON LAW OF THE UNITED STATES

The idea .that the United States had any common law jurisdiction, especially over seditious libel, was finally killed by the Supreme Court, February 13, 1812. The case arose out of an indictment for libel on the President and Congress of the United States contained in the Connecticut Courant, May 17, 1806, which charged them with having in secret voted $2,000,000 as a present for leave to make treaty with Spain. The judges of the Circuit Court had divided. The Supreme Court decided that—

The only question is whether the court has a common law jurisdiction. Although this question is brought up now for the first time to be settled by this court, we consider it as having been settled long since by public opinion . . . and the general acquiescence of legal men shows the prevalence of opinion in favor of the negative of this proposition.

United States versus Hudson and Goodwin,
7 Cranch 32.

STATE LIBEL LAWS AND FREEDOM OF THE PRESS

Even after the press had been freed form Federal interference, for over a generation two obnoxious doctrines of the English common law which had survived even the Revolution, were invoked in the states to limit the liberty granted by the constitutional guarantees. No one has ever claimed that freedom of the press means the right to injure private persons, even by telling the truth about them, when this served no public good. At least four states declare in their constitutions that men have a natural right to acquire, possess, and protect their reputations.[28] St. George Tucker admits such restrictions on freedom of the press in his admirable definition:

> Liberty of speech and discussion in all speculative matters consists in the absolute and uncontrollable right of speaking, writing, and publishing our opinions concerning any subject, whether religious, philosophical, or political; and of inquiring into and examining the nature of truth whether moral or metaphysical; the expediency or inexpediency of all public measures, with the tendency and probable effect; the conduct of public men, and generally of every subject without restraint except as to *the injury of any other individual in his person, property, or good name.*   (The italics are added.)

Libel laws are not denials of a free press. But two obsolete English doctrines concerning libel did affect the freedom of the press. The first was that the truth cannot be offered as a defense against a charge of libel because in criminal libel the English law once held that "the greater the truth, the greater the libel." The second was that the sole function of the jury was to determine the facts, while the judge was to determine the law. If a writer cannot urge the truth of his words as a justification, but must submit to an interpretation of them by a judge who may be ignorant or partisan, it is clear that the press has a dubious freedom. The right of the jury to judge the law as well as the fact had presumably been established by the Zenger case in New York in 1733; it had been won for England in the Fox Libel Acts, 1792. (32 *George III, c.* 60.) But in fact it was several decades after 1800 before all the states had liberalized these obsolete rules by new ideas of the sphere of free comment, and in many of their constitutions added positive provisions abrogating them.

The most important factor in this advance was the definition of freedom of the press by Alexander Hamilton in his brilliant *Brief in Croswell's Case* before the Supreme Court of New York in 1804. Croswell, a Federalist printer, was indicted for scandalizing, traducing, and vilifying the President, Thomas Jefferson, and for alienating from him the obedience, fidelity and allegiance of the citizens of New York by printing this malicious libel in *The Wasp*—

that Jefferson paid Callender for calling Washington a traitor, a robber, and a perjurer; for calling Adams a hoary-headed incendiary, and for most grossly slandering the private characters of men whom he well knew to be virtuous.

You will note that the Republicans (in power now) are here prosecuting a Federalist editor exactly as their own Republican editors had been prosecuted under the Sedition Act. The only difference is that this is a State prosecution, and that the power has shifted. During the trial, Hamilton laid down these rules:

I. The liberty of the press consists in the right to publish with impunity truth, with good motives, for justifiable ends, though reflecting on government, magistracy, or individuals.

II. That the allowance of this right is essential to the preservation of free government—the disallowance of it fatal.

III. That its abuse is to be guarded against by subjecting the exercise of it to the animadversion and control of tribunals of justice; but that this control cannot safely be entrusted to a permanent body of magistracy and requires the effectual co-operation of a court and jury.

IV. That to confine the jury to the mere question of the publication and the application of the terms, without the right of inquiry into the intent or tendency, referring to the court the exclusive right of

> pronouncing upon the construction, tendency and
> intent of the alleged libel is calculated to render
> nugatory the functions of the jury; enabling the
> court to make a libel of any writing whatsoever, the
> most innocent or commendable. . . .
> Alexander Hamilton, *Works,* VII, 333 to 373.

Hamilton's views of both doctrines were not admitted by
the court, which divided two to two, but created such a
favorable opinion that a declaratory bill as to the law of libel
was introduced into the Assembly by a Federalist member, and
at the next session enacted, only to be defeated by the Council
of Revision composed of the judges and the Chancellor. The
next year, the bill became law. And such, with limitations,
is now the law generally throughout the United States, either
by constitutional provision, legislation, or court decision.[29]
We cannot trace the details of the long struggle to give
this meaning to the guarantees of free speech and press. In
Massachusetts for example, in 1805, the House of Representatives made a report guaranteeing the guarantee,—that is asserting the new liberal doctrines. Yet in 1807 the court held in
Commonwealth v. Clapp (4 *Massachusetts Reports* 163) that
the constitutions merely gave the people the common law
rules under which the truth was no defense. The popular
demand was hearkened to by the Assembly in a declaratory
resolution in 1820, but in 1825 the court in Commonwealth
v Blanding (3 *Pickwick* 304) again denied the Hamiltonian
dicta, upheld the common law, and reasserted Blackstone. In
1826, finally, the liberal doctrine was made law in Massachusetts.[30]
The enlarging conception of freedom of the press as a necessity to democracy is shown in the attitude of the Massachusetts
judges towards privileged comment. In the Clapp case it
was charged that it was not libellous to comment on candidates for office, with the honest intention of informing the
people, and implied that a present incumbent might be regarded as a potential candidate for re-election, and so criticized. In the Blanding case, the judge declared that the truth

could be urged as a defence *only* for public men, and must be told in a decent manner properly to influence the electors' choice.

PROSECUTIONS FOR BLASPHEMY

Freedom of speech and of the press was also restricted by blasphemy prosecutions, based either upon the common law or upon old Colonial statutes which had been preserved by the American states. Many such statutes, some of great severity, had been passed by the theological-minded Puritan. Such prosecutions occurred in several States even as late as 1838. The constitutions had guaranteed religious liberty, and the courts had decided that "at the Revolution, the Episcopal church no longer retained its character as an exclusive religious establishment." [31]   But the fact remains that Christianity was the national religion, and it is held to be the religious basis of the nation in the following case under the common law, tried before Chancellor Kent of New York in 1811.

Indictment: . . . Ruggles was indicted for wickedly, maliciously, and blasphemously uttering and with a loud voice publishing in the presence of divers Christian people, of and concerning the Christian religion and of and concerning Jesus Christ the false . . . and blasphemous words: "Jesus Christ was a bastard and his mother must be a whore."

The defendent was found guilty by the Court of Common Pleas and sentenced to imprisonment for three months and to pay a fine of $500. The opinion of Chancellor Kent on the appeal to the higher court follows:

The reviling is still an offense because it tends to corrupt the morals of the people, and to destroy good order. Such offenses have always been considered independent of any religious establishment or the rights of the church. They are treated as affecting the essential interests of civil society. . . . There is nothing in our manners or institutions which has prevented the application or necessity of this part of the common law. . . . The people of this

State, in common with the people of this country, profess the general doctrines of Christianity . . . and to
scandalize the author of these doctrines is not only in a
religious point of view, extremely impious, but even in
respect of the obligations due to society, in gross violation
of decency and good order. . . .

The free, equal, and undisturbed enjoyment of religious
opinion, whatever it may be, and free and decent discussion on any religious subject, is granted and secured;
but to revile with malicious and blasphemous contempt
. . . is an abuse of that right. Nor are we bound by any
expressions in the constitution . . . either not to punish
at all, or to punish indiscriminately the like attacks upon
the religion of Mahomet or the grand Lama; and for this
plain reason, that the case assumes that we are a Christian people, and the morality of the country based upon
Christianity, and not upon the doctrines or worship of
these impostors. . . . Though the constitution has disregarded religious establishments, it does not forbid judicial
cognizance of those offences against religion and morality,
which have no reference to any such establishment. . . .
This constitutional declaration, noble and magnanimous
as it is, never meant to withdraw religion in general and
with it the best sanctions of moral and social obligations
from all consideration and notice of the law. . . . The
proviso guards the article from such dangerous latitude
of construction when it decrees "that the liberty of conscience hereby granted shall not be construed as to excuse
acts of licentiousness, or to justify practices inconsistent
with the peace and safety of the State." It was all that
reasonable minds could require. . . .

The court are accordingly of the opinion that the
judgment below must be affirmed.

People versus Ruggles, *Johnson's Cases*, VIII, 289.

There are few more humorous decisions in our not unhumor-
ous jurisprudence than Chancellor Kent's edict removing the
Grand Lama from the protection of the constitutional guarantees. Religious liberty plainly meant Christian religious
liberty.

In the course of an argument cn a religious question as a member of a debating association which met for discussion and mutual information, one Updegraph of Pennsylvania uttered the following (December 12, 1821):

That the holy Scriptures were a mere fable; that they were a contradiction and that, although they contained a great number of good things, yet they contained a great many lies.

He was indicted under a statute of 1700 entitled "An Act to prevent the grievous sins of cursing and swearing." Its provision was:

Whosoever shall wilfully, premeditatedly and despitefully, blaspheme and speak loosely and profanely of Almighty God, Christ Jesus, the Holy Spirit, or the Scripture of Truth, and is legally convicted thereof, shall forfeit and pay the sum of ten pounds.

Updegraph was found guilty and sentenced to pay five shillings fine and costs; but on appeal the judgment was reversed on the technical ground of insufficient indictment. The court, however, upheld the blasphemy charge, basing its opinion on a statute of 1662, declaring that:

Christianity—general Christianity—is and always has been a part of the common law of Pennsylvania; not Christianity founded on particular tenets, nor an established church with titles and spiritual courts, but Christianity with liberty of conscience to all men.[32]

THE LAST IMPRISONMENT FOR BLASPHEMY—1838

The most famous of the trials for blasphemy was that of the Reverend Abner Kneeland, who was convicted and sent to a Boston jail in 1838—the last of the blasphemers. Kneeland had been a minister, was a social radical, interested in many reform movements, and was a prolific writer as well as publisher. The indictments were founded on three articles in the free-thought magazine, *The Investigator,* of December 20, 1833, of which Kneeland was editor. The conviction, according to Kneeland, rested wholly upon the following sentence:

> Universalists believe in a god which I do not; but believe that their god, with all his moral attributes (aside from nature itself) is nothing more than a chimera of their own imagination.

The indictment was for blasphemous libel under a law of Massachusetts passed July 3, 1782:

> *Be it enacted,* . . . That if any person shall wilfully blaspheme the holy name of God, by denying, cursing, or contumeliously reproaching God, his creation, government, or final judging of the world, or by cursing or reproaching Jesus Christ or the Holy Ghost, or by cursing . . . the holy word of God . . . the Old and the New Testaments, or exposing any part of them to contempt or ridicule . . . every person so offending shall be punished by imprisonment not exceeding twelve months, by sitting in the pillory, by whipping, or sitting on the gallows with a rope about the neck, or to binding to good behaviour at the discretion of the Supreme Judicial Court before whom the conviction may be, according to the aggravation of the offence.

After many delays, retrials, appeals, and much public discussion, Kneeland was finally sentenced to sixty days in the common jail of the county of Suffolk. Meanwhile Kneeland republished his blasphemous articles, others publicly posted the blasphemous phrase, and still others published similar blasphemies in defiance of Justice Shaw's decision.[33]
The only preceding prosecution under this Massachusetts law was the indictment of a man named Avery in 1795 who was sentenced to be set on the gallows one hour and to be whipped twenty stripes.[34]

STATE PROTECTION OF MORALS

The same shift of the common law doctrine from the danger to religion to the danger to morality, and so to law and order, took place with respect to prosecutions for obscene publications. This was the entering wedge for the governmental control of public morals, afterwards the basis for the post-office department's censorship of the press. It illustrates the slow extension of state control to preserve the common standard of morals from innovations. The assumption of a common law crime to replace the old ecclesiastical crime is shown in the following case where the State of Pennsylvania in December, 1815, prosecuted one Sharpless for exhibiting lewd pictures in private to young men:

Opinion of Tilghman, C. J.:—In England there are some acts of immorality, such as adultery, of which the ecclesiastical courts have taken cognizance from very ancient times, and in such cases, although they tended to corrupt the public morals, the temporal courts have not assumed jurisdiction. . . . Although there was no ground for this distinction in a country like ours, where there was no ecclesiastical jurisdiction, yet the common law principle was supposed to be in force, and to get rid of it punishments were inflicted by the assembly. There is no act punishing the offense charged against the defendants, and therefore the case must be decided on the principles of the common law.

That actions of public indecency were always indictable as tending to corrupt the public morals, I can have no doubt. . . . The law was in Curl's Case (King v. Curl, *I George II, 2 Stat.* 788) established upon true principles. What tended to corrupt society was held to be a breach of the peace and punishable by indictment. The courts are the guardians of the public morals and therefore have jurisdiction in such cases. Hence it follows that an offense may be punishable, if in its nature and by its example it tends to the corruption of morals, although it be not committed in public. . . .

Yeats, J. *concurring:* Where the offense charged . . .

does or may affect every member of the community, it
is punishable at common law. The destruction of morality renders the power of the government invalid, for
government is no more than public order. . . . In such
instances courts of justice are, or ought to be, the school
of morals. . . .[35]

> Commonwealth versus Sharpless, 2 *Seargeant and
> Rawle* 91.

These cases make it clear that the Christian religion was
generally regarded as the religion of the separate States, regardless of how the First Amendment limited the power of
Congress. Kent identifies the Christian religion with civil
society, calling all others "impostors," and all of these judges
assumed that social morals were foundsd in the Christian
creed. The Pennsylvania judge frankly declared that Christianity had always been a part of the law of his State. They
interpreted the religious guarantee as meaning only a protection against any established state church of a special
Christian creed, and as guaranteeing liberty of conscience to
all the varieties of Christian, which the Pennsylvania court
oddly described as "Christianity with liberty of conscience to
all men." There was to be no freedom of act or word that
might undermine general Christianity or the morals founded
on it. Here is the beginning of that censorship of opinion in
the United States based upon "morals," "decency" or "good
order," that is, the morals of those in power!

This ends the first interpretations of freedom of speech
and of the press. This summary of Schofield gives the net
results:

> Reading the original declarations of liberty of the
> press . . . in the light of the then history and without
> reference to judicial opinions, evidently they obliterated
> the English common law test of supposed bad tendency to
> determine the seditious or blasphemous character of a pub-
> lication, and hence obliterated the English common law
> crimes of sedition and blasphemy; shifted the law of
> immoral and obscene publications from the region of

libel to the region of public nuisance; and left standing only the law of defamatory publications, materially modifying that, separating publications as they do into those on matters of public concern and those . . . of private concern, and applying only to the former, and truth being the dividing line between lawful and unlawful publications. . . .

As guardians and expounders of the declarations, the courts are a failure to date. (1912.) They cannot be a success until judges get rid of the notion that the declarations are only declaratory of the anti-Republican English common law of the days of Blackstone, Lord Mansfield, and Lord Kenyon.[36]

THE WRIT OF HABEAS CORPUS

The problem of the suspension of the privilege of the writ of habeas corpus in a war emergency arose twice in this period. The first occasion was the attempted insurrection by Aaron Burr when President Jefferson recommended to Congress that the privilege be suspended for three months. The measure was passed by the Senate, but failed in the House, 113 to 16, January 24, 1807, current events having changed to make it inexpedient. Here is a very clear recognition of the right of the legislature, not the executive, to suspend the privilege of the writ.[37]

GENERAL JACKSON DEPORTS A JUDGE

The war of 1812 offers evidence that war suspends civil liberty. The first great conflict between the military and the civil courts as to the writ of habeas corpus took place at New Orleans when General Jackson not only refused to honor the writ but deported the judge who issued it, and established a military censorship of the press with deportation of friendly aliens.

In December, 1814, the news of the destruction of the gunboats on Lake Borgne by the British, leaving New Orleans open to the enemy, led to a proclamation of martial law. The necessity for this measure seems to have been admitted by every one. On February 19, 1815, Edward Livingstone, who had been detained on the British fleet, returned with a newspaper story received by their admiral, stating that peace had been declared,—as in fact it had been. Two days later *The Louisiana Gazette* printed an article beginning:—"A flag has just arrived from Admiral Cochrane to General Jackson officially announcing the conclusion of peace, et cetera." Jackson at once sent a written order for the insertion of the following contradiction in the next issue:

> Sir: The Commanding General having seen a publication issued from your press to-day, stating that 'a flag has arrived' requires that you will hasten to remove any improper impression which so unauthorized and incorrect a statement may have made. . . . Henceforward, it is expected that no publication of the nature of that herein alluded to and censured will appear in any paper of the city, unless the editor shall have previously ascertained its correctness, and gained permission for its insertion from the proper source.

This letter, which many would declare is a righteous exercise of military censorship in the face of the enemy, was "a very famous document in its day, long stigmatized as an audacious attempt to 'muzzle' the press." The guilty editor replied in print thus:—

> . . . but as we have been officially informed that New Orleans is a camp, our readers will not expect us to take the liberty of expressing our opinion as we might in a free city. We cannot submit to having a censor . . . in our office and as we are ordered not to publish any remarks without authority, we shall submit to be silent until we can speak with safety—except making our paper a sheet of shreds and patches—a mere advertiser for our mercantile friends.

To escape the domination of the General some of the French troops claimed the protection of the French consul. Jackson met this by ordering the consul and all Frenchmen who were not citizens of the United States to leave New Orleans within three days, and not to return to within 120 miles of the city until official news of the peace was published. An indignant protest in French by "A Citizen of Louisiana of French Origin" was printed in *The Louisiana Courier*. It read in part—

> Is it possible that the Constitution and the laws of our country have left it in the power of the several-commanders of military districts to dissolve all at once the ties which united America to the nations of Europe? . . . The President alone has, by law, the right to adopt against *alien enemies* such measures as the state of war may render necessary; and for that purpose he must issue a proclamation. But this is a power he cannot delegate. . . . We do not know any law authorizing General Jackson to apply to *alien friends* a measure which the President himself has only the right to adopt against alien enemies. . . . It is high time the laws should resume their empire; that the citizens of the United States should return to the full enjoyment of their rights . . . the citizen accused of any crime should be rendered to their natural judges, and cease to be brought before special or military tribunals, a kind of institution held in abhorrence, even in absolute governments. . . .

Jackson sent an order demanding the name of the author, who was M. Louaillier, a member of the Legislature. He was arrested by a file of soldiers and imprisoned March 5. His lawyer at once appealed to Judge Dominick A. Hall and a writ of habeas corpus was issued. Jackson was informed that the writ was returnable on March 6, at 11 o'clock A. M. Jackson's retort was this order to Colonel Arbuckle:

> New Orleans, March 5th, 1815
> Seven O'clock, P. M.
> Headquarters, Seventh Military District—
> Having received proof that Dominick A. Hall has been aiding and abetting and exciting mutiny within my camp, you will forthwith order a detachment to arrest

and confine him, and report to me as soon as arrested. You will be vigilant; the agents of our enemy are more numerous than was expected. . . .

Andrew Jackson, Major General Commanding.

General Jackson himself took and kept the writ, giving the court's officer a certified copy. Louaillier was tried before a court-martial on the following charges, *all* based on the above article: exciting to mutiny; general misconduct; being a spy; illegal and improper conduct; disobedience to orders; writing a wilful and corrupt libel against the General; unsoldierly conduct; violation of a general order. On March 11 Jackson sent Judge Hall out of the city and set him at liberty, not to return until peace was regularly proclaimed. Peace was proclaimed two days later, when Hall returned and Louaillier was released. On March 22 in the United States District court it was ordered that—

the said Major General Jackson show cause on the 24th instant why an attachment should not be issued against him for contempt of court in having disrespectfully wrested from the clerk aforesaid an original order of the honorable judge of this court. . . ."

On March 24 the court refused to receive a paper from Jackson's representative, and ordered the General to appear March 31, which he did. Such a tumult arose that the judge directed the marshal to adjourn court, whereupon Jackson interfered and declared that he would protect the exercise of justice. The General refused to answer questions other than in the paper he had submitted, and the court sentenced him to pay $1000 fine.

The Acting Secretary of War wrote, April 12, 1815:

From these representations it would appear that the judicial power of the United States has been resisted, the liberty of the press has been suspended, and the consul and subjects of a friendly government have been exposed to great inconvenience by the exercise of military force and command. . . . The President is persuaded that there will be no dispositon in any part of the nation to review with severity the efforts of a commander acting in a crisis of unparalleled difficulty under the impulse of the purest patriotism.

There was not indeed any such dispositon in spite of this frank admission that war had played hob with the Constitution. The people approved and later elected Jackson President. His fine with interest to the total of $2,700, was refunded by Congress in 1844.[38]

CHAPTER II

THE RIGHTS OF THE PEOPLE
(1830-1860)

By 1830 the first interpretations of civil liberty had been made. These involved: (1) the rejection of the English traditions and laws found unsuitable to the new form of government or the spirit of the people; (2) the definition of the powers of the United States respecting the liberties of the citizens of the separate states; (3) and the new ideas consequent upon the transfer of sovereign power from a hereditary monarch to the people acting through a majority. For the first, the divorce from England had been declared final. For the second, the principle was laid down that the central government had nothing to do with protecting the liberties of the citizens of states. The third—the new ideas of democratic control—now engages us.

For forty years the "founding Fathers" had guided the nation. They had formed a sort of aristocratic succession to bridge the gap between monarchy and democracy. Now they were gone. The people were left alone with their government. The power had descended upon them, and through their new self-created leaders, Andrew Jackson first, they heard proclaimed the divine right of the people. They were easily flattered into a conviction of their wisdom, their power, and their final right to settle with the minority. Civil liberty became a question of resisting this new power, expressed either by law or by mobs.

The people had won important enlargements of political and economic rights: a greatly extended suffrage, generally without property or religious tests; equality of representation;

freedom for the bond-servant, redemptioner, and apprentice. The workers (among whom we find always least liberty) were securing some of the essential social liberties through their greater political power. Imprisonment for debt was slowly abolished; and such imprisonment had doubtless been a useful device for easily disposing of stray agitators against economic evils. Labor had made a gesture at political action and was winning a qualified right to organize simple unions. Systems of popular education were being demanded, and sometimes established. Yet the lack of any demand by the workers for civil liberty was not because the mechanic had any freedom, but because they had so little of it they did not recognize its violation just as they say, in the Far North, there is not sunshine enough to make an icicle.

One section of the workers had no civil nor any other liberty. The Negro through this period can be dismissed thus: "In the eyes of the law a chattel . . . not a civil right of any kind was his."[1] The importation of slaves had ended according to Constitutional provision after 1808. But even in the "free States" the freedom granted Negroes was so restricted as to be beneath being called civil liberty.

But on the whole the people were not so concerned with civil liberty as the Revolutionary generation had been. For the canonization of the populace brought the "popular mob." The people *were* the government (everybody told them so) — why worry about constitutional guarantees? The constitutions were theirs, too. If democracy means the rule of the majority, well, here is a majority now. Why wait for the tardy approval of the law? And so they rushed off to enforce by violence their economic necessities or instinctive prejudices. The dangers to civil liberty now were not from the dead hand of English kings, but from the living hands of the mob. The sophistry of the Federalists, that the Constitution needed no Bill of Rights to protect the people from themselves, was immediately disproved. The minority now needed that Bill more than anybody *ever* had needed it.

From 1828 to 1855, and especially from 1833 to 1843, came a veritable mob era. The masses, charmed by this idea of the rule of the people, were convinced that it made small difference whether you downed the minority by ballots or by brick-bats, which they understood better. This form of tyranny by majority had not been anticipated by the statesmen who expected the colder process of voting down the minority to prevail over the warmer sport of killing them.

Social conditions helped establish these notions. Urban centralization had begun. Immigration, encouraged to bring in cheap labor, first the Irish and later the Chinese, aroused economic, racial and religious prejudices. There was an ardent "nativism," by citizens who had themselves but yesterday come from foreign shores. There was an almost inexplicable dread of secret politcal or religious organizations, expressed in crusades against the Masons, Catholics, and Mormons. Beneath all, the growing machine industry was producing a proletariat. Wage-labor was slowly reaching economic self-consciousness, later to align itself against the wageless institution of Negro slavery. In a few places, direct action by the people approximated a rough sort of government, as in the Vigilantes and other extemporized "law and order" bodies of the frontier. They did some necessary natural policing before courts or State arrived. The question of whether "liberty" exists under such conditions, is so academic that it is not entered upon, and all cases in this category have been omitted.[2]

The early governing autocrats had tried to limit liberty by stifling interpretations of the Constitutions or by appeals to English precedents. The people simply appealed to force. To the interpretation by popular prejudice. The cases arise usually from a denial of rights to an individual or minority by another part of the community which claims to represent the will of the people,—the majority. As concerns the formal claims of civil liberty, they show how the State, organized ostensibly for law and order, failed to afford any real protection to unpopular groups.

THE MOB ERA

The mob seems to have come on the American scene late. In the Colonies there were a few race riots,—against Negroes in New York City early in the eighteenth century, against Indians in New Hampshire in 1753 because they had stolen two Negroes (an odd complication), and the celebrated "Paxtang riot" in Pennsylvania in 1763.

Some Scotch-Irish in frontier settlements exterminated twenty Indians, the entire remnants of a vanishing tribe. The settlers were actuated partly by religious motives, quoting the command of the Israelites to destroy utterly the heathen of Palestine. The Province, mostly Friends, was thoroughly aroused, for a lynching was a new thing in Pennsylvania, and excited more indignation than it would now.[3]

The Revolutionary mobs were manifestations of the war spirit and even so were surprisingly humane and orderly. From then on the American people showed little inclination to mob violence until about 1830. Possibly the instinct which makes for it found outlets in duelling, frontier violence, rabid politics and a madly vituperative press. Some force restrained the people from mob excesses, possibly reverence for the new political order or the general loose organization of a life chiefly rural or a lack of the need of this form of control. One terrible popular outbreak, in barbarity like the excesses of the French Revolution or our modern "lynching bee" did take place in Baltimore after the opening of the War of 1812. It was a flagrant case of political intrigue employing the popular passions to violate constitutional liberty.

"THE BALTIMORE RIOTS"

The editors of the Baltimore *Federal Republican* attacked the war and the President, and in an editorial on June 20, 1812, declared that his motives bore "marks of undisguised foreign influence" and that they meant to use "every constitu-

tional argument and legal means to render odious the con-
trivers of this highly impolitic war." The following Monday
the printing-office of the Federalists was pulled down and the
presses destroyed; and the next night the mob searched another
dwelling, dismantled several vessels lawfully bound for sea,
and burnt down the house of a free colored man who was
charged with having spoken in friendly terms of the British.
They were setting fire to an African church when dispersed.

These events were under legal investigation by the criminal
court until July 26 when one of the editors, Alexander Hanson, and some friends fortified the house of his partner, and
next day printed and circulated an issue of his paper containing severe reflections on the mayor, the police, and the people
of Baltimore. During the day a mob attempted to force the
doors of the printing shop, and several were wounded by gun-
fire from the defenders. One of the wounded later died.
The militia was sent for, and soon appeared, opening negotia-
tions with the defenders who finally surrendered and were
taken to jail on the assurance that the mayor and military
commander would protect them from violence. Meanwhile
a Dr. Gale had been killed by the Federalists.

The next day, about dark, the mob attacked the jail, overpowered the mayor, and forced a turn-key to let them into the
prisoner's room.[4] What followed is thus described by Richard
Hildreth in his *History of the United States:*

> Of those who fell into the hands of the mob, the fate
> was wretched indeed. Struck down by a butcher who
> had obtained access to the jail during the day, they were
> beaten in the most horrible manner, after which to the
> number of nine, they were tossed down the stone steps
> where they lay in a heap for three hours or more, the mob
> amusing themselves by beating their senseless bodies, stick-
> ing pen-knives into their cheeks, and dropping hot candle-
> grease into their eyes to ascertain if they were really
> dead. General Lingan expired amid these tortures, vainly
> reminding the infuriated wretches of his Revolutionary
> services. . . . General Lee barely escaped the same fate,

being made a cripple for life. . . . The jail physician who tickled the fancy of the mob by suggesting that these dead bodies, as they seemed to be, would make excellent Tory skeletons suceeded in obtaining permission to remove them to the jail.[5]

The rioters next went and demanded the copies of *The Federal Republican* deposited in the post office. The Democratic magistrates now ordered out a military force which charged the mob and protected the postmaster who refused to give up the newspapers.

The City Council laid the blame upon Hanson and his associates for having persisted in the publication of their newspaper in the time of war. The ring-leaders of the mob escaped punishment, because the Democratic attorney-general refused to exercise his right of changing the venue, and a Baltimore jury acquitted the prisoners without hesitation. Hanson and others were also acquitted after a trial for manslaughter at Annapolis. But the political effect was defeat for the mob and what it stood for.

The political aspect of the State of Maryland has been completely changed by the election. The House of Delegates now consists of 54 Federalists, and 26 Democrats. The Maryland representation in the 13th Congress will include Alexander C. Hanson in place of Mr. Key.[6]

The Baltimore event was imitated by mobs of military volunteers at Buffalo and Norfolk. The rarity of the event as well as its tragic enormity gave it such melodramatic prestige that it became famous as "Baltimore Club Law," was rebuked by papers such as *The Salem Gazette*, and was mentioned by DeTocqueville in his *Democracy in America* over a decade later, helping doubtless to form the European tradition of American violence. The whole transaction exemplifies the ferocity of war psychology, and the frequently amazing incapacity or deliberate negligence of local authorities in the face of popular passion.[7]

THE ANTI-MASONIC EXCITEMENT

Between 1826 and 1829, the Masons suffered the violation of their liberties by legal and political methods, by mob violence, and by social pressure, in·northern New York, in Pennsylvania, and other scattered spots. This is a fine example of the abiding fear in the American people of secret politcal societies, first expressed in the dread of the establishment of a monarchy by Washington and his officers through the Order of the Cincinnati. The excitement began in the alleged abduction and murder of one William Morgan of Canandaigua County, New York, by ·Masons, because he was about to print a so-called revelation of their secrets, having himself been a member of the fraternity. Attempts were made to burn the printing-shop and manuscript (showing the Mason's own respect for a free press), and then Morgan was seized as he left a court-room, placed in a carriage, and disappeared forever. What became of him was never learned, nor were his kidnappers discovered. But public clamor brought punishment on the Masons, and even became the basis for an anti-Masonic political party which exerted a limited influence for a short time.[8]

Some of the incidents of this agitation follow. The town clerk of Bethany, New York, disqualified a number of Masons as jurors although previous to 1827 they had been returned as able and sufficient jurymen, free-holders, men of understanding and integrity, some of them church-members, and one a representative of Seneca County in the Assembly for three years. The thing was so raw that the clerk was afterwards indicted by the unanimous vote of even an anti-Masonic grand jury, but acquitted. An attempt was made to break up a celebration of Masons at Batavia. In 1829, a county convention appointed a committee to investigate the affiliations of a land company so as to proscribe the Masons. A Colonel King was pursued by sheriffs all the way to Arkansas for suspected complicity in the Morgan kidnapping. He returned of his own will, but was never arrested. An instance of social pressure is shown by the fact that over one hundred meetings adopted resolutions that they would not support any person for office, or any minister who was a Mason. Batavia Church dismissed one of its deacons, and its pastor had to resign.

More significant of how the people were centering power in themselves as against minorities were the efforts in New York and Pennsylvania to abolish extra-judicial oaths, in order to outlaw the pledges of secret societies. In 1828 a select committee of the New York Assembly reported a bill, but it was never moved in either house. A memorial to Congress, May 12, 1828, was not received but was referred to President Adams, and never heard of again. A whimsical event was the removal of a Masonic sheriff, Eli Bruce of Niagara County, from office by Governor De Witt Clinton, himself the Grand High Priest of the General Chapter of the Masonic Order. Bruce had refused to testify at a trial of persons charged with the Morgan abduction on the ground of self-incrimination. Perhaps the old Governor was white-washing himself.[9]

RELIGIOUS LIBERTY AND THE PEOPLE

Constitutional religious liberty was not yet fully attained. Church and states were not quite divorced. Religious qualifications for the governorship persisted into the nineteenth century in New Jersey, New Hampshire, Connecticut and Vermont. In Maryland, no Jew could serve on a jury, sit as judge or magistrate, practice law or be a member of the Assembly until the passage of the "Jew Bills" in 1828; and it was only in 1851 that a special clause of a new Maryland constitution forbade all such discriminations.[10] There was not so much intolerance toward new creeds as we might expect, even though they preached new ideas of sex and property. These creeds had much freedom within their own groups, but a too vigorous evangelism among outsiders, especially when complicated by bad morals, resulted in rough discipline. As most of these sects were rural, their remoteness and the lack of communication made at least for the tolerance of ignorance.[11] They probably suffered both from social obloquy and various petty persecutions which small communities visit upon non-conformists. But it was only when economic competition aligned the Irish-Catholic against the native mechanic, or the Mormons against the land and slave-owning oligarchy that active suppressive measures were used.

THE "NATIVE AMERICAN" PERSECUTIONS

Let us take up the Catholic cases first. The "Native American" agitation with its political by-product, the Know-Nothing Party, was directed chiefly against the Irish-Catholics from 1835 to 1855. To the hatred of cheap Irish immigrant labor was added race prejudice and religious bigotry, making an appealing combination for persecution. Political partisanship augmented the trouble. The Know-Nothings, paradoxically also semi-secret, answering "I know nothing" when asked about their organization, depended upon this appeal to patriotic nativism. They gained control of a few states, and reached national proportions in the early fifties, only to be submerged in the strife over slavery. This movement is significant in the history of civil liberty because it shows the slow solidifying of the majority as a tyrannical force. The country belonged to the American mob. Foreigners would not be granted freedom to introduce competitive ideas. Things were already being standardized. This picture of a horde of hungry Irishmen rushing in to seize the very government of the people (and also their jobs) aroused such a gust of passion that politicians easily turned the resulting mob spirit to their own ends. As a result, the rise and fall of Know-Nothingism produced more voilence than any other political movement in our history, and involved a large diagonal slice of territory between the Catholic centers, Boston and New Orleans, extending politically into Virginia and the Ohio Valley.

The liberty lost was that of the body and possessions, which is always sacrificed to mob violence. The violence included orgainzed attacks on religious institutions or personages, miscellaneous fights, and terrorizing elections by rival political gangs. The free-for-all fights were perhaps generally enjoyed, and the election riots were a rude contest between the "outs" and "ins,"—with small choice for virtue between them. So the chief interest for us is in the cases of attacks on religious institutions.

THE BURNING OF THE URSULINE CONVENT

Convents were the objects of bitter anti-Catholic propaganda so that the sudden and secret flight of one Rebecca Reed in 1833 from the Convent of the Ursulines at Charlestown, near Boston, aroused great popular excitement. This was increased by her book *Six Months in a Convent,* a purported revelation of convent iniquities that rivalled in sensational success the later *Uncle Tom's Cabin.* In July, 1834, Sister Mary John got hysteria, secretly fled, but returned with her brother. From this the press spread the rumor that she was detained against her will and there was a demonstration by some of the ignorant and prejudiced. This led to an official visit by the selectmen of Boston who examined the Convent from cellar to garret and conversed with Sister Mary John, declaring that they would announce their satisfaction with conditions in the next day's papers.

About eight o'clock that night, August 11, 1834, a mob began to assemble, but no great alarm was felt as the city authorities were warned and presumably could keep the peace and protect property. But—

About ten that night about five or six hundred ruffians made a furious assault on the Convent . . . broke in the windows, battered down the doors, and ransacked and pillaged the building, and having broken and thrown out of doors such furniture as they could not carry away, finally burned it to the ground. No effectual efforts were made to extinguish the flames, the firemen probably being over-awed by the mob. The pupils, about fifty-five, all young ladies, were hastily dressed, and hurried out of the building, followed by the nuns, and found refuge in a neighboring farm-house.[12]

The next day in Faneuil Hall, a meeting led by Harrison Gray Otis passed resolutions of condemnation in the strongest terms. The Catholic Bishop, Fenwick, restrained his followers from acts of retaliation, and the excitement subsided. Of thirteen rioters tried, only one was convicted and he probably the least guilty. He was soon pardoned on petition from Bishop Fenwick as suffering unjustly for others. The Ursulines were forced to leave the vicinity.[18]

THE MASSACHUSETTS SMELLING-COMMITTEE

The following gives a second case of propaganda against convents, fortunately not without its humorous features:

The famous "Know-Nothing Legislature" of Massachusetts convened the first week of 1855. The upper house was solidly Know-Nothing, the lower with the exception of three. One of the opposition papers suggested as a text for the customary election sermon before the Legislature: "For we are but of yesterday, and know nothing." (Job I, 9.) There were about half as many farmers as in previous legislatures, but there were four times as many clergymen—twenty-four. . . .

The most notable event was the appointment of a committee to inspect the nunneries, the so-called "smelling-committee," which under the lead of one Hiss, a "Grand Worthy Instructor" of the Know-Nothing Council, became a junketing affair and carried along with it a number of invited guests. Its members lived at the best hotels and drank expensive wines at the cost of the State. The hotel expenses of a notorious woman were included among its many vouchers.

The gentlemen roamed over the whole Convent, not a part was spared. The ladies' dresses were tossed over in their wardrobes. The party invaded the chapel and showed their respect—as Protestants, we presume—for the One God whom all Christians worship, by talking loudly with their hats on; while the ladies shrank in terror at the desecration of a spot which they hallowed. . . . Under pressure of public clamor, the Legislature began to in-

vestigate its investigating committee. Hiss was finally
expelled from the House. The only distinctive nativist
measure passed was a proposed amendment to the Constitution restricting office-holding to native-born Americans, and requiring twenty-one years residence for naturalization.[14]

In 1853 at Cincinnati the militia had to disperse a mob of
two thousand moving on the residence of Archbishop Bedini,
papal nuncio to Brazil. In Baltimore he had to conceal his
presence. The next year, the "Angel Gabriel"—an eccentric
Scotch anti-Popery preacher—caused numerous out-breaks in
New England. A Know-Nothing mob attacked the Irish
quarter in Chelsea; the Catholic chapel at Coburg was burned;
the Dorchester chapel blown up; at Manchester, N. H., the
mob tore the American flag from the priest's house and
wrecked the interior of the Catholic church; and at Ellsworth,
Maine, Father Bapst was tarred and feathered. A mob led by
a notorious criminal attacked the Convent of Mercy at Providence, but the damage was slight as the Catholics rallied to
protect the institution. In August, St. Louis saw a riot which
resulted in ten deaths. At Washington, a Know-Nothing mob
captured a block of marble sent by the Pope as a tribute for
the Washington Monument, and threw the papal gift in the
Potomac.

Typical of the free-for-all-fight class, was the Broad Street
riot in Boston, June 11, 1837. It had a comedy opening: an
engine company returning from a fire came into collision
with an Irish funeral procession, and soon 15,000 people were
involved. The Irish were driven into their houses, and but
for the appearance of the military, the Irish quarter would
have been destroyed. No lives were lost. The City Council
decided that the blame rested about equally upon the firemen
and the Irish. Street fighting seems to have been a pleasant
recreation in those days. In June, 1854, an anti-Catholic
preacher was escorted through Brooklyn by a Know-Nothing
mob of 5,000. They collided (favorite word) with an Irish
mob, and a free fight ensued. The following Sunday it was

renewed. That this was a sort of game for spirited youths is
shown by the organization in New York City that same spring
of a nativist society for younger men. They were sometimes
called "Wide-Awakes" from their rallying cry. This organization attended to all street disturbances in behalf of their
order. Their wide felt "wide-awake" hats were recognized as
the insignia of their belligerency.[15]

The third class of cases concerns election riots. For example
at Mobile, Alabama, during the life of the Know-Nothing
party Catholic property near the city was burned.[16] Kentucky
witnessed a violent outbreak, the more singular because the
State had hardly any foreign population, and the native
Catholics were excellent and respected citizens. The election
for Governor which the Know-Nothing candidate won by
4,400 majority led the roughs of the "native American party"
to attack the Catholics, with the loss of twenty-two lives and
a large amount of property.[17] The devices against freedom
of speech and assemblage are noted thus:

> If a meeting was called to expose and denounce its
> schemes, it was completely drowned in the Know-Noth-
> ing flood which at the appointed time completely over-
> whelmed the helpless minority. . . . In my town thou-
> sands of men assembled as an organized mob to suppress
> the freedom of speech, and succeeded by brute force in
> taking possession of every building in which their op-
> ponents could meet, and in silencing them by savage
> yells.[18]

The reign of Know-Nothingism in Baltimore was a picturesque terrorism in which clubs called by such choice names
as the Tigers, the Black Snakes, the Rip Raps, the Blood Tubs,
and the Plug-Uglies roughed elections. In only one ward
could the Irish vote in safety. In others only the citizen who
gave the proper signal could get to the polls. A novel custom
was the use of coops to prevent voting. Many persons were
captured by the workers of the party and confined in cellars
and other convenient places so they could not vote. Often

beaten and robbed, the poor victims were thrown into these filthy places where as many as a hundred and fifty men were sometimes confined for several days without even the decencies of civilized life.[19]   Pitched battles with artillery were fought:

> Fighting and rioting occurred in various parts of Baltimore, but the most serious affair was around Belair Market. The fighting here began about three o'clock and continued desperately until dark. The Know-Nothings brought with them a small cannon mounted on wheels which was loaded with all kinds of missiles. The Democrats, however, overpowered them and got possession of the cannon, and the high constable and twenty policemen were not able to prevent the rioters from carrying it off. . . . We find a list of ten killed and over 250 wounded, making a total of fourteen killed in the two elections.[20]

The high constable seems to have been a sort of umpire in this pageant for which Baltimore seems to have an unequalled record. The city staged war riots in 1812, in 1860, and in 1917. In June, 1857, the Marines had to be gotten from the Washington navy yard to suppress a riot. Political manoeuvres paralleled the military. The Catholics fought for a division of the school fund. The Governor tried to make the Mayor protect the elections, but was himself forced to withdraw.[21] When finally the Democrats came into control of the Legislature, they merely reversed the injustice, illustrating the old point that who has power has liberty. They passed a Police Bill, to remedy the Baltimore situation which contained a clause that no Black Republican or endorser of the Helper book [22] should be appointed to any office under the Board. Schmeckbier says:

> This action shows that the Democrats were just as proscriptive as they charged the Know-Nothings with being, as it was just as much a part of the religion of the

Abolitionists to oppose slavery as it was for the Catholics to believe in the Pope's supremacy.

The Democrats learned nothing from persecution, but immediately fell to persecuting somebody else for something they did not like. The cry of "native Americanism" was used to proscribe whatever foreigners the party in power found in its way. Note how the slavery faction absorbed the idea:

> While in the North the crusade was carried on chiefly against the Irish, the South was chiefly concerned with insuring the harmlessness of the wicked Germans. Adams, of Mississippi, in assigning his reason for his Naturalization Bill, December, 1854, had laid special emphasis on the fact that the Germans had sent in so many petitions against the Kansas-Nebraska Bill, and had even burned Douglass in effigy.[23]

The final outburst of this brand of nativism came in Baltimore, as usual, when in April, 1861, the German Turner Hall was sacked by indignant Southern men because it was reported that a number of Germans had volunteered their services to the Government at Washington. The same night the office of the *Wecker*, a German paper, was attacked on account of the anti-slavery views expressed by that journal.[24] Startling evidence of the seizure of any pretext by those in power to limit liberty is that while the Irishmen of the Atlantic Coast were being mobbed as invading foreigners, other Irishmen on the Pacific Coast had set up the cry of "native Americanism" to outlaw the "heathen Chinese"—who were stealing "their" jobs, and "their" county!

FREEDOM OF EDUCATION

The "Native American" movement was too loose and unsubstantial to write any proscriptive laws against religion on the statute-books. Or perhaps the Catholic Church was too powerful. The only serious attempt to abridge religious liberty by formal act was the effort to prevent Catholics from giving their children the kind of education they wanted.

In the North throughout these years Catholic children endured much petty persecution in the public schools. At Ellsworth, Maine, a Catholic child was given corporal punishment for declining to read the Protestant scriptures. The Supreme Court of the State denied the claims of the child's parents, but the decision was not later approved by any court of last resort.[25] A hundred Catholic children were expelled from the Elliot school in Boston for refusing to participate in Protestant religious exercises. In the same city in 1858 a contest arose over discontinuing the reading of the Protestant Bible in the public schools, professedly non-sectarian and attended by many Catholics. One student was severely flogged for refusing to read the religious exercises, though he merely obeyed his parents' commands. An action for assault was brought against the teacher, but later dismissed. The Bishop advised the boys to submit, and took up the matter of changing the rule, but it was not adjusted until some years later. In Maryland a law for the control of persons in nunneries was proposed.[26] In Philadelphia the great riots of 1844 grew out of a controversy over Bible reading.[27]

THE PERSECUTIONS OF THE MORMONS

The Mormons have suffered longer and more bitter persecution than any other sect in the United States. The events of an entire decade after 1833 are unheard of by most Americans, yet they rival in terror the pogroms against Jews in Europe, and the horrors suffered by the Chinese and Negroes in this country. The origin of the hatred against them during this period was economic, not moral. They announced their determination to secure by thrift and absorption (never by illegal means) the land on which to build the new Jerusalem foretold in their scriptures. God had ordained them to own this land in spite of all mundane oppositon,—though in fact the ordained site had to be changed each time they were driven on. These people had a fanatic "will-to-land" which naturally threatened and terrified the communities in which they pitched their tents. In slave-owning Missouri the Mormons freed Negroes, and that fanned the flames. The conventional churches hated this usurping hierarchy with its picturesque appeals. There were many cases of personal immorality and peculation by leaders and members of the flock. Self-anointed religious leaders seem to fall into these sins.

But it must be held clearly in mind that the sufferings here recounted were not due to sexual immorality under the Church aegis. The doctrine of polygamy had not even been broached. It was not a tenet of their creed, nor was it even associated with the leaders until the very end of this period. The Mormons had broken no law to justify the treatment they received. They were just another alien and threatening power which the people with their new sense of solidarity dared not tolerate. They were a different sort of neighbor, and thrifty competitors. They seemed to hold out the threat of a secret society against the government. Later, of course, all other hatreds could be justified on the high moral ground of their sexual heterodoxy.

The Mormons had no politcal interests during their first period, which alone is covered here. They tried to run their communities under municipal ordinances secured by revelation, but they lived peaceably within the government, and rendered unto Caesar his due. Later when the democracy's demand for uniformity had driven them far west to found their own State—Deseret—they became a political power and a political issue. This new struggle, from the founding of the Utah regency to the abolition of polygamy by Congress, will be treated hereafter.[28]

THE TARRING OF A PROPHET

Joseph Smith, the Prophet, was a phenomenon,—an incarnation of pure will, the courage of endurance, duplicity in affairs, and that startling sexual vigor characteristic of early

Americans. In the first days of his Church in the East, he suffered the following atrocity, consequent on the public exposure of his financial methods by two seceding elders and the rumors of immoral practices in the fold. He describes it himself thus:

My wife heard a gentle tapping on the windows. Soon after, the mob burst open the door and surrounded the bed, and the first I knew I was going through the door . . . They seized my throat and held on until I lost my breath. I saw Elder Rigdon stretched out on the ground whither they had dragged him by the heels. All my clothes were torn off me except my shirt collar; and one man then fell on me and scratched my body with his nails like a madcat. . . . I pulled the tar away from my face so I could breathe. . . . I was naked and when my wife saw me she thought I was mashed all to pieces, and fainted. With my flesh all scarified and defaced I preached to the congregation as usual. The next morning I went to see the Elder Rigdon and found him crazy, for they had dragged him by the heels so high from the earth he could not raise his head from the rough frozen surface which lacerated it exceedingly; and when he saw me, he called to his wife to bring him his razor. . . . He wanted to kill me. During the mob one of my twins received a severe cold and died. The mobbers were composed of various religious parties, but mostly of Campbellites, Methodists, and Baptists.[29]

This and other outrages were not, as the Mormons claimed, outrages on the liberty of opinion. In this case, papers revealing a plot to take their property away from them and put it in Smith's control fell into the hands of some of the converts who thereupon organized a company to punish Smith and Rigdon. Smith was also tried on the financial charge, and vindicated. One commentator says:

Mormon writers have dilated on these persecutions, but the outcome of the hearings indicated fair treatment of the accused by the arbiters of the law, and the indignation shown to him by his neighbors was not greater than the conduct of such men in assuming priestly dignity might evoke in any similar community.[30]

The fact remains that these men were mobbed; and the fact remains that whatever their short-comings, hundreds of sincere believers suffered solely on account of their faith.

THE DEPORTATIONS IN MISSOURI

By 1833, the Church, now in Missouri, was busy at the New Jerusalem. Their spread alarmed the slaveholders of Jackson County and the following remarkable proscription was passed at a formal mass-meeting.

We, believing that an important crisis is at hand as regards our civil society, in consequence of a pretended religious sect of people, styling themselves Mormons, and intending to rid our society of them "peaceably if we can, forcibly if we must," and believing as we do that the arm of the civil law does not afford us a guarantee, or at least, a sufficient one against the evils which are now inflicted upon us, deem it expedient to form ourselves into a company for the easier accomplishment of our purpose . . . which is justified as well by the law of nature as by the law of self-preservation. . . . We believed them deluded fanatics or weak and designing knaves, and that they and their pretensions would soon pass away; but in this we were deceived. . . . More than a year since it was ascertained that they had been tampering with our slaves and attempting to sow dissensions and raise seditions among them. . . . In the "Star" published by leaders of their sect there is an article inviting free negroes and mulattoes to become Mormons and settle among us. . . . They declare openly that their God hath given them this county of land, and that sooner or later they must and will have the possession of our lands for an inheritance. . . . We therefore agree that if after a timely warning and receiving an adequate compensation for what little property they cannot take with them, they refuse to leave us in peace as they found us, we agree to use such means as may be sufficient to remove them.[31]

July 29, a meeting of 500 citizens demanded that no more Mormons come into the County, that those present pledge themselves to move, and that the editor of the *Star* discontinue his business. The latter refused and that same day the mob razed his printing-shop and home, and threw his wife and a sick infant out of the house. They also tarred Edward Partridge, bishop of the Church, in front of the Courthouse. The Mormons petitioned Governor Dunklin for troops to help regain their homes, assuring themselves that "no republican will suffer the liberty of the press and liberty of conscience to be silenced by a mob" and knowing "that every officer, civil and military, with a very few exceptions, has pledged his life and honor to force us from the country, dead or alive."

Governor Dunklin, who throughout this controversy showed a keen sense of the Mormons' constitutional rights but did nothing to protect them, advised that they get the circuit judge to have the offenders apprehended and "bind them to the peace." The futility of this advice was later proved, for Smith declares: "We made oath before Judge Ryland of the outrages committed upon us, but were refused a warrant; the Judge advising us to fight and kill the mob." [32]

THE MISSOURI POGROM

Between October 31 and November 7, the Mormons on isolated farms and in small communities were subjected to a reign of terror. Houses were destroyed, men beaten, and a pitched battle between sixty citzens and thirty Mormons took place near Independence. Several were wounded and one died. The militia was called out and the Mormons decided to give up their arms and leave the county. Certain leaders were given up for trial for murder on account of the battle, but were dismissed in a few days. Then, says Joseph Smith,

"By November 7, there was an exodus of over 1200 people out of Jackson County across the Missouri. . . . The mob continued depredations and outrages upon us

until November 13th . . . on which day they finished
the work of driving every Mormon out of the country.
Our crops became free booty to their horses, hogs, and
cattle. They also burned about 203 houses. I was chased
by about sixty of these ruffians five miles. I fled to the
South and my wife was driven north to Clay County, and
for three weeks I knew not whether my family was dead
or alive. . . . At one time I was three days without food.
. . . I found my family on the banks of the Missouri
River under a rag carpet tent, short of food and raiment.
In this deplorable situation, my wife bore me a son. . . .
Even our lands in that county were robbed of their timber, and either occupied by our enemies for years or left
desolate. . . ." [33]

The legal consequences of these events are especially interesting. The Circuit Judge investigated "the outrageous acts
of unparalleled violence," and declared "disgrace will attach
to our official character if we neglect to take proper means to
insure the punishment due such offenders." The Attorney-
General wrote: "I am warranted in saying that if the Mormons desire to be replaced in their property an adequate force
will be sent forthwith to effect that object. If the Mormons
will organize themselves into regular companies, they will, I
have no doubt, be supplied with public arms." The Mormons
refused this invitation to civil war, and again appealed to the
Governor. He replied in part: "Your case is certainly a very
emergent one. . . . For that which is the case of the Mormons
to-day, may be that of the Catholics tomorrow and after them
any other sect that may become obnoxious to the majority of
the people of any section of the State." And later he wrote:
"I am fully persuaded that the eccentricity of the religious
opinions and practices of the Mormons is at the bottom of the
outrages committed against them. . . . They have the right
constitutionally guaranteed to them, and it is indefeasible, to
believe and worship Jo Smith as a man, an angel, or even as the
only true and living God, and call their habitation Zion, or
the Holy Land, or even heaven itself. Indeed, there is noth-

ing so absurd or ridiculous that they have not a right to adopt as their religion, so that in its exercise they do not interfere with the rights of others."

Despite this libertarian philosophy, when the Court convened, it was protected by only one company of militia, and the Attorney-General decided that the bold front of the mob, "bound even unto death, as I have heard," was not to be penetrated by civil law or awed by executive interference. The Mormons next sent a petition of 114 names to President Adams, April 10, 1834, pointing out that such illegal violence had not been inflicted upon any sect since the Declaration of Independence (which was true); that it was a religious persecution, for the county court records held no name of a Mormon crime; and praying most humbly "in behalf of our society which is so scattered and suffering . . . to be restored to our lands in Jackson County and protected in them by armed force, and as in duty bound will ever pray." Lewis Cass, Secretary of War, made the usual reply,—that the laws of Missouri had been violated, not those of the United States, which could interfere only if the State applied for help on the ground that an insurrection existed. "But this state of things does not exist in Missouri, or if it does, the fact is not shown in the mode pointed out by law." This should be compared with the opposite action of President Tyler in the Dorr War, treated later. A petition to Congress was answered by the Judiciary Committee in the same tenor,—the grievance was against Missouri. Here ended the lesson. The Mormons secured neither protection in their rights or redress for their physical suffering, mental anguish, or lost property. Their only official consolations were these touching words in Governor Dunklin's refusal to endorse their petition to the President:—

Permit me to suggest to you that as you now have greatly the advantage of your adversaries in public estimation, that there is a great propriety in maintaining that advantage which you can easily do by keeping your adversaries in the wrong. The laws, both civil and military, seem deficient in affording your society the proper protection; nevertheless, public sentiment is a powerful corrector of error, and you should make it your policy to continue to deserve it.

After this humorous epistle, rather more truthful than most official apologies, the Mormons had only one course. They withdrew, and set about converting Clay and Caldwell Counties into Mormon colonies. They lost their peaceful habits, went into politics, and organized their own militia. In 1838 the Jackson County troubles were repeated, ending with a near-battle between the State and the Mormon militia, the court martial and later the civil trial of their leaders, and the final exile to Illinois. Two incidents show the character of this religious civil war.[34]

GOVERNOR BOGGS'S ORDER OF EXTERMINATION

Headquarters of the Militia
City of Jefferson, Oct. 27, 1838

Gen. John B. Clark,
Sir: Since the order . . . directing you to cause four hundred mounted men to be raised within your Division, I have received information of the most appalling character . . . which places the Mormons in the attitude of an open and avowed defiance of the laws. . . . Your orders are, therefore, to hasten your operations with all possible speed.

The Mormons must be treated as enemies, and must be exterminated or driven from the State if necessary for the public peace. . . .

I am, very respectfully, your ob't serv't,

L. W. Boggs, Commander-in-Chief.

THE HAUN'S MILL MASSACRE

In the afternoon of Tuesday, October 30, 1838, there occurred in Caldwell County a dreadful incident. At Jacob Haun's mill, on Shoal Creek, had collected about twenty Mormon families. . . . Perhaps four families had come in on the evening before, from Ohio, and were occupying their emigrant wagons. Not one member of the little community had ever been in arms against the "Gentiles," or taken any part whatever in the preceding disturbances. . . . Setting out from Woolsey's, Col. Jenning marched swiftly out of the timber towards the doomed hamlet. . . .

Taken wholly by surprise, the Mormons were thrown into extreme confusion. Perhaps 20 men, Captain Evans among them, ran with their guns to the blacksmith shop and began to return the fire. It was wild and ineffective; that of the militia, accurate and deadly. . . . Many were shot down as they ran. Captain Evans gave orders to retreat, every man to take care of himself. . . .

Coming upon the field after it had been abandoned, the Gentiles perpetrated some horrible deeds. At least three of the wounded were hacked to death with cornknives, or finished with a rifle bullet. William Reynolds found a little boy only ten years of age, named Sardius Smith, hiding under the bellows. Without even demanding his surrender, the cruel wretch drew up his rifle and shot the little fellow as he lay. Charley Merrick, only nine years old, ran out but received a load of buckshot. . . . He did not die, however, for nearly five weeks. Esquire Thomas McBride was 78 years old, and had been a soldier under Gates and Washington in the Revolution. He lay wounded and helpless but still alive. A Daviess County man demanded his gun. "Take it," said McBride. Rogers picked it up and finding that it was loaded, deliberately discharged it into the veteran's breast. He then cut and hacked the body with his cornknife. . . . The militia had not lost a man killed and only three wounded. The Mormons killed and mortally wounded numbered seventeen. The severely wounded numbered eleven, one boy and one woman, a Miss Mary Stedwell, shot through the hand and arm as she was running to the woods.[35]

THE MORMONS DENY FREEDOM OF THE PRESS

Driven from Missouri, the Mormons founded a new city, Nauvoo, Illinois, with their own municipal government, militia, and Church hierarchy. With the coming of power, their leaders became as intolerant as any of their persecutors. The practice of polygamy had been introduced, and a strong faction of the old Church tried to break it up by publicity, with this result:

> The first, and indeed, the only, number of the "Expositor," June 7, 1844, contained a scandalous attack upon the most respectable citizens of Nauvoo [e.g. revelations of immorality]. . . . The City Council immediately took into consideration what would be the best method of dealing with it, and resolved—
> "That the printing-office from whence issues the 'Nauvoo Expositor' is a public nuisance . . . and the Mayor is instructed to cause the said printing establishment and papers to be removed without delay, in such manner as he may direct."
> The Mayor (Joseph Smith) issued orders to the city marshal to destroy the press, and to Jonathan Dunham, acting Major-General of the Nauvoo Legion to assist, if called upon. The marshal with a small force demanded entrance. This was denied, whereupon the marshal broke in the door, carried out the press, broke it in the street, pied the type, and burned all the papers found in the office, and then reported to the Mayor, who sent an account of these proceedings to the Governor of the State.[36]

From this incident arose a sequence of events that culminated in the murder of Joseph and Hyrum Smith in the jail at Carthage by a mob, and then came the exodus to Utah. What they suffered here, they suffered for conscience sake, and at the hands of "the popular mob" made up of American citizens.

THE SOCIAL REFORMERS

About 1825 there first appeared in the United States what may be called "social reformers." They had no predecessors, though Thomas Paine was in the direct line, and Benjamin Franklin and Thomas Jefferson of kin. They were the forerunners of our later radicals and libertarians. The mark of all this group is the belief that society may self-consciously improve itself and direct its course, through research for facts, by propaganda and education, by legislation, and by changing public opinion. They rather definitely gave up the idea that salvation resides in religion alone, and they denied the millenial nature of the American democracy. They naturally came into conflict with both religion and government, for they disputed the old authoritarian, revelation-from-above idea in favor of a new experimental, revelation-from-below idea, with much studying of cases, statistics, and causes, and with the purpose of reconstructing the social system. Hence they were called "atheists" or "anarchists"—as indeed some of them were. Since they criticized the established order and advocated sharp changes, they were attacked and hampered and had early to take a real interest in civil liberty as a method of social progress.

THE ECONOMIC RADICALS

The economic radicals included the Utopian Socialists, certain religious communist bodies, a few mild anarchists, and the short-lived workingmen's parties in New York and Philadelphia, 1828-1830. These radicals suffered more from financial short-windedness than from persecution, though they did endure petty harassment by their neighborhoods. The moving spirits of the communist-labor groups were Robert Dale Owen, and Frances (Fanny) Wright, editors of the first radical organ, *The Free Enquirer,* an odd vehicle for philosophy, moral allegories, schemes for social salvation, and much excellent propaganda for education and labor reforms. The paper was abhorred as a thing tainted with immorality and atheism, and its editors suffered in modern fashion, thus:

Miss Wright, having been denied the use of the Walnut Street Theater to lecture in . . . made exertion through some of her friends to get Washington Hall; this was also refused, but finally Military Hall was secured. Miss Wright arrived, but was deterred, it is supposed, by the pressure of the crowd, from alighting. She addressed a few words to the crowd and drove away. Miss Wright wrote. "During the absence of Mr. Labbé, the proprietor, Washington Hall, was rented from his lady, the money paid, and receipt given. . . . During the course of the evening such active measures were taken to intimidate Mrs. Labbé, by threats of arrest, prophesies of riot and disturbance, and forewarnings of persecution and loss of patronage that the individuals who had rented the hall felt constrained in deference to her feelings to forego its occupany.[37]

Strike-breaking by the military arm was the most startling innovation in the field of labor. Although prosecutions for conspiracy were still invoked against labor unions, strikes and violence had increased. The military was first called out on strike duty, August 2, 1828.[38] The next year troops were again used on the Baltimore and Ohio railroad; and in 1834 riots on this railroad became such a nuisance that citizens along its way printed a set of resolutions against the Irish who were held responsible.[39] These troubles were chiefly casual fracases by immigrant laborers, mostly Irish, about the living conditions of their contract camps, the chief demand often being for more whiskey. But here we find the beginning of the long struggle by labor for liberty.[40]

FREEDOM FOR THE NEW SEX MORALS

The scrutiny of sex from an economic and semi-scientific rather than a religious view produced various doctrines and experiments, among both communal-religious and free-thinking groups, ranging from absolute chastity to community free-love. These experiments suffered less interference than might have been expected, perhaps less than they have suffered in later years. The economic and political implications of sex freedom were less realized by those in power then than afterwards. The societies practicing unusual sex relations suffered little persecution. Legal proceedings, of a kind not precisely within the field of civil liberty, were sometimes instituted. These concerned: (1) property rights and the rights of the children, (2) public morals, which might be injured by the reputed adultery, fornication and bigamy of some sects. But people and government seemed surprisingly indifferent until the later doctrines of the Mormons threatened the basic monogamous ideal of their society.

Even the doctrine of birth-control and the practice of contraception were somewhat widely preached in these years without much opposition. Charles Knowlton, M.D., a very respectable practitioner, who lived the end of his life in Ashfield, Massachusetts, was confined in East Cambridge jail, in 1833, and even set at hard labor. He was the author of the first treatise in the United States on these subjects, called *The Fruits of Philosophy, An Essay on the Population Question.* His seems to have been the single case of imprisonment. Robert Dale Owen's *Moral Physiology* ran into ten or more editions without interference. Alexander Noyes, a leader of socialist-communist thought suffered some unimportant prosecution for his tract, *Male Continence,* which attracted a good deal of attention.[41]

The study of prostitution and the social aspects of sex was rare, and met with reprobation when attempted, as in the case of a young minister, MacDowall, who felt called upon to go to New York, acquaint himself with the prostitute class, and publish their stories. His was a religious rather than a scientific effort, and he achieved little but a home for wayward girls, soon broken up by the pressure of public opinion and his own slackness in money matters.

He did, however, publish for a year or more a monthly, called *MacDowall's Journal,* which was attacked by the respectable newspapers, because it seemed to endanger both the reputation of the city, and the character of its leading citizens. "It is spoken of from Maine to Mississippi as a vile nuisance," declared one six-penny sheet. Editorial nagging finally produced the following action:

The Grand Jury presented the "MacDowall's Journal" as a nuisance which calls loudly for the interference of the civil authorities. Under the pretext of cautioning the young of both sexes against the temptations of criminal intercourse, it presents such odious and revolting details as are offensive to taste, injurious to morals, and degrading to the character of our city. We believe the representations therein made of the extent to which prostitution prevails within our limits is grossly exaggerated. . . .[42]

Nothing was done to MacDowall, and the "Journal" soon afterward failed. But the incident suggests the beginnings of "Comstockery," the later efforts to bar from the mails vice reports by scientific bodies and the general idea of censorship.

Other groups of the social reformers were interested in a higher social status for certain sections of society by the abolition of slavery and the emancipation of women; in free popular education with enlarged opportunities for the poorer classes, women, and Negroes; in temperance; and in freedom of thought, especially in the fields of religious criticism, scientific research, and experiments such as vivisection. The inter-relation of these groups, then as now, possibly because their adherents were so few in number, is shown in inter-locking directorates and common memberships. The movement for equal suffrage was partly in order that the votes of women might kill the liquor traffic. Communists like Owen furthered the labor parties, free education, and birth control because they were all to alleviate poverty. These movements may all be called humanitarian, but they had two sections,— one wing emotional and melodramatic, and the other practical and scientific. Although these years saw only the beginnings of such labors, their interest in relation to civil liberty is real, both in themselves and their later difficulties.

CRUEL AND UNUSUAL PUNISHMENTS

In spite of the prison reforms of this period, forced by humanitarian and labor movements, legal punishments existed that might well have brought them within the constitutional prohibition against "cruel and unusual punishments." In 1879, in Massachusetts, Connecticut and Rhode Island, ten crimes were punishable by death. "In 1822, a felon was flogged on the campus of Yale College in the presence of the students. . . . So late as 1817, in Philadelphia, a sailor was bound to the iron rings outside the walls of the Walnut street prison and flogged. . . . In 1811, the Superior Court of Georgia, at Milledgeville, sentenced one Miss Palmer to be ducked in the Oconee."

THE FIRST AMERICAN REVOLUTION

THE DORR WAR—1842

The Dorr War in Rhode Island was the first *American* Revolution. That of 1776 was begun by Englishmen. Its little-known history, and the invasions of liberty it caused, make it a necessary part of our study. In 1840, Rhode Island still lived under a Charter granted by Charles II in 1663 by which a Charter Assembly exercised uncontrolled power. Since 1666 suffrage had been limited to "freemen"—freeholders of certain property (at this time fixed at $134) and their eldest sons. Yet even such qualified persons had to be voted into suffrage by the other "freemen" of the town, and this they were not legally bound to do. Moreover no reapportionment of the representation of the towns had been made since the Colonial charter, and this had resulted in great inequalities, especially in the urban centers where modern industry had begun to concentrate great numbers of un-enfranchised working-men. Government was by a minority, a landed aristocracy, with the strange right of succession. The effect of this upon civil rights and civil liberty is thus indicated:

No person whatever, since the Revolution, had been permitted to bring suit in any court of law in the State, or have a writ out of the clerk's office unless he be a free-holder. The right of a trial by a jury of impartial peers is denied since none but freemen could sit on juries. Another law authorized the town council when any person whom "they shall determine to be an unsuitable person to become an inhabitant of the town, enters, to give notice to that person (he not being a free-holder) to depart out of the town within a certain period, on penalty . . . of being bound for one year into servitude to any citizen of the United States."

Reverend William Fuller, a respectable minister, was preaching (about 1830) in a house erected by the contributions of Christians, many of whom were disfranchised. . . . But his faithful testimony against rum-selling made him obnoxious to a number of free-holders by whom he was formally notified that he should be banished from the town unless he altered his style of preaching. He pursued the even tenor of his way. . . . Either by order of the town authorities or else by vote of the freemen in open town meeting he was authoritatively ordered to leave town with which orders he peaceably complied, and left the State.

An attack on freedom of assemblage may be found in the resolution enforced at Providence . . . excluding all persons except themselves (the free-holders) from the Town House during the Town Meeting.[43]

Finally in 1841 as a result of two Constitutional Conventions,—one voted by the popular suffrage associations, and the other held by the alarmed Assembly itself,—Rhode Island supplied itself with two constitutions in place of none. What the actual preference of the people was is not clear, though it seems that the "people's Constitution" got a majority of the new electorate of adult males, and even of the old Charter "freemen" electorate. At any event, on April 18, 1842, under the Peoples' Constitution, Thomas Wilson Dorr, an abolitionist, was elected Governor with 6,147 votes, and nearly a full House and Senate; while, next day, Governor King was reelected by the Charter group. Rhode Island attained the distinction since attained only by Utah Territory of having *two* governments. Meanwhile the Charter Assembly had proscribed possibly 180 citizens of the State, many of them prominent, for participating in this "revolution" or "rebellion." The method was by the famous "Algerine Laws," so called from their severity, akin to the barbarity of the Algerine pirates.

THE ALGERINE LAWS

After a preamble, explaining that "in a free government the duties of the citizen to authority should be plainly defined, and that the good people of the state have been misled by certain artful persons into a plan for the subversion of the government," it was enacted:—

> Section 3. If any persons, except such as are duly elected thereto, according to the laws of this State, shall, under any pretended constitution of government . . . or otherwise, assume to exercise any of the Legislative, Executive, Judicial, etc. functions of the offices of Governor, Lieutenant-governor, Senators, etc. of this State . . . either separately or collectively, or shall assemble for the purpose of exercising any such functions . . . every such exercise or meeting . . . shall be deemed to be an usurpation of the sovereign power of this State, and is hereby declared to be treason against the State and shall be punished by imprisonment during life. . . .
> Section 4. All offences under this act shall be triable before the Supreme Judicial Court only. . . . All indictments . . . and also all indictments for treason against this State, may be preferred and found in any county of this State without regard to the county in which the offence was committed; and the supreme Judicial Court shall have full power for good cause . . . to remove for trial any indictment . . . to such county of the State as they shall deem best for the purpose of ensuring a fair trial of the same, and shall upon conviction of any such offender . . . have full power to order, and from time to time alter, the place of imprisonment of such offender to such county jail . . . any act, law, or usage to the contrary notwithstanding.[44]

In spite of this remarkable recognition of the Judicial Court as a kind of Star Chamber, the People's government was organized in an old foundry in Providence, May 3, and Dorr sent a dignified message to his new Assembly. The Algerine

laws were repealed, and a few minor offices filled. Meanwhile
the Charter government met at Newport and sent commissioners to Washington.[45] Dorr's search for help from Tammany Hall in New York; the abortive attack on an Arsenal;
and the subsequent dilatory and futile military operations of
both governments are the records of a revolution so constitu-
tional-minded on the people's part that they could not be
persuaded to use force, and so uncertainly opposèd by the en-
trenched power that they seemed to admit their arms would
not be supported. The Charter Assembly finally declared
martial law over the entire State from June 25 to August 8,
when it was suspended by the Governor until September 1,
and later suspended indefinitely. The alleged violations of
civil liberty run into the hundreds, of which some specimens
are here recorded: [46]

A Providence blacksmith was arrested . . . marched
through the streets by a band of twelve men, nine of
whom were negroes, and confined in the armory over-
night. Sunday he was released by the colonel as no
charges were made against him. A farm employee, of
Warren, was arrested, kept in jail seven days, examined by
one of the commissioners, and discharged three days later,
there being no accusation against him unless it was that
of being employed as a moderator of a people's town
meeting. A minister was eating his dinner . . . when
three soldiers burst into his room and searched the house;
though they found no concealed weapons, they made the
clergyman a prisoner and marched him to a tavern. . . .
It causes no surprise to find that sixteen persons were confined for three days in one cell, twelve feet by nine. In
another, seven by ten, fourteen men were confined.[47]

A brother of Colonel Cooley, who had come on from
New York, but with no intention of taking any part in
the matter, having been arrested and confined for a long
time in the pestilent air of the prison, until he became
insane, died suddenly during the trial of his brother for
treason. August 11, after martial law had been suspended, Mr. Hoskins, a citizen of New Hampshire was

arrested. . . . The Justice had begun to get the warrant ready, but fearing to be too late, despatched the Deputy Sheriff without one, and Mr. Hoskins was arrested, examined and committed before the warrant was made out against him. General Carpenter urged that he should be set at liberty. Mr. Hazard, the justice, replied very pettishly, "I don't care a damn for the letter of the law. It is time the law was resolved into its original elements." They found nothing that could be construed as treason when Mr. Hoskins had been confined in prison for several days.[48]

"The Express," the organ of the Constitutionalists, though its prevailing voice had been for peace, even to the last, was marked as one of the first victims of the aristocratic triumph. . . . There are two accounts. . . . One that armed men presented themselves at the printing-office, and demanded that the publication should cease, or they would throw the types into the street; another, is that the landholder, the Charterist who owned the building, preemptorily ordered the printing to cease, and with a similar threat. After the suppression of "The Express," the "Republican Herald" began to publish some of the passing occurrences, but soon after announced that it had been taught that "the truth was not to be spoken at all times." It declined to publish the particulars of outrages committed by the Charterists.[49]

PRESIDENT TYLER'S THREAT OF FEDERAL INTERFERENCE

Appeals were made by both sides for the United States to establish the new or protect the old government. The issue concerned national politics, since an Abolitionist government in Rhode Island would injure the slave-states, perhaps changing the alliance of two senators. President Tyler's promise of armed help to the Charterists was a principal cause of the early downfall of Dorr's party, for it alienated possible aid both within and without the State. Tyler stated his position thus:

They are questions of municipal regulation, the adjustment of which belongs exclusively to the people of

Rhode Island . . . however, when an insurrection shall exist and a requisition shall be made, I shall not be found to shrink from the performance of a duty. . . . The Executive could not look into real or supposed defects of the existing government, in order to ascertain whether some other plan of government proposed for adoption was better suited to the wants and more in accord with the wishes of any portion of her citizens. To throw the Executive power of this Government into any such controversy . . . might lead to an usurped power, dangerous alike to the stability of the State governments and the liberties of the people. It will be my duty to respect the requisitions of that government which has been recognized as the existing government through all time past, until I shall be advised in regular manner that it has been . . . abolished and other substituted in its place, by legal and peaceable proceedings, adopted and pursued by the authorities and people of the State.[50]

The threat here given was made real on May 2, when the garrison of Fort Adams was raised from 10 officers and 109 men to 21 officers and 281 men. Later Major Payne was directed to obtain accurate information on the probability of conflict between the two parties. Tyler repeated his readiness "to succor the authorities of the State," on May 7. Such eagerness to intervene is in complete contrast with the failure of the United States to interest itself in the Mormons in Missouri who needed succor much worse than Rhode Island. But power was with the Southern States, and the Charter government increased that power, while the Mormons were freeing slaves, and so the group with power decided who should enjoy liberty.

Threatened with Federal action, and disintegrating within, the Dorr government disappeared. Dorr left the State, but was later arrested and tried for treason.[51] However, this only American revolution was, in fact, successful, for the Charter government held a new constitutional convention and proposed a more liberal constitution which was adopted November 23, 1843, by 7,032 votes to 59.

CHAPTER III

THE ABOLITIONISTS
(1830-1860)

THE Abolitionists were the radical *bloc* of the general and wide-spread oppositon to slavery. They wanted immediate abolition by federal act; and between 1830 and 1860 they carried on a vigorous propaganda for it. This was the peaceful and legal effort of very respectable citizens to change what they held to be a great economic and social evil; yet they suffered every possible denial of their liberties in the attempt. Their liberty was invaded by law and by the failure of the law, by mob and individual lawlessness, even by violence upon their representatives in Congress.

Their insistence upon the moral right of a minority to agitate for even the most radical changes, by free speech and a free press, by petition, and with full liberty and protection, was scarcely less important than their struggle against slavery. The Abolitionists were attacked by a powerful group—claiming to be a majority of the people—under that ancient pretext that the "safety of the community" is so superior to any constitution that this "majority" can set aside legal processes in favor of force. Yet all this time the real majority of the American people, including many in the Slave States, wanted in a luke-warm way to abolish slavery somehow, sometime. The claim of danger to the state from the abolitionists was unfounded, for, John Brown excepted, the Abolitionists never used force. William Lloyd Garrison, though he burned the Constitution as a "compact with Hell," was himself a non-resistant, and many of his supporters were Quakers. It is the irony of history that these Quakers, accused of "endangering the community," suffered later because they would not take up

84

arms for the cause for which they otherwise had fought. The purpose of the Abolitionists was so far from dangerous to the State, and so essentially right that in thirty-five years from the time the agitation started the North was in arms to enforce their ideas and save the union! Rarely has the purpose of a persecuted minority so quickly been vindicated.

The facts are treated in two parts; what happened to Abolitionists in the South and what happened in the North. Intertwined are the efforts of the Southern States by political coercion to make the North aid in the persecution of Abolitionists.

ABOLITIONISTS IN THE SOUTH

In the South until 1828, agitation against slavery by Southerners or by outsiders was tolerated. Itinerant Benjamin Lundy went around forming anti-slavery societies until there were more of these in North Carolina than in any other state.[1] After that time conditions changed, for slaves had increased in economic value:

> Even in the South slavery had not been formally established by statute in any State. It was a tolerated anomaly, an incongruity which had grown up since 1793, under the invention of the cotton-gin, and the vast development of cotton-culture into a gigantic moneyed interest, and then transformed into a political power. It was sectional and aristocratic.[2]

This change, and the irritation felt even by liberal Southerners at Northern demands for "immediate" abolition, soon closed the whole South against outside agitation, and outlawed the Southerner who dared advocate a change. Tolerance varied in the South, North Carolina remained liberal until late, but generally constitutional rights in opposition to slavery were abolished by law or violence. Nor did the rest of the Union try to enforce these guarantees until 1861. Rather the danger was that the South might enforce their code on the rest of the nation. James Bryce says:

The tie of obedience to the national government was palpably loosened over a large part of the country.[3]

Legal coercion and the crushing compulsion of Southern caste society presently stopped even the demand for the protection of civil rights for abolitionists. The significance of the period is not in the record of violated liberties, but in the silence.

Let the South define civil liberty in these years. Senator William C. Preston declared in the United States Senate:

> Let an Abolitionist come within the borders of South Carolina, if we can catch him, we will try him; and notwithstanding all the interference of all the governments on earth, including the Federal government, we will hang him.

A member from South Carolina declared in the House:

> I warn the Abolitionists, ignorant, infatuated barbarians as they are, that if chance throw any one of them into our hands, he may expect a felon's death.[4]

MOB VIOLENCE IN THE SOUTH

The record of actual violence against Abolitionists in the South is hard to compile. *The Liberator,*—an example but biased source, printed this on December 19, 1856:

> A record of the cases of lynch-law in the Southern States reveals the startling fact that within twenty years, over three hundred white persons have been murdered upon the accusation—in most cases unsupported by legal proofs—of carrying among the slave-holders, arguments addressed to their own intellects and consciences as to the morality and expediency of slavery.

Cutler in his accurate *Lynch Law* declares that no such record can be made out, and that many who did suffer mob violence were not peaceful abolitionists, but really slave-

stealers, gamblers, and inciters to slave insurrection for their
own ends. Charges of these other crimes were doubtless made
against Abolitionists too, to justify the attacks on them for
their opinions. But whether abolitionists or criminals, they
were entitled to legal trials. Professor Hart in *Abolition and
Slavery*, thinks the *Liberator* figure wildly partisan, and
notes but three cases,—an error in the other direction.[5] What
did happen in the South from year to year is shown by the
following facts:

In July, 1835 Amos Dresser, one of the former students of
Lane Seminary, who was selling Bibles and a few other books
in Tennessee was arrested as an Abolition agent. In his trunk
were found three books by Abolitionists, put in by Dresser for
private reading, and some old newspapers of the same character which he said he used to prevent his books rubbing together.

He was brought before a Committee of Vigilance con-
sisting of sixty-two of the principal citizens, including
seven elders of the Presbyterian Church. His private
journal was examined. The Mayor gave up the attempt
to read it aloud, observing that it "was evidently very
hostile to slavery." Private letters were then read
aloud. . . . At eleven o'clock the young man was sent
into an adjoining room to await judgment. It was with
horror he heard from the principal city officer that the
Committee were debating whether his punishment should
be thirty lashes, or a hundred, or death by hanging. The
Committee acknowledged through the whole proceeding
that Dresser had broken no laws; but pleaded that if the
law did not sufficiently protect slavery against the assaults
of opinion, an association of gentlemen must make law
for the occasion. He was found guilty of three things;
of being a member of an Anti-Slavery Society in another
state; of having books of an anti-slavery tendency in his
possession, and of *being believed* to have circulated such
in his travels. He was condemned to receive twenty
lashes on his bare back in the market-place . . . and
there by torch-light he was stripped and flogged with a

heavy cow-hide. Twenty-four hours were allowed for
him to leave the city. . . . Entire strangers bathed his
wounds . . . and furnished him with a disguise. . . .
He left the place on foot, early in the morning. Neither
clothes, books, nor papers were ever returned to him.[6]

Robinson, an English book-seller was whipped and
driven out of Petersburg, Va., in 1832, for saying that
"the blacks as men were entitled to their freedom, and
ought to be emancipated." John Lamb was tarred and
feathered, badly burned and whipped for taking the
"Liberator." [7]

Marius R. Robinson went to Berlin, Mahoning County,
to deliver several lectures . . . June 3, 1837 he was
seized by a band of ruffians . . . dragged out of the
house of the friend with whom he was staying, carried
several miles away and subjected to the cruel indignity of
a coat of tar and feathers . . . carried some miles
further, and having been denuded of much of his clothing, left in an open field. . . . The bodily injuries received on that dreadful night affected his health ever
afterwards, and even aggravated the pains of his dying
hours.[8]

A young Irishman, a stone-cutter, at work on the
State House of South Carolina, dropped a casual remark
that "slavery caused a white laborer at the South to be
looked upon as an inferior and degraded man. . . ." He
was at once seized, thrust into jail, taken out, and dragged
through the streets, tarred and feathered, and then without other clothing than a pair of pants, put into a
negro car for Charleston, whence, after a week's imprisonment, he was banished from the State. . . .

In the Spring of 1860 Reverend Solomon McKinney
went to Texas, a Democrat . . . he believed that the
Bible sanctioned slavery. In Dallas County he preached
on the relative duties of master and slave. A public meeting was held and he was warned not to preach there again.
He started for the North, but he and his companion

were overtaken, carried back and imprisoned. They were soon taken from the jail by armed men, and whipped with raw-hides, receiving eighty lashes each, until their backs were "one mass of clotted blood and bruised and mangled flesh. . . ." [9]

SUPPRESSION BY LAW IN THE SOUTH

The Southern states early enacted laws to suppress free speech or assemblage concerning slavery. This was one reason they had so little mob violence—fear of the law checked any such discussion:

When some people met at Smithfield, Virginia, in 1827, to form an abolition society, the meeting was broken up by the magistrates, on the ground that as there was no law authorizing such a meeting, it must be contrary to law. The author of *Americans as They Are*, published in 1828, refers to the extreme irritability of the South on the question, and the actual danger of death if a lawyer defended a slave.[10]

Virginians were ousted from membership in churches for attacking slavery, and one clergyman was tried for inciting to insurrection by his sermons. By about 1828 freedom of speech against slavery was dead in the South.[11] The lack of a law was soon remedied, and statutes appeared in almost every Southern state penalizing advocacy of abolition.[12]

STATUTES DENYING FREEDOM OF SPEECH

Such an ordinance follows:

If a person by speaking or writing maintain that owners have no right of property in their slaves, he shall be confined in jail not more than one year and fined not exceeding $500.[18]

By the Virginia Code in the fifties, publications which tended to incite insurrections were punishable by death. Granting slavery, there was excuse for this in the ever-present fear of rebellion in the South. But as usual the alleged "tendency" of words to excite acts was used to justify prosecutions for words which had no such tendency. The following case is an illustration:

> Dr. Reuben Crandall, a teacher of botany of high character, was arrested in Washington, (D. C.) and thrown into jail on the charge of circulating incendiary publications with a view to excite an insurrection of slaves. The evidence was that some of his botanical specimens were wrapped in old copies of anti-slavery papers . . . and that he had lent an anti-slavery paper to a white citizen. The passages read in court were no more inflammatory than the writings of Jefferson and Patrick Henry. The Prosecuting Attorney made a desperate attempt to secure conviction, though without success. But Crandall's close confinement for eight months in a damp dungeon brought upon him a lingering consumption which terminated his life in 1838.[14]

Where these laws did not exist or could not be applied, deportations on various pretexts were tried. Here is the case of a lecturer deported as a vagrant under a local ordinance:

> Licking County, Granville Township, ss.
> To H. C. Mead, Constable,
> Greeting.
>   Whereas, we, the undersigned overseers of the poor of Granville Township, have received information that there has lately come into said township a certain poor man named Robinson, who is not a legal resident thereof, and will be likely to become a township charge; you are therefore, hereby commanded forthwith to warn the said Robinson, with his family, to depart out of said township. And of this warrant make service and return. Given under our hands this first day of March, 1839.[15]

EXTENSION OF SOUTHERN LAWS TO THE NORTH

When the Northern states showed no great vigor in suppressing the leaders or presses of this "incendiary" movement, the South made repeated efforts to hale Abolitionist leaders

into its jurisdiction both by violence and by amazing uses of
the extradition laws. They were not successful.[16] For
example:

There came to New York harbor from Charleston,
S. C., a tender belonging to a United States revenue
cutter, with eighteen men on board, intent on capturing
Arthur and Lewis Tappan, Elizur Wright, and William
Goodell. Mr. Wright one day overheard in Gilpin's news-
room the plans for the capture; yet he and Arthur Tappan
walked leisurely home to Brooklyn that night.[17]

Governor Lumpkin, of Georgia, on December 26, 1831,
had signed an act of the Legislature which promised a
reward of $5,000 to the person who would bring Garrison
there to be judged according to the laws of the State.
That is to say, the State of Georgia offered a prize for the
commission of a crime.[18]

The Louisiana Journal carried this amazing offer:
The following has been handed to us by the Committee
of Vigilance of the Parish of East Feliciana, for publication:

FIFTY THOUSAND DOLLARS
REWARD

The above reward will be given on the delivery to the
Committee of Vigilance . . . of the notorious abolition-
ist, ARTHUR TAPPAN, of NEW YORK.
Papers opposed to abolition throughout the United
States are requested to give publicity to the above.
Jackson, La., Oct. 15, 1835.

In 1835, Governor Gayle of Alabama demanded of the
Governor of New York that Ranson G. Williams, publishing agent of the American Anti-Slavery Society should
be delivered up for trial under the laws of Alabama—a
State in which he had never set foot—on an indictment
by the Grand Jury of Tuscaloosa County. The words
on which he was charged with being a "seditious person,
greatly disaffected to the laws of the State . . . and in-

tending to produce insurrection among the slave population were given,—
'God commands, and all nature cries out, that men should not be held as property. The system of making men property has plunged 2,500,000 of our fellow-countrymen into the deepest physical and moral degradation.' " [19]

The Governor of New York naturally refused to honor such a demand. Indeed most of these offers were threats for publicity purposes never expected to secure any victims. Yet one did.

John B. Mahin, a citizen of Ohio, on requisition of Governor Clark, of Kentucky, was delivered up by Governor Vance of Ohio as a fugitive from justice . . . to be tried on an indictment for assisting the escape of certain slaves. He had not been in Kentucky for 19 years! Yet he was arrested at his residence, September 17, 1838, hurried to Kentucky and shut up in jail, without allowing him time to procure a writ of habeas corpus, or summon evidence in his behalf. He was tried by the Circuit Court of Kentucky. . . . It was admitted by the attorney for the Commonwealth that the prisoner was a citizen of Ohio and not in Kentucky at the time of the alleged offense, yet he made an effort to procure conviction. The jury returned a verdict of not guilty.[20]

ABOLITIONISTS IN THE NORTH

In the North the problem was twofold. First, how far the economic and political power of the South could coerce Northern people into stopping anti-slavery agitation. Second, how far race prejudice and economic antagonism against the Negro in the North would second the demands of the South. William Birney gives a very acute analysis of the forces at work to curtail liberty for anti-slavery agitation in the North:

1. The slave States were in possession of the patronage and power of the government.

2. The two parties were bound hand and foot to the slave power. "In 1836 it was no uncommon belief, even among the intelligent, that resistance to the demands of the slave-power was unlawful and akin to treason."

3. Many church organizations embraced both free and slave territory . . . and all the conservative forces were arrayed against a discussion likely to result in schism. This was also true of the large secret orders.

4. The commercial and manufacturing classes were generally hostile to agitation. They wished to be let alone.

5. The prejudice against the negroes among the Northern people indisposed them to resist the slave power. . . . Emancipation might mean the negroes would migrate *en masse* to the North.

6. The prevalent aversion among moral and religious people to take any part in political action greatly increased the difficulty of organizing resistance to the slave-power.

7. In July, 1836, there were 24 States, and the only ones in which slavery did not exist practically, were Maine, Massachusetts, Michigan, and Vermont.[21]

Whatever the cause, for a time neither states nor United States protected the liberties of Abolitionists.[22] The cases cover perhaps ten years. Few lives were lost, though as usual loss of life and property took place at the lowest economic level, i.e., among Northern Negroes, who were generally left defenceless to the mob after the Abolitionists had escaped. No restrictive laws got on the statute-books. There was little governmental action save a Congressional by-law against receiving anti-slavery petitions, and the postal censorship. And the agitation over these probably helped the Abolitionists by disclosing the South's power over the government. The South's attempt to invade the North by requisition or a demand for proscriptive laws failed. James G. Birney, himself a victim of mobs, declared: "The majority of the people are sound on free discussion and a free press."

Yet as was pointed out above, the Abolitionists suffered every possible violation of their liberties. We begin, as in the South, with mob violence against persons, institutions, and property.

THE MOBBING OF ABOLITIONISTS

The mobbing of Abolitionists for speaking or writing against slavery was a merry game all over the North from Maine to Missouri for a decade or more. It was one aspect of the "mob era." These mobs were not so dangerous to life as they were to liberty, especially freedom of speech and of the press. William Birney thus shatters certain melodramatic traditions:

> In the interest of historical truth, I wish to enter a protest against the customary conventional exaggeration of the Northern mobs. . . I must say they were, as a general thing not dangerous either to life or limb, or beyond the power of the police to suppress. . . . These minor forms of mobocratic annoyance were in a ratio probably less than one to a hundred anti-slavery meetings. More serious ones though largely talked of were very rare. "Tar and feathers" figured largely in newspaper articles and pro-slavery speeches, but of the thousands of anti-slavery lecturers only one was subjected to that indignity. The profuse rhetoric of certain Massachusetts writers about "abolition martyrs" might lead a careless reader to imagine that hecatombs of men were slaughtered on the altar of slavery; but I remember no abolitionist but Lovejoy who lost his life. The mobs were misdemeanors at law and political crimes, being aimed at the freedom of the press and speech, but very few persons were hurt. . . . James G. Birney used to say that not a single abolitionist had been mobbed half as often as John Wesley—a comparison which he thought was honorable to the American people.[23]

Birney also wrote in his *Philanthropist* in 1836:

> It is remarkable that no mob has ever attacked the abolitionists except after special training by politicians

who had something to hope from the favor of the South. The people of whom mobs are composed . . . care not a rush for the abolition of slavery, and, if left to themselves, would as soon think of attacking the phrenologists as the abolitionists.

The mobs began as early as Benjamin Lundy's time in the 1820's. He was "repeatedly assaulted on the streets of Baltimore, and once brutally beaten by Austin Woolfolk, a slave-trader." The most famous was the "Garrison Mob" in Boston.

"THE RESPECTABLE MOB OF GENTLEMEN OF PROPERTY AND STANDING"

The Boston Female Anti-Slavery Society advertised a meeting, whereupon this placard was circulated through the business portion of the city; Oct. 21, 1835.

THOMPSON
The Abolitionist!!

That infamous foreign scoundrel THOMPSON will hold forth *this afternoon,* at the Liberator Office. . . . The present is a fair opportunity for the friends of the Union to snake Thompson out! . . . A purse of $100 has been raised by a number of patriotic citizens to reward the individual who shall first lay violent hands on Thompson, so that he may be brought to the tar-kettle before dark.

Thompson, who was an Englishman, was not even in the city. William Lloyd Garrison, however, went to the office where he found the entrance crowded with rioters, and about thirty women meeting within. The Mayor came and told the ladies they must disperse for the sake of the peace, but they refused until they had transacted their business, when they left in a dignified manner, though insulted by the crowd. The Anti-Slavery sign-board was next demanded by the mob, and was thrown to them and danced into fragments. Garrison locked himself in an office until the crowd broke in a panel and "glared at me like so many volves." He narrates his experience thus:

> Unwilling or unable to protect me by an appeal to the military, but desirous that I should receive no harm, the Mayor endeavored (having cleared the building of rioters) to find some way of exit for me. . . . I was instantly discovered by persons on watch. Wilson's Lane was densely filled with rioters, the most active of whom found me in the second story of the carpenter's shop . . . and coiling a rope around my body let me down to the crowd. I was dragged bare-headed . . . into State Street where my clothes were nearly all torn from my body, their intention being as I understood to give me a coat of tar and feathers. . . . The Mayor and his constabulary succeeded in rescuing me with difficulty, and I was taken up into his office. . . . As the night was approaching . . . it was deemed necessary alike for the preservation of the Post Office and of my life, to send me to the Jail . . . as the only place of safety in the city. But I must be committed legally, of course; and so to obtain a writ, Sheriff Parkman had to take a false oath, that I was a disturber of the peace!—though I believe he was actuated by a friendly and sympathizing spirit. . . . I remained in jail until next day when the Court came to me and formally discharged me as one who had done no evil. . . .[24]

THE NEW YORK MOBS

The organization meeting of the New York Anti-Slavery Society was broken up by a mob in 1833. The sexton locked the iron gates of Chatham Street Chapel where the meeting had gone when the alarmed trustees refused the use of another building. The members transacted their business and left before the mob arrived from Tammany Hall. The crowd seized a Negro, whom they nick-named "Brother Tappan," and *made him make a speech*.[25] On July 4, 1834, also, the meeting of the American Anti-Slavery Society was broken up by a violent mob:

Houses and stores were attacked. They broke open the door of Lewis Tappan's house and burned his furniture. The store of Arthur Tappan was threatened, but iron shutters and thirty armed clerks protected it. On the 8th, the alarm was raised and a fight ensued in Chatham Chapel. The congregation was expelled. The night of the 10th they assaulted Dr. Cox's church with stones, then proceeded to his house, but he sent away his furniture and removed his family. A barricade of carts was built across the street to impede the horsemen of the military. The 11th the church of Rev. Ludlow was almost completely sacked; later an immense riot occurred in the neighborhood of Five Points. St. Philip's Episcopal Church (colored) was nearly torn down, while several houses of negroes nearby were entirely demolished. All the military in the city were under arms. Similar outbreaks occurred at Norwich, Connecticut, and Newark, N. J.[26]

For this series of riots, three participants were given one year of hard labor on Blackwell's Island, the heaviest penalty the Court could inflict; and six others, six months.[27] In Philadelphia, in August, 1834, a terrible riot lasted three nights. Forty-four houses of Negroes were attacked, and many destroyed. One Negro was killed, another drowned trying to swim the Schuylkill to escape his tormentors, and many seriously injured. When the colored people of Philadelphia attempted a celebration in commemoration of West Indian emancipation, August, 1842, a public hall and church were burned and private houses demolished. Fire companies refused to act. The hall, erected by the colored people for temperance and religious purposes only, was ordered to be demolished on a petition representing that there was well-grounded fear that it would be burned by a mob and was therefore a nuisance! Anti-slavery meetings were broken up in New Bedford and Pawtucket. Stephen S. Foster was mobbed in Portland, and with difficulty rescued.[28] When the New York State Anti-Slavery Society secured the use of the Court House at Utica, October 21, 1835, certain "prominent and respectable gentlemen," including one Samuel Beardsley, member of Congress from Oneida County, arranged to have a vociferous crowd occupy the room. The Convention went to a Presbyterian Church where a crowd rushed into the room and commanded the speaker to stop. The Convention listened to the leaders of the mob, a so-called "Committee of Twenty-Five," headed by the first Judge of the County. Threats of violence were re-iterated, the Committee besought them to adjourn, which they did, since no business could be transacted, and moved to Peterboro amid insults and threats.[29] In the evening the office of the *Standard and Democrat* received a visit from the "people" who threw its type and other material into the street.[30] The mob laid faggots against the house, in which some women delegates were guests, to burn it, but saw the women at prayer and stopped.[31]

Levi Lincoln and Patrick Doyle attacked Orange Scott, a distinguished minister speaking in the Town Hall at Worcester, Mass., seized the notes of his anti-slavery lecture, tore them up and started to drag the speaker out. This attack was typical of many occurring repeatedly up to 1851. Isaiah Rynders affords the first example of the gunmen who tried to break up anti-slavery meetings. Rynders was a Tammany leader who had engineered the Astor Place riot between Forrest and Macready, and broken up an anti-Wilmot proviso meeting. His effort to break up a meeting at Broadway Tabernacle, New York City, was foiled by the wit of Garrison and his negro colleagues.[32]

THE BURNING OF PENNSYLVANIA HALL

Perhaps the most startling event of this time was the burning of Pennsylvania Hall, Philadelphia, which had been erected at a cost of $40,000 by members of all sects and no sects in order "that the citizens of Philadelphia should possess a room wherein the principles of *Liberty* and *Equality in Civil Rights* could be freely discussed, and the evils of slavery freely portrayed." A majority of the holders of the twenty-dollar shares were working-people. The building was dedicated to "Liberty and the rights of man" before a large audience, May 14, 1838. Within three days it had been burned down.

During the three days a slavery meeting, temperance talks, a literary club, and a free produce convention met in the hall . . . a forum for those barred from free speech elsewhere. The mob began its attack almost at once: throwing stones the first evening, prowling around and inspecting the gas-pipes the next day, and in the evening, by disorder both without and within the hall, almost breaking up a meeting being addressed by Garrison and Angelina Grimke Weld. The 17th, the Managers addressed a letter to the Mayor setting forth the facts, "and we call upon thee—as chief magistrate of the city, to protect us and our property in the exercise of our right peaceably to assemble and discuss any subject of general interest." They enclosed placards, threatening the dispersion of the anti-slavery convention. The Mayor uttered this characteristic mayor's defence: "There are always two sides to a question—it is public opinion makes mobs!—and ninety-nine out of a hundred of those with whom I converse are against you." In the evening he addressed the waiting mob, saying in part: "I am sorry to perceive these disturbances, but I most hope that nothing will be transacted contrary to order and peace. . . . This house has been given up to me (the keys). The managers had the right to hold their meeting; but as good citizens they have at my request, suspended their meeting."
The mob then gave "three cheers for the Mayor" and soon after commenced their attack. They piled inflammable material in front of the forum, bent and broke the gas-jets, set fire to the gas, and in a few hours the building was consumed. They set fire to a new building intended for a "Shelter for Colored Orphans," and the next day attacked a Negro church.[33]

A Committee of the Council in a report on the Mayor laid the blame on the supporters of the meetings:

This excitement was occasioned by the determination of the owners of the building . . . to persevere in openly promulgating . . . doctrines repulsive to the moral sense of a large majority of the community . . . heedless of the dangers, or reckless of the consequences to the peace and order of the city. Of their strict legal and constitutional right to do so there can be no question . . . neither can there be any doubt of the duty of the city authorities to extend protection to all. But how far it was prudent or judicious, or even morally right—how far it became peaceful and good citizens to persevere in measures generally admitted to have a tendency to endanger the public peace—are questions on which public opinion is to a certain extent divided.[34]

The argument and action are identical, whether in Missouri against the Mormons, or in Philadelphia against the Abolitionists.

LEGAL ACTION BY NORTHERN STATES

There are few records of legal action in the North against Abolitionists. The inability of the law to protect was the chief complaint. But the following gives evidence that legal prosecutions occurred:

George Storrs, a Methodist preacher, addressing the anti-slavery society in Northfield, New Hampshire, December 14, 1835 . . . was dragged from his knees while at prayers by the deputy-sheriff, in virtue of a warrant issued by a Justice . . . charging Mr. Storrs with being "an idle and disorderly person . . . a common railer and brawler, going about . . . disturbing the public peace." On trial he was discharged. But on March 31, 1836, at Pittsfield, N. H., he was arrested again in the pulpit . . . tried the same day, and sentenced to three months hard labor in the House of Correction. He appealed from the sentence and we find no further account of the proceedings.[35]

FREEDOM OF THE PRESS

The Abolitionists, barred from the Southern states, had to use propaganda pamphlets and journals there and elsewhere. The first attack on their publications was that familiar device of the suppressor, a libel suit. It was against Garrison, who in 1829-1830 was helping Lundy edit *The Universal Genius of Emancipation* in Baltimore. Garrison was sued by Francis Todd, whom he denounced for taking a cargo of eighty slaves to New Orleans. He was fined fifty dollars and costs. Unable to pay, he served forty-nine days in jail,—the beginning of his fame! Whittier secured a promise of help for Garrison from Henry Clay, and the North Carolina Abolitionists sent a protest.[36] Jail is a great propagandist.

The next step was pseudo-legal action. The grand jury of Oneida County, New York, under the promptings of a law officer of the United States, presented abolition publications as nuisances. At Clinton, Mississippi, a town meeting on September 5, 1836 resolved against a paper proposed by James G. Birney, "that we would regard the establishment of an Abolition paper among us as a direct attempt to peril the lives and fortunes of the whole population, and that it will be the duty of every good citizen to break up by any means . . . any such nefarious design." [37] At Milford, Delaware, it was determined to suppress "an incendiary Republican sheet" by violence, but the plan met with such stubborn resistance that it failed.[38] This amateur suppression soon gave way to the destruction of presses in the border cities, by organized mobs of Southern sympathizers, and culminated in the murder of Elijah Lovejoy.

THE PRESS RIOTS AT CINCINNATI

James G. Birney, a Southerner who had sold his slaves and gone into exile, was candidate for president on the anti-slavery ticket. He established in Cincinnati a newspaper, *The Philanthropist*, in spite of threats. His experiences are significant as showing how good citizens foment "respectable mobs" to further their economic interests.   At midnight on July 12, 1836, a band of men attacked Birney's printer's shop, tore up next week's paper, dismantled the press and carried parts of it away.   The city night-watch offered no interference.   The next night this placard was posted:

ABOLITIONISTS BEWARE

The Citizens of Cincinnati, embracing every class, interested in the prosperity of the city, satisfied that the business of the place is receiving a vital stab from the wicked and misguided operations of the Abolitionists, are resolved to arrest their course. . . . The plan is matured to eradicate this evil which every citizen feels is undermining his business and property.

The business undermined was the very profitable commercial intercourse between the merchants of Cincinnati and the Southern States.   At the solicitation of the Abolitionists a reward of $100 was offered for the persons who broke up Pugh's press.   The mayor's proclamation contained the usual plea for the Abolitionists to abstain from . . . "such measures as may have a tendency to inflame the public mind."   But they would have abstained in vain, for on July 21, a card in the Cincinnati *Gazette* requested a meeting of citizens on Saturday evening at 6 o'clock . . . to decide whether they would permit the publication of *The Philanthropist*.   The alleged purpose of this meeting was to pass resolutions in order to forestall violence by the other citizens!   Although the Abolitionists claimed that the time and place of this meeting— in the mechanics' section of the town—were liable to provoke violence, Birney, with great courage, appeared and stated his intention to go ahead.   The meeting resolved in part:

That we entertain the most profound respect for the memories of the venerated patriots of more than sixty years since who in the harbor of Boston, without the sanction of the law, but in the plenitude of the justness of their cause, took responsibility of re-shipping the tea cargo . . . and that we in imitation of the noble and fearless example . . . declare that whenever we shall find an existing evil, aiming at the destruction and disunion of our happy government, and only prompted by those untiring engines of human ambition, hope of gain and love of notoriety, but shielded from legal enactment according to the usual practice of our laws so as to leave us but one channel through which we can rid our fair land from its withering influence, that in seizing that one point our exertions shall be firm, united and decided.

A committee of twelve prominent citizens was appointed, including Jacob Burnet, a supreme court judge and former United States senator; William Burke, minister and postmaster; Nicholas Longworth, most extensive property-holder of the city; and Oliver M. Spencer, a minister of the Methodist Church. Certain sly folks hinted that this Committee was named by political opponents of its members, who hoped they would get into trouble over the matter. But the Committee labored hard to secure a pledge from the Anti-Slavery Society that they would stop *The Philanthropist*. They failed and adjourned, with this final statement:

They owe it to themselves and those whom they represent to express their utmost abhorrence of everything like violence; and earnestly implore their fellow-citizens to abstain therefrom.

This was dated July 29. Then *The Cincinnati Gazette* records:

Saturday night, July 30, very soon after dark a concourse of citizens . . . broke open the printing-office of the "Philanthropist," scattered the type into the streets, tore down the presses, and completely dismantled the office. . . . The residence of Mr. Birney, the editor, was visited. . . . No person was at home but a youth, upon whose explanation the house was left undisturbed. The Exchange was then visited and refreshment taken. An attack was then made on the residence of some blacks in Church Alley; two guns were fired upon the assailants and

they recoiled . . . a second attack was made, and their
contents destroyed. It was addressed by the Mayor, who
had been a silent spectator of the destruction of the
printing-house. He told them they might as well now
disperse.[89]

THE MARTYRDOM OF ELIJAH LOVEJOY
(November 7, 1837)

"That an American citizen in a state whose Constitution repudiates all slavery, should die a martyr in defence
of the freedom of the press, is a phenomenon in the history
of this Union. Martyrdom was said by Dr. Johnson to
be the only test of sincerity in religious belief. It is also
the ordeal through which all great improvements in the
condition of men are doomed to pass. . . . Here is the
most effective portraiture of the first American martyr to
the freedom of the press, and the freedom of the slave."

Thus wrote John Quincy Adams, ex-President, about
Elijah Lovejoy. Lovejoy in 1835 was the editor of a religious
paper, *The St. Louis Observer* where he had been printing
articles regarding slavery with the eyes of justice and Christianity. In October, two white men were taken by a mob
of sixty influential white citizens and given 150 lashes for
suspected abduction of Negroes. Lovejoy's condemnation of
lynch-law, in spite of the efforts of his publishers to keep
silent, aroused bitter discussion ending as usual in a meeting
with resolutions condemning Lovejoy. His reply, *To My
Fellow Citizens*, (November 5, 1835), is a little known but
brilliant defense of freedom of conscience and of the press.
It shows he suffered not so much for opposing slavery as for
asserting the right to oppose it. Shortly afterward a mulatto,
McIntosh, was burned by a mob for murdering a deputy.
Judge Lawless justified mob violence in the trial of the lynchers. He said:

If, on the other hand, the destruction of the murderer
of Hammond was the act, as I have said, of the many—of
the multitude, in the ordinary sense of these words—not

the act of numerable and ascertainable malefactors: but
of congregated thousands, seized upon and impelled by
that mysterious, metaphysical, and almost electric frenzy
which, in all ages and nations, has hurried on the in-
furiated multitudes to deeds of death and destruction—
then, I say, act not at all in the matter; the case then
transcends your jurisdiction. . . . It is beyond the reach
of human law.[40]

This venture into mob psychology by a judge on the bench
to exonerate influential murderers is the unique possession of
the American people. Lovejoy promptly attacked the "electric frenzy."

We covet not the loss of property nor the honours of
martyrdom; but better far that editor, printer and publishers, should be chained to the same tree as McIntosh
and share his fate, than that the doctrines promulgated
by Judge Lawless from the bench should prevail in this
community. For they are subversive of all law, and at
once open the door for the perpetration, by a congregated
mob, calling themselves the people, of every species of
violence, and that too with perfect impunity. . . .

Convinced that Illinois offered greater freedom of opinion
than slave-holding Missouri, Lovejoy moved *The Observer*
to Alton, Ill., in July, 1836. His press was promptly destroyed as it lay on the Mississippi river bank. He secured
another and persisted for a year, until August 21, 1837, when
he was assaulted but escaped. His press was destroyed a second
time. The third press was broken and thrown into the river
September 21. About October 1, while on a visit to his invalid
wife in Missouri, a mob assaulted him in his bed-chamber, and
he was saved only by the desperate resistance of his wife and
her mother. The mob returned, but when his wife fell into
hysteria, Lovejoy escaped to relieve her. On November 3, a
meeting of the citizens of Alton under the leadership of the
attorney-general of Illinois, resolved to get rid of Lovejoy
who "was hurting the town." They passed resolutions de-

manding that he leave, and included the usual encouragement to mob violence which brought the tragedy four days later:

> *Resolved,* That a strong confidence is entertained that our citizens will abstain from all undue excitements, discountenance every act of violence to person or property, and cherish a sacred regard for the great principles contained in our Bill of Rights. . . .
>
> *Resolved,* That while there appears to be no disposition to prevent the liberty of free discussion, through the medium of the press or otherwise; it is deemed a matter indispensable to the peace and harmony of this community that the labours and influence of the late editor of "The Observer" be no longer identified with any newspaper enterprise in this city.

The persons who drew these resolutions naively gave lip service to the Bill of Rights while virtually ordering a man to leave the community because of his opinions. It is interesting testimony to the time honored unreality of phrases when a contrary purpose is really in mind. Lovejoy had already written—

> I hope to discuss the overwhelmingly important subject of slavery with the freedom of a republican and the meekness of a Christian. . . .

He now answered the threat in these splendid, pathetic words:

> I have been beset night' and day at Alton. And now if I go elsewhere, violence may overtake me in my retreat, and I have no more claim to the protection of any other community than I have upon this; and I have concluded, after consultation with my friends, and earnestly seeking counsel of God, to remain at Alton, and here to insist on protection in the exercise of my rights. If the civil authorities refuse to protect me, I must look to God, and if I die, I have determined to make my grave in Alton.

Lovejoy seems never to have thought at all that he might be safe if he kept silent. Here is one of those rare Americans, who, like Mary Dyer, the Quaker, and Albert Parson, the Anarchist, returned to death for conscience's sake. The fourth press arrived on November 6 and was stored in a warehouse under the protection of a group of citizens, supporters of Lovejoy, who had organized into a company of militia. The next day at about ten o'clock at night, a mob, many of them drunk, attacked the warehouse to burn it.[41] They had been driven off when—

> Our brother and Mr. Weller stepped to the door, and seeing no one, stood looking around just without the threshold, our brother being a little more exposed. Several of the mob had concealed themselves behind a pile of lumber. One of them had a two-barrelled gun and fired. Our brother received five balls, three in the breasts. He turned quickly around . . . ran hastily up a flight of stairs, and fell, exclaiming, "Oh, God, I am shot, I am shot," and expired in a few moments.[42]

To show the even-handed nature of justice, the defenders of the warehouse were indicted as well as eleven leaders of the mob, the latter "for riotously and routously attempting to destroy a printing press," and the former for "riotously and routously resisting this attempt." They were all acquitted.

But the death of this, the single martyr among Abolitionists in the North, brought a nation-wide protest. Citizens of Boston petitioned for the use of Faneuil Hall for a public meeting. This petition was refused by the Aldermen on the ground that it would not express the public opinion of the city, and would create disgraceful confusion in the Hall. Again protestants led by Dr. William Ellery Channing protested, demanded, and secured the Hall, where on this occasion young Wendell Phillips made his first brilliant address.[43]

LATER ATTACKS ON THE PRESS

Charles T. Torrey was excluded from a seat among the reporters at a Slaveholders' Convention at Annapolis, in

1842; afterwards forbidden to take notes in the gallery and finally arrested and thrown into prison. A few days later, on judicial examination, he was released on giving bail in $500, "to keep the peace till April." [44]

Cassius N. Clay issued, June 3, 1845, the first number of "The True American," a paper to urge the overthrow of slavery in Kentucky. . . . August 14th a committee waited upon him in his sick-bed, requiring him to suspend his paper. He wrote "I deny their power and I defy their action," and issued an appeal to the people of Kentucky. . . . On the 18th, a meeting, unmoved by his appeal, proceeded to the consummation of the purpose . . . by choosing a committee of sixty, which proceeded to the office of the offending journal, boxed up its press, and sent it out of the State . . . "as a nuisance of the most formidable character." [45]

Dr. J. E. Snodgrass, editor of the Baltimore "Saturday Visitor," aroused such opposition in 1846 that certain members of the Maryland legislature attempted to suppress his paper and imprison him.

In 1859, the Reverend Daniel Worth, formerly member of the Indiana legislature was arrested for circulating Helper's *Impending Crisis*. He was indicted and committed to jail to wait his trial in the Spring. His bonds, placed at an unreasonable amount, he could not obtain, and he was consigned to a cell "wholly unsuitable for a person to live in". . . . He was convicted for circulating the book, and sentenced to twelve months imprisonment—a sentence deemed light by many because . . . he might have been publicly whipped . . . according to law.[46]

THE BEGINNING OF THE POST OFFICE CENSORSHIP

The most novel and in its consequences the most significant event in the Abolitionist persecution was the first attempt to use the United States post office as a censor of ideas. This began in South Carolina at Charleston where a Committee of twenty-one citizens had made an "arrangement" with the local postmaster to stop delivering or forwarding the publications of the anti-slavery cause. *The Charleston Courier* said:

> The high character and standing of the gentlemen who compose this committee, and the perfect confidence imposed in the entire co-operation of the Postmaster . . . should quiet the apprehensions of our citizens, and induce every individual to give their countenance and support to the constituted authority.

It is not clear here whether "constituted authority" is the United States government or the Committee of Twenty-One, but it was clear after the postmaster had disregarded his agreement with the Committee:

> The recent abuse of the United States mail to the purpose of disseminating the vile and criminal incendiarism of northern fanatics, led to an attack on the Post Office which, although perhaps not to be justified, had much to excuse it. . . . A number of persons assembled about the Exchange wtihout any noise or disturbance, but with coolness and deliberation, made a forcible entry into the Post Office . . . carried off the packages containing the incendiary matter. . . . According to full notice published, the pamphlets . . . were burned the next evening at 8 p. m. opposite the main guard-house, 3,000 persons being present. . . .[47]

The burning was participated in by members of both political parties, and the postmaster was present and helped. To him, on August 4, Postmaster-General Amos Kendall wrote:

> I am satisfied that the Postmaster-General has no legal authority to exclude newspapers from the mails nor prohibit their carriage or delivery on account of their character or tendency, real or supposed. But I am not prepared to direct you to forward or deliver the papers. . . . We owe an obligation to the laws, but a higher one

to the communities in which we live; and if the former be perverted to destroy the latter, it is patriotism to disregard them. Entertaining these views I cannot sanction and will not condemn the step you have taken.[48]

He wrote to Samuel L. Gouverneur, Postmaster of New York City:

It was right to propose to the Anti-Slavery Society voluntarily to desist from attempting to send their publications into the Southern States; and their refusal to do so is but another evidence of the fatuity of the counsel by which they are directed . . . the postmaster-general has no legal authority to exclude from the mails any species of newspapers. . . . Such a power . . . would be fearfully dangerous, and has been properly withheld. But . . . if I were situated as you are, I would do as you have done. . . . You and other postmasters who have assumed the responsibility . . . will I have no doubt, stand justified before your country and all mankind. . . . Lawless power is to be resisted; but power which is exerted in palpable self-defense is not lawless. . . .[49]

The Southern bias of President Jackson and the power of the South in Congress and elsewhere was strong enough to make the President include this recommendation in his annual message, December 2, 1835:

PRESIDENT JACKSON SUGGESTS THE POSTAL CENSORSHIP

I must also invite your attention to the painful excitement produced in the South by attempts to circulate through the mails inflammatory appeals addressed to the passions of the slaves . . . calculated to stimulate them to all the horrors of servile war. . . . It is proper for Congress to take such measures as will prevent the Post Office Department, which was designed to foster an amicable intercourse and correspondence between all the members of the confederacy, from being used as an instrument of an opposite character . . . I would therefore . . . respectfully suggest the propriety of passing such a law as will prohibit, under severe penalties, the circulation in the Southern States, through the mail, of incendiary publications intended to incite the slaves to insurrection.[50]

A Select Committee was appointed December 21 on motion of Senator Calhoun (who was made chairman) to consider the President's recommendation. A bill was reported with a full and adroit discussion by Calhoun.[51] June 3, 1836, this bill came to its third reading by the vote of Vice-President Van Buren to break a tie, 18 to 18. The principal clause finally read:

> That it shall not be lawful for any deputy postmaster in any State, Territory, or District of the United States, knowingly to deliver to any person whatever, any pamphlet, handbill, or other printed paper, or pictorial representation, touching the subject of slavery where, by the the laws of the said State . . . their circulation is prohibited; and any deputy postmaster who shall be guilty thereof shall forthwith be removed from office.

In the debate on freedom of the press the leaders delivered these words:

> Henry Clay: This bill is unconstitutional, I believe, and if not so, it contains a principle of the most dangerous and alarming character.

> Daniel Webster: Congress may under this example be called upon to pass laws to suppress the circulation of political, religious, or other publications which produced excitement in the States.[52]

The bill was defeated April 12, 1836.

On the other hand, in this same year, to make certain that Abolitionist mail would be delivered, Congress passed a law prohibiting postmasters under severe penalty from "unlawfully detaining in their offices, any letter, package, pamphlet, or newspaper with intent to prevent the arrival and delivery of the same." (Act of July 2, 1836, 5 Stat. L. section 32, 87.)

This federal law was not obeyed. Southern postmasters followed the state laws against distributing anti-slavery literature. The laws of Virginia justified postmasters in excluding incendiary publications, and empowered any justice of the peace to "burn publicly" such condemned matter and to commit to jail anyone knowingly subscribing for and receiving it. Such laws were pronounced constitutional, not only by the Attorney-General of Virginia, but even by Caleb Cushing, Attorney-General of the United States under President Pierce. Judge Holt, Postmaster-General under President Buchanan, declared that his opinion had been "cheerfully acquiesced in by this department, and is now recognized as one of the guides of the administration." [53] Right up to the Civil War, the act of July 2, 1836 was void in Southern States. Their laws nullified freedom of the press under the First Amendment. For example:

> Post Office, Lynchburg, Va.
> December 2, 1859
>
> Mr. Horace Greeley:
> Sir:—I inform you that I shall not, in future, deliver from this office the copies of the "Tribune" which come here, because I believe them to be of that incendiary character which are forbidden circulation by the laws of the land, and a proper regard for the safety of society. You will, therefore, discontinue them.
> Respectfully,
> R. H. Glass, Postmaster [54]

Horace Greeley's reply is a fair statement of the whole issue:

> Sir:—I take leave to assure you I shall do nothing of the sort. The subscribers of the "Tribune" in Lynchburg have paid for their papers; we have taken their money, and shall fairly and fully earn it. . . . If they direct us

to send their papers to some other post office we shall obey the request; otherwise we shall send them as originally ordered. If you or your masters choose to steal and destroy them, that is your affair—at all events, not ours; and if there is no law in Virginia to punish larceny, so much the worse for her and our plundered subscribers. If the Federal Administration whereof you are the tool, after monopolizing the business of mail-carrying, sees fit to become the accomplice and patron of mail-robbery, I suppose the outrage must be borne until more honest and less servile rulers can be put into high places at Washington, or till the people recover their natural rights to carry each other's printed matter and letters, asking no odds of the government. Go ahead in your own base way. I shall stand steadfast for human liberty and the protection of all natural rights.

Yours stiffly,

Horace Greeley.

In December, 1859, a postmaster in Hardy County, at Linney's Creek, Virginia, having suppressed the "Religious Telescope" of Dayton, O. . . . Mr. Vallandigham addressed a letter to the Post Office Department. . . . The Virginia postmaster was immediately commanded to obey the law, and the "Telescope" had no more trouble.[55]

At the first appearance of this censorship issue, the Southern states had tried to get Northern states to pass laws against the freedom of the press. The winter of 1835-1836 brought from many legislatures resolutions like these:

By the General Assembly of North Carolina:—Resolved, that our sister States are respectively requested to enact penal laws prohibiting within their respective limits all such publications as may have a tendency to make our slaves discontented.

By Alabama:—That we call upon our sister States and respectfully request them to enact such penal laws as will finally put an end to the malignant deeds of the Abolitionists.

The efforts made in free-state legislatures then in session to pass laws against a free press all failed. Massachusetts passed resolutions against such measures. The law proposed in New York shows how extreme were the demands of the slave holders:

> All writings or pictures, made, printed, or published within this State, with a design or intent, or the manifest tendency whereof shall be to excite to, or cause insurrection . . . or civil commotion, or breach of the peace among the slaves in any part of America . . . or to create on the part of the slaves an abandonment of the service, or a violation of the duty which the master has a legal right to claim, shall be deemed a misdemeanor; all persons who shall make, print, publish, or circulate, or shall subscribe or contribute money or other means to enable any other to make, print, et cetera, shall be deemed guilty of the offense, and shall be punished by fine or imprisonment, or both, in the discretion of the court.

The failure of all these laws shows about how the lines were drawn. The end they aimed at was soon achieved by subverting the United States mails.[56]

THE RIGHT OF PETITION TO CONGRESS

The issue as to what should be done by Congress with petitions against slavery has raised the only Federal question affecting the right of petition. It first arose in the second session of the First Congress, in March, 1790, on two petitions praying for the abolition of slavery—one from the Quakers, and one from the Pennsylvania Abolition Society, signed by Benjamin Franklin as president. These petitions were received and referred to a special committee. In the debate James Madison urged his colleagues not to take any action "that would get the people interested." The report of the special committee for receiving the petitions was adopted.[57] But the people had already become interested.

Later Congress refused to pay any attention to certain petitions. One from Warner Mifflin, a Quaker, returned to its author, was described by a Southern member as "mere rant without any specific prayer." The erasure of the matter from the Journal, however, was not agreed to.[58]

The petitions continued year after year, for the abolition of slavery in the District of Columbia, for a constitutional amendment against it, and for other forms of abolition. At last the Abolitionist agitation forced Congress to other action than a mere reception of the petitions. On January 7, 1836, Senator Calhoun moved to refuse to consider any more petitions on slavery. No definite action was taken. But in the House of Representatives the determination to avoid the embarrassment of anti-slavery petitions finally led on May 26, 1836, to the adoption by vote of 117 to 68 of the following resolution proposed by the select committee on abolition, of which Henry L. Pinckney of South Carolina was chairman.

> And, whereas, it is extremely important and desirable that the agitation of this subject should be finally arrested, for the purpose of restoring tranquillity to the public mind, your committee recommend. . . .
> That all petitions, memorials, resolutions, propositions, or papers, relating in any way, or to any extent whatever, to the subject of slavery, or the abolition of slavery, shall, without being either printed or referred, be laid upon the table and that no further action whatever shall be had thereon.[59]

When the name of John Quincy Adams, once President, was called on the vote, he rose and said:

> I hold the resolution to be a direct violation of the Constitution of the United States, the rule of this House, and the rights of my constituents.

But this gag-rule was repeated in 1837, also in 1838, and in 1840 it was made Rule 21 of the standing rules of the House.

This practical denial of the right of petition helped center public attention on the slavery problem. The Massachusetts legislature on April 12, 1837, passed resolutions by a large majority declaring that "such disposition of petitions was a virtual denial of the right itself" and

> That the resolution above named is an assumption of power and authority, at variance with the spirit and intent of the Constitution of the United States, and injurious to the cause of freedom and free institutions; that it does violence to the inherent, absolute, and inalienable rights of man; and that it tends essentially to impair those fundamental principles of natural justice and natural law, which are antecedent to any written constitutions of government. . . .[60]

RIGHTS OF REPRESENTATIVES IN ASSEMBLY

While the right to protection of a representative in a legislative assembly is not affirmed in the Constitution, it is akin to the right of petition. Instead of sending written appeals the people send a personal agent to labor for their cause. He must enjoy protection from prosecutions for his words in debate, and from personal assault. The basis for the protection from prosecution for utterances in the legislature has been laid down as follows (1808):

> The freedom of deliberation, speech, and debate assured by the Constitution (of Massachusetts) to each branch of the legislature is part of the privilege of the individual members rather than of the house as an organized body; and being derived from the will of the people, the members are entitled to this privilege even against the will of the house. . . .
> The Constitutional provision securing such freedom should be construed liberally, so its full design may be answered; thus extending it to every act resulting from the nature of the member's office, and done in the execution of it, and exempting him from a liability for every-

thing said and done by him as a representative, whether according to the rules of the House or not. . . .

Coffin versus Coffin, 4 *Massachusetts Reports,* 1.

This is a somewhat larger view of the privileges of the representative than that held today.

SENATOR SUMNER ASSAULTED IN THE SENATE

Senator Charles Sumner of Massachusetts delivered before the Senate on May 19 and 20, 1856, in a set speech, *The Crime Against Kansas,* a terrible arraignment of the Southern representatives. Then—

Preston S. Brooks, a representative from South Carolina, either volunteered or was selected as agent for the infliction of punishment. After the adjournment of the Senate, May 22, Mr. Sumner remained at his desk. . . . Brooks, whom he did not know, approached him and said: "I have read your speech twice over. It is a libel on South Carolina, and Mr. Butler who is a relative of mine." . . . He commenced a series of blows with a bludgeon on the Senator's head, by which the latter was smitten down, bleeding and insensible on the floor of the chamber. . . . It was four years before he was pronounced convalescent.

On the House investigation committee's recommendation, it was voted to expel Brooks, 125 to 95 . . . a two-thirds vote being necessary, a vote of censure was adopted by a large majority. Brooks addressed the House. . . . "I went to work very deliberately, as charged," was his text. He announced his resignation and walked out. For the assault, the paltry fine of $300 was imposed by a Washington judge, without one word of disapprobation for the conduct of the culprit. . . . Brooks' constituents raised for him double the amount of the fine. . . . He was immediately re-elected without opposition, by 7,900 votes, on the single issue of whether he had done right or wrong. . . . The students and officers of the University of Virginia also voted him a cane.[61]

Northern indignation led Edward Everett to speak of "this act of lawless violence of which I know no parallel in the history of constitutional government"; and the Rhode Island Assembly passed a resolution that "this assault . . . shows a deliberate attempt to stifle freedom of speech in the national councils." [62]

FREEDOM OF TEACHING

Interference with freedom of Abolitionist teachers was shown in several localities in the North. For instance, the plan for a Negro college in New Haven, Connecticut, was abandoned after a public meeting on September 10, 1831, with Mayor Dennis Kimberley in the chair.   They listened to indignant speeches by distinguished citizens, and resolved 70 to 4 that: "The founding of colleges for the educating of colored people is an unwarrantable and dangerous interference with the internal concerns of other States . . . that the establishment of such a college in New Haven will be incompatible with the prosperity, if not the existence, of the present institutions of learning . . . and that the Mayor, Aldermen, and Common Council will resist the establishment . . . by every lawful means." [63]   The lawful means were not specified.

At Canaan, New Hampshire, a month was given to the preceptor and colored pupils of Noyes Academy in which to quit the town, on condition of forcible expulsion and under threats of death if resistance were made.   Before the ultimatum expired, a legal town-meeting appointed a Superintending Committee to remove the Academy, which was done by about 300 citizens of that and neighboring towns with nearly a hundred yoke of oxen.   They simply hauled the building away.   They then adopted an interesting resolution reading in part: "The Abolitionists must be checked and restrained within constitutional limits, or American liberty will find a speedy grave." [64]

Prudence Crandall, a young Quaker woman, had received fifteen or twenty colored girls in her school at Canterbury,

Connecticut, in 1832, in spite of threatening resolutions adopted at a public meeting in a Congregational Church.

> The store-keepers refused to sell her anything. . . . She and her pupils were insulted on the streets. The doors of her house were besmeared and her well filled with the most odious filth. The pupils were excluded from the privileges of public worship by the officers of the Congregational Church. An attempt was made to drive them away by the revival of an obsolete vagrant law, which provided that after warning by the selectmen, any person, not an inhabitant of the State, who did not depart from the town, should pay a dollar and sixty-seven cents a week, and on failure to pay this license, or leave in ten days, should be whipped on the naked back, not exceeding ten stripes. A warrant . . . was actually served on Eliza Ann Hammond, but not prosecuted. . . .[65]

An influential citizen, Andrew T. Judson, later a judge of the United States district court, found the "school for nigger girls so near him insupportable." So he with others secured this proscriptive law from the Legislature, May 24, 1833:

> Section 1. . . . That no person shall set up or establish in this State any school, academy, or literary institution for the instruction or education of colored persons who are not inhabitants of this State; nor instruct or teach in any school . . . nor harbor or board, for the purpose of being taught . . . any colored person who is not an inhabitant of the State, without the consent in writing, first obtained, of a majority of the civil authority, and also of the selectmen of the town. . . .

Miss Crandall was arraigned, bound over for trial, and thrust . . . into a cell just vacated by a murderer. The legal contest was ended by a technical error so no decision on the merits was ever secured.[66] The school was finally broken up by violence. Miss Crandall's house was set on fire in the night, but was saved because some rotten wood would not burn. Later the house was attacked at midnight by a mob armed with heavy clubs and iron bars. For these outrages there was no redress.[67] Miss Crandall finally left the town.

A like thing happened in the South.

Rev. John G. Fee, of Kentucky, with others, established a negro colony, and these people, negroes, of Berea made it a marked neighborhood . . . but no fidelity as citizens, no caution, no unobtrusiveness could hide their success. . . . A Committee of Sixty-five representing, it was said, "the wealth and respectability of the country," was intrusted with the cruel task of breaking up their homes and banishing them. . . . It was admitted they had broken no law . . . but, it was alleged, their principles were opposed to the public peace. They appealed in vain to the governor for protection, but were advised by that official "for the sake of the peace" to leave the State. This they did without resistance . . . the school-house was closed, the steam-mill dismantled, and again order reigned.[68]

ACADEMIC FREEDOM

Academic freedom in many institutions in the North did not include the right to advocate the immediate abolition of slavery. At Western Reserve College, Hudson, Ohio, Rev. Charles B. Storrs, and Professors Beriah Green and Elizur Wright aroused so much excitement by their views on abolition that the alarmed trustees thought the college would be ruined. The three men had to resign.[69]

James G. Birney, among his other trials for conscience, was rejected as professor of Ancient Languages in Center College, Kentucky. "Everything else was acceptable save my abolition views." [70]

During the intense excitement of the campaign of 1856, Benjamin Sherwood Hedrick was accused of inclination toward the hated "Black Republican" party. For political reasons the newspapers and alumni of the University of North

Carolina, in which Hedrick was a professor of astronomy, took up the charge. Hedrick answered the challenge with a *Defence,* in which he said: "To make the matter short, I say I am in favor of the election of Fremont to the presidency."

The Board of Trustees requested the President to use his influence to make Hedrick resign, and the rest of the Faculty whitewashed themselves in a resolution, declaring that "the course of Professor Hedrick . . . is not warranted by our usages; and the political opinions expressed are not those entertained by any other member of this body." His frankness at least was not the usage in most academic bodies. He was burned in effigy by the students and threatened with violence. The pressure upon the Trustees grew so great that on October 18, the Executive Committee (in spite of some question as to its power) dismissed Hedrick from the University and declared his professorship vacant. This was confirmed by the Trustees, January 5, 1857.[71]

Students suffered no less than teachers. In the North the power of the faculty and trustees was often exerted to prevent anti-slavery agitation. Students of Southern sympathies broke up abolition meetings at Yale and other schools. At Miami University an anti-slavery society was directed by the faculty to cease meeting. Illinois and Kenyon Colleges adopted similar gag-rules. But the students did not always submit. Fifty students of Phillips Academy, Andover, Massachusetts, asked dismissal from that institution because they were refused permission to form an anti-slavery society. A famous revolt for liberty took place among the maturer students at Lane Seminary, Cincinnati, founded a few years before under the presidency of Dr. Lyman Beecher to train ministers for the Mississippi Valley. Some eighty students between 21 and 35 years old formed a Colonization Society and debated slavery on eighteen evenings (February to April, 1834). Next came an Anti-Slavery Society, whose members did helpful service among the Negroes of Cincinnati. The resulting controversy, thought to endanger the Seminary and the interests of the Presbyterian Church, led during the next summer to the adoption of severe rules by the Trustees. They are good specimens of academic hair-splitting:

> The students shall not hold general meetings among themselves, other than those of a religious or devotional character, nor deliver public addresses . . . at the Seminary or elsewhere, in term time; nor make public addresses or communications to the students when assembled at their meals, or on other ordinary occasions. . . . The Committee are further of the opinion that no associations or societies among the students ought to be allowed . . . except such as have for their immediate object, improvement in the prescribed course of studies.

The Faculty interpretation of the rules followed:

> But while associations for free enquiry and voluntary public action, will within these limits be approved and encouraged, associations for public action, too absorbing for health, and the most favorable prosecution of study, and bearing upon a divided and excited community, and touching subjects of great national difficulty, and high political interest, and conducted in a manner to offend needlessly, public sentiment, and to commit this Seminary and its influences . . . we cannot permit.

The Anti-Slavery Society was commanded to disband and the Colonization Society, too. Nearly all the theological students and a number in the literary department requested and secured their dismissals.[72]

ECONOMIC AND RELIGIOUS PRESSURE

Social coercion is probably the most powerful force to secure conformity; it needs neither laws nor violence. Though not a violation of civil liberty, it fills in the picture to note how it worked against Abolitionists.

In Boston the directors of the Athenaeum Library excluded Mrs. Child because she was an Abolitionist. Harriet Martineau

was publicly ostracized.[73]   Arthur Tappan's business difficulties in New York were many. The insurance companies
refused to insure his property and the banks would not discount his paper. Threatening letters, pieces of rope as a
threat of the gallows, and even a slave's ear were sent him
from the South.[74] A meeting of merchants was called at
Charleston, S. C., to unite on a determination not to pur-
chase any more goods of Tappan, who had been supplying
the South Carolina merchants with silks.[75] The economic
aspect was clearly summed up by a partner in a prominent
mercantile house:

> There are millions and millions of dollars due to the
> merchants of this city alone, from the South, the
> payment of which would be jeopardized by any rupture
> between the North and the South. It is not a matter
> of principle with us. It is a matter of business
> necessity.[76]

THE PRELUDE TO CIVIL WAR

The Kansas Border Wars (1855-1859) present enough violations of civil liberty for a volume, but they are not detailed
here for they may well be viewed as the first chapter of the
Civil War. There were dual governments, disregard for law,
and armed violence. The neighboring state, Missouri, sent
its vagabond armies (unofficial, of course) into Kansas to
drive out the "nigger-loving abolitionists" who had been sent
in to colonize for a "free State." Meanwhile the colonization societies back in New England shipped in their Sharps
rifles. Political conditions in the rest of the nation kept the
Federal government from intervening to re-establish a constitutional regime. So what matter if William Phillips was
tarred and feathered. If *The Parkville Luminary* was
quenched in the Missouri? If duly elected legislators were
driven out into the plains? It was the overture to war, and
to that war we must now turn.[77]

As the North was won to the anti-slavery cause from

humane or economic motives, the Abolitionists gained their liberties. Power had shifted to their side. So after about 1845 we find no very serious interferences with their propaganda in the North. Yet even as late as 1862 a riot occurred at a meeting in New York where Wendell Phillips denounced the Administration's failure to free the slaves.[78] In the South as the cleavage became sharper there was less liberty than ever. Here from 1835 to 1885 constitutional liberty had no normal status since for two decades after the war it was submerged in the chaos of Reconstruction.

To sum up,—the events of the "mob era" and especially the attacks on Abolitionists blunted any sense of duty or need to protect the minority. The idea of the "respectable" mob was perfected and took an effective form. It was discovered that the Post Office could be used as a censor of ideas. The tyranny of the majority was carried further by the conception of controlling public opinion against a minority, and control of education by discipline of teachers and students was its significant expression. Most of the modern machinery for curtailing liberty was in full use after this period just before the Civil War.

CHAPTER IV

CIVIL LIBERTY AND CIVIL WAR

FOR civil liberty the Civil War (1861-1865) meant three things. First, it consummated the claim of one phase of the "tyranny of the majority," namely that a minority is not free to withdraw and set up a new state. Second, it proved again that war suspends constitutional guarantees. Third, it left the United States a legacy of violence and of weakened constitutional ideals.

The first is most important for liberty as an historic process. The majority of States in population and power finally asserted their rule over the rest—forbidding in effect any section from splitting off to install a new state guarantee in order to secure for itself some special liberty. The liberties the South wanted were: first, to own slaves, and second, to assert the opposite of tyranny by the majority of states, namely, tyranny by individual states under the principle of "states' rights." With the defeat of this second principle the Union established a "geographical tyranny" of the majority. A few years later the Mormons attempted to detach from the Union the Territory of Utah to create the polygamous state of Deseret. But the Union held Utah, and the Mormons have been denied liberty to practice polygamy.

In these cases the power of the majority achieved what are considered to be good ends. It freed the slaves and ended polygamy. But at the same time it created the machinery for crushing other minorities, which may not represent socially undesirable purposes. Now minorities must make their fight for existence inside the Union. They cannot set up independent states in which to function. Their liberty must be won at home, by education, not by migration. Outside, the earth is so occupied that no group can find room, as did the pioneering Puritans, to create a new state in which to establish their own freedom. This is the chief reason why a larger conception of evolutionary political liberty is now a supreme need.

As the Civil War blotted out the claims of geographical sections, it tended also to extend the majority's power in every direction, vertical as well as horizontal. It did away, at least in concept, with any undemocratic status like master and slave. The people were the only master. Everybody must belong to "the people," or the majority rule will not work. So they took the Negro from his owner and turned him over to a new master, the mob, to whom he was not only of no value, but was a rival to be persecuted as a "nigger" or "a scab."

The chief lesson of the Civil War from the standpoint of civil liberty is that "the people" (and their government) will control all sections or factions on any issue they think is vital to the democratic state. They will not allow any fractional liberty. The entire Civil War is evidence of that concept, regardless of whether the coerced minority was right or wrong.

The second lesson concerns civil liberty in the North and South. What happened to it under the impact of war is significant. In both sections there were minorities opposed to the entire war, and claiming the legal right to their dissent.

The facts in the North afford a peculiar test of civil liberty principles. The anti-slavery majority had just grown from an oppressed minority whose persecution was too recent to be forgotten. Now this majority is itself faced with a dissenting political group opposed to the war. Do they recall the old struggles? Do they protect this new minority? They do not! They pursue no abstractions. They follow the ancient rule—who has power has liberty—and put the dissenter in jail.

In the South there was less oppression because there was

less liberty and fewer dissenters. The constitutions of the Confederacy and of its states contained bills of rights on the old forms. But since the military power arose before the civil, there was no strength in the civil government. The urgency of defense was advanced as excuse for whatever the military did. In reality there was no law but military law. Jefferson Davis suspended the privilege of the writ of habeas corpus just as Lincoln did. The South showed the same invasions of civil rights as the North—by conscription, espionage, military rule and wholesale illegal arrests.

The political mind of the South was united for self-preservation and so did not resent military power. Opposition was negligible, compared with conditions in the North. Under the terrible pressure of Southern sentiment, none dared invoke constitutional forms that depended for their meaning entirely upon the success of the armies. No study of civil liberty in the South has significance except the cases of the Southern conscientious objectors to war.

We do not discuss here the *intersectional* problems of prisoners and the like that arose under the commonly accepted laws of war. Nor where the military power was in force have its decisions been questioned. They are noted only when they usurp the civil power.

There were of course extraordinary conditions in this war which have been urged in justification for the invasions of liberty in the North. First, it was a civil war,—the enemy was the same race and lived on the border of the loyal population. It was often difficult to distinguish the disloyal, so that measures intended to restrain the disaffected, were not infrequently invoked against the innocent whose acts might look disloyal. The long border between the states was a zone where allegiance was dubious and shifting. The instability of Maryland, the invasion of Pennsylvania, the constant threat of capture of Washington, demanded emergency measures which could not be particular about civil rights. The wide area involved, and the shifting operations made the theater of war hard to define and difficult to police.

Second, it was the first nation-wide war in which the morale of the whole people became a prime concern. New dangers arose in directions hitherto regarded as outside the theater of war;—from espionage, political and religious opposition to the war, resistance to conscription and from enforced labor. Fewer enlistments, curtailed production and a lowered morale meant defeat. How could such obstacles be overcome?

The practical answer was by force,—by replacing civil processes with military rule. Ordinarily martial law could not replace civil government until the courts were actually closed. But in the Civil War military rule extended into regions not invaded or remotely threatened. Men far up in New York State were arrested on executive order from Washington; a newspaper in Chicago was suppressed by a telegram from the commanding general. The civil courts were functioning and oddly enough their only danger was from the armies which were presumably defending them.

From the Civil War on we must recognize the extension of the field of war to the entire nation. Munitions are as important as the men on the firing-line; industry must be guarded against strikes and lowered production; the press must stimulate the war ardor. Political opposition, tolerated in time of peace, now becomes dangerous. People must be protected from opposition arguments, even if they lend no aid or comfort to the enemy. How such forces shall be checked becomes of great importance. President Lincoln, as head of both military and civil arms of the government, decided to use what he felt the necessities of any case demanded. Let us turn to his record.

DOES WAR SUSPEND THE CONSTITUTION?

Does war suspend the Constitution? Is the maxim *inter armis leges silent* always true? President Lincoln, his cabinet, his generals, and even Congress all answered yes. Here is what Lincoln said of his policy:

April 4, 1864.

. . . My oath to preserve the Constitution imposed on me the duty of preserving by every indispensable means that government, that nation, of which the Constitution was the organic law. Was it possible to lose the nation, and yet preserve the Constitution? By general law, life and limb must be protected, yet often a limb must be amputated to save a life, but a life is never wisely given to save a limb. I felt that measures otherwise unconstitutional, might become lawful by becoming indispensable to the preservation of the Constitution through the preservation of the nation. Right or wrong I assumed this ground and I now avow it. I could not feel that to the best of my ability I had even tried to save the Constitution, if to save slavery, or any minor matter, I should permit the wreck of the government, country, and Constitution, together.[1]

This is a classic statement of the old doctrine of necessity when power always justifies restrictions on liberty. Mr. Lincoln frankly admitted that the Constitution was suspended. James Bryce reached the same conclusion:

The executive and majority in Congress found themselves obliged to stretch this war power to cover many acts trenching on the ordinary rights of the States and individuals, till there ensued something approaching a suspension of constitutional guarantees in favour of the Federal government. . . . Only a few of these cases came before the courts, and the courts, in some instances disapproved them. Appeals made to the letter of the Constitution by the minority were discredited by the fact that they were made by persons sympathizing with the secessionists who were seeking to destroy it. So many extreme things were done under pressure of necessity, that something less came to be regarded as a reasonable and moderate compromise.

In theory war cannot suspend the Constitution. No word occurs in the Constitution authorizing its suspension—in war or peace—(save the clause on the suspension of habeas corpus). Nor apparently did its framers anticipate that it would at any time be suspended. The English Constitution had been enforced in war-time. The state constitutions made no mention of suspension,—ever. Delaware expressly prohibited it. "No power of suspending laws shall be exercised but by the legislature."

In fact, however, a serious war always suspends parts of the Constitution. The Revolution suspended the State guarantees for Tory and Quaker; the mere threat of war served as an excuse for the Alien and Sedition Acts; in the War of 1812, Jackson had proceeded on the thesis that in an emergency military power is above the civil. The Dorr War had proven the case in Rhode Island.

MR. LINCOLN SUSPENDS THE WRIT OF HABEAS CORPUS

April 27, 1861, scarcely a week after the fall of Sumter, President Lincoln authorized General Winfield Scott, if he found resistance that rendered it necessary, to suspend the writ of habeas corpus between Philadelphia and Washington, personally or through any officer in command. His purpose was to control border conditions, especially in Maryland, which daily threatened to go over to the South. Similar suspension was ordered on July 2, as far north as New York.

According to the Constitution the privilege of the writ is to be suspended only "in cases of rebellion or invasion when public safety requires it." Mr. Lincoln's order was widely disapproved on two grounds: first, by suspending the privilege himself he had usurped the powers of Congress; second, he suspended it in areas where the courts were functioning and no public danger of rebellion or invasion existed.[2] He was forced to defend himself in a message on July 4:—

It is believed that nothing has been done beyond the constitutional competency of Congress. . . . This authority has purposely been exercised very sparingly. . . . It is insisted that Congress . . . is vested with this power. But the Constitution itself is silent . . . and as the provision was plainly made for a dangerous emergency, it cannot be believed that the framers intended that in every case the danger should run its course until Congress should be called together, the very assembling of which might be prevented, as was intended in this case, by the rebellion.[3]

By February 14, 1862, the President, reassured that "the facilities for treasonable practices had diminished" and "anxious to favor a return to the normal course of Administration" directed that all political prisoners, or prisoners held in military custody, be released on a parole to render no aid or comfort to the enemy. Complete amnesty was granted for past offenses, and in the future extraordinary arrests were to be made by the military authorities alone.[4] A board of one military and one civil commissioner was appointed to determine whether military prisoners should be held, discharged, or remitted to the civil tribunals for trial. In November the Secretary of War ordered the release of all draft resisters and other war offenders in states where the draft quotas had been filled. He freed all prisoners from rebel States on parole, with permission to leave the North, not to return during the war.[5] The efforts of the joint-commission seem to have been half-hearted.

In spite of this generous house-cleaning President Lincoln, averring that "disloyal persons are not adequately restrained by the ordinary processes of law," ordered a general suspension of the writ of habeas corpus on September 24, 1862:

> During the existing insurrection . . . all rebels and insurgents, their aiders and abetters, within the United States, and all persons discouraging voluntary enlistments, resisting military drafts, or guilty of any disloyal practices . . . shall be subject to martial law and liable to trials and punishments by courts-martial or military commission;
>
> Second, that the writ of habeas corpus is suspended in

respect to all persons arrested, or who are now, or hereafter during the rebellion shall be, imprisoned in any
fort, camp, arsenal, military prison, or other place of
confinement, by any military authority, or by the sentence of any court-martial or military commission.[6]

Thereafter the civil authority was subordinate to the military, and every person guilty of the vague crime of "any
disloyal practice" was subject to martial law. The controversy over it became bitter. In the Congressional elections
of 1862 Mr. Lincoln suffered a distinct rebuke, in part attrib-
utable to his subversion of civil rights. It became necessary
to back up the President by an "Indemnifying Act," which
passed both houses in spite of a vigorous protest. It became
a law, March 3, 1863. It reads in part:

> Be it enacted, . . . that during the present rebellion,
> the President . . . whenever in his judgment, the public
> safety may require it, is authorized to suspend the
> privilege of the writ of habeas corpus in any case
> throughout the United States. And whenever and where-
> ever the said privilege shall be suspended . . . no mili-
> tary or other officer shall be compelled . . . to return
> the body of any person detained by him by authority of
> the President; but upon certificate, under oath . . .
> that such person is detained by him as a prisoner under
> authority of the President, further proceedings under the
> writ . . . shall be suspended by the judge or court, so
> long as said suspension shall remain in force. . . .
> Section 4. . . . That any order of the President, or
> under his authority, made at any time during the present
> rebellion, shall be a defence in all courts to any action,
> civil or criminal, pending or to be commenced, for any
> search, seizure, arrest, or imprisonment, made, done, or
> committed, or acts omitted to be done, under and by
> virtue of such orders, or under color of any law of
> Congress, and such defence may be made by special plea,
> or under the general issue.
> Section 2 required the Secretaries of State and of War
> to furnish to judges of United States circuit and district

courts lists of all citizens of states in which the administration of law remained unimpaired, who were held as "state or political prisoners"; and if after such lists had been furnished, no grand jury had indicted such persons, they were to be brought before the judge to be discharged; provided that the detained person take the oath of allegiance, and swear not to aid the rebellion, and that the judge might require bond to keep the peace if he deemed the public safety required it. Sections 5 and 6 provided that actions against officers might be transferred from the State Courts to the United States Courts; and must be commenced within two years.[7]

Under this act the President on September 15, 1863 confirmed his previous suspension in modified form for the duration of the rebellion. The writ could not issue against military, naval, or civil officers who under the President's command held

> Prisoners of war, spies, aiders and abettors of the enemy . . . or those for resisting the draft, or for any other offense against the military or naval service.

The President's power was limited only by interpretations of the vague terms "aiders and abettors of the enemy" and "any other offence against the military or naval service."

THOUSANDS OF POLITICAL PRISONERS

Under this authority from 1861 to the end of the War arrests continued. They constitute the largest record of official interferences with civil rights in the history of the United States. The total number is astounding, though exact figures are difficult to give because the records confuse State and Federal prisoners, political and military spies and draft-resisters. The evidence shows that they ran well into the thousands.

> The records of the provost-marshal's office in Washington show 38,000 military prisoners (political prisoners) reported there during the rebellion.[8]

The records of the commissary-general of prisoners from February, 1862 to the close of the war contains the names of 13,535 citizens who were arrested and confined in various military prisons. . . . Many cases do not show the charge on which arrests were made. There were also many imprisonments by military authorities in State prisons. . . . The assistant provost-marshal of Illinois reports, exclusive of deserters, 443 arrests from the organization of his office to May, 1865. . . . No lists of "state or political prisoners" were furnished to the Judges (by the Indemnifying Act) as far as I have been able to ascertain; and in truth the relish for autocratic government had so developed that in September of that year Chase was surprised that the provisions of the act were unfamiliar to the President and all the members of the Cabinet except himself.[9]

The *Official Records of the War of the Rebellion*, series 2, volume II, documents hundreds of cases in its 1,557 pages, with sixty pages of summaries added from the Record Book of the State Department. In *The American Bastile*, John A. Marshall details some one hundred and fifty cases of alleged illegal arrest and imprisonment.

Three statements on these arrests and imprisonments are of interest. Marshall contrasts our previous history with the Civil War cases. He says:

From the organization of the government to the Administration of the late President Lincoln, we know of no case in which an American citizen was arrested without warrant, imprisoned without charges preferred, and released after months and years of incarceration, without trial . . . although there was not only imaginary, but real "disloyalty" among citizens, dangerous to the common interests of the government, during former administrations.[10]

Rhodes in his history says:

While I have not lighted upon an instance in which the President himself directed an arrest, he permitted them all; he stands responsible for casting into prison citizens of the United States on orders as arbitrary as the *Lettres-de-cachet* of Louis XIV.[11]

James Bryce writes:

Abraham Lincoln wielded more authority than any Englishman has done since Oliver Cromwell. It is true that the ordinary law was for some purposes practically suspended during the War of Secession.[12]

THE ARMY DEFIES THE SUPREME COURT

John Merryman of Baltimore County, Maryland, was arrested May 25, 1861, under the original suspension of the writ, charged with various acts of treason and lodged at Fort McHenry under Gen. George Cadwalader. Merryman petitioned Chief Justice Roger B. Taney of the United States Supreme Court for a writ of habeas corpus, which was issued returnable May 27. Gen. Cadwalader refused to respond, alleging that he was duly authorized by the President to suspend the writ. The Chief Justice next issued a writ for the United States Marshal to produce the body of Gen. Cadwalader in court "to answer for his contempt." The marshal reported that he was not permitted to enter the fort, and was informed "there was no answer to his writ."

Justice Taney then delivered an opinion that the imprisonment was unlawful upon two grounds:

1. The President, under the Constitution and laws of the United States, cannot suspend the privilege of the writ of habeas corpus, nor authorize any military officer to do so.
2. A military officer has not the right to arrest and detain a person, not subject to the rules and articles of war, for an offense against the laws of the United States, except in and of the judicial authority and subject to its control. . . .

He further declared that the civil authority had been resisted by a superior force, and that therefore there was nothing he could do except reduce to writing his reasons, report them to the President, and call upon him to do his constitutional duty,—in other words to enforce the process of the court.[13]

This pitiful appeal of the Supreme Court was met by an opinion from the Attorney-General justifying Mr. Lincoln. When United States Judge Garrison of Brooklyn cited Col. Burke of Fort Lafayette for contempt in refusing to answer a writ sued out for four members of the Baltimore Police Board, the officer refused to appear, and the Judge, "submitting to inevitable necessity" dismissed the proceedings. The prisoners were subsequently released.[14]

Several states recognized the danger in these military arrests. The Wisconsin legislature approved Justice Taney's opinion, the Delaware legislature passed a bill to prevent illegal arrests by federal authority, but the Governor refused to recognize it and issued a proclamation that he would protect any persons prosecuted for making illegal arrests. Governor Horatio Seymour of New York in his first message, January 7, 1863, discussed "State Rights versus Martial Law." Governor Curtin of Pennsylvania sent a protesting message to his legislature.[15] Politics was of course responsible for some of this opposition, but there was behind it a wide-spread protest against the President's actions.

"GENERAL ORDER 38"

The famous General Order 38 was issued April 13, 1863, after the Indemnifying Act had passed, by General Burnside, commanding the Department of the Ohio in which there was strong opposition to the war. The text speaks for itself:

General Order 38.
The Commanding general publishes, for the information of all concerned, that all persons found within our lines who shall commit acts for the benefit of the enemies of our country will be tried as spies or traitors, and, if convicted, will suffer death. . . . The habit of declaring sympathy for the enemy will not be allowed in this de-

partment. Persons committing such offenses will be at once arrested, with a view of being tried as above stated. . . . It must be distinctly understood that treason, expressed or implied, will not be tolerated in this department.

By Command of Major-General Burnside.[16]

Freedom of speech is here denied, and the novel crime of "implied treason" created. But Burnside was not successful in stilling the opposition. The famous "Vallandigham case" presents a clear-cut issue between the President's military power in peaceful territory and the right of political opponents to criticize his acts. Clement Vallandigham was a Democrat, a member of Congress, and a vigorous political opponent of President Lincoln's. The Democrats moreover, espoused Vallandigham's cause.[17]

He was the chief speaker at a Democratic mass-meeting in Ohio on May 1, 1863. Two captains in civilian clothes took notes upon which General Burnside decided Order 38 had been violated. Vallandigham was arrested by soldiers at 2:30 on the morning of May 5, tried by a military commission two days later; found guilty and sentenced to close confinement during the continuance of the war. Rhodes sums up the case thus:

> From the beginning to the end of these proceedings law and justice were set at naught. . . . The right of General Burnside even to make the arrest may be questioned. The majority of the United States Supreme Court in the Milligan case maintained that the suspension of the writ of habeas corpus did not authorize the arrest of any one. The argument that Southern Ohio was the theater of war and therefore under martial law cannot be maintained. . . . The United States courts were regularly open in the Southern district of Ohio.[18]

The charge against Vallandigham was "publicly expressing . . . sympathy for those in arms against the government, and declaring disloyal sentiments and opinions with the object of weakening the power of the government in its efforts to suppress an unlawful rebellion." The specifications of utterances on which this charge was made included such statements as: "The present war is a cruel, wicked, and unnecessary war; a war not waged for the preservation of the Union . . . characterizing General Orders No. 38 as a base usurpation of arbitrary authority . . . that he firmly believed that the men in power are attempting to establish a despotism . . . more cruel and oppressive than ever existed before."[19] Vallandigham attempted no defence except this statement:

> I am not either in the land or naval forces . . . nor the militia in actual service, and therefore am not triable for any cause by such a court, but am subject by the express terms of the Constitution, to arrest only by judicial warrant . . . and am now entitled to speedy and public trial by an impartial jury of the State of Ohio . . . and evidence and arguments according to the common law and ways of Judicial Courts.
>
> And all these I here demand as my right as a citizen of the United States. . . . But the alleged "offence" is not known to the Constitution nor to any law thereof. It is words spoken to the people of Ohio in open and public political meeting, lawfully and peaceably assembled. It is the words of criticism of the public policy of public servants of the people by which policy it was alleged that the welfare of the country was not promoted. It was an appeal to change that policy, not by force, but by free election and the ballot box. It is not pretended that I counselled disobedience to the Constitution or resistance to laws and lawful authority. I never have.[20]

The sentence of the commission was commuted by President Lincoln as follows:

> May 19, 1863.
> Sir: The President directs that without delay you send C. L. Vallandigham under secure guard to the headquarters of General Rosecrans to be put by him beyond our military lines; and in case of his return within our

lines, he will be arrested and kept in close custody for the term specified in his sentence.

He went South, later to Canada, and returned to Ohio unmolested.[21] Mr. Lincoln was not very well pleased with Burnside, and wired that "all the Cabinet regretted the arrest, doubting its necessity. . . . but being done, all were for seeing you through with it."[22]

Two legal efforts were made to set aside General Burnside's stern action. Two days after the military trial Judge Humphrey Leavitt of the Southern District Court of Ohio refused a writ of habeas corpus on the grounds: (1) the arrest was legal; (2) even though it had been illegal it was "morally certain that the writ would not be obeyed." General Burnside submitted a paper claiming a legal right to make arrests as military commander of the Department, which he "chose to regard as a vast armed camp, every citizen within its limits being subject to military law." The Supreme Court of the United States denied Vallandigham a writ of *certiorari* to order the Judge Advocate of the Army to send up the proceedings of the military commission for review. Justice Swayne delivered the opinion that "whatever may be the force of Vallandigham's protest that he was not triable by a court of military constitution, it is certain that his petition cannot be brought within the 14th section of the Judiciary Act of 1789. . . . This court cannot originate a writ of certiorari to review or pronounce any opinion upon the proceedings of a military commission." [23]

The courts were unanimous in their impotence. They never actually passed upon the constitutionality of the President's acts though in most of the decisions one gets the impression that there were grave doubts as to the legality of what was done. The judges simply said they had to submit to a preponderant military power in the hands of those against whom their feeble writs might be issued; or else as did Justice Swayne, they sidestepped on a technical lack of jurisdiction.

Military power is necessarily unjust, particularly against the unknown and friendless. Here is an example of what must have happened generally:

> Not many months ago, this Administration, in its great and tender mercy towards the six hundred and forty prisoners of state confined for treasonable practices, at Camp Chase, Ohio . . . appointed a commissioner, an extra-judicial functionary, unknown to the Constitution and laws, to hear and determine the cases of the several parties accused, and with power to discharge, at his discretion, or to banish to Johnson's Island, in Lake Erie. Among the political prisoners called before him was a lad of fifteen, a newsboy upon the Ohio River, whose only offence proved upon inquiry to be that he owed fifteen cents, the unpaid balance of a debt due to his washerwoman—who had him arrested by the provost-marshal, as guilty of "disloyal practices." And yet for four weary months the lad had lain in that foul and most loathsome prison, under military charge. . . . [24]

Even after Lincoln's death and the close of hostilities, President Andrew Johnson prolonged the alleged war-power by suspending the writ by special order for the execution of Mrs. Mary Surratt, who had been found guilty by a military commission on June 28, 1865, of complicity in the conspiracy which led to the assassination of President Lincoln. Five members of the commission petitioned President Johnson to commute her sentence to life imprisonment on account of her sex and age—nearly fifty. He refused to intervene and she was sentenced to be hung between ten A. M. and two P. M. on July 7. At 7:30 that morning her counsel applied to Judge Andrew Wylie of the Supreme Court of the District of Columbia, for a writ of habeas corpus, to be returnable by Major-General W. S. Hancock of the Middle Military Division. The gist of her claim was "that she had been unlawfully tried by a military commission, although a private citizen and in nowise connected with the military; that the alleged offense was committed within the lines of the United

States armies, and not in enemy's territory, or in territory under the control of a military commission for the trial of civil causes; that she had the right to a public trial by jury in the criminal courts of the District which were and are open."

Judge Wylie endorsed the writ to General Hancock, returnable at the hour of ten o'clock A. M. It was served by the marshal, but when General Hancock did not appear at that time, Judge Wylie declared:

> The Court acknowledges that its powers are inadequate to meet the military power . . . the laws are silent . . . The court must submit to the supreme physical force that now holds the prisoner.

But at half-past eleven Hancock and Attorney-General Speed appeared with an apology and presented this return to the writ:

> That the body of Mary E. Surratt is in my possession under and by virtue of an order of Andrew Johnson, president of the United States . . . and that I do not produce said body by reason of the order of the President, endorsed upon the said writ:

Executive Offices,
July 7, 1865, 10 A. M.

W. S. Hancock . . . I, Andrew Johnson, President of the United States, do hereby declare that the writ of habeas corpus has been heretofore suspended in such cases as this, and I do hereby especially suspend this writ and direct that you proceed to execute the order heretofore given on the judgment of the Military Commission, and you will give this order in return to the writ.

Andrew Johnson, President.

The Court replied: "The Court finds itself powerless to take any further action . . . and therefore declines to make orders which would be vain for any practical purpose." That afternoon Mrs. Surratt was hanged.[25]

LIBERTY RESTORED AFTER THE WAR

The United States Supreme Court finally repudiated the whole doctrine upon which these arrests and orders rested—but unfortunately for the deported Vallandigham or the dead Mrs. Surratt, not until some time after the close of the War. Then came before them the case of Lamdin P. Milligan of Indiana, arrested October 5, 1864, by the military commission on the usual charges,—conspiracy against the government, inciting insurrections, affording aid and comfort to the rebels, violations of the laws of war. The specification was that he had joined a secret society known as the Order of American Knights for the purpose of overthrowing the government . . . conspiring to liberate prisoners of war . . . resisting the draft, etc. He was found guilty, sentenced to be hanged, and his execution set for May 19, 1865. He petitioned the United States Circuit Court for Indiana to be turned over to a civil tribunal or discharged, advancing the usual argument of these petitioners, namely that he had never been in the military service, nor in any State engaged in rebellion, and that the grand jury, which had convened during his imprisonment, had returned no indictment against him.

The Circuit Court judges divided and certified the case to the Supreme Court, which decided that a writ of habeas corpus should be issued, that Milligan should be discharged, and that the military commission had no jurisdiction legally to try or sentence Milligan. The decision contains these fine words on civil liberty:

No graver question was ever considered by this Court nor one which more nearly concerns the right of the whole people, for it is the birthright of every American citizen when charged with crime to be tried and punished according to the law. . . . By the protection of the law human rights are secured; withdraw that protection and they are at the mercy of wicked rulers or the clamor of an excited people. . . . By that Constitution and the law authorized by it, this question must be determined.

. . . One of the plainest constitutional provisions was therefore infringed when Milligan was denied a trial by jury . . . If this government (martial law) is continued after the courts are reinstated, it is a gross usurpation of power. Martial rule can never exist when the courts are open and in the proper and unobstructed exercise of their jurisdiction; it is also confined to the locality of actual war.

The privilege of this great writ (habèas corpus) had never before been withheld from the citizen. . . . The suspension of the writ does not authorize the arrest of any one, but simply denies to one arrested the privilege of the writ in order to obtain his liberty. . . . Those great and good men foresaw that troublous times would arise when rulers and people would seek by sharp and decisive measures to accomplish ends deemed just and proper, and that the principles of constitutional liberty would be in peril unless established by irrepealable law. The Constitution of the United States is a law for rulers and people, equally in war and peace, and covers with the shield of its protection all classes of men at all times and under all circumstances. . . . No doctrine is more pernicious than that any of its great provisions can be suspended during any of the great exigencies of government. That leads directly to anarchy and despotism. . . . Whatever his desert or his punishment may be, it is more important to the country and to every citizen that he should not be punished under an illegal sentence, sanctioned by this court of last resort than that he should be punished at all. . . .[26]

SUSPENSION OF THE WRIT DURING RECONSTRUCTION

One suspension of habeas corpus during Reconstruction occurred as a consequence of the Civil War. President Grant, having issued a proclamation against certain lawless bodies in South Carolina on March 24, 1871, an act outlawing the Ku Klux Klan was passed on April 20, empowering the President to suspend the writ. He issued a proclamation calling attention to the recent law, and on October 17 suspended habeas corpus in nine counties in South Carolina.

Federal troops were sent in and over 1,800 arrests were made. The suspension lasted until November 10. The President's act was authorized by Congress, but whether actual conditions in South Carolina justified the suspension, was then, and remains now, unsettled. This is the last suspension of the writ by the President of the United States.[27]

FREEDOM OF SPEECH AND ASSEMBLAGE

The mob violence and suppression of minority opinion that characterize all wars occurred throughout the Civil War. Peace meetings and expressions of peace sentiments were quickly put under the ban. Persons were arrested or mobbed for chance remarks, as when a talkative stagedriver was charged with "sedition." Philadelphia witnessed violence against Southern sympathizers; but the Mayor had the ringleaders of the mob arrested. In New Town a peace meeting was postponed for fear of violence. At Middleton, New Jersey, Thomas Dunn, an Englishman, was locked up because he promoted a peace meeting.[28] Here are two incidents:

A number of tories at New Fairchild, Conn., had a white flag up, which certain Union men in Danbury determined to take down. Some thirty or forty of them repaired to the location of the obnoxious rag, taking an American flag to put in its place. . . . They were attacked by a party of tories some two hundred strong . . . the weapons being spades, axes, and clubs. Being soon overpowered the Union men fled, carrying away with them Andrew Knox, John Allen, and Thomas Kinney of their party, all very badly cut around the head with spades. . . . Of the tories two were probably fatally wounded. . . . A peace flag was taken down in Easton on Thursday . . . and preparations were making on Sunday to proceed to Hattertown. . . .[29]

A peace flag was to be raised at Stepney . . . to be addressed by a well-known stump-speaker in the last campaign. Five or six omnibus-loads of people, including many returned volunteers went out, broke up the meeting and replaced the peace flag with the American flag. Calls were made for the speaker, but none appearing P. T. Barnum mounted the platform . . . immediately surrounded by returned volunteers who, revolvers in hand, promised death to any one who should fire on the platform. Mr. Barnum then called for the speakers advertised, promising them in the name of the Union men, a fair hearing provided they uttered nothing treasonable.

Since no one accepted, a regular Union meeting was organized with P. T. Barnum as secretary, which adopted a threatening resolution, ending:

> Until this war is ended in the complete suppression of this wicked rebellion, we will stand by the old Stars and Stripes and hereby pledge our lives, our fortunes, and our sacred honor to defend it to the last.[30]

Soon there were laws against sedition:

> The sheriff of this county went to Chestnut Hill, Penn., and took down a secession flag, to-day. A new law of the State authorizing the constable in any town, or the sheriff of any county to take down treasonable flags has been enacted, and their owners are liable to not less than 30 days' imprisonment or a fine of not less than $100. Prudential committees are being formed throughout the State to put down secession.[31]
>
> Chicago: An ordinance was passed by the Common Council requiring all newcomers to take the oath of allegiance or leave the city. The people have formed a vigilance committee.[32]

The colleges reflected the general intolerance. A student at Princeton was subjected to indignities by fellow-students for secession sympathies. The faculty suspended three of the students concerned, and warned the Southerners against "inflammatory utterances." This sort of suppression of opinion was nation-wide.

FREEDOM OF OPINION IN CHURCHES

The military authorities repeatedly interfered with church services to prevent disloyalty or to force expression of allegiance to the government. For example:

The Catholic bishop of Natchez, Mississippi, having refused to read the prescribed prayer for the President, and having protested in an able and temperate manner against the orders of the commanding general in this respect, the latter ordered him expelled from the Union lines, although this order was almost immediately rescinded.

A young officer rose in his seat and requested an Episcopal minister to read the prayer for the President, which he had omitted. Upon the minister's refusal, the soldier led him, loudly protesting to the door, and then quietly returning to the altar himself read the prayer—not much, it is to be feared, to the edification of the congregation.

General Rosecrans issued an order in Missouri requiring the members of religious convocations to give satisfactory evidence of their loyalty to the United States as a condition precedent to their assemblage and protection. . . . In answer to protestations from many loyal church members, he said that if he should permit all bodies claiming to be religious to meet without question, a convocation of Price's army (Confederate) under the garb of religion, might assemble with impunity and plot treason.[33]

General Butler arrested a clergyman at Norfolk, Virginia, and placed him at hard labor for "disloyalty in belief and action." But the President reversed this sentence to exclusion from the Union lines.[34]

In 1862 a difference between the Reverend Dr. McPheeters of the Vine Street Church in St. Louis and his congregation grew so bitter that the provost-marshal finally intervened, ordered the arrest of Dr. McPheeters, excluded him from the pulpit, and took the control of the church out of the hands of his trustees. The only offenses discoverable were that he would not declare himself in favor of the Union, and that he had baptized a baby with the name of Sterling Price, a rebel general.   President Lincoln repudiated this action, writing General Curtis:

> Now . . . I tell you frankly I believe he does sympathize with the rebels, but the question remains whether such a man, of unquestioned good moral character, who has taken such an oath as he has, and cannot even be charged with violating it, . . . can, with safety to the government, be exiled upon suspicion of his secret sympathies. . . . I must add that the United States government must not undertake to run the churches. When an individual in a church or out of it becomes dangerous to the public interest, he must be checked . . . but it will not do for the United States to appoint trustees or other agents for the churches.[35]

Later, however, Mr. Lincoln refused to restore Dr. McPheeters to his church.

Lincoln was aroused to anger in the last year of the war by discovering that Secretary of War Stanton had virtually given the Northern Methodist Church possession of certain churches, and lent military aid to Bishop Ames in taking possession of them.   He wrote:

> This, if true, is most extraordinary. I say again, if there be no military need for the building, leave it alone, neither putting anyone in or out of it, except on finding some one preaching or practising treason, in which case lay hands on him just as if he were doing the same thing in any other building or in the streets. . . .[36]

FREEDOM OF THE PRESS IN THE CIVIL WAR

The first interference with freedom of the press came, as usual, in attacks upon editors and their properties.   The first weeks of the war witnessed the forcing of many newspapers to display the flag.   After the fall of Sumter a mob collected around *The New York Herald* office, and were prevented from violence only when Gordon Bennett displayed the Union flag from his window. In August after the battle of Manassas and the return of the first "three-months volunteers," the mobs, often led by returned soldiers or departing recruits, grew more vicious. On August 25, *The New York Journal of Commerce* listed all newspapers forced to suspend by mobs. Ambrose L. Kimball of the Essex, N. J., *Democrat*—a "weekly secession sheet"—was tarred and ridden on a rail until he promised to quit writing. William Halsey was deported from town for trying to get subscribers to the New York *Daily News* on a Connecticut railroad. The Cumberland *Alleghanian* was destroyed; the Wilmington *Gazette* attacked; a sheriff's posse was called to protect the Allentown (Pa.) *Democrat and Republican*. At Terre Haute, Ind., the office of the *Journal and Democrat* and several private dwellings were demolished by members of the 43rd regiment declared to be under the command of their colonel. He denied it and asked for an investigation by the civil authorities. The Westchester (Pa.) *Jeffersonian* was cleaned out by a mob. The prevalent attitude is clear in the naive press report that "there was no disturbance."

This violence continued in less degree throughout the war. In the spring of 1863 the Columbus (Ohio) *Crisis* was destroyed by 150 soldiers; the Richmond (Ind.) *Jeffersonian* demolished by 800 paroled prisoners, and the Keokuk (Iowa) *Constitution* wrecked by convalescents in a hospital. Here are the details of an early case which show their character:

> The paper of Archibald McGregor, coming out every week, kept alive the animosity of the war party, and made him a constant object of their vindictiveness. This they manifested in various ways—withdrawal of patronage, loss of subscribers, threats of personal injury and destroying his office. . . . The night of August 22, 1861, the newspaper and job-office of the *Stark County Democrat* was broken into by a squad of new recruits, mostly sons of prominent families of Canton. . . . The marauders did their work effectively, making a bon-fire in the

street, and burning wood, type cases, type and all that was combustible. . . . The old newspaper hand-press was the only article of value that escaped.[37]

McGregor himself was afterwards imprisoned on executive order without trial. *The Advertiser and Farmer* of Bridgeport, Conn., suffered almost identical treatment for "its disloyal and traitorous course."[38]   A newspaper office at Concord, New Hampshire, was attacked by armed soldiers, and the publishers had to be rescued by the citizens and carried to the State Prison for safety, considerably bruised but not seriously injured.[39]

NEWSPAPERS AND GRAND JURIES

The first attempt to suppress the minority newspapers by law was through actions before grand juries. A New Jersey grand jury reported five papers to the United States court, declaring:

> They feel it their duty to repudiate and denounce the conduct of these journals. . . . They recommend all loyal citizens, all public officers, all municipal corporations, vigorously to withhold all patronage from such newspapers as do not hereafter give their unqualified support to the national government.

The United States attorney at Pittsburgh warned an editor that the tone of his paper might lead to prosecution. The grand jury of the Southern District of New York asked the advice of the Court on the following presentment of facts:—

> There are certain newspapers within this district which are in frequent practice of encouraging the rebels . . . by expressing sympathy and agreement with them. . . . The New York daily and weekly *Journal of Commerce, News, Day Book, Freeman's Journal . . . Brooklyn Eagle.* The first named has just published a list of newspapers in the free states opposed to what it calls "the present unholy war." . . . If the utterance of such language in the streets or through the press is not a crime, then there is a great

defect in our laws, or they were not made for such an emergency. . . . The Grand Jury will be glad to learn that such conduct is subject to indictment and punishment. . . .[40]

No action was taken, however, against these papers. The judge of the circuit court of Westchester County, N. Y., told the grand jury that reported on four local papers that they had violated no law. But the report on the New York papers started governmental action against the press in three ways: first, denial of the use of the mails; second, the imprisonment of editors by executive order; and third, the suppression of newspapers by the military authorities.

NEWSPAPERS DENIED THE USE OF THE MAILS

The use of the mails was denied according to the following order:

August 22, 1861.

To the Postmaster, New York City

Sir:—The Postmaster-General directs that from and after your receipt of this letter none of the newspapers published in New York City which were lately presented by the grand jury as dangerous, from their disloyalty, shall be forwarded in the mails. . . .

T. B. Trott, Chief Clerk.

Circulation was denied some of these papers in other ways. In Philadelphia, Marshall Millward and his officers examined all the bundles of papers arriving on the New York train and seized every copy of the New York *Daily News*. He also seized all bundles at the express office marked for the West and South. The sale was totally stopped. He also took possession of the office of *The Christian Observer*.[41] The Secretary of State wrote to the Postmaster-General recommending that *The Franklin Gazette* (N. Y.) be barred from the mails "for its treasonable character." The Post Office replied that the order had been given at Malone, N. Y., almost two weeks before.[42] This cooperation of the two departments is

the more interesting because the editors of *The Gazette*—
F. D. and J. R. Flanders—were political opponents of the
Administration. Both were finally cast into prison without
trial.[43]

An extra of *The Democrat*, Bangor, Maine, was held up
by the postmaster who awaited orders from Washington.
The Democrat's office had been destroyed by a mob two
weeks before. Two "Rebel" papers in Baltimore, *The South*
and *The Exchange*, were excluded●September 31, 1861, and
similar orders followed later during the war.

Some of the papers were stopped altogether—*The True
American* of Trenton, N. J., a Democratic organ and one of
the oldest papers in the State suspended, declaring that the
government had virtually forbidden the publication of every
newspaper that did not support the Administration. The
New York *News* and the *Day Book* suspended. The Brooklyn
Eagle and *The New York Journal of Commerce* agreed to
abandon their previous policies and were soon restored to
the mails. The order against *The Freeman's Journal* was not
revoked until April 4, 1862. Postmaster-General Blair rescinded all exclusion orders against so-called disloyal papers
on December 15, 1862.

Investigations of the exclusions were made by both House
and Senate. The House Committee on the Judiciary made
two reports, January 20 and March 3, 1863. It white-washed
the Postmaster-General with the usual formula:

> It being a time when extreme vigilance was demanded
> by the executive departments . . . to preserve the in-
> tegrity of the Union . . . your committee believes the act
> of the Postmaster-General was not only within the scope
> of his powers, but induced solely by consideration of the
> public good.[44]

The letter of Postmaster-General Blair is a historical document in the development of the postal censorship:

> The freedom of the press is secured by high constitu-
> tional sanction. But it is freedom and not license. . . .

It cannot aim blows at the Government and the Constitution . . . and at the same time claim its protection. While, therefore, this department neither enjoyed nor claimed the power to suppress such treasonable publications, but left them free to publish what they pleased, it could not be called upon to give them circulation. The mails· established by the United States could not upon any known principle of law or public right, be used for its destruction. . . . I would not, except in time of war, have adopted the arguments of my predecessors. . . . These citations show that a course of precedents has existed for twenty-five years—known to Congress, not annulled or restrained by act of Congress—in accordance with which newspapers and other printed matter decided by the postal authorities to be insurrectionary or treasonable, or in any degree exciting to treason or insurrection, have been excluded from the mails . . . solely by authority of the executive administration. This, under the rules as settled by the supreme court . . . as applicable to the executive construction of laws with whose execution the departments are specially charged, would establish my action as within the legal construction of the postal acts. . . .

Upon the like considerations, I have at different times excluded from the mails obscene and scandalous printed matter on exhibition of its immorality. This power should not devolve on the 28,000 postmasters but be reserved to the postmaster-general . . . and he cannot in time of peace exclude matter obnoxious to some special interest, but not to the government, law or public safety.[45]

This states all the elements of postal censorship. It is here based on the exigency of war and specifically limited to war emergencies, but in the same document it is extended to peace-time control by the assumed right to exclude so-called "obscene matter" on the sole judgment of the postmaster-general acting for the "moral police power." It also shields itself behind the judicial doctrine that the courts cannot question the acts of an executive officer in the exercise of his discretion unless manifest wrong is done.

That postal officials were suspected of interfering with private letters is indicated by a resolution offered in Congress on July 15, 1861, asking the Postmaster-General to inform the House whether he had authorized any postmaster or other person at any post-office to open letters or violate seals . . . or if he knew whether private correspondence had been violated. By law, letters can be opened only by authority of a search warrant. The resolution was lost by a refusal to suspend the rules to consider it.[46]

IMPRISONMENT OF EDITORS

There were a few cases of imprisoning editors for their attitude to the war. A case typical of the method was that of James W. Wall of New Jersey:

James W. Wall was arrested by order of the Secretary of War, at Burlington, New Jersey . . . and committed to Fort Lafayette, September 11, 1861. From papers on file in the Department of State it appears that Wall was a contributor to the columns of the New York *News*, and an active supporter of the obnoxious and dangerous principles disseminated by that sheet previous to the withdrawal from it of mail facilities, and its subsequent suppression. He was also represented as a noisy, brawling secessionist and as having exulted over the defeat of the United States troops at the Battle of Bull Run.[47]

After two week's imprisonment on charges no more precise than the above, Wall appealed to the Governor of New Jersey:

I have endeavored in vain to learn the cause of my arrest. I am denied my rights as a citizen of the United States. I now ask if I have any rights as a citizen of New Jersey under her Constitution, or if not, at what time my rights ceased and by virtue of what provision in that constitution?

The Governor dropped this delicate hint to the Secretary of State, Seward:

I suggest that the charges upon which persons are arrested and imprisoned should be communicated to them and be made public so that it may be known that they are arrested for good cause, for some actual wrong-doing, and thus the Government may be justified. . . . Thinking men among us feel uneasy lest the confidence of the people in the government should be impaired.

Seward made this retort:

It is to be regretted that you have not given me more precise information in regard to the cases of arrest in New Jersey which are represented to have been made upon insufficient grounds so that correction might be applied in those cases if injustice should be found. . . .

Wall was however shortly released on taking the oath of allegiance to the United States still quite ignorant of what his crime had been. Wall's fellow-citizens evidently held him in esteem for they later elected him to the United States Senate.

Henry A. Reeves of the Greenport, L. I., *Republican* was sent to Fort Lafayette for the treasonable character of his paper.[48] James A. McMaster of the New York *Freeman's Appeal* was arrested by order of the Secretary of State, September 14, 1861, charged with editing a disloyal newspaper. He was released a month later on taking the oath, which he did under protest. The effect of the paper's suspension is shown in a letter from McMaster's wife to Lincoln:

I am now advised that the continued suspension of the "Appeal" will be followed by the complete loss of its subscription list, its advertising patronage, and by such pecuniary damage as will require the discharge of its employees. . . . I respectfully ask that it may be allowed to pass through the mails.[49]

Though these imprisonments of editors were comparatively few they terrorized other editors into silence and so achieved a far-reaching censorship.

MILITARY SUPPRESSION OF NEWSPAPERS

In addition to the postal censorship and executive orders, military force was used against the press, both in suppressing particular papers and in forbidding their circulation within prescribed areas.   Here is one case:

> Headquarters, U. S. Reserve Corps,
> St. Louis, July 12, 1861.
>
> To the People of the State of Missouri:
> The "Missouri State Journal" . . . is continually giving aid and comfort to those who are in active rebellion. . . . It has not only encouraged them by its pertinacious appeals to the People to take up arms . . . but by its constant and continual publication of intelligence known to be false respecting the troops of the United States, it has indirectly incited disaffected citizens to the commission of overt acts of treason. . . .
> For these reasons . . . I have by order of General Lyon, . . . suppressed the publication of the "Missouri State Journal" for the present.   Its further publication will be prohibited as long as the public peace and safety require it.   John McNeil, Col. 3d Regt.

Upon issuance of this order a detachment of Home Guards surrounded the office and removed the forms.[50]   The St. Louis *Herald* and *Evening News* were suppressed in August and September.   Later all Missouri newspapers, except in St. Louis, had to furnish an advance copy of each issue to the provost-marshal for his inspection.

The suppression of the Chicago *Times* by telegraphic despatch of "General Orders 84" from the headquarters of the Department of the Ohio, June 1, 1863, aroused a bitter controversy, especially because Chicago was so remote from the seat of war.   The order follows:

> 1. The tendency of the opinions and articles habitually published in the newspaper known as the New York "World" being to cast reproach upon the Government, and to weaken its efforts to suppress the rebellion, by creating distrust of its war policy, its circulation in time

of war is calculated to exert a pernicious and treasonable influence, and is therefore prohibited in this department.

2. Postmasters, et cetera, will govern themselves by this order.

3. On account of the repeated expression of disloyal and incendiary sentiments, the publication of the newspaper known as the Chicago "Times" is hereby suppressed. . . .

By Command of Major-General Burnside.
Official Records, Series 11, XXIII, part II, 381.

On June 3 at three o'clock in the morning videttes galloped up to the Chicago *Times* office. . . . An hour later two companies of infantry took possession, stopped the press, destroyed the newspapers which had been printed, placed a guard over the establishment, and patrolled the entire block. The proprietors at once secured an injunction from Judge Drummond of the United States Court, and under it issued their paper for six mornings. Excitement was high throughout the city and nation. A meeting of prominent citizens was held, the Mayor presiding, and by unanimous vote the President was asked to rescind Burnside's order. The State House of Representatives denounced the order by a resolution. Twenty thousand loyal citizens, half of them Republicans it is said, assembled and passed resolutions that freedom of speech and the press must not be infringed by the military power. The next day President Lincoln ordered the rescinding of Burnside's order affecting the *Times* and the *World*. In New York on June 8 a meeting of prominent journalists was held to protest against this suppression.[51] At the same time, however, the so-called "Copperhead" press generally was suppressed, including the South Bend, Ind. *Forum* and the Columbia City *News*.

CONFLICT OF CIVIL AND MILITARY POWERS

The last important military interference with the press was in New York City. On May 18, 1864, *The Journal of Commerce* and *The World* printed a proclamation purporting to have been issued by President Lincoln calling 400,000 into the service:

> This paper was delivered at the offices of these journals late on the night of May 17, and in the news bureau form of a Washington despatch. Soon after its publication it was found to be a forgery, whereupon the fact was announced by the journals on their bulletin-boards, and a reward of $500 offered for the author of the fake. The editors at once informed General Dix of the forgery. . . . He issued orders to seize the offices, to suppress the publications, and imprison the editors and proprietors in Fort Lafayette—the American Bastile. The order for the arrest . . . was rescinded the same day, but publication of their papers was suspended for two days. The author of the proclamation was discovered, arrested and imprisoned, however, before the printing offices were restored to their owners. He was detained several months and then discharged without further investigation.

Governor Horatio Seymour wrote to A. Oakey Hall, district attorney of the County of New York:

> . . . If the owners of the above named journals have violated State or National laws, they must be proceeded against and punished by those laws. . . . Any action against them outside those laws is criminal. . . .

The district attorney laid the matter before the Grand Jury who found it "inexpedient to examine into the subject." Then on June 21, he appeared before a Judge of the city and county who issued warrants for General Dix and others. They appeared and were paroled, the counsel for the defence announcing that the President had ordered General Dix to disregard the process of Court. Governor Seymour on July 7 ordered Hall to enforce the law without regard to the President's order. On August 1 the Judge rendered his decision to hold General Dix and others subject to the action of the Grand Jury, declaring:

If that provision of the Indemnifying Act is constitutional it assimilates the President of the United States during the existence of the present rebellion, to an absolute monarch, and makes him incapable of doing any wrong.

Apparently the Grand Jury took no action, the civil authorities being content to have the military power appear in court.[52]

Military suppression of newspapers continued as long as war conditions made it seem necessary. May 18, 1864, Major-General Wallace suppressed *The Baltimore Evening Transcript*, and on May 26 *The Metropolitan Record* was forbidden to circulate in the department of the Missouri, and *The Cincinnati Enquirer* in Kentucky.

LIBERTY OF THE PRESS UNDER "RECONSTRUCTION"

During the first years of "Reconstruction" while the Southern states were still under military control, civil liberty was denied by the very status of the people, and freedom of the press was restrained. In many states newspapers were suppressed. This order from General Schofield to the Richmond, Virginia, *Times* reveals the condition:

Sir:—The commanding general directs me to call your attention to an editorial article in the Richmond, Virginia, "Times" of this morning, headed "A Black Man's Party in Virginia," and to say that while he desires not only to permit but encourage the utmost freedom of discussion of political questions, the character of the article referred to calls for severe censure. . . . Especially the following words . . . are an intolerable insult to our soldiers of the U. S. A. and no less so to all true soldiers of the late Confederate Army. . . . The efforts of your paper to foster enmity, create disorder and lead to violence can no longer be tolerated. It is hoped this warning will be sufficient.[53]

An amusing example of the spirit of censorship is the following "resolution" adopted by the Constitutional Convention of South Carolina in redrafting the State Constitution.

> *Resolved,* That this Convention take such action as it may in its wisdom deem compatible with its powers and conducive to the public weal to expunge forever from the vocabulary of South Carolina, the epithets, "negro," "nigger," and "Yankee."
>
> *Resolved,* That the exigencies and approved civilization of the times demand that the Convention or Legislative body created by it enact such laws as will make it a penal offense to use the above epithets in the manner described against an American citizen of this State, and to punish the insult with fine and imprisonment.[54]

CONSCRIPTION AND CIVIL LIBERTY

Conscription for military service was practiced on a large scale for the first time in the United States by both Federal and Confederate governments. Enforced military service is not commonly regarded as affecting civil liberty except when it conflicts with religious scruples. It is not mentioned in the federal Bill of Rights and in only a few state bills where exemptions on religious grounds are authorized. Yet conscription is the greatest possible interference with the liberty of body and soul of the individual. The soldier has no freedom of opinion, speech, assemblage, or of movement. He has no voice in making the laws or selecting the officers he must obey on penalty of death. He has no civil rights. He becomes an automaton. Despite the silence of the constitutions and the decisions of courts, this conflict between personal liberty and state power is most significant.[55]

We may note at once that the courts have invariably upheld the constitutionality of the conscription laws, declaring that they do not violate individual rights.[56]

The first conscription law in the Union during the Civil War, act of March 3, 1863,[57] contained no provision for exemption on conscientious grounds, religious or other. A man could, however, secure exemption by providing a substitute or paying a bonus of $300 with which a substitute could be hired. This law produced a crop of "draft resisters" who without any scruples against war *per se*, refused to be forced into military service. As most of these refused service for selfish reasons, and expressed their objection by flight, desertion, and riots, they are of little interest from the viewpoint of civil liberty. It is an interesting commentary on national unity that in the spring of 1863 desertions from Union armies had reached such a number that troops had bloody encounters with bands of resistants in Illinois and with the "Butternuts" in Indiana.

In some few cases, however, the draft-resisters seemed moved by some sense of personal liberty, and of a local right to refuse a national service they did not endorse. This seemed partly the case in Columbia County, Pennsylvania, where such resistance was on such a large scale that troops had to be sent in, martial law declared, and many participants punished.[58]

The chief resistance arose in cities where the laboring classes were angered by seeing the wealthy escape the draft by paying a bonus or hiring a substitute. The sense of injustice was sharpened by economic and race antagonism. Negro strike-breakers had been introduced in the cities on the docks, and clashes and murders were frequent.

> The draft in the minds of a large part of the industrial classes, already deeply stirred, was another name for forced military service in behalf of their hated negro rivals, and at the head of the rioting mobs were angry and defeated longshoremen. Industrial discontent was a fundamental cause of the riots.[59]

The most tragic of these draft riots was in New York, July 12-17, 1863—exceeding in loss of life any similar event in our history.[60] This violent resistance is not a matter of concern to civil liberty.

Efforts to make foreigners with their first papers liable to the draft also aroused a storm of wrath, and was one of the causes of the New York riots. The foreign consulates were crowded with "first-paper men" claiming the protection of their countries.[61] There were no "political" objectors, such as the Socialists in the World War.

The "conscientious objectors" were chiefly Friends, with fewer Dunkards, Mennonites, and numbers of pacifist smaller sects, whose creeds forbade engaging in war. Among them were a few "absolutists," that is, men whose scruples forbade even non-combatant service, or any service rendered under military direction, or furnishing a substitute. They were sincere men whose record has significance for civil liberty.

CONSCIENTIOUS OBJECTORS IN THE NORTH

The Union government was on the whole lenient with the comparatively few real objectors, in part because the Quakers had been the first and strongest opponents of slavery. The President himself was descended from Friends and had a "Quaker Cabinet." Stanton's mother was the head of a Friend's meeting, Bates and Chase were connected with Friends, and General Halleck remained by accident a member of a Meeting during the entire War. Quakers were exempted from the first draft. But Congress judged this unjust to others, and would not permit it to continue. At the suggestion of government officials, when the draft was about to be extended, a conference of Friends from about twenty-five Meetings in New York, New England and elsewhere, was held in Baltimore (December 7, 1863). It unanimously adopted the following minutes:

> We believe it right for us to record our united sense and judgment that Friends continue to be solemnly bound unswervingly to maintain our ancient faith and belief that war is forbidden in the Gospel and that as followers of the Prince of Peace we cannot contribute to its support or in any way participate in its spirit; that to render other service, as an equivalent for, or in lieu of, that requestioned for military purposes is a compromise of a vital principle which we feel conscientiously bound to support under all circumstances and

notwithstanding any threats to which we may be subjected. . . . We greatly appreciate the kindness evidenced
at all times by the President and Secretary of War when
we have applied to them for relief from suffering for
conscience sake, and honor them for their manifest regard
for religious liberty.[62]

A delegation from this Conference, with Stanton's help,
secured the following exemption clause in the amendatory
Enrollment Bill of February 24, 1864:

> Members of religious denominations who shall by oath
> or affirmation declare that they are conscientiously op-
> posed to the bearing of arms, and who are prohibited
> from doing so by the rules and articles of faith and prac-
> tice of said religious denominations, shall, when drafted
> into the military service, be considered non-combatants,
> and shall be assigned by the Secretary of War to duty in
> the hospitals, or to the care of freedmen, or shall pay the
> sum of $300 to such person as the Secretary of War shall
> designate . . . to be applied to the benefit of sick and
> wounded soldiers: Provided that no person shall be en-
> titled to the benefit of . . . this section unless his deport-
> ment has been uniformly consistent with such declara-
> tion.[63]

Stanton even tried unsuccessfully to have this $300 put
into a special fund for colored refugees of which Friends
should have the disbursement. The Friends felt they would
have been granted unconditional exemption but for the embarrassment it might cause the Government. Mr. Lincoln's
attitude is shown in his reply to the letter from Mrs. Gurney,
which he was carrying in his pocket when he was shot:

> Your people, the Friends, have had, and are having, a
> great trial. On principle and faith opposed to both war
> and oppression they can only practically oppose oppres-
> sion by war. In this hard dilemma some have chosen
> one horn, and some the other. For those appealing to
> me on conscientious grounds, I have done, and shall do,
> the best I could and can, in my own conscience, under
> my oath to the law.[64]

He expressed similar sentiments in letters to the Iowa Quakers (January 5, 1862) and to Samuel Boyd (March 19, 1862). "This promise Abraham Lincoln faithfully kept and the Northern Friends had no just grounds for complaint. The three hundred dollars was accepted for hospital supplies, service in hospitals was granted, and where conscience was not free to accept either, or it seemed inexpedient, they were "paroled until called for and never called for." Occasional cases of hardship did occur, as in that of Cyrus Pringle of Vermont, who had taken the absolutist position, refusing to take part in the war in any way.[65] Parts of his very moving diary follow:

> For more than a week we have lain here, refusing to engage in hospital service; shall we retrace the steps of the past week? or shall we go South as overseers of the blacks on the confiscated estates of the rebels, to act under military commanders . . . ? What would become of our testimony and our determination to preserve ourselves clear of the guilt of this war?
>
> P. S.   We have written Henry Dickensen that we cannot purchase life at the cost of peace of soul?
>
> . . . This morning the officers told us we must yield. . . . We were threatened great severities and even death. . . . We seem perfectly at the mercy of the military power, and more, in the hands of inferior officers, who from their being far removed from Washington, feel less restraint from those regulations of the Army . . . for the protection of privates from personal abuse . . .
>
> I went back to my tent and lay down for a season of retirement, endeavoring to gain resignation to any event. I dreaded torture and desired strength of flesh and spirit. The lieutenant called me out and pointing to the gun . . . asked me to clean it. I replied to him that I could not comply with military requisitions. . . . Two sergeants . . . bade me lie down on my back, and stretching my limbs apart, tied cords to my wrists and ankles and these to four stakes driven into the ground somewhat in the form of an X. I was very quiet in mind as I lay there on the ground soaked with the rain of the previous day,

exposed to the heat of the sun, and suffering keenly from the cords binding my wrists and straining my muscles. And, if I dared the presumption, I should say that I caught a glimpse of heavenly pity. . . . About the end of another hour his orderly came and released me. . . . I arose and sat on the ground. I did not rise to go away. I had nowhere to go, nothing to do. . . .[66]

Friends of Pringle intervened with Lincoln, who finally said: "I want you to go and tell Stanton that it is my wish all those young men be sent home at once." But Pringle fell into a delirious fever from which he recovered only after many weeks.

MARTYRS FOR CONSCIENCE IN THE SOUTH

When the South was being bled white for soldiers, the objectors to war suffered extraordinary martyrdoms. The Southern Quakers earned hatred on two scores: they opposed slavery, and they refused to participate in war. In North Carolina many Abolition societies had existed since the 1820's; in one strong Quaker county the vote was 2,370 to 45 against secession. These Southern pacifists were patriotic:

It has often been charged that non-resistant peace-men are bad patriots, real enemies to their country. Nothing could be further from the truth. . . Their patriotism was an intelligent and discriminating one, and no blast from the hot furnace of persecution was able in the least to make it yield.[67]

As early as December, 1861, the North Carolina Legislature passed an act for a test oath of loyalty. All males above 16 were required to renounce the United States and defend the Confederacy. A few Friends were included in the first military drafts, but appear to have obtained relief through unofficial action. In July, 1862, Friends petitioned both State and Confederacy and were released from State service on payment of $100 each. Their real difficulties began in the same month when the Confederacy conscripted all men between 18 and 35 years.   But on October 11 the Confederate Congress exempted all friends, Nazarenes, Dunkards, and Mennonites upon payment of $500, or the provision of a substitute, or entrance upon hospital service.   The later sufferings seem to have come upon those who refused to take any service or to pay the bonus; or else resulted from the inefficiency of the exemption machinery or from the brutality of individual officers.[68]

THE SUFFERINGS OF THE MACONS

Abijah Macon, after securing an honorable discharge as a volunteer and paying the $500 exemption fee, was, nevertheless, hurried on to Richmond, and immediately required to take a gun and fight.   But he was in no mood for fighting, so they put him under guard and for food gave him only cotton-seed meal.   This was followed by severe illness . . . and he soon passed away—having laid down his life for the gospel of peace.

Isaiah Macon was forced into the battle of Winchester. But he stopped no bullets.   He had nothing to do but to trust in God and await the end of the terrible scene. He seemed to possess a charmed life.   His comrades fell all around him, their places being filled with others who wondered at the strange sight—a man with plain citizen's clothes, having neither pistol, sword, nor gun, and no military cap, calmly filling his place in battle line, but taking no part in the battle . . . As his company turned to flee he calmly laid down upon the ground. Northern soldiers soon discovered him, peaceful amidst all; no shot had he fired, no part had he taken. . . . He was soon in Point Lookout prison, where in a few days he died, doubtless from mental suffering.[69]

In Randolph County, N. C., forty-three young men were taken for the army.   Some accepted substitute service in the gristmills and salt mines, some fled to the West.

Yancey Cox, 17 years old, who weighed but 84 pounds, was taken from his widowed mother, but officers tried in vain to make a soldier of this boy. He refused to take a gun or to wear military clothing. . . . He was made to march until the blood ran from his feet. . . . He was pierced in the thigh with a bayonet. . . .

By confinement, punishment, and torture they endeavored to extort from these aged people information as to the hiding places of their sons. The soldiers placed the hands or fingers of the aged men and women between the lower rails of the fence, and with its crushing weight upon them would wait to be told what they wished. . . . One mother, who would ere long have given birth to another child, was hung by a rope around her waist to a tree (a usual torture) in order to make her reveal the hiding place of her boy, and she died as a result of this cruelty.

Solomon Frazier was so meek and endured all their persecutions with such patience that the Captain got very angry, and told him he must now take a gun or die. While the officer was tying a gun to his arm, Solomon remarked to him: "If it is thy duty to inflict this punishment upon me, do it cheerfully; don't get angry about it." The Captain then left him, saying to his men, "If any of you can make him fight, do it. I cannot."[70]

CIVIL WAR AND LABOR

Military interference with the right to work was comparatively rare. The workers were not organized to take advantage of the Government's need, and there were few strikes. In numerous cases the mere organization of a union was sufficient to secure the demands.[71] There were a few cases of the use of the military to make men work, or to forbid strikes, in the last two years of the war when losses of life and the increased cost of living had made the workers rebellious. They are the only cases in our history where men worked under governmental coercion:

On March 10, 1864, a strike took place among the laborers at Cold Spring, N. Y., . . . in the employ of R. P. Parrott, who was engaged in the manufacture of shot, shell, et cetera, for the government. The men were receiving from a dollar to a dollar and a quarter a day. Owing to the very large advance in the price of the necessaries of life, they requested that their wages be advanced to a dollar and a half. This was refused. . . . Two days after the strike took place, four of the strikers were arrested and sent to Fort Lafayette where they remained for seven weeks, when they were liberated without a trial, though a trial was demanded. Two companies of United States soldiers were ordered to Cold Springs and martial law was proclaimed, and the men forced to resume work at the old rates. . . . Three of these poor men were not permitted to return to their homes and their families forced from town. . . .[72]

A strike by tailors, and one by machinists and blacksmiths occurred in St. Louis, Missouri, April, 1864. Because martial law was in effect the employers demanded military interference by the commanding general of the district, who issued the following "General Order No. 65" on April 29:

It having come to the knowledge of the Commanding General that combinations exist in the city of St. Louis, having for their object to prevent journeymen . . . and laborers from working in manufacturing establishments, except on terms prescribed to the proprietors by parties not interested therein, which terms have no relation to the matter of wages to be paid employees, but to the internal management of such establishments; and it appearing that in consequence of such combination . . . the operation of some establishments where articles are produced which are required for use in the navigation of the Western waters, and in the military, naval, and transport services of the United States, have been broken up, and the production of such articles stopped . . . the following order is promulgated:

1. No person shall, directly or indirectly, attempt to deter or prevent any person from working on such terms as he may agree upon in any manufacturing establishment, etc., etc.

2. No person shall watch around or hang about any

such establishment for the purposes of annoying the employees thereof, or learning who are employed therein. 3. No association or combination shall be formed or continued, or meeting held, having for its object to prescribe to the proprietors . . . whom they shall employ, or how they shall conduct the operation thereof.[73]

The order further provided for listing the members of all such combinations and for military enforcement of the order and protection for the employees against interference. And Major-General Rosecrans "confidently relied on the help of the city authorities and of all right-minded men." Several members of the two unions were arrested with intense excitement. A demonstration could not be made by the workingmen because the city was ruled by martial law.

A similar occurence took place in Louisville, Kentucky, where Brigadier-General Burbridge issued an identical order. It was charged against Burbridge that "he was in the confidence of the employers, aware of their plans and objects and that he was actuated by the most selfish and dishonorable motives."

Other incidents were the arrest in Tennessee of two hundred striking mechanics by General Thomas who sent them north of the Ohio river; the seizing and running of the Reading railroad in Pennsylvania which had been tied up by striking engineers; (2) The breaking-up of the Miners' Association in the Eastern coal fields by Government interference; and the confiscation of the back pay of the moulders in the Brooklyn Navy Yard when they struck for higher wages. In New York the striking longshoremen stood idly by while government transports were loaded by deserters under strong guard.

CHAPTER V

RACE PROBLEMS AND CIVIL LIBERTY

WHAT liberty is accorded minority races among the people of the United States? The question affects chiefly the native Indian and native-born Negro, and the aliens living among us.

The liberties given to aliens are not constitutional, but are based on international law, on treaties and on the power of the home-land to protect these far away rights. Our history shows how these factors were strengthened by the ideas of democracy, equality, and the rights of man; and by a pride in affording an asylum to political and religious refugees. And how often we forget that we were all once aliens in the land possessed by the Indians.

In spite of these ideas minority races in the United States have enjoyed only the liberty indicated by the general principle: he who has power has liberty. Aliens backed by a great power at home, have enjoyed our best brand of liberty—often more than native citizens. But the weaker races—especially the Indians, Negroes and Chinese—because of economic as well as race antagonism, have suffered persecution of an extent and brutality unexampled in our history. The record is too long to be more than sketched.

AMERICAN LIBERTY FOR THE AMERICAN INDIAN

The colonial Indians had what liberty they could defend against invaders. The conflict was tempered by occasional friendship and tolerance where the land-hunger of the white was not too great, and where zeal for the Indian's salvation encouraged charity. Quaker gentleness provided for example in an ordinance of 1681:

> That the Indians shall not be abused . . . but have
> liberty to do all things relating to improvement of their
> ground and providing sustenance for their families that
> the planters shall enjoy.

Generally however the Indian had no rights and few privileges. When the Union was formed the single mention of
him in the Constitution assigns him the status of the Negro.
(Article I, section 2, clause 111.)   Since then, he has had
no real liberty either as a resident in the United States or as
a citizen of his own presumably autonomous tribe.   When
he was ceded along with land to the United States by foreign
powers no mention of his rights was made.   He has been
an anomaly—neither in the nation nor out of it, neither
citizen nor alien.   Though his own nations were destroyed
because of their fierce love of liberty, he has known only
the supervised liberty of a dependent.   He passed early into
the ill-defined state of a "ward of the nation," and was never
recognized as a citizen.   The treaties with his tribes were
never respected.   They were mere bargains over property and
secured no rights to the Indian.   The determining factors
were force, greed, and fraud.[1]
The Indians have suffered ceaseless exploitation, robbery,
violence and murder.   They have suffered as "inferior races"
always suffer, by a lack of bodily safety, freedom of movement, protection against violence or against the law itself
when accused of crime. . . . The illegal and selfish spoliation
of their lands by the government, by lawyers, politicians,
ranchmen, everybody, does not fall within our province.   We
need not go into the records of injustice to the Indians.   The
case can be summed up by generalizations such as:

> The history of the Government's connection with the
> Indians is a shameful record of broken treaties and unful-
> filled promises.[2]
> There is not among the 300 bands of Indians, one
> which has not suffered cruelly at the hands of the gov-
> ernment or the white settlers. . . . The tales of the

wrongs, oppressions, the murders or the Pacific Slope Indians in the last thirty years would be a volume in itself, and is too monstrous to be believed. It makes little difference, however, where we open the record of the history of the Indians, every page and every year has its dark stain.[3]

The Indian is the only human being within our territory who has no individual right in the soil. He is not amenable to or protected by, the law. The executive, the legislative, the judicial departments . . . recognize that he has a possessory right in the soil; but his title is merged in the tribe—the man has no standing before the law.[4]

Here is a concrete example:

A few years ago, former Commissioner Leupp arbitrarily ordered the confinement of eight Navajos in the military prison at Fort Huachuca, Arizona, at hard labor, for an indeterminate period. Although charged with being bad men, they had been given no trial, military or civil. Commissioner Leupp . . . stated in effect that those Indians would be held . . . until he was ready to release them, "law or no law." . . . The Association instituted habeas corpus proceedings. The Arizona supreme court . . . decided that the commissioner was wrong, and that an Indian could not be deprived of his liberty without due process of law. The Navajos were subsequently released and returned to their reservation.[5]

Within the tribe the Indian had no individual status; outside in relation to the whites, he had duties. The conscription of the Indian in the World War expresses these. Slowly the Indian is now becoming a citizen, and his survivors will probably enjoy the average liberty of minority races in the American commonwealth.

LIBERTY IN OUR ISLAND POSSESSIONS

Similar problems have arisen in our island possessions. The natives have not been usually in control of their affairs, although they had previously achieved a status in relation to European or native rulers. Though called "backward" races, they are often well educated and aspire to self-government. Their aspirations have fostered demands for civil rights—freedom of speech, assemblage and the press. They ask whether the Bill of Rights follows the flag; whether constitutional guarantees protect native Porto Ricans, Filipinos and Virgin Islanders. There has not yet been a definition of what rights these peoples have. There is a persistent disinclination to give them any, because of the great probability they will use them for agitation against American rule in favor of independence. The usual mixture of military with civil government further complicates island rule, and hampers civil liberty. Exploiting economic interests also restrict liberty. Numerous cases have arisen in Porto Rico, Haiti, San Domingo, Samoa, and the Virgin Islands—and a few in the Philippines. In all of these places there is continuous agitation against either the fact or form of American rule.

THE NEGRO AND CIVIL LIBERTY

The Negro presents the most important "race problem" for civil liberty in the United States. He is first of all of a very different color and origin. He has passed from the status of an imported African slave, first landed in Virginia in 1619 to that of a so-called free citizen, though in fact with a very inferior position. He forms a considerable and increasing part of the population—now about one-tenth. He is not a ward like the Indian nor an alien who can be deported. These ten million nominal citizens are entitled to all the constitutional guarantees, some of which were especially framed for their protection. But these do not so apply, and over a large section of the country they are deliberately and studiously denied. The Negro is in reality a sort of half-citizen—a citizen on probation to the whites.

THE COLONIAL PERIOD

In this period (1619-1776) the English Colonists recognized no rights for the Negro slaves.

As a slave the negro had none of the ordinary civil or personal rights of the citizen. In criminal cases, he could be arrested, tried, and condemned with but one witness against him, and he could be sentenced without a jury. ... Zealous for religion as the colonists were, they made little attempt to convert the Negroes in the earlier decades of the 17th Century, there being a very general opinion that neither Christian brotherhood or the law of England would justify the holding of Christians as slaves. In course of time, however, they lost their scruples, and it became generally understood that conversion and baptism did not make the slaves free, Virginia in 1667 enacting a law to that effect.

The fear of Negro insurrection caused violent measures to be taken. In New York in 1712, twenty-four Negroes were put to death, some in cruel ways, and in 1711 on the mere rumor of an intended rising occurred an organized persecution of the blacks.

Every one of the eight lawyers in town appeared against the Negroes, who had no counsel and were convicted on most insufficient evidence. Fourteen of the unfortunate people were burned at the stake, eighteen were hanged, and seventy-one deported.[6]

This has a modern ring though distinguished by the fact that the victims had the form of a trial. The Negroes' status was ordinarily beyond the reach of any civil process.

The negro slave in the eyes of the law was a chattel, could be bought and sold, bequeathed by will, given away, mortgaged, or seized in satisfaction of a judgment. Not a civil right of any kind was his. He could not make a contract, or give testimony against a white man in any court, nor acquire property in any way. Whatever he found, whatever he made, whatever was given to him, reverted at once to his master. To teach a slave to write was not allowed anywhere; to teach him to read was allowed in a few colonies.[7]

THE CONSTITUTIONAL PERIOD

This period (1776-1863) may be so called though slavery was never explicitly recognized in the American constitutions. No provision on the subject appears in any State constitution except in Delaware's of 1783. The Federal Constitution implicitly recognized slavery in providing that representation shall be determined on the whole number "of free persons, three-fifths of all others." (Article I, section 11, clause 3.) It permitted the importation of slaves until 1808. In the "free States" where the Negroes were not numerous or economically important they advanced to a relative liberty. The Supreme Judicial Court of Massachusetts held that the provision in the State Bill of Rights that "all men are born free and equal" prohibited slavery. The status varied:

> In New England slaves were regarded as possessing the same legal rights as apprentices, and if masters abused their authority, they were liable to indictment. Each State had its own slave code . . . and it is difficult to make general statements about the legal side. . . . If he did not get what was due him, he had no redress, for he had no legal voice. His marriage was not considered binding and he was not supposed to have any morals.[8]

Mob violence against the Negro was ferocious in the "free States" because the Negro was not a valuable chattel but a competitor with white workers. The fields of employment were limited rather by social control than by law. Education was generally denied, Negroes being refused admission to schools and even theological seminaries.

In the Southern States the Negro had no rights and no liberties. The laws penalized teaching slaves to read and even talking to them.[9] In South Carolina the law authorized the arrest of English sailors under the English flag if the sailors were black and labor was needed in the rice swamps. Owners had absolute control of the slave's body; and treatment ranged from kindness to cruelty.

The summary execution of negroes, did not, however, become a serious evil previous to the Civil War. So long as the negroes were valuable as slaves it was a direct economic loss to the slaves-holder if any able-bodied slaves were put to death. In general it was only in cases of real or supposed conspiracy or insurrection that negroes were killed in a summary manner. There was of course a regular slaughter in such cases as Nat Turner's rebellion, when scores of negroes, innocent or guilty, were hunted down and killed.[10]

No record of cases during this period is attempted for the reason well stated in Gilbert Stevenson:

A greater reason for the futility of discussion of race distinctions before 1865 is that prior to that date the Negro was considered to have no rights which the white man was bound to respect. The Dred Scott decision in 1857 virtually held that a slave was not a citizen or capable of becoming one.[11]

THE RECONSTRUCTION PERIOD

Neither Slavery nor involuntary servitude, save as a punishment for crime whereof the party shall have been duly convicted, shall exist within the United States or any place subject to their jurisdiction.

Thirteenth Amendment to the Constitution

All persons born or naturalized in the United States, and subject to the jurisdiction thereof, are citizens of the United States and of the State wherein they reside. No State shall make or enforce any law which shall abridge the privileges or immunities of citizens of the United States; nor shall any State deprive any person of life, liberty, or property, without due process of law; nor deny to any person within its jurisdiction the equal protection of the laws.

Fourteenth Amendment to the Constitution

These two new additions to the Federal Bill of Rights covered most of the questions concerning civil liberty during the Reconstruction Period, here roughly fixed between the Emancipation Proclamation, January 1, 1863, and 1883, when the Civil Rights Bill of 1875 was declared unconstitutional.[12]

The Thirteenth Amendment is clear enough. It abolished slavery. There has been no return to this institution unless peonage for debt in the South may be so called. It freed the Negro, and left him just there. The Fourteenth Amendment is the effort to assure his political freedom by forbidding States to pass laws limiting his civil rights. It took the Fifteenth Amendment to give him the right to vote.[13]

THE FOURTEENTH AMENDMENT

The Fourteenth Amendment is of prime importance to civil liberty. "Fairly considered, these amendments may be said to rise to the dignity of a new Magna Carta." Thus speaks Justice Swayne of the United States Supreme Court. A commentator adds: "The Fourteenth Amendment nationalized the whole sphere of civil liberty. . . . Our Constitutional history during years (to 1898) with comparatively few exceptions may be said to be but little more than a commentary on the Fourteenth Amendment."[14]

The guarantee of life, liberty, and property under the law should indeed be a new magna carta, but the Supreme Court has not so interpreted it save as it affects property. Its protection was in law extended to all who came within the rule, not limiting it to the negroes who had occasioned it.

But the Supreme Court has not interpreted it in the interest of civil liberty. The principal report of the Federal Commission on Industrial Relations (1915) says:

We are informed by counsel who have examined the cases involved that the fourteenth amendment has had no appreciable effect in protecting personal rights. According to the existing decisions, the due-process clause does not guarantee the right of trial by jury, nor does it necessitate indictment by grand juries, nor has it restrained arbitrary arrests and imprisonments on the part of the State governments when men are kidnapped in one State and carried into another. . . . It is quite clear that it not only has failed to operate to protect personal rights, but has operated almost wholly for the protection of the property rights of corporations. (Pages 47, 49.)

The Fourteenth Amendment attempted, (1) to establish the fact of citizenship in the United States as well as in the States; (2) to prevent States from taking away the privileges or immunities belonging to national citizenship; (3) to reaffirm the already stated rights of the citizens in the law of the land, and to equality before the law. (See Constitution of the U. S. III, ii, 3 and Amendments V and VI.) It does not, however, define "privileges and immunities" nor does it enforce the provisions of the Bill of Rights.

In Maxwell versus Dow (176 United States Reports 581) the court emphasized the doctrine that the adoption of the fourteenth amendment had not had the effect of making all the provisions contained in the first eight amendments operative in the State courts . . . on the ground that the fundamental rights protected by these amendments are, by virtue of the fourteenth amendment to be regarded as privileges or immunities of the citizens of the United States.[15]

On the whole the Civil War amendments did not have an appreciable effect on the general principle of civil liberty under the Constitution. Let us turn then to the Negro after the Civil War.

THE NEGRO UNDER RECONSTRUCTION

The freedom declared in the Emancipation Proclamation had no effect on the status of the Negro in the South until the rebellion was defeated. Then on December 18, 1865, the thirteenth amendment was added to the Constitution. The new state constitutions adopted in the South during the next five years, mostly under some sort of Northern influence, also prohibited slavery. For example the Georgia constitutions of 1865 (article I, section 20) and of 1868 declared that: "The social status of the citizens shall never be the subject of legislation." Further national action to assure the newly freed slave equal rights as a citizen was taken in the first Civil Rights Acts, passed over the President's veto in April, 1866. Meanwhile the various new governments attempted to handle the problem of the Negro—masterless, without land, wandering over the country. These legislative efforts are important as fixing an attitude toward the Negro's liberty that has influenced his status ever since.

> The slave codes were obsolete; the few laws for free negroes were not applicable to the present conditions; most laws and codes were expressly for whites. The task of the law-makers was to express in the law the transition from slavery to citizenship; to regulate family life, morals and conduct; to give the ex-slave the right to hold property, the right to personal protection, and the right to testify in the courts, . . . to protect the whites in person and property from the lawless blacks. In general the laws relating to whites were extended to the blacks. . . . But one principle was never lost sight of, viz., that the races were unlike and unequal and should be kept separate. . . . The sources of these laws are found in the ante-bellum laws for free negroes, in the Northern and Southern vagrancy laws, in the freedmen's codes of the West Indies, in the Roman law of freedmen, and in pure theory to some extent, and to a great degree in the regulations for blacks made by the United States army and treasury officials in 1862-1865 and in the Freedmen's Bureau rules. . . . The laws were never in force in any of the States. . . . Since the downfall of the Reconstruction régime, the essential parts of this legislation have been re-enacted in the Southern States, especially the laws relating to the definition of race, to the separation in schools, et cetera. . . .[16]

The spirit of these "Black Codes" is expressed as follows:

> Almost every act, word, or gesture of the negro, not consonant with good taste and good manners, as well as good morals, was made a crime or misdemeanor for which

he could first be fined by the magistrate and then be consigned to a condition of almost slavery for an indefinite time, if he could not pay the bill.[17]

The foundation of peonage for debt to the state (fines) or to private persons is here early disclosed; as well as the cleavage of races which could not be obliterated by legislation. To protect the Negro other national legislation was enacted: on May 1, 1870, a revision of the Civil Rights Bill of 1866, which had proved ineffective; the guarantee of political rights in the Fifteenth Amendment, proclaimed March 30, 1870, and a more drastic Civil Rights Bill in March, 1875 (18 *Statutes at Large* 335). The first two sections of this were declared unconstitutional in 1883, and here ended the Reconstruction efforts of the Nation.[18]

Meanwhile in the South despite Federal laws and "black codes" the Negro was denied even bodily safety and free movement by the organized violence of the southern whites. This systematic terrorization is the history of his "liberty" for a decade after 1866. The first expression of it was the Ku Klux Klan. The Klan arose from fear of Negro dominance. It substituted a reign of violence for law, terrorized the blacks, and abrogated every liberty of the new citizen. The evidence has been gathered in official form and need not be restated here.[19]

These conditions lasted into the seventies, and include murder, whippings, terrorism, deportation, and every form of violent coercion.

> The movement lasted under one form or another until the close of Reconstruction, and the lynching habits of to-day are due largely to conditions, social and legal, growing out of Reconstruction.[20]

NEGRO MASSACRES

The "knight" of the Ku Klux Klan was in some States merged into the "regulator" whose duty it was to "keep the Negro in his place," scared and defenceless, and by murder and terrorism to prevent him from voting, or to make him vote "right." In Louisiana and a less degree in other states between 1866 and 1876, thousands of Negroes were massacred by armed bands. The details of these horrors are to be found in government reports. The general outline is indicated by this statement to President Grant by General Philip Sheridan.

> Since 1866 nearly 3,600 persons, a great majority of whom were colored men, have been killed and wounded in this state (Louisiana). In 1868 official records show 1,885 were killed and wounded. From 1868 to the present time, 1875, no official investigation has been made and the civil authorities in all but a few cases were unable to arrest, convict, or punish the perpetrators. . . . There is ample evidence to show that more than 1,200 persons have been killed and wounded during this time on account of their political sentiments. Frightful massacres have occurred in the parishes of Bossier, Caddo, Atahoula, St. Bernard, St. Landry, Grant and Orleans. . . . In St. Landry in 1868 in a massacre of three to six days, 200 to 300 colored men were killed. . . . The total summing up of murders, maimings, and whippings for political reasons in September, October and November, 1868, as shown by official sources is over 1,000. . . .[21]

In a report on Negro atrocities, President Grant on December 6, 1876 transmitted to Congress a report on Negro atrocities listing persons maimed, whipped or murdered and the perpetrators of the crimes for the period 1866-1876. It covered ninety-eight pages of fine print averaging a victim a line, and the list was estimated to include about 4,000 cases. Another report in two volumes by a Congressional Committee of which the late John Sherman was chairman deals with the Louisiana election frauds in connection with the Hayes-Tilden contest. One case will show their nature:

> November 23.
> Benjamin Morgan, being sworn, says: I am the coroner of the Parish of East Baton Rouge. . . . I was informed on April 13, 1876, that two men had been killed. I

went to hold an inquest. I found the body of Jerry Myers hanging by the neck, dead. I collected a jury and cut him down. The evidence showed that the deed had been committed by a party of bull-dozers, who hung him in my opinion because he was a Republican. Within 100 yards of the house I found Samuel Myers . . . shot in the back with six balls . . . and dead. Both the deceased were honest, hard-working farmers; neither of them held any office, and had for the last five years put the first bale of cotton on the market in the parish. On the 17th I received a letter through the Post Office:

Mr. Ben Morgan, Coroner:

You will please bear in mind that your absence is required in the county, and I further inform you that if you are caught therein any more your fate shall be as those you came to hold your inquest over.
Yours truly,
Captain of Regulators.[22]

This same report lists these murders alleged to have been committed by white regulators in East Baton Rouge Parish in 1876:

Jan. 5—Taylor Hawkins, murdered; Jan. 6—Major Selve, hanged; Jan. 14—John Jackson, shot; Jan. 16—George Washington, shot, then burned with oil; Feb. 3—Peter Henderson Painter, shot to death; Feb. 16—Johnson Stewart, shot dead; Feb. 17—Charley Robertson, hanged; April—Job Johnson, burned to death in his house and shot. Occurred in the 11th Ward where he was constable. Alice Gilbert was roped and threatened with hanging. April 13—W. Y. Payne taken from house, rope put around his neck, the other end tied to a saddle, and then dragged until he died when his body was thrown in the River. Sept. 1—Sanford Smith, Paul Johnson, Arch Stewart, shot to death.

One of the bloodiest riots on record occurred in St. Landry Parish where the Ku Klux Klan killed and wounded over 200 Republicans, hunting and chasing them two days and nights through fields and swamps. Thirteen captives were taken from jail and shot, and a pile of 25 dead bodies was found buried in the woods.[23]

Much of this evidence is from politically partisan investigators who were seeking political capital and trying to make a case.[24]   But allowing even a generous discount the record is black.   The so-called exodus of Negroes to certain Northern States in 1876-1878 showed the force driving the Negro from his home.   A Congressional committee learned that a committee of 500 Negroes had secured the names of 98,000 possible emigres.   This investigating committee declared:

> Nearly all the witnesses gave as the causes of the exodus: the feeling of insecurity for life and property; the denial of political rights as citizens; long continued persecution for political reasons; the system of cheating; the inadequacy of the school system; and the fear of being reduced to peonage.[25]

To sum up the Reconstruction record the fact is perfectly clear that with the passions of war still running strong with political blunders on both sides, with race prejudice and economic re-adjustment, the Negro in the South had no liberty.

NEGRO LIBERTY IN OUR DAY

The period between 1883 and 1920 is one in which the Negro has achieved a greater measure of civil rights.   But in spite of a constant struggle and help of his friends, his status is still far from the level of personal and constitutional liberty enjoyed by the most disadvantaged whites.   The struggle may be described under three heads: first, for bodily safety against illegal violence; second, for civil and political rights with equality before the law; third, for such social and economic rights as free education and a free race press.   Violence constitutes the larger field of attack on the Negro, with its long and shameful record of lynching and mob outrages.

LYNCHING

During these years lynching has become a national institution and constitutes the most flagrant and comprehensive violation of civil processes in the United States. The Negro has suffered and still suffers at the hands of lawless mobs which regard themselves as the agents of an extra-legal popular will. Back of the failure to punish lynching is an idea of "popular justice." Says J. D. Cutler in his *Lynch Law:*

"In the course of this investigation into the history of lynching, it has become evident that there is usually more or less of public approval, or supposed favorable public sentiment, behind a lynching. Indeed, it is not too much to say that popular justification is the *sine qua non* of lynching. It is this fact that distinguishes lynching from insurrection and open warfare. A lynching may be defined as an illegal and summary execution at the hands of a mob or a number of persons, who have in some degree the public opinion of the community back of them. . . .

In the last analysis lynch-law in this country is without any justification whatsoever. In a government founded on the idea that the ultimate power and authority shall rest with the people, and in which sufficient facility has been given to the expression of the collective will of the people so that the acts of the government, the formulation of the law, and the administration of justice ought to adequately represent this collective will, there is no tenable ground on which to vindicate the practicing of punishing criminals other than by the regularly constituted courts."[26]

The alleged justifications for lynching need no discussion, the rights to trial and legal punishment are basic no matter what the offense. There is a growing agreement that action by the Federal government alone will work effectively to end lynchings. Cutler, however, puts more weight on public sentiment. He says:

Until there is a sentiment in every community in which a lynching occurs, which will demand the punishment of those who take part, it can scarcely be expected that sheriffs will risk their lives to protect prisoners, or that prosecuting attorneys, judges, and juries, will cooperate to secure the conviction of lynchers and to make them feel the full penalty of the law.[27]

The number of reputed lynchings is given in this table:[28]

Number of White and Colored Persons Lynched in United States, 1889-1918*

YEARS	TOTAL	WHITE	COLORED
1889	175	80	95
1890	91	3	88
1891	194	67	127
1892	226	71	155
1893	153	39	114
1894	182	54	128
1895	178	68	110
1896	125	46	79
1897	162	38	124
1898	127	24	103
1899	109	22	87
1900	101	12	89
1901	135	27	108
1902	94	10	84
1903	104	17	87
1904	86	7	79
1905	65	5	60
1906	68	4	64
1907	62	3	59
1908	100	8	92
1909	89	14	75
1910	90	10	80
1911	71	8	63
1912	64	3	61

YEARS	TOTAL	WHITE	COLORED
1913	48	1	47
1914	54	5	49
1915	96	43	53
1916	58	7	51
1917	50	2	48
1918	67	4	63
	3,224	702	2,522

*Victims of the Atlanta, Ga. (1906), and East St. Louis, Ill. (1917), riots have been excluded from this and subsequent tables.

Since 1889 eleven white and fifty Negro women have been lynched. In this period 2,834 lynchings took place in the South, 219 in the North, 156 in the West and 15 in Alaska and places unknown. The Negroes lynched were 78.2 per cent of the total. The following were the crimes charged against the victims in a "low year":

LYNCHINGS IN 1911

Murder	36
Rape	7
Attempted rape	7
Suspected rape	1
Insulting women	4
Assault to kill	3
"Prejudice"	2
Threats	1
"Desperado"	1
Robbery	1
	63

The following abstracts from *Thirty Years of Lynching* show the variety of attacks:

Louisiana. The fellow took fright, was followed and finally climbed a magnolia tree. . . . One of the pursuers went for a rope. Presently, the man deliberately slid down out of the tree, and halfway down he was shot to death. The man's clothing marked No. 43 was found to be that worn at the State Insane Asylum in a neighboring town. The insane occupant had escaped a few days before, and the helpless fellow, wandering at large, had suffered death for a crime he had not committed.[29]

Two innocent negroes had been shot previous to this by a posse looking for Holbert, because one of them who resembled Holbert, refused to surrender when ordered to do so.

Tennessee. Ed. Johnson, a Negro, convicted of rape and sentenced to be hanged, was granted an appeal by the Supreme Court of the United States. Johnson was in jail at Chattanooga. . . . A mob hanged him.

South Carolina. The mob was led by Joshua W. Ashleigh, a local member of the State Legislature, while Victor B. Cheshire, editor of a local newspaper, after taking part in the lynching got out a special edition telling about it. . . . The then Governor, Cole Blease, absolutely refused to use the power of his office to bring the lynchers to justice, and the Coroner's jury found that the Negro came to his death "at the hands of parties unknown."[30]

Oklahoma. Marie Scott, a 17-year-old Negro girl, was lynched because her brother had killed one of two white men who had assaulted her. She was alone in the house when the men entered, but her screams brought her brother to her rescue . . . one of the white men was killed. The next day the mob came to lynch her brother, but as he had escaped, lynched the girl instead. No one was ever indicted for the crime.

Georgia. At Jackson, Henry Ethridge was lynched, April 26, 1912, for being active in securing recruits for a colony in Africa.   Race prejudice is also given as the cause.

The following excerpts picture a fraction of the terrible cruelties which here characterized many lynchings.

"The lynching was devoid of the minor brutalities that frequently mark such occasions."

"The woman was raped by members of the mob before she was hanged."

"Before the torch was applied to the pyre, the Negro was deprived of his ears, fingers and other portions of his body with surprising fortitude."

It was really only ten minutes after the fire was started that smoking soles and twitching of the Negro's feet indicated that his lower extremities were burning. . . . The Negro had uttered but few words.   When he was led to where he was to be burned, he said quite calmly, "I wish some of you gentlemen would be Christian enough to cut my throat," but nobody responded.   When the fire started he screamed, "Lord have mercy on my soul," and that was the last word he spoke though he was conscious for fully twenty minutes after that.   His exhibition of nerve aroused the admiration even of his torturers.[31]

Mrs. Turner (a Negro) made the remark that the killing of her husband on Saturday was unjust, and that if she knew the names of the persons in the mob . . . she would have warrants sworn out against them and have them punished in the courts. . . . The mob determined to teach her a lesson. . . . She was captured at noon on Sunday. . . . Mary Turner was in her eighth month of pregnancy. . . . Her ankles were tied together and she was hung to the tree, head downwards.   Gasoline and oil from the automobiles were thrown over her clothing and while she writhed in agony . . . a match applied and her clothes burned from her person. . . . While she was yet alive, a knife, evidently such a one as is used in splitting hogs, was taken and the woman's abdomen was cut open, the unborn babe falling from her womb to the ground. The infant, prematurely born, gave two feeble cries and then its head was crushed by a member of the mob with his heel. Hundreds of bullets were then fired into the body of the woman, now mercifully dead, and the work was over.[32]

LYNCHERS ARE NOT PUNISHED

The lynching of Negroes is the more significant since the States make no real effort to punish the lynchers.

A member of the Maryland bar writing in 1900 said that less than a dozen lynchers had even been tried for their crimes, and only two had been punished. The present writer has been able to obtain no information that would warrant the statement that as many as twenty-five persons had been convicted of a crime and punished for participating in the lynching of over 3,000 persons in the last twenty-two years.[33]

Here is evidence of the state of mind which leads to lynching.

Judge Charles H. Brand ordered Allen brought to Munroe for trial although it was known that the citizens had organized a mob to lynch him. The judge was offered troops by the Governor to protect the prisoner, but refused. . . . The same judge had refused to ask for troops on a previous occasion, saying that he would "not imperil the life of one man to save the lives of a hundred Negroes."[34]

In North Carolina on one occasion heroic efforts were made to prevent a lynching and punish lynchers:

Realizing that if a lyncher is permitted to remain unpunished the decency of the community is greatly endangered, Judge B. F. Long . . . sentenced fifteen white men to serve from fourteen months to six years in prison. The men were found guilty of attempting to lynch Russell High, a prisoner in the city jail. . . . The fifteen men were a part of a mob that for a night and a morning terrorized Winston-Salem in their effort to lynch a black man, innocent of the crime of assault for which he had been arrested on suspicion . . . and incidentally killed four people, one a little white girl. The Mayor of the city acted with promptitude and courage, calling out the Home Guards and the fire department . . . nearly every policeman was hurt. The Governor rushed troops from Camp Green at Charlotte. For many days cannon guarded the streets.[35]

RACE RIOTS

Race riots are more than mass lynchings; they frequently become local wars against Negroes. They involve murder, whipping, deportation and destruction of property. The elements in such conflicts are too complex to be given here, and the list too long. They are not confined to the South. Some of the most serious have been in Springfield, Illinois, Chicago, and in Washington, D. C. Perhaps the most shocking of modern race riots occurred in East St. Louis, Illinois, in 1917. It is summed up thus:

> On the 2d of July, 1917, the City of East St. Louis in Illinois added a foul and revolting page to the history of all the world . . . a mob of white men, women and children burned and destroyed at least $400,000 worth of property belonging to both whites and Negroes; drove 6,000 Negroes out of their homes; and deliberately murdered by shooting, burning and hanging between one hundred and two hundred human beings who were black.[36]

The disastrous effects of such riots have been officially recorded in a report on the Atlanta riots in August, 1906, by a white committee headed by W. G. Cooper, secretary of the Chamber of Commerce, and George Muse, a prominent merchant. The sensational exaggeration of reported attacks on white women brought on a clash that lasted several days, with this result:

1. Among the victims there was not a single vagrant.
2. They were earning wages in useful work up to the time of the riot.
3. They were supporting themselves and their families or dependent relatives.
4. Most of the dead left small children and widows, mothers and sisters, with practically no means and very small earning capacity.
5. The wounded lost from one to eight weeks' time, at 50 cents to $4.00 a day.
6. About seventy persons were wounded and among these there was an immense amount of suffering . . . in some cases prolonged and excruciating pain.
7. Many of the wounded are disfigured and many are permanently disabled.
8. . . . most of them were honest, industrious, and law-abiding citizens and useful members of society. . . .
10. Of the wounded ten are white and sixty colored. Of the dead, two are white and ten colored; two female and ten male. . . .
13. It is clear that several hundred murderers or would-be murderers are at large in this community.
14. Although less than three months have passed . . . events have already demonstrated that the slaughter of the innocent does not deter the criminal classes from committing more crimes. Rape and robbery have been committed in the city in that time.
15. The slaughter of the innocent drives away good citizens. From one small neighborhood, twenty-five families have gone.
16. The crimes of the mob include robbery as well as murder . . . the property of innocent and unoffending people was taken . . . the victims, both men and women, were treated with unspeakable brutality.
17. All this sorrow has come to people who are absolutely innocent of wrong-doing.[37]

For these crimes, the Grand Jury indicted sixty Negroes fo murder and sixteen whites for riot.

SELF DEFENCE BY THE NEGRO

The cases cited show that the Negro cannot expect protection from violence by the civil or military authorities. Practically their only protection is by using arms in self-defence, which means miniature civil war. Yet in spite of the Second Amendment guaranteeing the right to keep arms and many similar State guarantees, he is not permitted to defend himself. "The right of the people to keep and bear arms shall not be infringed" does not apply to the Negro. The local police power in most Negro sections is so exercised that Negroes cannot keep arms for defense against attack. Pawn-shop regulations and laws against carrying concealed weapons are used to disarm them. Nor are Negroes allowed to organize military companies even in sections where the race predominates. The Southern states keep Negroes out of the state militia. Georgia in 1905 permanently disbanded all colored soldiers in the State militia.[38] In Connecticut, West Virginia, and New Jersey, Negro troops are kept separate from white. There is no objection to Negro soldiers in the Federal Army, and in the drafts of 1917-1918 a larger percentage of the Negro Race than of the White Race was accepted for service.

THE NEGRO'S RIGHT TO LAW

Not only does the Negro fail to get the protection of the law, but he is continuously the victim of police persecution. He is arrested on what amount to general warrants—"round-ups for the Chief"—in which vagrancy, disturbing the peace, and other general offences are invoked to harass him. Negroes are frequently given the "third degree," beaten, and deported by being "given hours." For example:

In Atlanta, on October 15, thirty-seven laborers were arrested at night in their lodging-house as "vagrants." In Texas, five laborers were arrested as vagrants, and proved their steady, hard jobs. The Galveston "Tribune" says: "But the State chose to prosecute under a different portion of the law, alleging loitering around a house of ill-fame. The court explained, as it had done before, that a person can be a vagrant, yet be steadily employed, the law being general in its effect and covering many points upon which a conviction can be had on a charge of vagrancy.[39]

Although no law prevents Negroes from entering any park in Indianapolis, they are excluded from at least one of them by the danger of being assaulted by so-called "bungaloo gangs." In many parts of the country, both North and South, the Negro's coming and going is ordered by law or threatened violence.

In three places, at least, in North Carolina, a Negro is not allowed to stay over night—Canton, Haywood County, Mitchell, and Madison Counties . . . Negroes may work unmolested all day, but, if they linger after nightfall, they are reminded that it would not be healthy for them to remain during the night.[40]

At Syracuse, O. . . . and Lawrenceburg, Ellwood, and Salem, Ind., Negroes have not been permitted to live for years. If a Negro appears, he is warned of conditions, and if he does not leave immediately he is visited by a crowd of boys and men and forced to leave. A farmer who lives within a few miles of Indianapolis told me of a meeting by 35 farmers . . . in which an agreement was passed to hire no Negroes, nor to permit Negroes to live anywhere in the region.[41]

From Atlanta "Georgian," March, 1907. Peter Zeigler, a Negro, was last night escorted out of town by a crowd of white men. Zeigler has been here for a month and passed himself off as a white man. A visiting lady recognized him as a Negro who formerly lived in her city. . . . It developed regarding this news item from Albany, Georgia, that immediately after suffering the indignity of being expelled . . . Mr. Zeigler communicated with his friends and relatives, a delegation of whom came from Charleston . . . and proved to the satisfaction of every one that Mr. Zeigler was in reality a white man connected with several old families in South Carolina.[42]

The effect of the law in the South is to deny freedom of movement to Negroes in certain sections. He is deported if not wanted; he is restrained from leaving if wanted. He is sent to labor either on public works or for private employers to pay off fines imposed for minor offenses. Ray Stannard Baker says:

Laws in Southern States keep men from employing Negroes to go to work in other places . . . to a certain extent interfering with their freedom of movement. . . . Many other laws have been passed designed to keep the Negro on the land, and having him there, to make him work. The contract law, the abuses of which lead to peonage and debt slavery is an excellent example. . . . The criminal laws, the chain-gang system, the hiring of Negro convicts to private individuals . . . limit liberty. . . . The vagrancy laws, not unlike those of the North, and excellent in their purpose, are here sometimes executed with great severity. In Alabama, the Legislature passed a law under which a Negro arrested for vagrancy must prove he is not a vagrant.[43]

FREEDOM OF SPEECH AND PRESS

Freedom of speech for the Negro has not been violated by law. That has not been necessary when violence or deportation are far more effective. Freedom of the Negro press has never raised a serious issue.

The race has not been militant nor radical enough to invite suppression. Intimidation kept them in order, too. The great increase of Negro publications in recent years and their growing vigor indicates the advances being made by Negroes toward independence of thought in their own problems. Stray cases may be noted of attacks on Negro editors.

Miss Ida B. Wells, colored editor of the "Free Speech" at Memphis, Tenn. had her paper suppressed because she so fiercely denounced the lynching of some young colored men and arraigned the authorities for failing to punish the lynchers.[44]

For a time A. L. Manley published a Negro newspaper at Wilmington, N. C., but during a race riot in that city a number of years ago, he was driven out, and his office burned to the ground. He lived as a white man some years.[45]

Free speech on the Negro problem has been a more serious issue for white sympathizers than for the Negroes. This is especially true of teachers.

Professor Emory Slade was compelled to resign from Emory College in Georgia because he published an article in the "Atlantic Monthly" taking a point of view not supported by the majority of Southern sentiment. . . . Professor John Spencer Bassett was saved from a forced resignation from Trinity College in North Carolina after a lively fight in the Board of Trustees, which left Trinity with the reputation of being one of the freest institutions in the South. . . . George W. Cable, the novelist, was practically forced to leave the South because he advocated "the continual and diligent elevation of that lower man which human society is constantly precipitating," and advocated justice for the negro.[46]

Harvey Jordan, professor of embryology in the University of Virginia, was called upon to resign by the press in Virginia for some biological observations concerning Negroes published in a scientific journal. He was supported by his university but gave up the line of research that embarrassed him.

Two cases of more active measures taken against white advocates of Negro rights in the South may be noted though they occur after 1917.

Austin, Texas, August 22, 1919. John R. Shillady, of New York, secretary of the National Association for the Advancement of Colored People, was severely beaten in front of a hotel here to-day and ordered to catch the first train out of town . . . following a meeting held with Negroes by Shillady.

Two weeks ago local officials ordered the disbanding of a local branch of the National Association on the ground that the Association had no permit to do business in Texas. . . . His meeting was not interfered with. . . .[47]

THE NEGRO AND "FREEDOM OF EDUCATION"

A free education is not a civil right but the problem of Negro education is so full of difficulties that some of their aspects should be at least mentioned. It involves such questions as:

Is a fair share of the taxes paid by Negroes spent on Negro education?

Shall Negroes be educated in general public schools, or if not, shall they receive equal advantages in separate schools?

Shall the co-education of whites and blacks be forbidden even in private schools?

The question of separate schools has been tested many times in the courts, and they have uniformly affirmed the right of the community to provide separate schools for different races. This is therefore not an infringement of any right guaranteed under the Fourteenth Amendment. The Negro in the South has, as yet, little access to a free education, still suffering from the slave idea of keeping the Negroes ignorant and servile.

CIVIL LIBERTY FOR ALIENS

Let us now consider the status of white aliens.

Alien immigrants to the United States have no inherent right of entry. That right may be granted by treaty, but except for such limitation Congress may debar aliens for any reason it chooses. If an alien gains entrance, he may be held, examined before an immigration official and deported by executive order. His single right is to be brought before a court on a writ of habeas corpus for examination of the basis of the deportation. But the courts always refuse to intervene unless gross abuse of executive discretion can be shown.

Two clauses of the Constitution alone concern aliens directly:—that authorizing Congress to establish uniform rules of naturalization; and that giving the Senate and President jointly the power to make treaties.[48] Naturalized aliens become full citizens but we are here concerned only with those of alien status.

The treatment of aliens depends on several factors largely outside the control of law. First, degree of difference in color and culture from the predominant Anglo-American type. The sharper the differences, the greater the race prejudice, and the consequent invasions of personal liberty. This antagonism is deep and instinctive, not to be checked by law. There is a fundamental human reaction expressed in calling a man a "dago," "yid," "ginney," or "nigger."

> It denotes a consciousness of difference that common human qualities cannot quite transcend . . . an inheritance from the days when tribal distinctions were of profound importance in the progress of society.[49]

The second factor in determining the treatment of aliens is economic rivalry. The alien is generally regarded by the native worker as a competitor who may take his jobs, and undermine his standard of living. The aliens who have suffered most have been those who were imported by business interests to do hard work because they were cheap. The Irish suffered until they became a political force; the Chinese coolie suffered until he was excluded altogether; the Italian and Southeastern European suffers serious disadvantages today.

The third factor is religious antagonisms. These usually are a cloak for race and economic antagonisms, and are unimportant.

White Europeans backed by strong governments have suffered comparatively little in the United States. When they do, apology and reparation usually follow quickly on the demand of their governments. English-speaking aliens for instance have never suffered serious disadvantages here. But Latin and other European races have. As early as 1850-1851 there were anti-Spanish mobs, especially in New Orleans.[50] In 1891, in the same city, eleven Italians were killed in a race riot. The United States Government, though denying any legal international obligation, paid a damage claim.[51] Sporadic cases of this sort still occur, as witness the killing by mobs in Illinois of Albert Piozza, October 12, 1914, and of Joe Spreanza, June 12, 1915.[52] Jews have endured an unrecorded amount of intense social discrimination, business boycott and petty violence. They have had to endure them without appeal to home governments who have rarely concerned themselves with their Jewish nationals. Their economic power alone has prevented worse treatment.

The problem of the alien has been difficult along the Mexican border. Mexicans in the United States have suffered grave injustices, but singularly little attention has been paid to them. Twenty-one Mexicans were lynched in Texas alone in 1915. This is a high record due to the strained relations between the countries at the time, but the lynchings of Mexicans every year must reach a considerable number.[53]

As far back as the early fifties, Mexicans were excluded from the mines of California and deported along with the Chinese. The problem is complicated by the factors of border brigandage and violence by Mexicans, by the raids and gun-running of Revolutionary movements, by race antagonism, by whatever system of local protection obtains in the Border States resembling the Vigilantes. There is no record of the violence used against Mexicans in the United States but press reports and knowledge of conditions in border states make it clear that it has been great.

PERSECUTION OF THE CHINESE

The Chinese have suffered probably more than any other aliens, chiefly in California. Chinese immigration to the United States began shortly after 1850 and continued until the exclusion act of 1882. For about two years they were unmolested, but thereafter became the victims of every type of legal and illegal persecution. The reasons for it were deep-seated race antagonism and hostility by the working-class to a competitor who worked hard and needed little. The non-resistant philosophy of the Chinese made them safe victims, and they had no strong government behind them to demand protection. The slang phrase "a Chinaman's chance" tells the story. He had no chance.

The first anti-Chinese movement in California drove them from the better mines and settlements by intimidation, violence and deportation. They retreated to dumps and abandoned claims where less perseverance than a Chinaman's could not work them at a profit. Here they were terrorized, and mulcted of their earnings by the Miner's Tax Law, which became a source of considerable income to the State of California. The tax collectors gouged all they could from the Chinese by threats, outrages and even murder, until mining became so dangerous they gave it up. Then upon the adoption of the Fourteenth Amendment, this tax law was declared unconstitutional![54]

In 1855 we have the interesting paradox of the native Protestant Know-Nothing Party mobbing Irish Catholics in the East and in California Irish Know-Nothings mobbing the "heathen Chinee" for stealing *their* country and *their* jobs![55]

The Chinese fled from the mines to the towns. The people were led to believe them the root of all evil. From 1866 to 1877 they were attacked by violence, law, unjust taxation and police persecution. In 1869 the California State Democratic platform opposed the Fifteenth Amendment for fear it might enfranchise the Chinaman. Finally the fear of coolie competition became the inspiration for an organized propaganda of violence along the entire Pacific Coast especially during the labor agitation of the seventies. In 1869 a Chinese Protective Association was formed by the Chinese.

> Since 1855 no other class of foreigner on the Pacific Coast has such a roll of outrage, robbery, and murder to show as the Chinese. . . . It would be impossible to estimate the number of victims unrecorded who were driven from their claims, robbed, mal-treated, or mur-

dered. The Chinese were inevitably the prey of every
lawless adventurer and criminal. The total undoubtedly
mounts into the thousands. . . . There was an untold
series of petty outrages in the West and over the entire
country—of queue-cutting, snatching ornaments off
women. . . .[56]

In 1855 it was estimated that thirty-two Chinamen were
killed. *The San Francisco Bulletin* had an excellent index
which listed 262 outrages against Chinese before the fire of
1906. B. S. Brooks listed over two hundred cases in 1876
and adds: "Hundreds of Chinese have been slaughtered in
cold blood in the last five years."[57] In 1862 a Senate Committee of the California Legislature acknowledged that "there
had been a wholesale system of wrong and outrage practiced
on the Chinese population." In 1876-1877 the agitation
against "coolie labor," imported by business interests for
cheap construction of trans-continental railroads, was seized
upon by such political leaders as Dennis Kearney and his Sand-
Lotters, to turn the discontented workingman into an instrument for their political power.[58]

Incidents taken from over the entire period are here
given: March 9, 1857, at Alder Creek, a mob of 150
persons expelled all the Chinese. They made a circuit
of ten miles, driving 19 away, tearing up their sluices,
razing their dwellings, beating and mal-treating them.
. . . October 24, 1871, began the big Los Angeles riots,
over the arrest of a hoodlum for Chinese-baiting. Fifteen Chinamen were hung by the mob, and the Grand
Jury later found indictments against thirty-two rioters.[59]
July 23, 1877 and for several days thereafter, the mob
in San Francisco burned twenty-five washhouses, and
indulged in an orgy of arson, robbery, and torture, which
was finally suppressed only by the organization of a
Vigilance Committee under the old chairman of the
"Vigilantes" of 1850. It secured aid directly from the
United States Government, with no appeal to the Governor, and illustrates one moment at which the popular

police power worked for the protection of liberty. These riots spread from town to town, and similar ones broke out in the East. There were the deportations from Rocklin; the Chico murders in Montana. In the Truckee riots of 1878, a thousand or more Chinese were deported from one community. In San Francisco it was unsafe to attend the mission schools; laundries had to be barricaded against hoodlums with wire nets; the property of men employing Chinese was raided and burned. In Denver in 1880 trouble arose which led to the death of one Chinaman, and a property loss of $20,000.[60]

When the agitation against the Chinese had grown powerful, national action was taken to exclude all further immigration of Chinese. The Chinese Immigration Act was passed May 6, 1882; and the Chinese Exclusion Act September 13, 1888. The exclusion Act[61] ended any possible Chinese "menace," for no more Chinese could enter and those already here were not increasing. But this action did not stop the persecution. Let us note how the law treated the Chinese during this period.

LAWS RESTRICTING CHINESE LIBERTY

Law itself was frequently invoked in California against the Chinese. For example a California statute of 1850 excluded Negroes and Red Indians from giving testimony in courts of justice against whites. In 1854 in a murder case where the testimony of a Chinese witness was needed for conviction an appeal to the California Supreme Court brought this startling essay in ethnology;

> The term Indians includes all Mongolians . . . as in the days of Columbus all the countries washed by Chinese waters were denominated "the Indies" . . . therefore, all Asiatics are Indians, and inhibited by the statute from testifying against white men. . . .[62]

That this was no empty ruling was shown seventeen years later:—

February 2, 1871.—A woman was arrested for stealing $38.50 from a Chinese. She was discharged on the ground that there were no white witnesses to the theft. The Chinaman speaks and writes English very well, yet he could not testify to the loss of the money.

After this date Chinese were permitted to testify.

A case of indirect attack on Chinese religious liberty by ordinance is significant as illustrating how the law discriminated. San Francisco in 1873 passed the "Cubic Air Ordinance" requiring 500 cubic feet of space for each person in any room of an apartment. Regular raids on crowded Chinese quarters caught 147 victims in 1873, whose fines averaged $10. No whites were ever arrested though thousands violated the ordinance nightly. Moreover, these same Chinese had been imported on ships with 96 cubic feet of air per capita, and were kept in city jails with less than 100 cubic feet, and a State Prison with only 25 feet per inmate. When 177 Chinese were mulcted of $2,060 in fines in 1874 they found it cheaper not to pay their fines and go to jail,—which they did in such large numbers as to embarrass the supervisors until they decided on both punishment and deterrent by cutting off the Chinaman's queues in jail, a serious loss to them.

This queue-cutting measure was first proposed as an ordinance in 1873, but defeated by the veto of Mayor Alford who quoted the Civil Rights Act of 1870 as applicable to the Chinese, and the Treaty provision of 1868:

Chinese subjects in the United States shall enjoy entire liberty of conscience, and shall be exempt from all disability or persecution on account of their religious faith or worship.

But three years later (June 14, 1876) the order was passed:

Each and every male prisoner incarcerated or imprisoned in the County Jail of this city and county under or pursuant to a judgment or conviction, had by any court having jurisdiction of criminal cases . . . shall immediately upon their arrival at said County Jail . . . have their hair of their head cut or clipped to a uniform length of one inch from the scalp thereof. It shall be, and is hereby made, the duty of the Sheriff to have enforced the provisions of this order.[63]

Three years later the ordinance was declared unconstitutional by Justice Field of the United States Circuit Court for California.

> . . . the Supervisors had no power or authority to prescribe what amounted to an additional penalty. . . . The ordinance being directed against Chinese only, imposing on them a degrading and cruel punishment is also subject to the further objection that it is hostile and discriminating legislation against a class, forbidden by the Fourteenth Amendment which declares that no State "shall deny to any person within its jurisdiction the equal protection of the laws." . . . The complainant avers that it is the custom of Chinamen to shave the hair from the front of the head and to wear the remainder of it braided into a queue; that the deprivation of the queue is regarded by them as a mark of disgrace, and is attended, according to their religious faith, with misfortune and suffering after death . . . and that the plaintiff has suffered great mental anguish, been disgraced in the eyes of his friends and relatives, and ostracized from association with his countrymen. . . .
>
> Probably the bastinado, or the knout, or the thumbscrew, or the wrack would accomplish the same end; and no doubt the Chinaman would prefer either of these modes of torture to that which entails upon him disgrace among his countrymen and carries with it the constant dread of misfortune and suffering after death. It is not creditable to the humanity and civilization of our people, much less to their Christianity that an ordinance of this character is possible.[64]

This is apparently the only legal attack on the Chinese religious customs. But the popular attitude and consequences are shown here:

Sacramento, November 4, 1873,—The Chinese have been occupied for several days past in their joss-house, it being holidays. On Sunday evening some white rascals visited the joss-house, and after various insulting performances one of them set fire to the immense paper image. . . . It was discovered in time. . . . Later in the evening some wretch cut off a Chinaman's queue. . . .[65]

The problem of the Asiatic in California schools had already arisen, as this testimony shows in 1877:

A Chinaman wanted to go to school. . . . I wrote a letter to the school-board . . . that he was cleanly in person, well-behaved, and had such and such scholarship. They said personally they would not object, but that they did not think the public sentiment would allow it, and they did not dare admit him. . . . It was race prejudice. . . . I think there is no law against it. . . . I think the Chinese child has a right to go to the schools.[66]

The Exclusion Act of 1882 ended Chinese immigration, but not persecution.

In spite of the complete cessation of Chinese labor immigration, and in spite of the promises of our government to provide protection and "most favored nation treatment," the unjust treatment of the Chinese did not cease. The outrages on them during the eighties were even more inexcusable than those of the preceding decade.[67]

Former President W. H. Taft, in *The United States and Peace*, cites the cases of 50 Chinamen who suffered death at the hands of mobs in the Western States, and 120 others who suffered wounds or robberies after 1885. The list is far from complete.

The most terrible of these events was the massacre at Rock Springs, Wyoming Territory, on September 2, 1885, in which at least twenty-eight Chinese laborers were killed, fifteen of whom had wives and children. Many others were driven into the hills and exiled, suffering both from wounds and exposure. $148,000 worth of property was wantonly burned. President Cleveland declared in a special message:

> The facts . . . are not controverted or affected by any exculpatory or mitigating testimony. . . . There is no allegation that the victims by any lawless or disorderly act . . . contributed to bring about the collision; on the contrary it appears that the law-abiding disposition of these people, who were sojourners in our midst under the sanction of hospitality and express treaty obligations, was made the pretext for an attack upon them by a lawless mob. The oppression of Chinese subjects by their rivals in the competition for labor does not differ in violence and illegality from that applied to other classes of native or alien labor.[68]

The economic motive for this and other attacks is clear. This was a year of vigorous labor agitation by the Knights of Labor. The low-wage Chinese workers who had been imported to work on mines and railroads were easy victims. The overt cause at Rock Springs was a difficulty over the rights of Chinese workmen. A fight ensued down in a mine where four Chinamen were wounded, of whom one died. The following account is from the anti-Chinese local newspaper:

> On Wednesday all the Chinese in Rock Springs to the number of about six hundred were driven out by the long suffering miners. . . . The fact that white men had been turned off the sections . . . while the Chinese were being shipped in by the car-load . . . strengthened the feeling against them. . . .
> After dinner the saloons were closed. . . . It was finally decided that John must go; and the small army of sixty or seventy armed men went down the tracks toward Chinatown. . . . They sent forward a committee to warn the Chinamen to leave in an hour. Very soon there was a running to and fro, and gathering of bundles. But the men grew impatient. . . . An advance was made

with much shooting and shouting. The Chinamen snatched up whatever they could lay their hands upon and started east on the run . . . like a flock of frightened sheep scrambling and tumbling down the steep banks of Bitter creek. . . . Men, women, and children were out watching the huried exit of John Chinaman . . .

Soon black smoke was seen issuing from the peak of a house in "Hong Kong," then from another . . . half-choked with fire and smoke numbers of Chinamen came rushing from the burning buildings, and with blankets and bed-quilts over their heads to protect themselves from stray rifle-shots, they followed their retreating brothers into the hills. . . . Joe Young, the sheriff, came down from Green River in the evening and guards were out all night to protect the property of citizens in case of disturbance. But everything was quiet in town. . . . Over in Chinatown, however, the rest of the houses were burned. . . .

Thursday morning, in the smoking cellar of one Chinese house the blackened bodies of three Chinamen were seen. Three others were in the cellar of another, and four bodies were found near-by. From the position of some of the bodies, it would seem that they had begun to dig a hole in the cellar to hide themselves; but fire overtook them when about half way in the hole, burning their lower extremities to crisp—another body was found, charred by the flames and mutilated by hogs. The smell that arose from the smoking ruins was horribly suggestive of burning flesh. . . .

Judge Ludvigsen summoned a coroner's jury . . . and they returned a verdict that eleven had been burned to death, and four shot by parties unknown to the jury. . . . Every one was sober, and we did not see a case of drunkenness. Some sixteen arrests were made, and the men put under bonds to appear at the next term of the Sweetwater County Court. The grand jury failed to indict, reporting instead:

We have diligently inquired into the occurrence at Rock Springs . . . and though we have examined a large number of witnesses, no one has been able to testify to a single criminal act committed by any known white

person on that day . . . and therefore, while we deeply
regret the circumstances, we are wholly unable, acting
under the obligations of our oaths, to return indictments. . . .

> "The Rock Springs Independent" quoted in a
> pamphlet *The Chinese Massacre*.[69]

The effects of this wave of hostility by native workers
spread widely:—

A few months since when the news came of the Wyoming massacre . . . there had been scarcely a ruffle on
the quiet waters of Puget Sound concerning the now
vexed Chinese question. A few days later there appeared
an Irish agitator from California, who proceeded to har-
angue the laboring people and to organize them into
lodges of the "Knights of Labor." . . . Ere thirty days
passed four Chinese laborers had been murdered cowardly
in their beds, and a camp outfit worth some thousands
of dollars burned at midnight, the inmates being driven
half naked into the woods. Within ninety days these
so-called Knights arose en masse at Tacoma, and drove
two hundred Chinese residents from their homes . . .
herded them on the open prairie in a drenching rain, and
the next morning drove them into cars on an outgoing
train, excepting two poor wretches that had to be carried, having died from exposure. . . . Seventeen persons,
including one woman, were indicted for conspiracy against
the Chinese . . . and Mr. Nixon who was president
of the Young Men's Christian Association of Tacoma,
and a member of the Presbyterian Church . . . resting
under five well-earned indictments for unlawfully abus-
ing and driving Chinese people from their homes.[70]

Dr. Gulick adds these details:

In an official report of February 15, 1886, riots were
reported at Bloomfield, Redding, Boulder, Eureka, and
other towns in California, involving murder, arson, and
robbery, and it was added that thousands of Chinese had
been driven from their homes. . . . None of the crimi-

nals were punished in spite of the article in the treaty expressly providing that—

In case Chinese laborers meet ill-treatment at the hands of other persons, the Government of the United States will exert all its power to devise measures for their protection and secure them the same rights, privileges, immunities and exceptions as may be enjoyed by citizens or subjects of the most favored nations, and to which they are entitled by treaty.

Since 1886 there has been no organized attack on the Chinese, although there had been repeated violence, mostly simple "hooliganism." People have grown indifferent to the inconspicuous Chinaman, whose numbers are so few. But he like other aliens has suffered under the Immigration laws, from unjust arrest, unwarranted deportations and from the large powers granted executive officers to control the movements of immigrants without court review:[71] Such abuses of power are exemplified by the following case when 250 Chinese residents of Boston were simultaneously arrested (October 11, 1902) on suspicion that they were in the United States illegally:

In many cases no demand was made for certificates of entry. The captives were dragged off to imprisonment, and in some instances the demand was not made until late at night or the next morning when the certificates were in the possession of the victims at the time of the seizure. . . .The case of one old man was particularly sad. In the upsetting of the police wagon, two of his ribs were broken, and he was otherwise injured. . . . He informed the officers that his certificate was in his trunk upstairs, but he was not permitted to get his papers even under guard. This innocent man who under treaty had a perfect right to reside in this country free from molestation was made to suffer untold tortures in body and mind. . . . Two hundred and thirty four Chinese were imprisoned . . . 121 were released without trial or requirement of bail . . . only five were deported, but the officials hoped to secure the conviction and deportation of fifty more. . . . Although earnest complaint was made by the Chinese minister to the government at Washington, not a single officer was punished, or even censured for his illegal and brutal conduct and no reparation was secured by the Chinese.[72]

Sidney L. Gulick writes: "Chinese, even those lawfully in the United States, are still liable to arrest and deportation under circumstances that deny them even the most rudimentary justice." He cites the Case of Chin Loy You, brought before Judge Morton of Boston on a writ of habeas corpus to try the issue on an administrative order of deportation, February 16, 1915.[73] Granting the writ, Judge Morton declared:

It is apparent that many of what we are accustomed to regard as the essential safeguards of individual liberty are ignored. . . . The prisoner was not allowed to see any of the witnesses against him while they were testifying, nor to cross examine them. All oral testimony was taken behind his back. The petitioner was denied the assistance of counsel. . . . The proceedings were plainly not of a judicial character. Why were the ordinary safeguards against injustice refused or ignored? It does not seem to me that the opportunity here given to present evidence and to argue the case rendered the proceedings fair or in accordance with due process of law. . . . The proceedings present, to my mind, a plain violation of the fundamentals of fair play by the immigration inspectors. . . . The next case of this kind may be one of an American citizen endeavoring to protect himself against exile by administrative order made in this way.[74]

THE JAPANESE QUESTION

The Japanese in comparison with the Chinese have suffered comparatively little loss of rights granted by treaty. They resist, and they have behind them an active government. The Japanese question centered in the right to own land, to attend the public schools and to become citizens.[75]

Freedom of education is closely related to the constitutional freedom, so mention of the Japanese and the schools in California since 1906 is in place. A California law of 1872 empowered school trustees to establish separate schools for Indian children and those of Mongolian and Chinese descent, and to segregate them in such schools, if provided. The Chinese rarely wanted occidental culture through public schools so the law was disregarded. But in May 1905 the Board of Education of San Francisco passed this resolution:

> That it is determined in its effort to effect the establishment of separate schools for Chinese and Japanese pupils, not only for the purpose of relieving congestion . . . but also for the higher end that our children should not be placed in any position where their youthful impressions may be affected by association with pupils of Mongolian race.

On October 1, the Board directed all principals to send all Chinese, Japanese or Korean children to the Oriental public school after October 15.[76] The insult implied in the Board's resolution produced international complication. The Japanese of San Francisco protested; the Japanese Government questioned the United States, and President Roosevelt sent Secretary Metcalf to report and conciliate.[77]

The existing treaty with Japan provided that Japanese "enjoy the same kind and degree of protection for persons and property that nationals enjoy and have free access to the courts to secure such treatment."

It was held by the courts that separation in the schools was no violation of this clause. Investigation revealed only 93 Japanese students in 28,736 children. It was shown, however, that mature Japanese students were in classes with much younger students,—31 were above 16 years old, six being in primary grades and one of these was 19 years old. The issue was compromised. The Japanese over 14 years of age were permitted to attend the higher schools,[78] thus preventing grown men sitting with children. The later attempts at restrictive measure against Japanese land-ownership et cetera are not within our field.

CHAPTER VI.

CIVIL LIBERTY AND LABOR

THE power which exercises the greatest control over liberty
is economic. It often acts through military and political
power,—but it remains at bottom control by those who
govern business and credit. That is why the industrial struggle, the "Fifty Years War" of Labor and Capital from 1870
to 1920 involved more numerous and more complex attacks
on civil rights than any other conflict in our history. Doubtless, a very small degree of personal liberty has ever been
the lot of the wage-worker. But as he gained education and
began to organize, he demanded more and more liberty to
carry on his struggle for higher wages and better conditions.
The record of this conflict would fill volumes; we here outline
simply the major facts.

The labor movement has progressed along three lines:—
the trade unions, political activities, and the radical propaganda of a small section.

The bulk of the attacks on the civil liberty of the workers
has arisen out of conflicts between the unions and employers.
The concrete issues have been the right of labor to organize,
to strike, to picket and to boycott. The worker needed all
the liberties guaranteed in the constitutions:—freedom of
speech and assemblage, with the use of public halls and streets;
freedom for propaganda presses; protection from unlawful
police and military control; and all the hallowed safeguards
of criminal justice in the inevitable prosecutions for the exercise of these rights.

Against the workers were lined up the capitalist—employer
combinations creating as the workers declared an "invisible
government" superior to the constitutions, that could both

make and enforce its own laws, or control the enforcement of laws long in existence. They bought immunity from prosecutions, or defeated them by long delays and confusion in the courts; and through them plus the respect in which wealth is held, were able to establish their case in public favor, while misrepresenting both the purposes and the acts of the workers. Generally, they acted with a loose understanding through employers' associations, "citizens' committees," chambers of commerce, all moved by a common purpose.

A third element in the conflict was government. The government was seldom able to remain neutral and by its police function was usually drawn in on the side of the employing class to resist what was characterized as "labor violence;" the employers invoked the laws for themselves and did what they could to prevent legal protection to the workers. They used the military power of the states in strikes and through it enforced the most sweeping restrictions on the workers.[1]

The struggle has been fought chiefly by strikes, and the methods used to break these constitute conspicuous violations of civil rights. The rights of employers have but rarely been an issue, for those involved have been chiefly those concerning organized vs. unorganized labor, strikers vs. strike-breakers. The history of these strikes is only incidental to our discussion.[2]

As late as 1874 it could be said, "Strikes in this country have not been very serious nor long protracted." The first signs of the bitter struggle to come were the "Molly Maguires," a secret labor organization in the Pennsylvania coalfields. They were a link with the past, for the members, who were mostly Irish, had shared in the Know-Nothing agitation (See Chap. III) and many of their numbers had been draft-resisters, in 1863. Some of the agents used against the "Mollies" had been in the secret service during the Civil War and naturally turned to this new form of warfare. These "Pinkerton Men" and their employers first learned here some of the methods so commonly used later against organized labor. The causes that produced the Molly Maguires and the

methods used, constituted a variety of violations of civil
rights; but as the Mollies often used violence themselves, the
whole record is dubious. No details need be given.[3]

The great railroad strikes of 1877 called "The Great Riots"
were uprisings of jobless and hungry men who burned and
plundered. They demanded no rights; they wanted bread
and work. They were suppressed by State and federal troops.
The methods, used at this time for punishing those accused
of inciting the riots, the appearance of newspaper distortions
of the worker's struggles and the bitterness everywhere
aroused by this volcanic outburst, all laid the foundations for
further trouble.[4] These riots roughly marked the dividing
line between the previous peaceful semi-agricultural civilization which was passing and the complex industrial era of
today.

VIOLENCE BY THE WORKERS

The only attack on civil rights of others by the workers
has been through violence. The have not had power to deny
liberty to others by other means. Their violence has been
almost entirely directed against strike-breakers, occasionally
against the property of employers. This violence is due
partly to the instinctive reactions of determined men; partly
to the bitterness of the industrial struggle, and partly to the
Civil War and the weakened public morale which followed
it. After the War, violence was the resort of the Ku Klux
Klan in the South, of the private coal and iron police against
the Molly Maguires in the East, and of the Vigilantes and
"citizens' committees" in the West. The philosophy of the
Anarchist in the labor movement encouraged the workers'
resort to violence.

The workers, of course, have used violence extensively,
though usually only to meet the violence of the employer or
to intimidate the strike-breaker. The extent of such violence
can not even be estimated. But even when we admit its outrages the total amount is greatly exaggerated. The large
majority of such cases of violence have been intimidation and

minor assaults ending in the police court. The resort to violence is always opposed by labor leaders. And they have been usually successful in checking it. In recent years employing groups have hired spies and *agents provocateurs* to incite the outbreaks that would let violence loose in order to discredit the strike with the public and the authorities, and to justify their own resort to force.[5]

The following cases merely show the types:

July 3, 1894, John Kneebone who had been the principal witness for the prosecution against the Union men in 1892 and who had been many times threatened, was murdered in cold blood and broad daylight by 40 masked men who came from the town of Burke. . . . Four men were deported . . . the Grand Jury was unable to obtain testimony such was the terrorized condition of the country . . . . December 22, 1894, a number of non-Union men were called from their beds and deported; and on April 5, 1895, and on other occasions . . . they entered the bedroom of John Kopf and threatened to kill him. . . . December 23, 1897, Fred D. Whitney, foreman of the Helena and Frisco concentrator was brutally murdered.[6]

In 1899 the blowing up in Idaho of the Bunker Hill concentrator by several hundred union miners, resulting in the death of one employee of the company and one miner, started naturally an insurrection. The men seized the railroad train, loaded a supply of dynamite from the company's arsenal and ran the train out on to another railroad's main line. This led to cutting in of United States troops on the ground of interference with mail and inter-state commerce.[7]

The record of violence in one of the most turbulent trades—that of founder—is given by the President of the National Founders' Association (1908). It consists of nearly 100 pages of cases of threats, violence, dynamiting, intimidation of boarding-house keepers and deliverymen, and the hiring of labor "sluggers." Many of these are based on affidavits or court records. But this is the extreme statement of the case by employers in an industry noted for the bitterness of its labor struggle. It covers the troubles of four years:

Affidavits, on violence, intimidation, coercion.......... 400
Injunctions asked for.. 34
Injunctions granted... 34
Approximate contempts charged............................... 36
Convictions on contempt charges............................. 32

A specimen case follows:

Pickets were immediately stationed around the plant to intimidate new employees . . . from six to twenty or over being around at opening and closing hours. Threats, intimidating tactics, and slugging were employed. Customers of the firm were stopped and questioned with reference to their business associations with the firm and attempts were made to persuade or intimidate these customers to withdraw their patronage. Union pickets followed our delivery wagons to destination and attempted to persuade men not to handle products, especially those in building trades. Attempts were made to get other workers to refuse jobs on this material. The firm was compelled to enclose its entire property with a high board fence and station watchmen at the gates . . . to employ guards continuously to watch premises and escort workmen in and out . . . and to their houses. . . . Firm was forced to open a boarding house upon the premises to house its non-Union men who feared violence if they attempted to leave the plant.[8]

About as serious an interference with personal rights as violence is enforced emigration or deportation. Strikebreakers have been frequent victims. Here is a case:

On July 27, 1903, non-Unionists were forced to leave Victor. . . . Five Austrian miners from Butte had arrived . . . the unwritten law of many Western mining camps that no Italian should be allowed to live in the camps had been strictly enforced. These five men were mistaken for Italians, suspected of being an advance guard of non-union men to be brought into the camp in anticipation of the strike. . . . Two miners interviewed them and learning that they were not members of the Federation, informed them that they could obtain work as railroad laborers a mile or two outside the town and that they would be directed there. A committee of three miners called at their boarding-house . . . and the foreigners, carrying their grips, went with them in the direction of Hollywood. With a warning never to return . . . they were started off down the Florence and Cripple Creek tracks, and the crowd was ordered to go no further. After the five men had gone fifty yards a volley of revolver shots were fired after them.[9]

In a Michigan copper strike when riots occurred at the mine shafts, " . . . Many employees of the companies had been sworn in as deputies, but they had no firearms. The strikers overpowered these deputies, took away their badges, and in some cases beat them."[10]

VIOLENCE BY THE EMPLOYERS

Violence by the employers has worked indirectly through paid agents and through the State. Its avowed aim has been to defend their property and protect strike-breakers. Often enough the real purpose has been to intimidate the strikers, embroil them with the authorities and then to use the forces of the State to help break the strike. Their own violence was veiled behind the law and often ended in military rule. Before they became so well organized, violence consisted of riots that quickly subsided before the police. Military rule never superseded the courts. The most effective weapon of the "fighting" employer is to have the troops called out. He is thus relieved of all responsibility. Lacking the troops, he has his own agents of violence, while the local police and the courts are usually with him.

"PINKERTON MEN"

This use of detectives by private employers, "Pinkerton Men," strike-breakers, gun-men, thugs, "special deputies" or even the state constabulary has been a powerful cause of most violent outrages on the elementary rights of workers. These men often constitute a private army, and in some states were regarded as so serious a menace as to be forbidden by law. Generally, they are paid and housed by the employers, and this relationship is naturally reflected in their acts. Thomas Beet, formerly with Scotland Yard, London, writes thus:

> The private constabulary system, by which armed forces are employed during labor troubles has worked untold damage in America. It is a condition akin to the feudal system of warfare, when private interests can employ troops of mercenaries to wage war at their command. . . . In no other country in the world, with the the exception of China is it possible for the individual to surround himself with a standing army to do his bidding in defiance of law and order. . . . The conditions I have outlined could never obtain in England. During labor troubles the government looks after the policing and under no circumstances permits the meddling of private detectives. . . . During a famous strike in a western city . . . the country rang with details of acts of extreme violence, alleged to have been committed by the strikers. . . . There were probably instances in which strikers were responsible, but to my knowledge, much of the lawlessness was incited by private detectives who led mobs in the destruction of property.[11]

The coal mines, especially of Pennsylvania and West Virginia, have been centers of the armed guard system. As early as 1865, in Pennsylvania, a law was passed, permitting railroads and mine owners to appoint their own police, duly commissioned by the Governor. To the number of these, there was apparently no limit; "they could have 1,000 if they wished". From them grew the infamous "Coal and

Iron Police" which anteceded the more orderly State Constabularly of today.   Other States produced equally lawless types.   The strike-breakers of the Baldwin-Felts agency are described as follows in the official report of the West Virginia Mining Commission investigation in 1912:

> There emerges clearly and unmistakably the fact that these guards while personally brave men, openly, recklessly, and flagrantly violated, in respect to the miners on Paint and Cabin Creek . . . the rights guaranteed by natural justice and the Constitution, to every man, however lowly his condition and estate.   Many crimes and outrages laid to their charge were found to have no foundation in fact; but the denial of the right of peaceable assembly and freedom of speech, many and grievous assaults on unarmed miners show that their main purpose was to overawe the miners and their adherents, and if necessary, beat and cudgel them into submission. We find that the system employed was vicious, strife-promoting, and un-American.   No man worthy of the name likes to be guarded by others armed with blackjacks, revolvers and Winchesters, while he is endeavoring to earn his daily bread.

The difficulty of securing these deputy-sheriffs, often privately paid and obtained from strike-breaking agencies outside the state, and the cost of such service to the employers is told in the Report on the Michigan Copper Strike, 1913.   The characteristic methods of these armed guards are shown in this:

> Thereupon the Waddell detectives and deputies surrounded the house on two sides and began firing at the inmates.   They claimed a shot was fired from the house. When the firing began, there were 15 people in the house, including 2 women and 4 children . . . 4 men were shot and a baby in its mother's arms was powder-burned. One man was killed instantly, another died next day . . . one killed while at a table eating supper.   The neighbors testified that the deputies had gathered up stones and bottles and had put them around the house to indicate

that they had been used as missiles against them . . .
the prosecuting attorney denounced it as wanton murder . . . and the men were indicted for murder in the
second degree. . . . Mary Frazakas was shot in an early
morning parade of the strikers (probably by a militia-
man).[12]

A United States Bureau of Labor report on a Pennsylvania
strike contains this testimony by a sheriff as to the State Constabulary.

> The State Constabulary shot down an innocent man,
> Joseph Szambos, who was not on the streets but who was
> in the Majestic Hotel, when one of the troopers rode up
> on the pavement at the hotel door, and fired two shots
> into the bar-room . . . shooting one man through the
> mouth, . . . Szambos, through the head. . . . There was
> no disturbance of any kind. . . .
> One of the troopers jumped off his horse, caught a
> man by the throat, pulled his collar and tie off, without
> any reason as I have been told and turned him over as a
> prisoner to a police-officer. . . . No charge has been
> preferred to date (Feb. 26th to March 24th). I kept
> this man until the afternoon and released him on a cash
> bail of $25.00.[13]

J. H. Maurer[14] gives other details and C. D. Wright tells
of a picturesque uprising of 1,100 unpaid deputies during a
miner's strike . . . their martial adventures and progress in
search of their pay, amply justifying the term "mercenaries."
One use of detectives to instigate such violence that the
law might be brought down is given in this testimony before
the Industrial Commission of 1901.[15]

> A strike was inaugurated in Vallens' and Co.'s cigar
> factory. . . . During the trial (for conspiracy) it de-
> veloped that the Vallens had entrusted the suppression of
> the strike to Mooney and Boland's detective agency; that
> Dittbrenner, in the employ of this agency had pretended
> to be a cigar-maker,. and also pretended he was about
> to apply to Vallens for work, but permitted himself to be

dissuaded . . . joining the strikers . . . on picket duty.
Immediately, he commenced advising violence of almost
every description; advised the making of assaults on Vallens' family . . . to lay for Vallens and maim and dis-
figure him; he advised clubs, acids, hot irons . . . even
the burning of the plant. In the presence of other
strikers he got into a fight with a Mooney and Boland
detective, and when apparently getting the worst of it,
he called to the strikers for help and got none. In fact,
the only violence or attempt at violence shown upon that
trial was the pretended fight between two detectives, the
one in uniform, the other pretending to be a striker.

These private and mercenary agents have produced "the
plant," "the frame-up," the "fake confession" and other devices for manufacturing evidence which may convict workers
of crime or bring about violence to discredit organized labor.
The "labor spy" is essential to many of these achievements,
. . . a detective who joins the union, to secure a knowledge
of its plans, and who often attains in the union an office of
considerable power. Thus James McParland, first of this
profession secured the conviction of the Molly Maguires. He
is also credited with securing the "confession" of one Harry
Orchard, used in the attempt to convict Moyer, Haywood
and Pettibone of murdering the Governor of Idaho. This was
picturesque enough to be printed, but the workers declared
it was concocted simply to convict the union officials.[16] The
methods of a "plant" were well revealed in the strike at Lawrence, Mass., 1912.[17]

Dynamite was discovered in a house on Oak Street, in
the Syrian quarter, by the police. Five men and two
women were arrested. . . . Later, dynamite was found in
a cobbler shop on Lawrence Street and in a sand-bank.
. . . The cobbler was arrested. The strikers emphatically
declared the innocence of those arrested and claimed that
the dynamite had been "planted" by some. one who
wanted to discredit the strikers and make them lose
public sympathy. . . . All cases arising directly from

the dynamite were dismissed . . . Jan. 29th, a business man of Lawrence who had no connection with the strikers, was arrested for conspiracy and charged with having planted the dynamite nine days before. . . . On May 16th, he was convicted of conspiracy to injure by the planting of the dynamite and was fined $500.00.

DEPORTATIONS

The expulsion of an individual or a group from a community by violence was probably first employed by workers to get rid of strike-breakers. But since the nineties, it has been an accepted form of lawlessness, resorted to by "citizens committees," private detectives, the police and even the State Militia. It is, of course, a violation of constitutional liberties, yet there is no successful recourse to law, even where the members of a mob are known. The deporters usually represent public sentiment and control the local officials.

After a dynamite outrage during a strike at Idaho Springs, 1903, at a meeting of the Citizens' Protective League (an organization of mine-owners and businessmen) a bank president said: "If it is good law for the Western Federation of Murderers (Miners) at Victor to walk five Austrians out of town, it is good law for us. . . . I now move that we go to the calaboose and there take the prisoners and escort them to the edge of the city limits and tell them firmly to go and never to return." After some objection from the deputy district attorney on the ground that there was no evidence that the 23 men in jail were guilty, the motion carried with a shout. The guards gave up their keys, and 14 men were deported in an orderly, almost friendly manner. . . . Some of the men had lived in Idaho Springs several years . . . four or five had families there. The Citizens' League issued a statement claiming to have protected the miners from violence. . . . The deported men petitioned Gov. James H. Peabody, praying that "as citizens of this State, you will tender us such protection as will return us to our homes . . . and that we be guaranteed no further molestation from a lawless association. . . ." The Governor calmly replied that until he was called upon by the sheriff or mayor because the civil power was exhausted, he was not empowered to call out the militia. . . . The Citizens Alliance of Denver passed a companion resolution in the same old formula—"the business men of Idaho Springs acted within that higher and unwritten code to which resort must always be had . . . when there is no speedy and adequate remedy at law."

Judge Frank W. Owers granted an injunction restraining each and every member from interfering with the deported men or preventing their return to their homes and business. He said: "The action of the mob—I take pains to use the accurate word—in running out of town with threats of violence, the officials of the miners' union, was sheer anarchy, an outrageous violation of the rights guaranteed by the Constitution to the humblest person." He also pointed out that the miners' union was under very rigid investigation by the district attorney, while "the other union" (the League) seemed to be escaping investigation.

Judge Owers issued bench warrants for 129 citizens of Idaho Springs, charging them with rioting, making threats, and assault. . . . Most of these men were arrested, and gave bond for their appearance at $500. . . . February 8, 1904, District Attorney Thurman entered a nolle prosequi in each case. The attorney who had been engaged to help prosecute said that it seemed that pressure had been brought to bear, and that there was one law for influential citizens, and another for poor people.[18]

This is one of the few cases in which the whole event is recorded. Members and officers of the Industrial Workers of the World have been repeatedly deported. This organization of migratory workers with a radical philosophy has been, in many sections, practically outlawed, and its members have been denied any pretence of personal liberty. In a strike in Louisiana, against the Santa Fe and Southern Lumber Co.—

Three hundred gunmen seized fellow-workers Charles Cline, the local secretary, and Charles Deeny, and gave them a terrible beating and drove them out of town; tore down the tent in which the soup kitchen (for strikers) had been, pulling it down on the heads of the women, and shipped it with a part of the contents of the Union hall to De Ridder, La. . . . Men drifting into town who had never heard of the union were seized and thrown into jail, brought into court and given the option of going to work for the American Lumber Company, or being run out of town. Mayor Pressly of De Ridder had his resignation demanded because he refused to issue a proclamation prohibiting a mass-meeting.—They tried to run him out of town.[19]

FREEDOM OF SPEECH AND ASSEMBLAGE

Denials of freedom of speech and assemblage for workers, especially workers on strike, was constant during this whole period. The cases are so numerous that only a few notes are given.[20]

During the financial depression of 1873-4 the unemployed of New York City were organized to make an impressive demonstration. Permits to pass through the streets and use Tompkins Square for a meeting on Jan. 13th, were secured from the police and the Board of Parks. On Jan. 12th, these were revoked, but the workers not knowing this, began to gather in the Square. . . . About ten o'clock when they were standing about peaceably, platoons of police rushed in on the unarmed crowd, violently assaulting them with clubs, wounding many and dragging some 30 or 40 off to the station-house.[21]

The freedom of speech and of meeting were subsequently violated over and over again. The police by menaces and other means, prevented the meeting called in Assembly Hall to protest against the action in Tompkins Square; and again they tried intimidation with the Cooper Institute meeting until at last the aggrieved workingmen and their sympathizers felt as though they had no rights which the municipality was bound to respect,

The record piles up year by year. Governor Altgeld of Illinois cites this event in an official statement (Nov. 14, 1891).

> On Wednesday night . . . there was a meeting of working people at which there was no breach of the peace and no call for police interference of any kind. Yet Inspector Hubbard forcibly entered with a squad of officers and in a dramatic manner, stopped the proceedings . . . ordered those assembled to go and get an American flag declaring that unless they did so he would adjourn the meeting, indulging in other threats . . . and practically breaking up the meeting. . . . Not a single man was arrested or prosecuted. . . . The act of the Inspector was an outrage . . . a clear violation of the law, for which he should have been dismissed. The law guarantees to every person, liberty of speech, the protection of the person and the protection of property; one is no more sacred than the other."

Strike after strike has witnessed similar attacks on the most elementary rights, and today no strike occurs without such. From 1909 to 1917 the "free speech fights" of the Industrial Workers of the World most dramatically embodied that issue.

When denied the rights to speak on the streets, the I. W. W. have deliberately invited arrest, imported all members available, and filled the jails to overflowing until the cost and annoyance to the community brought concession. This ingenious nuisance was invented about 1909, and used vigorously as at Spokane, Wash., where the city council had passed an ordinance forbidding all street speaking within the fire limits—this being the only district, where workingmen congregated in any numbers. This law was amended to permit religious bodies like the Salvation Army to hold meetings. James Thompson, an I. W. W. spoke, was arrested, and tried on Nov. 2. . . . The religious amendment was declared unconstitutional by Judge Mann, but the original restriction was upheld. Then all the local I. W. W. members went out and spoke. They were arrested under another ordinance—

for disorderly conduct and some were sentenced to jail for thirty days. If one of them said "Fellow-Worker" on the street, he was liable to a fine of $100.00 and costs. Frank Little was declared to have been given thirty days for reading the Declaration of Independence. There were over 100 arrests the first day. Calls for volunteers were answered by 40 from Portland and many from elsewhere. The I. W. W. headquarters was raided. They replied that their plan was to make this as expensive as possible to the tax-payers of Spokane. The prisoners were locked up in school buildings and subjected to unsanitary conditions with rough treatment by the police until 344 sick men were reported as treated. The struggle ended without any clean cut victory either way though the I. W. W. secured the right to talk unmolested.[22]

Other free speech fights were conducted in 1909 at Missoula, Mont., and Newcastle, Pa. . . . By 1913 some twenty had been made, lasting from a few days to more than six months. They occurred at Wenatchee and Walla-Walla, Wash.; Fresno, Calif.; Denver, Colo.; Portland, Ore.; San Diego, Calif.; and Lawrence, Mass.

THE SAN DIEGO FREE SPEECH FIGHT

The most celebrated of these conflicts was in 1912, at San Diego, Calif. The causes were general labor troubles and antagonism to the I. W. W. It opened with a petition from eighty-five citizens, mostly business men asking the Council to prohibit street-speaking in certain congested districts. The results were reported to the Governor by a special investigator, Harris Weinstock, a business man of San Francisco. He says:

Public meetings are not permitted in any part of the city unless a permit is granted by the Chief of Police, despite the fact that there is no law requiring a permit. The I. W. W. charge that in recent weeks they have not been permitted to conduct street-meetings, the police justifying their refusal, under the existing circumstances, and by an alleged use of slanderous and abusive language by I. W. W. speakers. . . . No body of men should be deprived of their constitutional right of free speech beyond the legally restricted district, and since there is a law against the use of slanderous language in public places, the I. W. W. should be arrested and punished by due process of law. . . . Much testimony is that there has been needless brutality on the part of police officers while meetings were being dispersed. . . . Kilcullen had been assaulted by a group of policemen and brutally handled. . . . He was not arrested, but picked up on the streets unconscious. . . . An armed body of men, under the orders of Harry Place, a constable . . . under the directions of District Attorney H. S. Utley . . . maintained a guard on the Northern boundary of the county, interfering with the passage of pedestrians and vehicles on the public highway.

Forty-three sworn affidavits were submitted that members of the I. W. W., their sympathizers and others, had been arrested, on the streets or at I. W. W. headquarters, and without being charged with a violation of the law, and many of them without being guilty of a violation of the law, had been taken out of the city by autos a distance of 22 miles, and there subjected to an inhuman brutal treatment by a body of men, part of whom were police officers, part constables, and part private citizens. Local commercial bodies have encouraged and applauded the acts of these so-called vigilantes. The Merchants' Association passed a resolution commending the authorities and citizens' committee on ridding the city of all lawless and undesirable people. . . . The "Evening Tribune" (April 6, 1912) declared in an editorial: "If the sword of our own law is turned against us, we claim the right, under the unwritten law, to resort to the law of nature."

At a public inquiry Captain of Detectives Myers testified that although 200 arrests had been made, these had been solely for violating the street-speaking ordinance, no acts of violence had been committed that could be directly charged to the I. W. W., no I. W. W. arrests for drunkenness, nor resisting an officer.

For his bold utterances, A. R. Sauer, editor of "The San Diego Herald" was kidnapped, hurried out of town and a rope placed about his neck. The other end was flung over a tree and Sauer was hauled clear of the ground. He was constrained to promise that he would leave San Diego and never return. . . . If he divulged the names of his captors he would suffer the penalty of death.[23]

The investigator added that every member of the so-called vigilance committee had laid himself open to criminal charges under the federal law (Sec. 5,508, Revised Statutes). "The question naturally arises—who are the real anarchists,—the real violators of the constitution, these so-called and unfortunate members of 'the scum of the earth' or these presumably respectable members of society?"

Outside these organized fights, I. W. W. members have suffered numerous outrages. For example, in Lawrence, Mass. in 1912

> Peaceful women went to a meeting, March 1st . . . returning home about 15 of them were suddenly surrounded by fifty or more metropolitan police officers. . . . There had been no provocation, nor shouting, even, nor noise. . . . The clubbing they received was shameful and atrocious. . . . Not until one of the women, Bertha F. Crouse, 151 Elm Street, had been beaten into insensibility did the thugs in uniform desist. . . . The beaten woman was carried unconscious to a hospital, and pregnant with new life, this was blown into eternity by the fiendish beating and was born dead, murdered in the mother's womb.[24]

There was even a movement in Massachusetts at that time to make it a crime for any one to speak in criticism of the military, which had been called out, on the ground that it was an interference with military control. This was intended to silence W. D. Haywood, one of the I. W. W. leaders, but it was scarcely needed.[25]

By summary action the police have forbidden the I. W. W. to talk in Manchester, N. H. and they are obliged to hold meetings across the river. At Wakefield, Mass., the owner of the hall already hired, revoked permission for its use and the strikers were told they could not even conduct outdoor meetings. Even a meeting held within a private dwelling was dispersed by the police, who invaded the home.

On Friday night, July 18, 1913, in Seattle, Wash., a large number of enlisted men from the U. S. Navy, together with U. S. soldiers from the forts, led a riotous and lawless outbreak against constituted authority—said to be seeking vengeance for "an alleged prior assault upon some two or three enlisted men by street speakers who advocated doctrines antagonistic to their ideas of law and order". . . . It is persistently contended to the contrary that the one or two enlisted men, intoxicated, attacked a woman speaker on the street. . . . It is asserted that the crusade for vengeance . . . has been endorsed by officers of the Navy, and that the men's conduct was actually encouraged by some of their superiors. . . . The rioters, not only invaded the halls and buildings where the I. W. W. met, but they tore into the Socialists' halls, removed pianos, song-books and lodge paraphernalia, and made a bonfire of it. They then entered a Salvation Army place and continued their lawlessness tearing down mottoes "God Is Love."

Congressional Record, July 29, 1913.

ILLEGAL ARRESTS AND DETENTION

Illegal arrests and detention are frequent in the history of industrial conflict. The report of the Federal Industrial Relations Committee, 1915, says:

It is charged by the workers that during strikes, innocent men are in many cases arrested without just cause, charged with fictitious crimes, held under excessive bail, and treated frequently with unexampled brutality for the purpose of injuring the strikers or breaking the strike. . . . The Commission has been furnished with evidence showing that in a number of recent strikes large numbers of strikers were arrested, but that only a small number were brought to trial and relatively few were convicted of any serious offense . . . were as a rule required to give heavy bail . . . or detained without trial until their effectiveness as strikers was destroyed. . . . In each of the strikes investigated the charges as made were in essentials substantiated. . . .

In Paterson, N. J. . . . 2,238 arrests were made charging unlawful assembly or disorderly conduct. . . . In all, there were 300 convictions in the lower courts. Men arrested for unlawful assembly were held in bail of $500 to $5,000. The right of trial by jury was generally denied. Men were arrested for ridiculous reasons, as, for example, standing on the opposite side of the street and beckoning men in the mills to come out. This was the allegation on which the charge of unlawful assembly was placed against four men, and for which they were sent to jail in default of $500 bail, and although never indicted, the charge still stands against them as a bar to their rights as citizens and voters. . . . One was fined $10 for permitting strikers to sit on a bench in front of his house. . . . Not more than $25 worth of damage was done during the entire strike, involving 25,000 workers, and there was no actual violence or attempt at violence on the part of the strikers during the entire strike.[26]

In the Lawrence strike, 900 arrests were made without warrants and without the right of getting bail.

Sometimes the illegal detention is by guards and detectives who keep imported strike-breakers from leaving their precarious jobs. In a car of miners imported during the West Virginia strike, in 1912, two guards watched the doors at Philadelphia; at Washington, when the strike-breakers changed cars they passed through a lane of guards, some armed. Here is the affidavit of James A. Fleming:[27]

I was assigned to house 56 in Kayton, Kanawha County, West Virginia. Once I tried to lead a break from this house and they threatened me with jail. There was a little Jew boy by the name of Heim. . . . He had been picked up, he said, in New York on the East Side. He was crying night and day and begged the bosses to send him home. They put him in the mines. He was undersized and sickly and couldn't eat. My buddie and I escaped by climbing out the window one night and we never heard anything more about this boy.

EXTRADITION VERSUS KIDNAPPING

A new form of illegal arrest developed in the industrial struggle was the sudden and forcible extradition of labor leaders from one state for trial on charges in a second state, under circumstances which prevented them from exercising their constitutional rights.

The first important case was the seizure of John Moyer, who was wanted for trial along with W. D. Haywood and G. A. Pettibone, all officers of the Western Federation of Miners. This was on a charge of having murdered the former Governor of Idaho, Frank Steunenberg, on Dec. 30, 1905 at Caldwell, Idaho, by exploding a bomb at his gate. Moyer averred, in his petition for a writ of habeas corpus, that he had not been in the State of Idaho for more than ten years and that the Governor of Idaho knew he had not been in the state the day the murder was committed nor at any time near it. The actual events as stated by Supreme Court Justice McKenna were:

A conspiracy is alleged between the Governor of Idaho and his advisers, and that the Governor of Colorado took part in this conspiracy, the purpose of which was "to avoid the Constitution of the United States . . . and to prevent the accused from asserting his constitutional right under clause 2, section 2, of Article IV. . . . The agent of the State of Idaho arrived in Denver, Thursday, February 15, but it was agreed between him and the officers of Colorado that the arrest . . . should not be made until some time in the night of Saturday, after business hours—after the courts had closed and judges and lawyers departed for their homes; that the arrest should be kept secret, and the body of the accused should be clandestinely hurried out of the State of Colorado with all possible speed, without the knowledge of his friends or his counsel; that he was at the usual place of business during Thursday, Friday, Saturday; that no attempt was made to arrest him until 11:30 P. M. Saturday when his house was surrounded and he was arrested . . . thrown into the county jail. . . . On Sunday morning, the officers of the State, and "certain armed guards, being a part of the forces of the militia of Colorado," provided a special train for the purpose of forcibly removing him from the State. . . . He was forcibly put on said train, and removed with all possible speed to Idaho; that prior to his removal and at all times after his incarceration in the jail at Denver, he requested to be allowed to communicate with his counsel, and the privilege was absolutely denied him. The train, it is alleged, made no stop at any considerable station, but proceeded at great and unusual speed, and that he was accompanied by and surrounded with armed guards, members of the state militia of Colorado, under the orders of the adjutant-general of the state. . . .[28]

Moyer and Pettibone both petitioned the Supreme Court of Idaho for release on a writ of habeas corpus. Their petitions were denied by this court and by the U. S. Circuit court, and the U. S. Supreme Court upheld their refusal on these grounds:[29]

Even if the arrest and deportation of one alleged to be a fugitive from justice may have been effected by fraud and connivance arranged between the executive authorities of the demanding and surrendering states so as to deprive him of any opportunity to apply before deportation to a court in the surrendering state for his discharge, and, even if, on application to any court, state or Federal . . . he would have been discharged, he cannot so far as the Constitution or the law of the United States are concerned, when actually in the demanding state, in the custody of its authorities for trial and subject to the jurisdiction thereof . . . be discharged on habeas corpus by the Federal court. It would be improper and inappropriate in the circuit court to inquire as to the motives guiding or controlling the action of the governors of the demanding and surrendering states. . . .[30]

Justice McKenna (dissenting); In the case at bar, the states, through their officers, are the offenders. They by an illegal exertion of power deprived the accused of a constitutional right. . . . And Constitutional rights the accused certainly did have. The foundation of extradition between the states is, that the accused should be a fugitive from justice from the demanding state, and he may challenge the fact by habeas corpus immediately upon arrest. If he refute the facts, he cannot be removed. . . . It is the right to be free from molestation. It is the right of personal liberty in its most complete sense. . . . No individual could have accomplished what the power of the two states accomplished . . . could have made two arrests of prominent citizens by invading their homes; could have commanded the resources of jails, armed guards, and special trains; could have successfully timed all acts to prevent inquiry and judicial interference. . . . At the first instant that the State of Idaho relaxed its restraining power, he invoked the aid of habeas corpus. He should not have been dismissed from court.[31]

THE ILLEGAL EXTRADITION OF JOHN J. MCNAMARA

On the afternoon of Saturday, April 22, 1911, a requisition for the return to California of John J. McNamara of Indianapolis was presented to the Governor of Indiana. McNamara was charged with complicity in an alleged dynamite explosion in Los Angeles, and with being a fugitive from justice. At 5:30 o'clock of the same afternoon when the higher courts were adjourned and would not again be opened for 36 hours, McNamara was arrested . . . taken before a police judge, and after having been denied counsel was turned over to the Los Angeles authorities by whom he was rushed out of the city. . . . McNamara was not a fugitive from justice. It was not seriously contended that he was in Los Angeles at the time of the Llewellyn explosion. The Governor of Indiana made no proper effort to determine whether Mc-

Namara was a fugitive. The police judge had no proper jurisdiction in the case since the law specifically provides that the accused shall be brought before the circuit, superior, or criminal court. The police and private detectives had no legal right to make the arrest since the law provides that such arrests must be made by a sheriff or constable. The seizure of McNamara's private papers was illegal. The Indiana statutes (Acts of 1905, section 56) define the right of search and seizure. No such act as was exercised by McNamara's abductors is therein permitted. (cf. Fourth Amendment of the United States Constitution.) He was refused the advice of counsel. It is thus certain that in the kidnapping of McNamara and in all attending circumstances a series of flagrant violations of State law and of the Federal Constitution have been committed. (Statement of Victor Berger, congressman.)

An affidavit, by the assistant district attorney of California, sets out a telegram received from W. J. Burns on the 15th of April, week previous to the arrest, which reads as follows:

Chicago, Ills. 4/15/11.
I have arrested and am holding in Indianapolis, Ind. J. J. McNamara.

As I understand the practice in the executive department of California, before a requisition will issue there must be a showing that the party has been apprehended. . . . In order to obtain that requisition Burns sent this telegram on the 15th of April. . . . He was not arrested until one week later so that the information was—to use the only correct term—a lie. A brother of McNamara and this man McManigal were arrested in the city of Detroit. They did not go through the forms of extradition. They simply arrested them, took them into a flat in the city of Chicago, held them ten days, and then carted them to California. . . . These police officers under the guise of this search warrant for dynamite . . . drilled into the safe and abstracted the check-books, et cetera. . . . I went to the court to which the return was supposed to have been made of this search warrant and he referred me to the chief of police . . . and he referred me to the court. . . . They were not returned by either of them. . . . The chief of police said: "We will take whatever we please."   (Testimony of Attorney Rappaport, p. 13.)

So far as the taking of this man from Indiana was concerned he was not taken under the forms of law . . . there is no question about that.   (Statement of Congressman Madison of the Committee.)

Ample evidence is at hand that the safe-guards guaranteed by law were flagrantly disregarded and John J. McNamara surrendered without a moment's preparation or opportunity to avail himself of his lawful rights. (Letter of Samuel Gompers, president of the American Federation of Labor.) [32]

THE CHILDREN'S EXODUS FROM LAWRENCE

A novel form of detention was applied to the children of the textile strikers at Lawrence, Mass. in 1912. The strikers had been sending their children to sympathizers in other cities, to save expense and get them better care. On February 17, one hundred children were sent to New York and elsewhere. Colonel Le Roy Sweetzer, commanding the Massachusetts militia on duty in Lawrence, then issued this ultimatum:

Mr. William Yates,
Lawrence, Mass.
   Sir: I herewith notify you and through you the strike committee that hereafter while I am in command of the troops in Lawrence I will not permit the shipping of little children away from their parents to other cities, unless I am satisfied that this is done with the consent of the parents of the said children.

A few days later, the Marshal of Lawrence stated publicly that no more strikers' children would be allowed to leave the city. Two days later, the strikers undertook to send about 100 children to Philadelphia. One of the committee relates the facts:

We saw the street lined all around the station with police and a company of soldiers marching up and down. . . . Some of the children tried to get in the station and the police would not allow them. . . . But when we got in the station there were about forty children, and we bought tickets for those forty children for Boston. . . . When it came time for the train to start, and I was on the point of going out of the station with two children in hand, when a soldier put a bayonet across the door and said I could not get out. . . . He wouldn't tell me any reason. . . . When I got out of the station two policemen grabbed me. They beat me with a club. I saw them take up little children and pick them up by the leg and throw them in a patrol wagon. I saw one of the women put up a little resistance and a policeman grabbed her by the neck and choked her. *(Testimony of Max Bogatin.)*

I had an auto truck in use by the military department at the station and when they started for the train I formed two lines of policemen and we prevented them from going on the train, and we put them into the auto truck and took them to the police station. *(Testimony of City Marshal Sullivan.)* [33]

Five women were held for "neglect of children," but no case came to trial. In most . . . a fine of $1 was imposed . . . a number of children were detained, but after the police judge had heard two of the cases, he referred the rest to a committee and all the cases were ultimately dismissed. . . . March 1, forty or fifty were sent to Philadelphia, with no interference on the part of the police except they secured a list of the names and addresses of all children sent. . . . It was rather because the sending of the children away from Lawrence seemed an un-American and an unnecessary war measure which hurt the community's pride that vigorous steps were taken to prevent the children going. . . . The police authorities are entitled to the credit of having acted with sincere good intentions and upon grounds not wholly unreasonable. . . . The strikers felt that the refusal of the authorities to allow the children to leave Lawrence was a serious interference with their rights. They had undertaken in all cases to secure the consent of the parents. . . .[34]

There is a feeling today however that the police partly in answer to a public demand, overstepped their powers. . . . Summary restriction of the liberty of the parents to send their children out of town because their purpose is disapproved of or because the authorities feel that it is not necessary, encroaches upon the natural rights of parents to control them.[35]

Governor Foss of Massachusetts wrote to the Attorney-General ordering an investigation and the taking of any necessary action to assure all citizens free and untrammelled exercise of their rights. No action was taken.

CRUEL AND UNUSUAL PUNISHMENTS

There are nowadays no "cruel and unusual punishments" in the sense of the constitutional prohibition, inflicted by any courts. Plenty of them are inflicted by the police and by officials of penal institutions. Torture is used for disciplinary purposes or to secure confessions from suspects. This cruelty is general and is used against workers as well. Here is an instance in the class struggle:

Among the strikers gathered in by the police (of Paterson, N. J.) was a mother with a nursing baby. She was fined $10 and costs with the alternative of 20 days in jail. She was locked up but the baby was not allowed to go with her. In 24 hours the mother's breasts were filled to bursting but the baby on the outside was starving. He refused to take any other form of food. In a few hours the condition of the mother and baby was so dangerous that Elizabeth Gurley Flynn went to see the Recorder. She told him the baby would die. . . . He replied, "That's none of my business."[36]

110 HOURS IN A STRAIGHT-JACKET

Jacob Oppenheimer, confined in San Quentin penitentiary, California for murder, tells this experience with disciplinary punishment:

The straight-jacket, made of coarse canvas, was about 4 feet long and on one side had brass eyelets about 4 inches apart. On the inside were two canvas pockets. . . . The guard ordered me to put my arms into the pockets. Then he wrapped the canvas folds about me and . . . began lacing it tight across my back. He then jerked me off my feet and flung my face down on the floor. He braced his foot against my back and laced the cord still tighter until my breath came in short, hard gasps. . . . No conceivable torture can be worse than 110 hours continuous compression in that canvas constrictor that I suffered . . . my first experience in the jacket that has killed and maimed many prisoners. . . . I had not been in it fifteen minutes when sharp, needle-like pains began shooting through my fingers, hands and arms, which gradually extended to my shoulders . . . within half an hour these pains shot back and forth like lightning. Cramping pains clutched my bowels; my breath pained with a hot dry sensation. The brass rivets ate into my flesh, and the cord ground into my back until the slightest movement, even breathing, was an added agony. My head grew hot and feverish, and a burning thirst seized me which compelled me every few minutes to ask the guard for water. . . . As the hours and days passed the anguish became more and more unbearable. I slept neither night nor day. . . . The bodily excretions over which I had no control in the canvas vice, ate into my bruised limbs adding pain to pain. My fingers, hands and arms finally became numb and paralyzing shock stunned my brain. . . .

Had I been offered a dose of poison I would have drunk it with gratitude. Thus I suffered for 4 days and 14 hours incessantly. . . . Released I reeled off to my cell where I sank on my mattress in utter collapse. . . . I managed to drag off my saturated clothes. . . . What a sight I beheld. My hands, arms, and thighs were frightfully bruised, and had all the colors of the rainbow. My body was shrivelled like that of an old man and a horrible stench arose from it. I sank down on my mattress and never arose from it for a week. . . .

Prisoners have been killed and crippled for life in the

jacket. I know of four prisoners who in one year attempted suicide rather than be subjected to its tortures.[37]

MARTIAL LAW

The year 1892 witnessed the beginning of "state martial law" in industrial conflicts. Militia had been used against strikers as early as 1828, and both state and federal troops were called out in the eastern half of the country in the Great Riots of 1877. Before about 1892, the military was regarded as an extension of the civil power. They assisted the civil officers and the courts to preserve order and protect life and property. The so-called "martial law" meant only that the soldiers were called in as police. It did not mean, as it has come to mean since, the imprisonment of men by hundreds, a trial by military commissions, suspension of the writ of habeas corpus and a supplanting of the courts. At this time, the soldiers had no more right than a chief of police to exercise such powers.[38]

The assumption of this authority under "martial law" came about from their function of protecting life and property as the employers conceived it. Protecting the strike-breakers brought the strikers and troops into collision. The local civil authorities sometimes favored the strikers and often remained neutral; therefore effectively to accomplish the protection of the strike-breakers the Governor or the commander proclaims "martial law." The effect is thus stated by federal investigators:

> In Colorado martial law has been in effect ten times since 1894. Similarly in Idaho . . . on several occasions. . . . Not only have strikers been imprisoned by military courts, but thousands have been held for long periods in "bull pens." Hundreds have been deported from the State, and so arrogant have the troops become upon occasions that they have refused to obey the mandates of the civil courts. . . .
> In West Virginia, during the strike of the coal-miners in 1912, martial law was declared and the writ of habeas

corpus denied in spite of the fact of a direct prohibition by the constitution of the State, in spite of the fact that the courts were open and unobstructed. Persons outside the military zone were arrested, dragged before military courts, tried, and sentenced under so-called martial law Upon appeal to the Civil courts . . . the military authorities were upheld, in spite of the oath of the judges to support the constitution . . . which provides that—

No citizen unless engaged in the military service of the State, shall be tried or punished by any military court for any offense which is cognizable by the civil courts of the State.
and
The writ of habeas corpus shall not be suspended.

Although uniformly held that the writ of habeas corpus can only be suspended by the legislature, in these labor disturbances the executive has in fact suspended or disregarded the writ. In labor cases the judiciary either disregards the fact that the writ has been suspended by the executive or evades the issue. In non-labor cases the courts have protested emphatically when the executive attempted to interfere. In cases of military operation because of non-labor disturbances, the judiciary has almost without exception protested against the exercise of any arbitrary power. . . . In labor agitations the judiciary has uniformly upheld the power exercised by the military, and in no case has there been any protest against the use of such power or any attempt to curtail it, except in Montana, where the conviction of a civilian by a military commission was annulled.[39]

This statement cites the cases of the Kentucky Night Riders when in an almost real insurrection, the writ of habeas corpus was not suspended.[40]

IN IDAHO

Martial law first supplanted civil processes in industrial conflicts during the strike in the Coeur d'Alenes mines, Idaho, in 1892. The Mineowners' Association had secured an injunction restraining the striking miners from interfering with the Association's imported strike-breakers. The Governor issued a proclamation warning the men against even using moral suasion to keep others from working, and threatened martial law. The Frisco mine and mill were shortly after destroyed and several men were killed. Martial law was then declared, the troops arriving the next day. It was claimed that the sheriff and marshals, having been elected by the striking miners would not act against them. General Curtis of the national guard removed them from office and by "Special Order, No. 3" said:

> Dr. U. S. Sims, of Wallace, Idaho, is hereby appointed acting sheriff of the county of Shoshone, and is empowered with all the authority of that office under martial law now in force in said county. Dr. Sims was the physician employed by the mine-owners. . . . Immediately more than 500 men were arrested and thrown into the "Bull Pen"—one at Kellogg and one at Wallace. . . . Of the 500 some were released on parole, some on bonds, and about 75 were held for two months against most of whom no charges had been made. . . . Of all who were tried only sixteen were convicted . . . and those for contempt of court. They would not refrain from moral suasion. The decisions were all reversed by the United States Supreme Court. . . .[41]

The idea of a military officer appointing a civil officer like a sheriff shows that the only law was armed force.

Seven years later in the second Coeur d' Alenes strike, the military went even further. The trouble arose over a demand for recognition of the miners' union; and the sheriff underestimated the danger. The leaders organized about 1,000 miners, seized powder, put it on a commandeered train, ran it over a different railroad, and blew up the Bunker Hill concentrator. Four days later, federal troops arrived. Governor Steunenberg proclaimed Shoshone County in a state of insurrection. The sheriff and county commissioners were removed from office—a proceeding later approved by the Idaho Supreme Court; and Dr. Hugh France, an employee of the mine-owners, was appointed "agent for the State of Idaho," a new office. The candidates for county commissioner who had been defeated at the last election were put in office. Finally, Dr. France, assisted by soldiers, arrested some 800 miners and threw them in the "Bull pen."

> . . . Eight hundred men were taken from the mines in their working-clothes and driven like sheep into a few box cars and an old barn. For 24 hours they remained without food or drink; and for three weeks they were kept in these places, where there was not a bed and not sufficient room for all of them to lie down at the same time. The food was nauseating. . . . From this inhuman treatment several of the men died, and many contracted diseases which still linger with them. . . . The authorities were pressed either to prefer charges, try them, and punish them, or to release them. The local officials insisted that as long as martial law prevailed they had no power to act; while the State and Federal authorities insisted they were only to preserve peace and had no power over the men. Thus they held them for months with these evasive excuses. . . .[42]

Of the hundreds arrested, only fourteen were convicted of any crime, a seventeen year old boy for murder in the second degree, and the others for obstructing the U. S. mails, though the mail train was declared to have been on time the day of the trouble. A justice of the peace named Flannagan, elected by the people, was arrested and held almost five months because he would not surrender his office on demand of the state officers. He was finally released without being charged with a crime. The defense of these acts by the Attorney-General is a remarkable admission:

> It was almost impossible not to make a mistake in the arrests in the bull-pen. Some persons were arrested by

mistake and these were released in a few days—a very
large number, technically guilty, but not morally guilty
were discharged as soon as the situation was discovered.
It is sometimes stated that a large number of innocent
persons were arrested and detained without warrant . . .
held in custody an unreasonable time. . . . To have proceeded by complaint before a magistrate would, owing
to the nature of the crimes, the large number of witnesses to be examined and the large number of persons
involved, have taken a much longer time and thereby
occasioned a longer imprisonment, and added greatly to
the public expense.[43]

Governor Steunenberg, asked why he kept men in jail for
months, replied: "I do not think it safe for them to have
their liberty." The Governor received judicial absolution
from the Supreme Court of Idaho which laid down these doctrines:

(1) That in case of an insurrection, the governor or
military commander may for the purpose of suppressing
it, suspend or disregard the write of habeas corpus;[44]
that the truth of the governor's recital of causes for his
acts will not be inquired into or reviewed; that if the
local officers fail in their duty to apply to the governor
to proclaim an insurrection in existence, he may issue
such proclamation without their application.

IN COLORADO

The power of the executive to use troops has arisen both
with respect to the President (see below, page 248) and
governors.

The usual rule has been that troops will not be ordered
until asked for by the local authorities, with convincing proofs
of the necessity. An interesting case in 1894 of how the
Populist governor of Colorado met this effort to discredit the
workers in a local strike should be noted. In response to the
appeal of the sheriff, he sent three companies of militia to El
Paso County. He also sent the Adjutant-General who reported:

No person in the county had been charged with **any** offense in regard to the existing labor trouble. . . . Neither the sheriff nor his deputies had ever been resisted in any way. I told Sheriff Bowers that the troops were there at his solicitation, on his showing no process had issued from the courts, the military was not subject to his order, and that the facts would at once be made known to the governor.[45]

The governor promptly ordered the troops withdrawn. When the local authorities fail to call for troops where they really are needed, the courts in Idaho and Utah have upheld the governor sending troops into a district upon his own initiative. The Colorado decision came after suspensions of civil laws, during the Cripple Creek troubles of 1903-4.[46]

The first arrests were made by the militia on September 10, 1903, when Charles Campbell, H. H. Kinney, and three others were held on the grounds of military necessity. No charges were filed against them. They applied to Judge W. P. Seeds of the district court for writs of habeas corpus . . . which were issued to Adjutant General Bell and Brigadier General Chase, returnable on September 18. . . . On the 18th, for return to the writs, General Chase acknowledged that the petitioners were in his custody, but set forth the order of the Governor calling out the national guard in justification. . . . Judge Seeds decided that it was imperative that the petitioners be produced in court. . . .

September 21, about 90 cavalrymen marched through Cripple Creek, surrounded the Court House . . . permitting no person to pass unless an official or a press representative. A company of infantry escorted the four petitioners to the court-house and 14 soldiers entered and with loaded guns and fixed bayonets guarded them until the court was called to order . . . took their seats and removed their hats which was construed as a submission to the court. . . . September 23, thirty-four armed soldiers brought the prisoners into court. . . . Eugene Engley stated that the court was no longer a constitutional court, but an armed camp, refused to proceed with the military present, and left the court with the other attorney for the petitioners. . . . The court ordered that the petitioners be discharged from custody, deciding that though the military had the right to make arrests, the persons arrested must be immediately turned over to the civil authorities, and commenting on the troops as "offensive to the court . . . unwarranted and unnecessary . . . tolerated because it was the national guard. . . . If I had insisted upon its withdrawal a conflict would probably have arisen, with the entire national guard on one side and a mere posse comitatus on the other."

General Chase arose and saluting the court, said: "Acting under orders of the commander-in-chief, I must at this time decline to obey the orders of the court." But later in the day, acting on instructions telegraphed by Governor Peabody, he released the four prisoners.[47]

A similar case, suggesting the Merryman case during the Civil War (see above, page 135) arose when the same Judge Seeds during this strike ordered Colonel Verdeckberg to release one Victor Poole from custody. Coroner James Doran who attempted to serve the order was forcibly ejected from military headquarters. The military kept Poole in custody, appealing from Judge Seeds to the Supreme Court of the state. While the matter was pending, a charge of assault to kill was brought against Poole and he was turned over to the sheriff. He was tried shortly, before a magistrate, but there being no witnesses against him, he was discharged.[48]

During the military regime at Cripple Creek Governor Peabody is reported to have declared "There is no martial law in Cripple Creek and there will be none." A Lieutenant McClelland of the militia declared, when it was pointed out to him that his proceedings were in violation of the Constitution "To Hell with the Constitution. We aren't going by the Constitution." Assistance to families of the strikers was forbidden except through military channels. Deportations were also ordered by the military.

The arrest and detention by the military of Charles Moyer,

an officer of the Western Federation of Miners, from March 30 to June 15, 1904, resulted in two important decisions which have since buttressed martial law.[49]   Moyer's petition for a writ of habeas corpus was refused by the Colorado Supreme Court on these grounds:

> The governor has the power to call out the militia and his determination cannot be controverted; the militia so called has the right to arrest and detain; a person imprisoned for aiding and abetting insurrection is legally arrested and his detention is legal.[50]

Justice Steele dissented denying the governor's power saying:

> He has no power to arrest a person who may commit a crime. As the privilege of the writ has not been suspended, as the courts are open, as martial law does not prevail, and as no charge has been preferred against the petitioner, he should be discharged.

Moyer brought action for damages against Governor Peabody and others in the U. S. Circuit Court. claiming that he had been deprived of liberty without due process of law guaranteed by the Constitution, especially the Fourteenth Amendment.[51]

The Court affirming the general principle that the executive's decision as to an insurrection cannot be questioned and that military officers may lawfully arrest, declared it could not act unless the governor was guilty of wanton abuse of his power. An appeal was taken to the U. S. Supreme Court where the decision was upheld, as it claimed that public danger warranted the substitution of executive for judicial process, and that *no rights under the federal constitution* had been violated.[52]

In 1912 the struggle between the striking coal-miners in Cabin Creek, Paint Creek and other West Virginia fields and the armed guards acting for the operators had produced a state bordering on civil war. Governor Glasscock ordered out the militia and issued a proclamation of martial law. This was later cancelled but shortly renewed again. The case of one Nance will show how martial law worked. Nance was tried by a military commission for the crime of telling a private policeman formerly in the militia that he had no right to place a man under arrest without a warrant. The incident grew out of a fist fight between an Italian and a Negro. The order of the Governor following the second proclamation reads:

> The military commission is substituted for the criminal courts of the district covered by the martial law proclamation, and all offenses against the civil laws as they existed prior to the proclamation of Nov. 15th shall be regarded as offenses under the military law and in punishment therefor the military commission can impose such sentences either heavier or lighter, than those imposed under the civil law, as in their judgment the offender may merit . . . cognizance of offenses against the civil laws as they existed prior to Nov. 15th, committed prior to the declaration of martial law and unpunished will be taken by the military commission.[53]

Nance petitioned for a writ of habeas corpus on the facts:

> The petitioner, a civilian in private life, having at no time been a member of the military forces of the State . . . was arrested by the military forces and incarcerated in a military guard-house at the town of Pratt, . . . under military guard. He was taken before a military commission appointed by the governor and arraigned upon a charge of having violated sec. 143, Code of West Virginia . . . said offence was charged in the specification and conclusively proven by the evidence to have been committed, if committed at all, on the 7th day of Nov. 1912, eight days before the declaration of martial law of the governor. . . . He was tried and convicted by the military commission, sentenced to five years in the State penitentiary at Moundsville . . . the sentence was

affirmed by the governor and he was imprisoned . . . at
the time of the alleged commission of the crime (and
since) the civil courts of the county were in full and
undisturbed exercise of all the powers and functions con-
ferred upon them by law.[54]

The Supreme Court of West Virginia denied the writ basing
its decision upon the Idaho and Colorado cases, cited above.
Justice Robinson dissented, citing two provisions in the West
Virginia Constitution that look conclusive to a layman:

> Article I, section 3; The provisions of the Constitution
> of the United States and this state are operative alike
> in a period of war as in time of peace and any departure
> therefrom or violation thereof under the plea of necessity
> is subversive of good government and tends to anarchy
> and depostism.
> Article III, section 4; The privilege of the writ of ha-
> beas corpus shall not be suspended.

In a second important case involving "Mother Jones" and
others arrested for helping conduct the strike, Justice Robinson gave this dissenting opinion:

> Petitioners were arrested in the city of Charleston on
> a warrant of a justice of the peace, a civil court, charg-
> ing them with civil offenses, that of a conspiracy to
> inflict bodily injury on persons whose names were un-
> known and other offenses. They were taken before the
> justice in sight of the court house where the civil courts
> of the county were open and in exercise of their powers.
> Instead of giving the accused preliminary examination,
> and upon the finding of probable cause holding them to
> answer the grand jury, the justice directed the special
> constable having them in charge, by endorsement on the
> warrant to deliver them to the military authorities in
> the so-called military district. They were so delivered
> and were about to be put on trial before a military com-
> mission . . . for the same offenses charged before the
> civil court. . . . That court in absolute disregard of

their rights and the law governing it, sent them to the military authorities in a distant part of the county. . . . This illegal procedure alone entitled the petitioners to be remanded to the civil courts. . . . Yet it simply illustrates the extreme to which disregard of the Constitution and legal procedure has run. Instead of recognizing the true order of the statute whereby a militia is to aid the civil authorities, the law is reversed and the civil authorities used to aid the military power. Verily, indeed, has the military power been made absolutely independent and dominant in West Virginia.[55]

Other incidents of this strike, of interest in this connection, are affidavits by the five members of the military commission that although the defendants were guilty of all the charges "there was not a county justice in West Virginia who would find them guilty;" the Judge Advocate's declaration that "This court is not bound by the Code of West Virginia" and the sentencing of one Joe Raines to five years imprisonment for obstructing a train "by words."[56]

In sharp contrast to the courts which have legalized martial law, students of constitutional law see no authority for it. Stimson says there is no martial law in reality, save in an enemy's country in time of actual warfare. Martial law is the will of the commander, not law at all.

H. W. Ballantine, another student says:

It is believed that there is no warrant in the history of constitutional government for vesting in the governor as commander of the military forces of the State the absolute discretionary power of arrest and as a logical consequence, of life and death, so that his command or proclamation may take the place of a statute, and convert larceny into a capital offence, or going beyond legislative power deprive citizens unreasonably and arbitrarily of life or liberty without review in the courts. . . .

The true view, undoubtedly, is that during a riot or other disturbance, militiamen and their officers are authorized to act merely as a body of armed police with the ordinary powers of police officers.   Their military character cannot give them immunity for unreasonable excess of force.   The governor of the State as commander of militia is merely the chief conservator of the peace and entirely destitute of power to proclaim martial law . . . punish criminals, or subject citizens to arbitrary military orders.[57]

THE USE OF FEDERAL TROOPS

Federal troops have rarely been used against strikers and almost exclusively in railroad strikes which interfere with the mails or commerce between states.   The use of the U. S. soldiers during the railway strike of 1894 aroused an almost threatening situation in several states involving the right of the federal government to send troops into a state against its will.   Several governors protested vigorously, and Waite of Colorado declared that "President Cleveland had no right to make war upon his state."   A squad of federal troops arrested forty-eight of his constituents and took them before a federal judge for trial.[58]

The most significant controversy arose between President Cleveland and Governor John P. Altgeld of Illinois.   Illinois had not asked for federal troops to protect her citizens.   But the federal officials in Chicago, judges, district attorney and marshal, appealed for help "to move the mails and enforce the court orders."   President Cleveland without consulting the state authorities ordered troops to Chicago.   He justified his act under sections 5298-9 of the Revised Statutes passed in 1861 to strengthen Mr. Lincoln's war powers.   They provide:

That when on account of unlawful combinations, assemblages, or rebellion against the authority of the United States, it becomes impracticable in the judgment of the President to enforce by judicial proceedings the laws, it shall be lawful to call for the militia. . . .

That when domestic violence, insurrection, or conspiracies in any State oppose or obstruct the laws of the

United States or the due execution thereof, it shall be lawful and the duty of the President to suppress such by force.

Governor Altgeld telegraphed the President:

Surely the facts have not been presented to you. . . . It is entirely unnecessary and, as it seems to me unjustifiable. . . . The State of Illinois is not only able to take care of itself, but it stands ready today to furnish the Federal government any assistance it may need elsewhere. . . . I protest against this and ask the immediate withdrawal of Federal troops. . . .

President Cleveland: Federal troops were sent to Chicago in strict accordance with the Constitution and laws of the United States, upon the demand of the post-office department that obstructions to the mails should be removed, and upon the representation of the judicial officers . . . that process of the Federal Courts could not be executed . . . and upon abundant proof that conspiracies existed against the commerce between the States. . . .

Governor Altgeld: Your answer to my protest involves some startling conclusions and ignores and evades the question at issue—that is that the principle of local self-government is just as fundamental as that of Federal supremacy. You calmly assume that the Executive has the legal right to order Federal troops into any community in the United States in the first instance, whenever there is the slightest disturbance, and that he can do this without any regard to the question as to whether the community is able to and ready to enforce the law itself. . . . Inasmuch as Federal troops can do nothing but what State troops can do there . . . and believing that the ordering out of the Federal troops was unwarranted, I again ask their withdrawal. . . .

President Cleveland: . . . It seems to me that in this hour of danger and public distress, discussion may well give way to active efforts on the part of all in authority to restore obedience to law and to protect life and property.[59]

INJUNCTIONS

One of the repeated grievances of organized labor is that its rights have been invaded in wholesale fashion by injunctions.

> It is charged by the workers that the courts by the unwarranted extension of their powers in the issuance of injunctions, have not only grievously injured the workers individually but have by contempt procedure, consequent upon disobedience to such injunctions, deprived the workers of the right, fundamental to Anglo-Saxon institutions to be tried by jury.[60]

Since early in the eighties there has been a constantly increasing use of the injunction against the rights to organize, strike, and picket. In the mass of material and issues we can only indicate how injunctions have been used to curtail these rights by forcing men to work, by denying the right to a trial by jury, and by curtailing freedom of movement and assemblage.

An injunction is an order by a judge of a court of equity (not a criminal court) forbidding the persons enjoined from doing certain acts that may injure the property of others, especially if the injury is one difficult or impossible to be repaired by an award of damages. Refusal to obey the injunction—that is, the doing of the forbidden act—is contempt of court, and may be punished by the judge who issued it, with a fine or jail sentence. In labor cases the injunction came to be an order forbidding strikers or their leaders from doing certain acts in furtherance of the strike, on the ground that injury to the employers would follow. The workers claim that these anti-labor injunctions are made so broad as practically to forbid strikes. Peaceful acts are enjoined, such as sending telegrams or paying out strike monies, acts not in themselves criminal but for which they can be tried and sentenced by a judge. Through the injunction, the judge becomes a censor over the striker's acts, before they are committed. Men are punished not for actual crimes but for not obeying an injunction.

The whole issue is well illustrated by the case of Eugene Debs in 1894, during the railway strike in Chicago of 150,000 members of the American Railway Union in sympathy with a strike against the Pullman Palace Car Company. The union forbade any of its members handling Pullman cars in trains. The strike spread over the entire country and in a few days tied up the traffic of the central and western United States. The federal government interfered on the ground that refusal to haul the trains was an obstruction of the mail and of inter-state commerce:

> The attorney general (of the United States) indicated that it might be advisable instead of relying entirely upon warrants issued under the criminal statutes against persons actually guilty of the offense of obstructing the United States mails, to apply to the courts for injunctions which would restrain and prevent any attempt to commit such offense . . . basing such proceedings on the proposition that under the Constitution these subjects were in the exclusive care of the United States . . . that Federal courts could intervene under general principles of law . . . and under the Act against conspiracies in restraint of trade, July 2, 1890.[61]

The U. S. attorney applied to the judges of the Circuit Court at Chicago, and they issued on July 2, 1894, the famous "Gatling Gun" Injunction, the first important injunction against strikers. It reads in part:

> To Eugene V. Debs, George W. Howard, and L. W. Rogers, of the American Railway Union, Sylvester Kelliher . . . (twelve others named) . . . and to all other persons combining and conspiring with them, and to all other persons whomsoever: You are hereby restrained, commanded, and enjoined absolutely to desist and refrain from in any way or manner interfering with, hindering, obstructing, or stopping any of the business of any of the following named railroads:—

Atchison, Topeka, and Santa Fe Railroad,
Baltimore and Ohio Railroad,
   . . . (20 others named).
as common carriers of passengers and freight between or
among any States of the United States, and from in any
way interfering with . . . or stopping any mail trains,
express trains, whether freight or passenger, engaged in
inter-state commerce . . . and from in any manner
interfering with any train carrying the mail . . . any
engines, cars, or rolling stock . . . from injuring or
destroying any of the property of said railroads, engaged
in or for the purpose of, or in connection with inter-
state commerce, or the carriage of the mails of the United
States; . . . from entering on the grounds or premises
. . . from injuring or destroying any part of the tracks,
road-bed, or road, or permanent structures . . . displac-
ing or extinguishing any of the signals . . . spiking any
of the switches . . . uncoupling or in any way hamper-
ing the control of cars, etc., . . . and from compelling
or inducing, or attempting to compel or induce, by
threats, intimidation, persuasion, force, or violence any of
the employees of the said railroads to refuse to perform
any of their duties as employe of the said railroads in connection with interstate business . . . or carriage of the
mails; and from compelling . . . or inducing . . . by
threats, intimidation, etc. . . . any of the employes of
the said railroads . . . to leave the service of such railroads, and from preventing any person whatever, by
threats, etc. . . . from entering the service . . . and
from doing any act whatever in furtherance of any conspiracy or combination to restrain either of said railroad
companies or receivers in the free and unhindered control
and handling of interstate commerce . . . and from
ordering, directing, aiding, assisting, or abetting, in any
manner whatever, any person or persons to commit any
of the acts aforesaid. . . .
And it is further ordered that the aforesaid injunction . . . shall be in force and binding upon such of the
defendants as are named in the bill from and after service
upon them of the writ . . . and shall be binding upon
said defendants whose names are alleged to be unknown

. . . after the service of such writ upon them respectively by the reading of the same to them or by the publication thereof by posting and printing . . . and shall
be binding upon all persons whatsoever who are not
named herein from and after the time when they shall
severally have knowledge of the entry of such order and
the existence of said injunction.[62]

(Signed) William A. Woods,

P. S. Grosscup,

Judges.

Comparison of the terms of this omnibus injunction with
the charges against the earlier strikers (see above, page 15)
will show that the liberty enjoyed by them had not greatly
changed, at least in the courts. Debs and others were arrested
"for open and defiant disobedience" of the injunction, refused
to give bail, and at a hearing, December 14, they were
found guilty of contempt and sentenced to three and six
months imprisonment. The court held that it could restrain
a public nuisance such as it declared this strike to be; that
the punishment for contempt was not a denial of the right
to a trial by jury because the proceeding was limited to equity
cases; and that its jurisdiction arose out of the act of July
2, 1890, against conspiracies in restraint of inter-state commerce.[63]

The U. S. Supreme Court affirmed the decision May 27,
1895, declaring that trial by jury had not been denied, but
basing its conclusions on the general right of the United
States to enforce its laws, rather than on the specific authority
of the Inter-State Commerce Act.[64]

Outside the legal doctrines involved, these facts are clear.
Debs had committed no crime, and had urged peaceful measures. The charge of contempt was based on the sending of
telegrams concerning the strike. The omnibus injunction was
so broad that the strike could not be conducted without violating it. Debs claimed the injunction and the arrests broke
the strike. An attempt to convict him of crime failed. He
and three others were arrested during the strike on indict-

ments for complicity in obstructing the mails and interfering with inter-state commerce, but the case was never brought to trial.[65]

The Report of the Federal Commission on Industrial Relations in 1915 cites the Debs case in illustrating the different attitude assumed by the courts on the same question:

> The inconsistency between the decision in the Debs case wherein it is held that the control of Congress over inter-state commerce is so complete that it may regulate the conduct of the employees engaged therein to the extent of enjoining them from going on a sympathetic strike, and the decision in the Adair case wherein it is held that Congress has so little power over the conduct of those engaged in inter-state commerce that it cannot constitutionally forbid employers engaged therein from discharging their employees merely because of their membership in a union. (208 *United States Reports*.) [66]

How the injunction may be used to deny freedom of assemblage is shown by one issued by Judge H. P. O'Brien of the Michigan Circuit Court in 1913 restraining miners in the copper strike:

> from picketing in or about or in the vicinty of the mines . . . or on or near the highways used by the employees of said mines . . . from gathering or parading in large numbers or in any numbers at or in the vicinity of the premises of the said complainants or on the highways over which the employees of said complainants pass to work.

Ninety-nine men were arrested by the militia for violating this injunction and haled before the court for contempt. The Michigan Supreme Court dissolved this injunction but re-established it later with the significant omission of any restraint upon peaceful meetings and parades.

In the Ann Arbor cases in 1893 the workers claimed that men were practically ordered to work by an injunction. The case was decided by Judge William Howard Taft. The men had gone on a sympathetic strike in accordance with a by-law of their union. This was declared inoperative and illegal, and they were directed to return to work or be in contempt of court. They returned and the strike was broken.

THE CHICAGO ANARCHISTS

By 1886 the propaganda of the Anarchists had excited the public mind.[67] May 1 of that year had been set for a country-wide demand for an 8-hour day, backed by strikes, and inspired by the success of the powerful Knights of Labor. The entire nation was at tension, dreading an outburst. At this psychological moment came the "Haymarket bomb" in Chicago ending in what labor has always charged was the judicial murder of the so-called "Chicago Anarchists," members of the International Workingmen's Association. The facts are told by the Governor of Illinois, John P. Altgeld:[68]

On the night of May 4, 1886, a public meeting was held on the Haymarket Square in Chicago; there were from 800 to 1,000 people present, nearly all of them being laboring men. There had been trouble growing out of the effort to introduce an 8-hour day, resulting in some collisions with the police, in one of which several laboring people were killed (riot at McCormick Reaper Strike, May 3, 1886), and this meeting was called as a protest against alleged police brutailty. . . . The meeting was orderly and was attended by the Mayor (Carter Harrison, Sr.) who remained until the crowd began to disperse and then went away. As soon as Capt. John Bonfield . . . learned that the Mayor had gone, he took a detachment of police and hurried to the meeting for the purpose of dispersing the few that remained, and as the police approached a bomb was thrown by some unknown person, which exploded and wounded many, and killed several, among the latter being one Mathew Degan. A number of persons were arrested, and after a time August Spies, Albert R. Parsons, Louis Lingg, Michael Schwab, Samuel Fielden, George Engel, Adolph Fischer, and Oscar Neebe were indicted for the murder of Mathew Degan.[69]

Their dramatic trial began June 21, 1886, before Judge Joseph E. Gary, and attracted international interest. Parsons, the only native American of the group had escaped capture and was in hiding at the opening of the trial, but moved by what he deemed the injustice of the proceedings he suddenly returned to share the fate of his companions. The trial was based on a novel theory of "constructive crime." A contemporary account declares:

> The prosecution could not discover who had thrown the bomb and could not bring the really guilty men to justice, and as some of the men were not at the Haymarket meeting, it was forced to proceed on the theory that the men indicted were guilty of murder because it was claimed they had at various times in the past uttered and printed incendiary and seditious language, practically advising the killing of policemen, etc. . . . and were therefore responsible for the murder. . . . Oscar Neebe was sentenced to 15 years imprisonment and all the other defendants were sentenced to be hanged. . . .

The conviction was appealed to the Supreme Court of Illinois which affirmed the verdict on September 20.[70] Of this decision *The Chicago Enquirer* said:

> The evidence manufactured by the detectives . . . did not satisfy the higher court, and dutifully the latter furnished what was lacking. . . . In short the Supreme Court of our State has made out an entirely new case against the defendants; the original one, it is presumed, was no good.

Application for a writ of habeas corpus was made in behalf of Spies and others to the United States court, but denied, and the denial affirmed by the United States Supreme Court.[71] Soon after this Lingg committed suicide. The sentence of

Fielden and Schwab was commuted to imprisonment for life, and Parsons, Fischer, Engel and Spies were hanged on November 11, 1886. Six years later Governor Altgeld pardoned the three men in prison, giving his reason in part as follows:

It is clearly shown that Ryse was appointed special bailiff at the suggestion of the State's attorney, and that he did summon a prejudiced jury which he believed would hang the defendants; and further that the fact that Ryse was summoning only that kind of man was brought to the attention of the court before the panel was full, and it was asked to stop it, but refused to pay any attention. . . . The State has never discovered who it was that threw the bomb . . . and the evidence does not show any connection whatever between the defendants and the man who did throw it. The trial judge said: "The conviction has not gone on the ground that they did have actually any personal participation in the particular act which caused the death of Degan, but proceeds upon the ground that they had generally by speech and print, advised large classes of people, not particular individuals . . . to commit murder. This case is without a precedent." No judge in a civilized country has ever laid down such a rule before.

It is shown here that the bomb was, in all probability, thrown by some one seeking personal revenge, that . . . for a number of years there had been labor troubles, and in several cases a number of laboring people, guilty of no offense, had been shot down in cold blood by Pinkerton men, and none of the murderers were brought to justice.

It is further shown that much of the evidence was a pure fabrication; that some of the prominent police officials . . . not only terrorized ignorant men by throwing them into prison and threatening them with tortures if they refused to swear to anything they desired, but that they offered money and employment to those who would consent. . . . Further that they deliberately planned to have fictitious conspiracies formed in order that they might get the glory of discovering them. . . .

I have examined all the evidence against Neebe, and it utterly fails to prove even the shadow of a case against him. Some of the other defendants were guilty of using seditious language, but even this cannot be said of Neebe. . . . It is further charged that the judge conducted the trial with malicious ferocity, that every ruling was in favor of the State . . . that page after page of the record contains insinuating remarks of the judge, made in the hearing of the jury, and with the evident intent of bringing the jury to his way of thinking. . . . I do not care to discuss this. . . . I therefore grant an absolute pardon to Samuel Fielden, Oscar Neebe, and Michael Schwab, this 26th day of June, 1893.[72]

The final statements of the defendants, while colored by the drama in which they acted are significant of the issues involved. August Spies said to the Court:

Now these are my ideas. I cannot divest myself of them, nor would I, if I could. And if you think you can crush out these ideas that are gaining ground more and more every day . . . by sending us to the gallows; if you would once more have people suffer the penalty of death because they have dared to tell the truth . . . and I defy you to show where we have told a lie . . . I say, if death is the penalty for proclaiming the truth then I will proudly and defiantly pay the costly price! Call your hangman! Truth crucified in Socrates, in Christ, in Giordano Bruno, in Huss, Galileo still lives . . . they and others whose name is legion have preceded us on this path. We are ready to follow. . . .

Spies' last words were:

There will come a time when our silence will be more powerful than the voices you strangle today.

The memory of the Chicago anarchists is still a profound inspiration to large masses of laboring people, and November 11 every year is marked with solemn memorial services for them.

THE COURTS AND THE WORKERS

The administration of the law as it concerns the constitutional rights and personal liberties of the workers was attacked as defective and partisan to the interests of property, throughout this period.   The best statement of this view is in the principal report of the Commission on Industrial Relations (1915, pages 38-61).

With regard to the federal courts it is startling and alarming to citizens generally, and in particular to the workers, to learn that the consensus of federal decision is to the effect that the section of the Constitution defining the rights of citizens (The Bill of Rights) apply only to federal jurisdiction and in reality protect the citizen only against the action of the federal government.   The only sections protecting the citizens under ordinary circumstances are the thirteenth amendment, prohibiting involuntary servitude, and the fifteenth protecting the right to vote.[73]

With the "bills of rights" of the states, the situation as far as the workers is concerned is somewhat different, since in many jurisdictions these have been used on numerous occasions to afford substantial protection to them in their personal rights.   The workers call attention particularly, however, to the long list of statutes, city ordinances and military orders abridging freedom of speech and press which have not been interfered with by the courts, and when tested have almost uniformly been upheld by the state and federal courts.   They also point to the grave injury done to the worker, individually and collectively, by the thousands of arrests that have been made in labor disputes with no just cause and with no relief from either the courts or the executive; to the denial upon numerous occasions of the writ of habeas corpus; to the fact that where workers have been grievously injured, brutally treated, or interfered with in pursuit of their guaranteed rights by other classes of citizens or officials, the courts have not interfered and the perpetrators have gone unpunished."

Commission on Industrial Relation (1915) *Report* I, pages 47-49.

Other grievances against the courts complained of by the workers are that biased juries are selected to try labor cases and that the law's costs and delays often make it impossible for them to secure justice because they cannot afford the time or money required to take their cases to the highest courts.

To sum this up we quote from the Report of the Committee on Industrial Relations *On Justice and Liberty*, page 97:

When governmental institutions are thus corrupted and used as instruments of oppression men can only resist with such power as they have, not alone for the protection of themselves and their families but for the preservation of the fundamental rights of themselves and their fellow-citizens. Resistance to the usurpers of governmental power and to those who pervert to base uses the official power with which they are clothed was made the key-stone of the American nation, and Abraham Lincoln on a most solemn occasion said:

"If by mere force of numbers a majority should deprive a minority of any clearly written constitutional right, it might, in a moral point of view justify revolution . . . certainly would if such a right were a vital one." (Inaugural, March 4, 1861.)

The grave danger in the United States is that on account of the enormous area and the sense of isolation of each section as regards the others, the encroachment upon fundamental rights and the subversion of local government will be permitted to gain ground without the effective protests of the entire nation until the liberties of all citizens are hanging in the balance.

CHAPTER VII

FREEDOM OF SOCIAL THOUGHT

THE climax of the struggle for liberty has been the conflict during the last fifty years between reformist and radical groups seeking to change society by some definite theory, and on the other hand, the police power of the state. Since the chief way to change society is by changing its mind, these groups need the widest freedom of organization and propaganda—the right to what Mill called "freedom of communication," and which is here roughly termed "freedom of social thought." This is a complex modern need, and includes freedom of belief and of research, freedom to organize and agitate in every way with protection against mob violence and any arbitrary interference. This chapter lists denials of these rights.

These social reformers believe that eugenics or anarchism or universal suffrage for example, will work a conscious amelioration in man's lot. They are moved often by humanitarian benevolence; more recently by a serious design to reform mankind by science. They are not new; their first activities in the United States were discussed in chapter III. After about 1825 they preached Utopianism, the rights of labor, sex equality, and the like. Then, one movement— the abolition of slavery—came to overshadow the others for half a century, though temperance and the rights of women were not neglected. Meanwhile, exiles from the older European civilizations, from about 1848 on, had brought more sophisticated ideas on social progress,—in anarchism and Marxian socialism. Then came the theory of evolution to give the social reformers a philosophy on which to base their hope of directing change. Thus, when the national intellect recovered from the prostration of the Civil War, it began organizing for enquiry and propaganda along many lines.

The new ideas met two opposing forces: the conservatism of the authoritarian classes, and the inertia of the herd mind. The first opposed them because their privileges and profits were best maintained by the status quo. The masses opposed them from their instinctive fear of change, bulwarked by traditional religion and morality. This popular antagonism has sometimes been native and spontaneous; oftener it has been aroused and exploited by the ruling classes. They have even been clever enough to align the people against movements clearly in behalf of the people and against these exploiters. Popular opposition to birth-control, for example, has been fostered by the classes who profit by surplus labor, yet who themselves limit their own families.

The struggle resolved itself into one issue—to enjoy freedom of communication in spite of the police powers. Both the necessity for this freedom and also the nature of the police power must be better understood if the cases are to be clear.

You can change a democracy only by education. The rule of a tyrant is forbidden; and you can't use force,—for the people *are* the force, either by mobs or votes. You must change their minds. In a sense the entire modern struggle for liberty is for possession of the means of changing the people's minds, the means of education and the means of communication. They may be viewed as one, for communication in a large sense is but a public way of teaching. The social reformer, therefore, must enjoy the freest communication,—communication from a picket to a scab, from a nurse to a woman weary of child bearing, from a Socialist on a soap-box to a crowd in the public street, from the crowd to the President, from the press of an anarchist to his fellow-anarchists through the mails. Anti-liberty means to silence the picket by an injunction, the nurse by a birth-control ban, the Socialist by a nuisance ordinance, the crowd by breaking up meetings, the anarchist by a postal censorship. And all these, please observe, are legal methods. Of course, both the advocate and his audience must have freedom of conscience— the right to believe whatever they think they find in the facts. They must also enjoy protection and the right to law, but these are the means, not the end. The end is communication; not indeed a new problem, but one in which new factors have been introduced by the mechanical extensions of communication, and by the fact that public opinion has become an almost ponderable force. For example, the postal censorship forbidding the mailing of a motion-picture film presenting problems of birth-control meant to be shown in clinics exclusively for women, presents a complex problem in liberty.

The question next arises then; "how has freedom of communication for ideas that are repugnant both to conservative interests and the people been denied?" Once it would have been done by mobs; but we find little violence against these social movements which is at all comparable to that used against Mormons or Abolitionists in the thirties. It is hard to mob an idea, and moreover an idea is not realized as a threat to the community. The mob spirit is not easily aroused against an abstraction. To mob a negro or a scab is a different matter.

Therefore, the suppression of disturbing ideas was turned over to the police power. Violations of liberty in this field are not extra-legal, but are achieved through the state itself. The new coercion was by laws, executives, and courts. It was far more effective than violence because it was legal and had the organized force of the community behind it. The effect is the same,—to enforce the will of the majority upon the rest of the community for what is claimed to be the welfare of the whole. The tyranny of the majority is given a new name—"the police power."

Let us add at once that the police power is necessary, and that it has in its modern form accomplished many beneficial things. But let us add that it has been extended to permit very dangerous invasions of civil liberty. Moreover this new

power of suppression is precisely the same whether inspired
by popular prejudices or the selfish intrigues of privileged
classes.

This conflict between liberty and the police power is frankly
admitted by the legalist:

> Before the doctrine of evolution, natural rights were
> regarded as immutable, substantive, eternal, not to be
> changed by external conditions. . . . About the middle
> of the 19th century the courts of the country invented
> what is spoken of as the police power, which may be said
> for all practical purposes to be unaffected by the private
> rights theory. The government may exercise the police
> power unrestricted by the constitutional limitations to
> be found in the Bill of Rights.[1]

The following reconciliation is attempted by an authority:

> Civil liberty is the freedom of entering into legal re-
> lations with others and of appealing in any manner to
> public opinion or sentiment. This liberty must be sub-
> ject to manifold restaints in behalf of the public wel-
> fare, and as a constitutional right has no specific con-
> tent. . . . But certain spheres of liberty may be singled
> out as withdrawn from the police powers in this sense
> that the pursuit of certain objects, or certain forms of
> activity cannot in themselves be regarded as elements
> of public danger. Such special recognition is given by
> our courts to freedom of religion, of speech and press,
> and of assembly, and by foreign constitutions and laws
> to the freedom of migration, occupation and associa-
> tion.[2]

Most Americans would be surprised to learn that their
cherished "constitutional liberties" have no specific content;
and are only withdrawn from the police power as harmless
forms of activity. When they mean anything, the police
power is alert to interfere. It is therefore of supreme importance that we understand this vast power.

All the definitions are vague, as when Goodnow calls it

"the power which is exercised in the interest of public safety or convenience." Roughly, it is the supreme coercive force of the community exerted upon its members for the sake of "safety, health, or morals." In its prime function—the protection of life and property—it is the basis of our organized states, and cannot be objected to except by those who do not believe in organized states. In the emergency of war it protects life and property against external force, and is recognized as inherent in sovereignty. Both war and peace powers hold dangers to civil liberty. But in practice, the state's duty of protecting life and property must be conceded, and so also the dangers of its misuse.

But the police power proves to be extremely variable—at one moment reaching out to forbid the dissemination of birth-control, and at another so shrinking that it cannot prevent the toil of little children in field or factory. Civil liberty is chiefly concerned in its extensions. First, in its function of protector, it reaches out to cover acts such as speaking or printing, that present no danger to life or property, but are declared to have a "tendency" to create conditions from which such danger may arise. The police claim a duty to disperse or even forbid meetings and to censor publications that may conceivably sometime, somewhere, incite somebody to crime. Since there are no tests for such "constructive" crimes, the police power seizes a wide field for suppression.

The next step seems even more logical. If the police power is useful to protect us against loss of life and limb by violence why not let it protect us against such losses by disease? Goodnow makes this interest in health the origin of the modern developments of the police power. Urban industrial conditions demand good health and at the same time menace it. The success of preventive medicine enabled the government to take measures against disease,—first against disease itself, then by the same logic against the causes of disease. It invented quarantines, vaccination, pure food regulations, safety laws and traffic cops. How beneficial much of this has proven! These protections of a man's bodily welfare were justified on two grounds: first, sickness and death are both a current expense and a capital loss to society; second, the sick may communicate many of their diseases to the well. There were bitter struggles over the right to live and die your own way, even if you killed others en route. But generally in the field of health the police power has won out all along the line.

But when the police power discovered that the causes of crime and diseases were not only physical but also social and moral, it forgot its common-sense basis in safety and health and undertook transcendental tasks. It was extended finally to protect us against states of mind or morals that were declared to be diseased and so to threaten the safety or health of the community. The psychological crimes of which the police gradually took cognizance were of four main kinds: (1) beliefs that were in some way inimical to bodily health (Christian Science); (2) beliefs that tended to undermine the moral basis of society (the Mormons' polygamy, or the advocacy of birth-control); (3) beliefs that threatened the form of the state (woman's suffrage or Socialism); (4) beliefs that denied the state itself, and so attacked the police power and its officers (anarchism).

Three interpretations of police power complete the machinery of suppression: first, its extension to cover words or acts which might have a tendency to produce mental states from which overt dangers might spring; second, the justification of preventative measures to keep persons from uttering words or performing acts with this dangerous tendency; third, the recognition by the courts of the right of executive officials to issue regulations which have far-reaching effects. The courts will not, for example, review an order of deportation by the Secretary of Labor or a revocation of second-class mail privileges by the Postmaster-General.

It begins by enforcing things that are good for the body and ends by enforcing things that are not good for the soul. It works by the quaint but dangerous analogy that quarantine prevents small-pox, therefore, censorship will prevent bolshevism! It proceeds from preserving the peace to preserving the status quo. This force for safety soon translates safety into "law and order" and this into "the established order." It changes health into comfort, and comfort into peace of mind, which means no agitation, no freaks, no tampering with things as they are.

So we find the police power dabbling in all sorts of mysteries. It prosecutes the Mormons for polygamy and the Spiritualist for necromancy. It pursues the ignorant or avaricious for not sending their children to school. It amends the Constitution and prevents the drinking of alcohol. It forbids the circulation of knowledge of birth-control, yet itself experiments with the sterilization of the feeble-minded, and so tampers with a liberty of grave import though one not mentioned in the Bill of Rights. And it does all this, not because ignorance or drunkenness are bad for the fool or the drunkard, but because the fool and the drunkard are bad for the rest of us. The community takes to enforcing on the individual what it thinks is good for itself: and the only possible curb on it is to persuade the public that a given police measure has no value for safety and comfort.

The lover of liberty must concede the social worth of these achievements of the police power. But he must, when it oversteps the limit of protection from physical dangers, condemn it. He must resist when it asserts the right to police ideas. The only standard by which to test a change in ideas is trial and error. But the inevitable tendency of the police power is to make everybody conform to a common standard. It must quell every disturbance of mental peace; it obeys one law,—the law of averages. It never concedes that the individual has any right, capacity, or desire that cannot find satisfaction in the self-preserving purposes of the majority. Least of all can the police power be persuaded that the safety and health of society demand freedom of change. In theory of course, it accepts individual liberty as a healthful thing for society. Freund says:

Public policy assumes the superiority of the social over the individual interests. The highest conception of the state, however, repudiates the absolute and unquestioning subordination of the individual to society and insists upon the preservation of individual liberty as an essential factor in civilization, and one which will lead ultimately to a more perfect social welfare though it may produce temporary disturbances or delays in the accomplishment of what is believed to be the public good. . . . It is, however, regarded as contrary to constitutional liberty to exercise compulsory control over public opinion and agitation which refrains from the practice or incitement of violence, or from injury to private rights, and the constitution's attempt, in part at least, to secure this liberty by special guarantees.[3]

Unfortunately governments do not act upon this "highest conception of the state," nor will they tolerate "temporary disturbances or delays in what is believed to be the public good." In many constitutions the guarantee of religious liberty contains a police power clause excepting from protection "acts against public safety or morals." Nor will the post office transmit information on contraception though there is herein neither incitement to violence or injury to private rights.[4] Freund neatly sums up the whole danger thus:

The exercise of the police power might conceivably serve the purpose of guiding or checking intellectual movements so as to further the ideas of the government of what is beneficial to society or state. Such a purpose is, however, disclaimed by liberal governments, and the guaranty of freedom of religion and of speech and press removes the pursuit of ideal interests on the whole from the operation of the police power.[5]

This seems too naive; the phrases "might conceivably" and "such a purpose is disclaimed by liberal governments" hint that the author's tongue was in his cheek. The cases presented here prove that governments habitually use the police power to "guide and check intellectual movements," and that the pursuit of "ideal interests" is not removed from its operation.

FREEDOM OF CONSCIENCE

Freedom of conscience is the foundation of freedom of communication. We must be free to study anything and believe anything. These rights have been pretty well won, and science has the largest possible right of research.

In the religious field, liberty today means that you may believe and preach whatever you wish; but the police power will not accept your religious belief as justification for any *act* judged dangerous to the safety or morals of the community. You may hold any old faith or invent a new one. You may utter praise or contempt of the Christian religion, or of any other in comparison with the Christian religion. Religious belief is so assured that in New York it was held to be a violation of the Constitution to ask a witness if he were an agnostic.[6] The old crime of blasphemy is almost dead. To call Christ a bastard and the Virgin Mary a whore, once fined by Chancellor Kent because it "undermined the government" is now held to be neither lewd or lascivious.[7] There is an occasional effort to punish blasphemy:

> Michael X. Mockus, a free-thought lecturer . . . came to Waterbury, Conn., to deliver a series of lectures in the Lithuanian tongue to an incorporated Lithuanian Free Thought Association. He uttered some phrases alleged to be blasphemous under a statute passed in 1642. He was arrested, tried in the City Court, and found guilty . . . and sentenced to ten days in jail. An appeal to the District Court was taken where the jury disagreed, and a retrial was ordered for December 6, 1916. The case was apparently never heard.[8]

The Catholic Church suffered an occasional attack, due not so much to religious antagonism as to the fear that Irish and Latin Catholics were invaders who might be by priests formed into a secret political machine to capture the state. The principal discrimination against them is in the public which often reflect Protestantism. In the nineties a rev the Know-Nothing spirit produced a considerable ant olic agitation, half-sectarian, half-political, in the West. Its organ was the "A. P. A." or American Pro Association. The old issue of religious instruction in schools was dragged out, and a few minor political v were won on it.[9] There was no serious trouble, thou Democratic Party, with which most of the Irish Catholics were affiliated, found it expedient to re-affirm the constitutional guarantee of religious liberty in its platform in 1896.[10]

Against Jews social discrimination exists, especially respect to clubs, employment and exclusions from s. This antagonism is racial and economic as well as religious. But all of these discriminations against Catholics and Jews involve no real interference with belief.

There has been complaint that religious liberty is not plete because the state exempts church property from tion and enforces laws for the protection of the Ch n Sabbath, and against blasphemy of the Christian religion y. These are at once justified because they strengthen the ice power, "for the good of society:"

> It is alone needful to note that the justification of all such legislative action resides not in the demands of religion nor in the competition of one form of religion with another, but solely in the demands of social order, safety, and propriety . . . opposition to tax-exemption loses all force when the exemption is made for the good of society.[11]

Here we have the church used as an adjunct of the police power. The modern state is not concerned with man's religious ideas so long as he does not act contrary to the purposes of the state itself. If he does his religion is no excuse. The Constitution of New York asserts the superiority of the police power thus:

. . ..ut the liberty of conscience here secured shall not
be s.. construed as to excuse acts of licentiousness or
jus...g practices inconsistent with the peace or safety
of the state.

And the courts have fortified this in such decisions as:

No man can be permitted to set up his religious belief
as a defense to the commission of an act which is in plain
violation of the law of the state.[12]

The statement of this doctrine for the nation touches the
Mormons.   In 1852 their Church proclaimed the dogma of
plural marriages.   They sincerely believed that women so
"sealed to an elder of the Church stood a better chance of
salvation; polygamy was the will of God.   Congress on July
1, 186 , passed an act declaring that every person who had
a husband or wife living, yet married another person in the
Unit d Territory was guilty of bigamy and punishable by a
fine o, not over $500.00 and by imprisonment for not more
than fi years.[13]   When the test cases under this law came
before the United States Supreme Court, the following answer
was ma e to the defense of polygamy under the First Amendment, garanteeing religious liberty:

Congress was deprived of all legislative power over
mere opinion, but was left free to reach actions which
were in violation of social duties or subversive of good
order . . . there never has been a time, in any State in
the Union, when polygamy was not an offense against
society, cognizable by the civil courts, and punishable.
. . . It is impossible to believe that the constitutional
guarantee of religious freedom was intended to prohibit
legislation in respect to this most important element in
social life—marriage: while, from its very nature the
sacred obligation is, nevertheless, in most civilizations, a
civil contract, and usually regulated by law. . . .
Laws are made for the government of actions, and
while they cannot interfere with mere religious belief

. . . they may with practises. . . . Suppose one religiously believed that human sacrifices were a necessary part of religious worship, would it be seriously contended that the civil government could not interfere to prevent sacrifices? Can a man excuse his practices . . . because of his religious belief? To permit this would be to make the doctrines of religion superior to the law of the land; and in effect be to permit every citizen to become a law unto himself. Government could exist only in name. . . . It matters not that his belief was a part of his religion; it was still a belief and a belief only.[14]

The complete repudiation by the Supreme Court of the power of religion to dictate our acts would surprise our Puritan, Quaker and Huguenot forefathers. It leaves nothing to religion but what the Court contemptuously refers to as "religious belief and opinions." We are in this dilemma: if we want to preserve the idea of freedom of religion we must believe that the civil law by some gift of infallibility always expresses the true will of God; and this at once leads to an established church, in this case the church that believes in monogamy. That becomes the government church. This view was frankly stated by Justice Bradley in the Mormon Church Cases;[15] that the religious argument was no defense since the prohibition of polygamy was based on "enlightened civilization and Christianity." Or, second, we can throw religious freedom overboard and admit that the police power over religious practices arises from the ideals of the majority, the sort of tyranny already described.

What happened in Utah during the Mormon regency is too confused for this study. The Mormons violated the liberties of their opponents to the same degree their own had been violated. Their history is one of tumult, massacre, riot and official gunmen, called "Danites." On the other hand their own rights to law and civil rights in politics were constantly denied. In other states Mormon missionaries in conflict with the community morality have suffered violence and deportation. Here is an example:

Elder W. S. Berry and Henry Thompson were laboring as missionaries. . . . A meeting was appointed on August 10, 1884, at the house of James Condor, on Cane Creek, Lewis County, Tenn. Elder Jones was reading a discourse at Mr. Garrett's house when suddenly a mob of men in fantastic garbs and masked faces . . . made him prisoner and proceeded to Mr. Condor's. They made the latter prisoner. . . . David Hinson entered the house where Elder Gibbs was engaged in selecting texts from the Scripture. . . . He took a gun from its hooks over the door and shot Elder Gibbs down. Elder Berry observed other of the mobocrats enter. . . . He simply bowed his head and received the bullets of the assassins and fell dead at their feet. Martin Condor engaged in a struggle with David Hinson, and while engaged some members of the mob shot him down and murdered him. . . . J. F. Hudson, step-son of James Condor was seized by two of the murderous ruffians, but tearing himself loose he shot and killed David Hinson, and then in turn was slain.[16]

Governor B. H. Bate offered a reward of $1,000 for the assailants. The violence was said to have been caused by the circulation in Lewis County by certain orthodox Christian ministers of the so-called "Red Hot Address," purporting to have been made by a Mormon bishop. It was later proved fake.

The treatment of Christian Scientists very clearly shows the conflict between conduct prescribed by a religious faith and the police power. Criminal action has been taken against Science healers for the illegal practice of medicine, against parents and others for failure to provide orthodox medical attention for their dependents, and to enforce local quarantine and vaccination regulations on Scientists in spite of their denial of disease.[17] Various attempts have been made by the States to forbid the practice of Christian Science, beginning in Rhode Island in 1887, but with little success. There is practically no interference with Christian Science as a religion though it is said that such a Church was once refused a charter in Philadelphia. The interference has been with their theory of bodily healing as it has come in conflict with orthodox medical ideas. Certain other theories of medicine or healing have met with similar treatment.

In New York City, ordinances have been passed forbidding the practice of clairvoyance and other so-called spiritual revelations for money on the ground that defrauding of innocent persons resulted from the pretensions of charlatans. This has in some ways handicapped the scientific study of spiritism and embarrassed those who profess Spiritualism as a religion.

FREEDOM OF SPEECH AND ASSEMBLAGE

Violations of freedom of speech and assemblage have been so constant and wide-spread during this period that no attempt has been made to list them. But some general evidence and an outline of the methods of interference are given. It is significant that the American Sociological Society devoted its entire annual meeting in 1914 to "Freedom of Communication." [18] Here, Professor Edward A. Ross said:

> During the last dozen years the tales of suppression of free assemblage, free press, and free speech, by local authorities or the State operating under martial law have been so numerous as to have become an old story. They are attacked at the instigation of an economically and socially powerful class, itself enjoying to the full the advantages of free communication, but bent on denying them to the class it holds within its power. . . . It is inexpressibly surprising that the rights of free communication, established so long ago at such cost of patriot blood, time-tested rights which in thousands of instances have vindicated their value for moral and social progress, accepted rights which in the minds of disinterested men are as settled as any principles of human conduct can be, should with increasing frequency be flaunted by strong employers and set at naught by local authorities.[19]

Most of this suppression was accomplished through ordinances such as those against disturbing the peace, obstructing traffic, unlawful assembly, vagrancy, unlicensed parades, un-regulated use of halls, misuse of the parks, and the distribution of printed matter. The enforcement of such laws is usually a matter of discretion with the police—some of them are interpreted technically, as in the rule that three persons may constitute "an unlawful assemblage." Some, such as disturbing the peace, are so vague that they cover a multitude of cases. The burden of proof, too, is always on the defendant. He is not allowed free exercise of his civil rights as the constitution intended, but must prove them as against the police.

The police themselves are not particularly to blame. Their function necessarily creates a tendency to suppression. They feel they should break up what they do not understand. The economic and political powers behind the machinery of government provide through bosses and bribery or through control of public opinion an aggressive attitude by the police toward radical movements.[20] Judgment and sentence after arrest are usually a matter of summary action by police magistrates, who are a part of the machinery of suppression.

These ordinances are obviously necessary for other purposes and cannot be attacked on general grounds. It is difficult to prove that in a specific case intentional injustice has been done.

The use of streets and parks illustrates the situation. These are the natural meeting-places of the people, they hold a perpetual audience, they cost nothing, they are the forums of the poor.

> The common use of the streets is, however, far more than a license. . . . It must be looked upon as one of the constitutional rights of the individual in so far as the individual is part of the general mass of the people which is designated as the public.[21]

Yet John Graham Brooks declared:

> In more than one recent instance, the guardians of the law had to run to the books, after the emergency had

arisen, to learn what free assemblage meant, and what the law was in the bailiwick.

He quoted this specimen of absolute cloture on free speech in the parks of Los Angeles—which we do not believe became the law:

> It shall be unlawful for any person to discuss, expound, advocate, or oppose the principles or creed of any political party, partisan body, or organization, or religious denomination or sect or the doctrines of any social or economic system in any public speech, lecture, or discourse, made or delivered in any public park in the city of Los Angeles.[22]

The control of meetings in public halls is exercised through the interpretation of fire, health, and building ordinances, nuisance laws, and intimidation of the owner or lessee, who is dependent on the police in many ways, especially for the renewal of licenses. Under these various threats, the hall-owner is forced to refuse the use of his hall whatever his own sentiments. Even meetings in private places are sometimes dependent upon how far the police can extend their power. A charge of nuisance or of conspiracy offers the opportunity to break up a meeting even if it is not later pressed. The use of publicly owned buildings is so regulated almost everywhere as to prevent real freedom of speech.[23]

The cases resulting from these various types of control are too numerous to cite. But typical violations of freedom of speech and assemblage are noted in connection with the Anarchists, birth control advocates and suffragists.[24]

The right to speak or write in any language should be noted in relation to freedom of speech. If a person knows only one language and that is under certain conditions forbidden, his rights are manifestly denied. English is specified as the state language in the constitutions of four states. In Oklahoma the public schools must be conducted in English; and there are similar requirements for the use of English in legal and other public relations in various states.

ADVOCACY OF BIRTH CONTROL

The advocates of birth control have had a difficult time
as to freedom for agitation for their cause, and freedom to
conduct a public clinic for information. Here are some of
the facts:

In Portland, Ore., about 1915, Emma Goldman and
Ben Reitman were arrested at one of Emma Goldman's
public meetings for the distribution of a leaflet giving
information as to the means of preventing conception.
The meeting was broken up, and at the police station bail
was fixed at $500, which the police sergeant declared
must be in cash. With great difficulty owing to the late
hour, the money was raised to release Emma Goldman.
Reitman remained in jail. At the trial, Judge F. W.
Stadter, sitting in place of the regular incumbent, imposed a fine of $250 each. On appeal to the Circuit
Court of Multnomah County, Judge William Gatens
discharged the defendants, remarking that the leaflet
gave only in a dignified way information which every
woman ought to know and which the wives of the rich
did know through the family doctor.

1916—April. The police of Akron, Ohio, refused to
allow Margaret Sanger to speak on birth control.

May. The police of St. Louis, Mo., prohibited Margaret Sanger from speaking in the Victoria theater after
the contract was signed, and the deposit for the theater
paid.

July. Margaret Sanger was arrested for speaking in
Portland, Ore., and five others for distributing a pamphlet, "Family Limitation." At the conclusion of her
lecture, they were taken in the police wagon to the police
station where they spent the night, having refused to
give bail. At the trial, Police Judge Languth, held that
the pamphlet was in violation of the city ordinance and
the law, but probably having Judge Gaten's decision
in mind, he discharged the defendants with a reprimand.

October. Margaret Sanger opened a birth control
clinic in Brooklyn, New York. She and Ethel Byrne, a
nurse, were arrested for imparting oral information on

contraception under section 1142 of the Penal Code of New York. Fania Mindell, the translator who had given away or sold the book, "What Every Girl Should Know," was arrested under the same section. They were released under $500 bail. Mrs. Sanger, having re-opened her clinic was arrested on a charge of maintaining a public nuisance, violating section 1530 of the Penal Code. The landlord was also served notice to eject her from the premises as harboring a public nuisance. This case had not been tried to July 1, 1919. The court refused a jury trial to the defendants. The Mindell case was carried to the Court of Appeals, the decision of the lower court reversed, and the fifty dollar fine returned, though no costs were allowed. Ethel Byrne went on a hunger strike when removed to jail and was pardoned by Governor Whitman.

1917—April. The police of Albany, New York, closed the doors of a theater in which Margaret Sanger was to speak.

1919—December. An article on abortion was considered obscene by the police of New York City, and Margaret Sanger and Kitty Marion were taken before a judge for writing and selling this article in "The Birth Control Review." The case was dismissed, chiefly on the ground that the information was largely the same as in the book "What Every Girl Should Know," declared not obscene by the Court of Appeals.

In New York City, William Sanger, Rose Pastor Stokes, Jessie Ashley, Emma Goldman, Ben Reitman and Kitty Marion have been arrested, some serving prison terms. In Boston, Van Kleek Allison was arrested for the same offence. In Pennsylvania, a woman, the mother of six children, was given nine months imprisonment for distributing "Family Limitation" in an Italian translation to the wives of coal miners.[25]

FREEDOM OF THE PRESS

The most important means of communication to-day is the press. Public opinion is power; whoever controls the press enjoys power, and therefore liberty. The right of free, cheap publication has become fundamental to all other liberties. The press has become the first instrument of social force. Word of mouth or in meetings is still powerful; but in these days of vast numbers and magnificent distances, when to insure the strength of a movement a whole nation must be organized behind it, the press is the chief tool. Hence the first thought of the social reformer nowadays is publicity. Naturally the police power seeks some means of controlling so extraordinary an agency for change. Once again the police face the difficult task of drawing the famous line (as imaginary as the Equator) between liberty and license.[26] We discover that the police power attempts to limit freedom of the press locally by various censorships and nationally by restricting the privilege of cheap mail service. And the entire matter is confused by the supreme difficulty of setting any standard by which the state can censor or suppress. National restrictions are treated first as the most important.

THE POST OFFICE CENSORSHIP

The post-office department exercises a life and death veto on periodical publications by its control of cheap circulation through the mails. This censorship was first suggested in 1836 by the effort to exclude Abolitionist publications from the mails. Before that the government had concerned itself solely with the physical contents of the mails, not the psychological content. By 1860, though no law justified it, it had become customary not to deliver this so-called "incendiary" matter in the Southern States.[27] The next step was the exclusion from the mails during the Civil War of certain pro-Southern newspapers published in the North. Postmaster-General Blair justified this exclusion as a war power of the government to protect itself from overthrow by the use of one of its own agencies. But his defense admits the beginning of a peace-time censorship. For he declared that *he had, on his own executive discretion, excluded what he judged to be obscene matter.* We have shifted from the protection of public safety to that of public morals; and in the legitimate effort to prevent debauching public morals began the post-office censorship.[28]

Congress perceived that the executive must have authority for such acts, and passed a series of laws against the transmission of obscene matter and later forbidding information on abortion and contraception. (Acts of March 3, 1865; June 8, 1872; March 3, 1873; July 12, 1876, et cetera.) Extensions of the principle soon followed. In 1868 it was made a crime to mail letters or circulars regarding lotteries, so-called gift concerts, and similar enterprises (15 *Statutes at Large* 196); in 1872 the law against fraudulent matter was passed (17 *Statutes at Large* 323, c335, section 301); and in 1917 the South secured the principle it had vainly fought for in 1836, when the Randall-Bankhead law forbade transmission by mail into prohibition States of publications containing advertisements of alcoholic beverages. In 1917, Congress, using its war-power, passed the Espionage Act (June 16) which excluded from the mails matter that might interfere with the conduct of the war; and by amendment (May 18, 1918) extended the exclusion to matter opposing the form of government or criticising public affairs or public officers. The century-old rule of no verbal treason laid down in Respublica v Dennie was reversed. (See Chapter II.)

THE CENSORSHIP IS CONSTITUTIONAL

The Supreme Court has invariably declared each new extension of the censorship not to limit freedom of the press. The principle is laid down in a case under the obscenity statute of 1873.

> In excluding various articles from the mails the object of Congress had not been to interfere with the freedom of the press, or with other rights of the people; but to refuse its facilities for the distribution of matter deemed injurious to the public morals. . . . But we do not think that Congress possesses the power to prevent the

transportation in other ways, as merchandise, of the matter which it excludes from the mails. . . . Nor can any regulation be enforced . . . so as to interfere in any manner with the freedom of the press. Liberty of circulating is as essential to that freedom as liberty of publishing; indeed without circulation the publication would be of little value.[29]

Ex parte Jackson, 106 *United States Reports* 727.

This decision recognizes two points that serve the cause of liberty: first, that denial of liberty of circulation is in effect a denial of freedom of the press; second, that if the government mail monopoly be closed as a vehicle of circulation there shall be no denial of the right to circulate in other ways. The essence of the matter for civil liberty, however, was stated in a separate opinion by Justice Field:

> The difficulty attending the subject arises not from want of power in Congress to prescribe regulations as to what shall constitute mail matter, but from the necessity of imposing them consistently with rights reserved to the people of far greater importance than the transportation of the mail.

It may be more important that the people communicate freely among themselves than that certain uncommon offenses against public morals be punished.

There are three other factors in the working of the postal censorship: (1) the mail monopoly declared by the United States forbids private mailing organizations (*Revised Statutes* 3982, c. 9-40); (2) the refusal of the courts to review a postmaster-general's exclusion order on the general ground that an executive must enjoy discretionary power; (3) the refusal of the post-office department to pass upon the contents of periodicals in advance of actual mailing.[30] The purpose of this refusal to interpret the statutes on obscenity, et cetera, is to prevent the charge of a pre-publication censorship; and the result is that a publisher can never tell in advance what he will be allowed to mail.

The procedure of exclusion is as follows.   Any postmaster can, if he thinks a publication non-mailable under these statutes, hold up an entire issue while he sends a copy to the third assistant attorney-general at Washington.   The latter who acts as counsel to the post-office department, renders a decision, and the postmaster-general if he affirms the finding, then orders the issue excluded.   There is no hearing or appeal.   An order of exclusion may be the first notice the publisher gets and this merely gives the reason as "Number .... of the Postal Regulations."   There is no specification as to the offensive clauses, and since the meaning of the statutes necessarily depends upon the interpretation of general terms, the publisher cannot find out what the post-office objects to, or deduce any definition for future guidance. Consequently he must always play safe.   Usually the barred copies are returned.   But even if the issue be finally admitted to the mails the delay in a business in which regularity of distribution is essential, injures the publisher and if repeated may destroy his property.

The procedure for the total revocation of a second-class mailing privilege is similar, except that the publisher is granted a hearing at Washington (nowhere else), and may present such defence as the indefinite nature of the specifications permit.   The restoration of the privilege, once suspended, depends solely on the will of the postal authority.

The objections to the censorship were summed up by Louis F. Post after investigation of exclusions on obscenity charges:

1. Any periodical though it contain nothing obscene is subject to exclusion peremptorily from the mails . . . upon the mere order of an administrative official.

2. Exclusion orders are made in accordance with precedents created by rulings in particular cases . . . but these rulings are secret and by refusing to define their limitations upon request the Department

prevents publishers from guarding against the penalties. . . .

3. Publishers . . . are accorded no protection in the courts against unjust exclusions, not even if the exclusion be made in manifest bad faith. . . . The postmaster-general's dictum, right or wrong, and with good or evil intent, is absolute.

4. In practice the Post Office Department excludes periodicals . . . for publishing articles denounced as obscene which in fact are not obscene.

5. The law . . . affords officials of the Department a degree of opportunity for corrupt discrimination . . . unsafe to repose in any official and which ought to be carefully safeguarded by Congress.[31]

Further evidence of the distrust of the postal censorship was the petition of the American Newspaper Publishers Association to Congress that the publishers be given the right to judicial review of the exercise of the authority of the Post Office Department in the granting, withholding or withdrawal of the second-class privilege, the exclusion of improper matter or the interpretation and construction of the postal laws.[32]

First-class mail, that is, private sealed letters, are held exempt from scrutiny by the postal authorities except upon a specific warrant as sacredly as if they rested in the desk of the addressee in his home. The Supreme Court declared:

The Constitutional guaranty of the right of the people to be secure in their papers against unreasonable searches and seizures extends to their papers thus closed against inspection (sealed) wherever they may be.[33]

There were charges, however, during the Civil War and the late World War that the postal authorities were permitting the scrutiny of first-class mail either by their own officials or by agents of the Department of Justice. It has been held that the obscenity laws applied to sealed letters.[34] And in connection with the revocation of second-class privileges under fraud or other orders, a sort of indirect censorship is exercised, since the post-office returns as "non-deliverable" all letters addressed to the alleged illegal receiver.[35]

THE CENSORSHIP OF MORALS

The chief interest here is in the application of the obscenity statute to restrict discussions of sex. The merit of the police power over frauds, lotteries, et cetera is not in dispute.[36] As sex has become less a mysterious medley of religious tradition and *tabu*, and more a scientific study in a self-conscious society, to be dealt with for the good of both the individual and the race, the desire for freedom of discussion has brought many serious and idealistic persons into conflict with laws based on conventional morality or on the concept that women or children are best protected from immorality by silence and ignorance. The control of vice is admitted necessary. No one desires obscene matter conceived in viciousness or for gain to pass through the United States mails. But as usual it has proved extremely difficult to preserve useful freedoms while punishing deliberate vice. The effect of mere words on sex themes is incapable of measurement; and the courts themselves have supplied no consistent standards. The net result has been that discussions of the morals of marriage (sex relations, divorce, eugenics, and birth-control), of radical ideas of sex freedom (the double standard of morals and "free love"), or of the health aspects of sex (prostitution, venereal disease, marriage certification and stirpiculture) have been attended with danger for the person who gave frank publicity to his views.[37]

"THE COMSTOCK LAW"

The suppression of publications by the Post Office, and the criminal prosecutions in the courts, were both based on the obscenity statute—the so-called "Comstock Law"—passed by Congress March 3, 1873.[38] The form of the statute follows:

Every obscene, lewd, or lascivious, and every filthy book, painting, picture, paper, letter, writing or print, or other publication of an indecent character . . . and every article or thing designed for . . . preventing conception or producing abortion . . . or the giving of information directly or indirectly, where or how or from whom or by what means any of these articles can be obtained is a crime. . . .

Anthony Comstock who fathered the act, had himself appointed a special agent of the post-office department without salary, and shortly afterward perfected an organization for the enforcement of the statute, which still exists as the "New York Society for the Suppression of Vice." Later the New York Code of Criminal Procedure was amended to permit proceedings in that State against persons who could not be reached under the postal law.[39]   Only a few specimen cases are given here for Comstock himself gave the number of his prosecutions as 3,648, with 2,682 convictions.   Most of these do not of course involve principles of liberty.   He is credited with having destroyed fifty tons of books, 28,425 pounds of stereotype plates, 16,900 photographic negatives, and 3,984,063 photographs.

The first important prosecution was against S. D. Woodhull.   A famous violator of the statute was Ezra H. Heywood, who was arrested November 2, 1877, for the alleged mailing of two books, *Cupid's Yokes,* a treatise on marital morality by Heywood, and Trall's *Sexual Physiology.*   He was convicted in the United States Court at Boston and sentenced to two years hard labor in Dedham jail, June 25, 1878.   He was unconditionally released by President Hayes, December 19.   On October 26, 1882, he was lodged in Charles Street jail, Boston, for violating the amended act, but was acquitted by the United States Court, April 12, 1883.[40]   There was a famous trial of D. M. Bennett, March 18, 1879, in the Circuit Court at New York.[41]

Moses Harman was prosecuted for twenty years beginning in April, 1888, when the U. S. District Court in Kansas

imposed a fine of $300 and a five-year term at hard labor
for mailing an obscene paper (June 18, 1886). He did not
serve the term. In 1891, he was convicted and imprisoned
for certain articles in his journal *Lucifer*. This sentence
was later reversed because it omitted "hard labor."[42] In
1903 Harman was still editing *Lucifer* (now in Chicago)
dealing with sexual matters. The edition of December 17
was barred from the mails by the Chicago postal authorities, and confiscated under section 497 of the postal regulations. Harman was tried and sentenced to one year's imprisonment in Joliet penitentiary, Illinois, which he entered
February 27, 1908. Other numbers of *Lucifer* were excluded (August 3 and 17, and October 12, 1905) for such
crimes as referring to a book on the Post-Office *index ex-
purgatorius* because it dealt with birth-control methods; the
republication of an editorial from the *Woman's Journal*
of Boston (though the original was not suppressed); and
(high irony) the republication of an agricultural report by
the United States Department of Agriculture! [43]   Editors
found it dangerous even to comment on the case:

> In June 1890, J. B. Caldwell printed an article on the
> Harman case in his small weekly in Chicago, which was
> devoted to advocating continence in the marital rela-
> tion. A proof of the article was furnished the superin-
> tendent of the mails. . . Washington stated that "the
> Department did not decide upon proofs submitted." . . .
> Caldwell invited McAfee (agent for the Vice Society
> in the west) to inspect all the publications of his paper,
> "The Christian Life." McAfee replied he was not a
> censor of the press and did not decide upon the mail-
> ability of matter. On October 15, Caldwell was arrested
> for mailing obscene publications. The specification was
> that one copy contained an article by the Rev. C. E.
> Walker, entitled "Marital Purity." His bail was fixed at
> $500. Hearing has been deferred.

In 1907, *Eugenics*, successor to *Lucifer*, was threatened with
the loss of its second-class mail privilege.

In 1895 a man named Wise of Clay Center, Kansas, sent a quotation from the Bible through the mails, and was found guilty of obscenity.   In October, 1897, Henry Addis, Abner Pope and other members of the Ruskin Colony in Tennessee, were arrested for mailing obscene literature, and No. 34 of *The Firebrand* was confiscated by the postal authorities at Portland, Ore.   In September, 1911, the *Report of the Chicago Vice Commission* was forbidden the mails, though this was the production of a very respectable and presumably scientific body.

We may note that in most of these cases the alleged offenders were radical or free-thinkers, or more generally social and religious idealists, some of whom instead of painting the beauties of sex, believed it a very sinful and morbid thing. They were often opposed to licentiousness inside of marriage, and they sometimes achieved a sane conception of evolutionary eugenics.   They were not scientific and were frequently foolish, but they were not intentional corrupters of public morals, nor indeed did their publications contain anything that could rightly be called unintentionally corrupting.   They were pioneers and suffered the penalties.   They won a freedom later used by others.

We cannot go into the procession of cases in which the courts have wrestled with the whole matter of obscenity and the interpretation of the statute.   The central doctrine is derived from an English case; "that is obscene which has a tendency to deprave and corrupt those whose minds are open to such immoral influences, and into whose hands a publication of this sort might fall."   (Regina v. Hicklin, 2 L. R. Q. B. 569. Ex Crum Case, 19/1868. Trials of Charles Bradlaugh and Annie Besant.)   A critic of the law gives the following summary:

A glance at the decisions handed down during the forty years of Comstock's chief activity shows a truly amazing willingness to accommodate him in his pious enterprises.   On the one hand there was gradually built up a court-made definition of obscenity which eventually embraced almost every conceivable violation of Puritan prudery, and on the other hand the victim's means of defence were steadily restricted and conditioned, until in the end he had scarcely any at all. This is the state of the law to-day. It is held in the leading cases that anything is obscene which may excite "impure thoughts" in the minds . . . of persons that are susceptible to impure thoughts,"[44] or which "tends to deprave the minds" of any who, because they are "young and inexperienced," are "open to such influences"[45] . . . in brief that anything is obscene that is not fit to be handed to a child just learning to read, or that may imaginably stimulate the lubricity of the most foul-minded . . . Words that "abstractly considered may be free from vulgarism" may yet be assumed by a friendly jury to be likely to "arouse a libidinous passion . . . in the mind of a modest woman" . . . The court failed to define "modest woman."[46] Yet further it is held that any book is obscene "which is unbecoming, immodest.[47] Almost any printed allusion to sex may be argued against as unbecoming in a moral republic, and once unbecoming it is also obscene. . . . The defendant cannot allege in his defence that the offending work was put forth for a legitimate, necessary, and decent purpose.

FEDERAL ACTION AGAINST BIRTH CONTROL PROPAGANDA

The propaganda for the dissemination of information on the control of conception, known in the United States as the "birth control movement," led by Mrs. Margaret Sanger, a nurse, has resulted in the suppression of publications and prosecution under the Federal obscenity statute. The following gives the facts:

In February, 1913, the Sunday Magazine of the Socialist daily, "The New York Call," was held up on account of a series of articles, entitled, "What Every Girl Should Know." The specific matter complained of was a discussion of the effects of venereal diseases. After much protest and discussion the Post Office Department reversed the exclusion order. In March, 1914, the first

number of "The Woman Rebel" was refused mailing
privileges, and the copies submitted for mailing were
confiscated. The May, July, August, September, and
October numbers were also excluded and the copies confiscated. One of the paragraphs for publishing which
the March issue was barred from the mails read: "It
will also be the aim of THE WOMAN REBEL to advocate the prevention of conception and to impart such
knowledge in the columns of the paper." [48]

After three issues of the "Woman Rebel" had been
excluded from the mails, without the editor being able
to discover what was the exact nature of the obscenity,
the journal printed a "Defense of Assassination," by
Herbert A. Thorpe. This was done to force definite
action, assassination and arson having been included as
'obscene' by the amendment to the section 211 of the
United States Penal law. In July, Margaret Sanger
was arrested for violating the obscenity statute, but released on her own recognizance. October 5, a postponement of the trial was refused, and Mrs. Sanger went to
England. She returned in November, 1915, and on
February 18, 1916, all the cases against the "Woman
Rebel" were dismissed.

The detained copies were never returned to the owners.

"The Birth Control Review," successor to "The Woman Rebel" was detained by the Post Office for advertising a book, "Married Love," by Marie C. Stopes. This
book had been barred from the mails, although it was
allowed to circulate in England. The November, 1918,
issue was detained, without notification to the publishers,
who discovered the detention only when the subscribers
complained of not receiving the journal. Two enquiries
elicited no information from the Post Office, but a letter
dated November 20 declared the publication mailable.
The effect of such delays on a periodical publication's
circulation is apparent. [49]

THE OBSCENITY STATUTE AS A CLUB

The obscenity statute has been used as a club with which
to attack other groups as well as those interested in freedom

of discussion on sex. Socialists, anti-Catholics and physical culturists have been charged with obscenity in order to suppress their propaganda.

In 1912 Hobart Coomer who published a Socialist paper in Oklahoma was sentenced to six months imprisonment for publishing an advertisement of a proposed edition of his periodical. The advertisement which was attacked as "obscene, lewd, lascivious, and filthy" read in part as follows:

FREE LOVE EDITION OF SOCIAL DEMOCRAT, JULY 10, . . . The master class has always taught and paid their hireling teachers, preachers, authors (editors) and other able idiots to teach that woman is merely a multiplication table for the human species; that her only business on God's green footstool is to fry steak and onions and bearing soldiers and politicians. . . . They never, until recently, allowed her to exercise anything but her sexual apparatus. The Socialists have made a great discovery. They have discovered that women are human beings. They are getting paid for this great discovery by having "free love" and many other stupid hee-haws brayed in their ears. We are going to tell you in the Free Love edition why the Socialists believe women are human beings.

There was nothing about free love in the paper. The above words formed the basis for the indictment. The case was taken to the United States Circuit Court which refused to change the decision.[50]

In a previous case, Fred Warren, of Girard, Kansas, had published in a widely circulated Socialist weekly, *The Appeal to Reason*, charges based on affidavits against a deputy warden of the Federal penitentiary at Leavenworth, accusing him of sexual irregularities including homo-sexual practices with prisoners in his charge. He was brought into the United States District Court in Kansas for violating the obscenity statute.   Judge Pollack sustained a demurrer to the indictment, declaring the publication justified by the purpose it sought to accomplish.[51]   Warren and *The Appeal to Reason* had been actually punished under a different postal law in 1903.   The Socialists claimed it was an attack on their party and its chief organ.   The prosecution was based not on matter published in the newspaper, but on the mailing of envelopes on which was printed: "$1000 will be paid to any person who kidnaps ex-Governor Taylor and returns him to the Kentucky authorities."   Taylor was at the time under indictment for murder, but was safe in Indiana because a Republican governor refused to sign extradition papers. Warren was indicted under part of the Act of September 26, 1888 making it a crime to put on the outside wrapper of mailed matter any language of a "defamatory or threatening character obviously intended to reflect injuriously on the character or conduct of another."   Warren was convicted and punished, but pardoned by President Taft, who was of the opinion that the action taken against him was too severe and actuated by antagonism to his Socialist activities.[52]

The Menace, an anti-Catholic journal in Missouri was prosecuted under the obscenity statute for publishing extracts from the works of a former priest, these extracts having to do with the morality of the priests and the conduct of the confessional.   The defendant claimed that a leading official of a Catholic organization had furnished the material to the district attorney, and that a number of Catholic societies had written to the Postmaster-General for the purpose of bringing a prosecution.   The jury acquitted the editors.[53]

The next case concerns a person who claimed an interest in physical culture, personal hygiene, and so in right sex morals.

The defendant was the publisher of a physical culture magazine in which in October, 1906 began an article "Growing to Manhood in Civilized(?) Society" . . . the career of a young man as an example.   Through the activities of some unknown person with a motive, the attention of a Post Office Inspector was attracted to the three numbers; he purchased the same through the mail, and the arrest, indictment, and conviction of the defendant followed.　He was sentenced to two years hard labor in the penitentiary and fined $2000. . .

The suit against me was of local origin in the little village in New Jersey where the "Physical Culture Magazine" was then published.　No intimation of impropriety in the story was received from any reader, and while in Washington the day following my arrest I was informed that the officials of the Post Office Department had received no complaints against my magazine. . . . In addition to personal obloquy resulting from this prosecution, and many false and slanderous statements concerning it, I have been made to suffer large financial loss . . . it will probably reach $200,000.

    Bernarr Macfadden, *Statement on His Trial*, p. 17.

The United States Circuit Court upheld the conviction for obscenity:　"It caters to a prurient taste. . . . The test is the tendency to deprave and corrupt the mind of those open to such influence."[54]

IS ANARCHISM INDECENCY?

The federal executive authorities found the postal laws inadequate to suppress publications that discuss social questions in ways they opposed.　They could not reach the anarchists, for example, and were forced to resort to technical rulings, thus:

We moved in 1905 to St. Louis to publish our paper *Regeneracion* (an organ of the radical Revolutionaries of Mexico). . . .　Diaz used diplomatic channels. . . . We had complied with all the provisions of the postal laws in order to avoid this . . . and yet Mr. Cortelyou, the Postmaster General, with neither justification nor shame, declared that *Regeneracion* could not enjoy second class privileges because over fifty per cent of the copies were destined for circulation in Mexico.[55]

There is some evidence that these technical postal regulations have been invoked against publishers whose real offence was the expression of radical political or social ideals. Here is how President Roosevelt attempted to supply the deficiencies of the statutes by his own ukase:

> *To The Attorney-General*, March, 1908; By my direction the Postmaster General is to exclude *La Question Sociale* of Paterson, N. J., from the mails and it will not be re-admitted unless by order of the court, or unless you advise me that it must be admitted. . . .
> *Attorney-General Bonaparte to the President*: I am obliged to report that I can find no express provision of law directing the exclusion of such matter from the mails . . . In the absence of any express provision . . . or binding adjudication, . . . in my opinion the Postmaster General will be justified in excluding from the mails any issue . . . which shall contain any article constructively a seditious libel, and counselling such crimes as murder, arson, riot, and treason. . . . Such action would be perfectly safe since at common law it is settled that the owner of a libelous picture, et cetera, is entitled to no damages for its destruction. . . . Hence Federal Statutes for punishing the Postmaster for detaining mail . . . would not operate.[56]

This is a rare exhibit even in our history; the Attorney-General trying to nullify the First Amendment by such ancient devices as constructive crime, seditious libel, and the common law interposed to protect the Postmaster from federal statutes. There was "neither statute nor binding adjudication" to justify Roosevelt, yet the act was declared "perfectly safe" because they could not be punished.[57] The periodical was actually excluded, but on a technical postal violation, not for its views. President Roosevelt transmitted the Attorney-General's opinion to Congress with a special message; and as result of the agitation we have (1909) the following hybrid addition to the obscenity statute, an excellent example of how the censorship on moral grounds is extended to other fields:

And the term "indecent" within the intendment of this section shall include matter of a character tending to incite arson, murder, or assassination.[58]

WHEN IS ART OBSCENE?

The obscenity club has been used against the artist, graphic, plastic, literary, and dramatic. In 1882, Osgood and Company, Walt Whitman's publishers, submitted to the poet twenty-four passages in *Leaves of Grass* for censorship.[59] Backed by a threat of the United States attorney, they ordered these passages expunged before the book was allowed on sale in Boston. Foreign authors whose works have been proscribed in one way or another, are Rabelais, Boccaccio, Zola, Daudet, Balzac, Hardy (*Jude the Obscure,* and *Tess of the d'Urbervilles*) and Harold Frederic, (*Damnation of Theron Ware*). Frank Harris was deprived of a publisher for his *Life of Oscar Wilde.* George Moore's *Memoirs of My Dead Life* was expurgated. D. H. Lawrence's works were forbidden for a time; and attacks were made on Theodore Dreiser's *Genius,* David Graham Phillips' *The Career of Susan Lennox,* and Alfred Kreymborg's *Edna.*

Scientific sex studies suffered equally with fine arts: Forel's *The Sexual Question* was brought into court as pornography; Havelock Ellis' works on sex barred from the mails at one time; and the publishers of Przybyszewski's *Homo Sapiens* were forced to withdraw the volume. Not all of these interferences were based on the Federal mail statute. James Lane Allen's *A Summer in Arcady,* for example, was barred from libraries, as were many other suspected books.[60]

Plays have of course been barred under local ordinances. The list includes Du Maurier's *Trilby,* Bernard Shaw's *Mrs. Warren's Profession,* (later revived quite innocuously), Oscar Wilde's *Salome,* and the plays of Eugene Brieux. In Cleveland, Ohio, in 1906, Olga Nethersole had to omit the staircase scene in the play from Daudet's

Sappho. A play was suppressed in Philadelphia because it was obnoxious to the Negro population.

In the representative arts we have such incidents as a raid on the Art Students' League (New York City), August 2, 1906; and the removal from a confectioner's window in that city of a painting *Triumph of the Chaste* because it contained a nude woman. The confusion in municipal esthetic standards was humorously shown when a bronze Bacchante by MacMonnies was exiled from the Public Library by prudish Boston, only to find sanctuary in the Metropolitan Museum, New York. We must admit that the distinction between pornography and art is not always easy to make; indeed in some of the above cases there remains the uneasy suspicion that art was secondary to publicity and profits. But it is certainly dangerous to freedom in art to let commonplace and inexpert minds decide the possible effects of the nude or the sexual in literature.[61]

THE CENSORSHIP OF MOVING-PICTURES

The moving-picture may be treated here as a combination of the art and postal censorship. Here is a new and popular and powerful means of communication. Does it fall within the protection of the guaranty of a "free press"? Certainly not in words; and in fact there are very real differences. The press for example was conceived of as an instrument in relation to government, but the screen can hardly be so viewed save as it is profoundly educational. The more vivid emotional reaction to the picture than to the printed word taking place in crowds differentiates the problem from that of freedom of the press. Since the status of many pictures is so uncertain we only sketch the facts.

Efforts have been made to create a federal national board of censors to pass upon films intended for inter-state shipment. This has not been done. The federal censorships have been of three kinds: First, censorship of all films imported into this country was created in the tariff act of 1909, to be exercised by the Secretary of the Treasury. This does not appear to have been widely applied.[62]   Second, films of prize-fights have been barred from importation and from inter-state transportation, by the mails or common carriers.   It is a crime either to deposit the film for shipment or to receive it from shipment.   This is based on the brutalizing effect of such contests, though pictures of bayonet practice go through the mails freely.   Third, it has been decided that the First Amendment does not cover the transportation of picture films in the mails.   "The United States could refuse transportation to any film not subjected to its censorship.   Pictures are far worse on public morals than mere words."[63]   The court is here evidently extending the principle of the obscenity and lottery statutes that a government utility cannot be forced to carry what is regarded as immoral.

The censorships and police regulations of moving-pictures by states and municipalities are too complex and as yet unsettled to be more than mentioned here.   Boards have been quite generally granted the power to ban or excise parts of films or order their change.   The police acting as ex-tempore censors, sometimes with the help of the clergy and other experts in art and morality, have forbidden exhibitions and revoked the licenses of halls.   Pictures liable to cause race feeling or stimulate immorality have come under the ban.[64]

THE COURTS AS CENSORS OF THE PRESS

The courts also have acted as censors of the press by the use of their power to punish for contempt.

Recently (1900-1914) in Colorado, Ohio, and New York, editors have been punished for contempt of court, which consisted in criticism published in their news-papers, and not in the presence of the court; and, there-fore, having no direct tendency to disturb its orderly proceedings.   In Colorado, perhaps in other States also, proof of the truth was excluded.[65]

In Colorado, one Patterson was punished by a State court for contempt in publishing certain opinions on the conduct of a case before the Court.[66] His appeal finally reached the United States Supreme Court which denied him redress.[67] This method of bridling the press to the judicial hand was comparatively new, and its employment promised to be widespread during the first years of this century. It aroused this comment from an expert on free communication:

> The judge-made law of contempt of court for publications censuring judges is simply intolerable in a land of equality where judges are no more important to the universe than executives and legislators.[68]

Justice Harlan dissented in the Patterson case, and declared:

> I go further and hold that the privilege of free speech and of free press belonging to every citizen of the United States, constitute essential parts of every man's liberty, and are protected against violation by that clause of the Fourteenth Amendment forbidding States to deprive any citizen of his liberty without due process of law.

CENSORSHIP UNDER LOCAL POLICE POWERS

Censorship of the press involving the suspension of publication and the raiding of publication offices with the destruction of property has been not unusual in the last forty years, under police powers granted by local and State laws, especially with respect to Socialist papers. The following list does not exhaust the evidence, but it exemplifies the various kinds of restriction:

1888—The *Alarm,* Chicago, was suspended from April 8, to July 14, on account of its alleged anarchistic tendencies.[69]

1893—*The Free Speech* edited by Miss Ida B. Wells, a Negro, was suppressed because she so fiercely denounced the lynching of some young colored men, and arraigned the authorities for failing to punish the lynchers. She was driven from Memphis, Tennessee, and formed an anti-lynching league in England, securing as members, the Duke of Argyll, the Archbishop of Canterbury, and others.[70]

1906—Emil Ruedebusch, of Maysville, Wis., was fined for publishing *Old and New Ideals*, a pamphlet of radical social and sex philosophy.

1910—*The New Castle Free Press*, in a free speech fight in New Castle, Pennsylvania, was charged with seditious libel under the revival of the obsolete doctrine of the common law. Four men, McKeever, Hartman, McCarty, and White, were tried. The jury disagreed. In the celebration after this vindication the Socialists were forced to rent an orchard for a meeting, and, it being Sunday, narrowly escaped a new prosecution under a local blue law.[71]

1912—On September 5, the Socialist paper of Butte, Montana, went out with three columns of white censored spaces, far more eloquent than the expurgated text, creating a curiosity that could hardly be met when the censorship was removed.[72]

1913—*The Weekly Issue* of Passaic, N. J., suffered from police action during the strike of the silk weavers in the latter town. The police entered Socialist headquarters and seized 500 copies of the "Weekly Issue," the organ of the Socialist Party. Charges of theft were made against the police later, and four of them were brought before a Socialist judge and held in bail of $200 each. Next a warrant was issued for the arrest of the editor, Alexander Scott, charged with "aiding and abetting hostility to the government," a crime punishable by 15 years at hard labor. He was arrested at a meeting held to protest against this persecution, locked up over night, and released next day on $2000 bail. He had compared the conditions in Paterson with the rule of the Cossacks. Four men who sold the paper on the street were also arrested. Scott was tried and convicted in the lower court, but the verdict was set aside by the Supreme Court of New Jersey, while the four men, after being held several days in default of bail, were released without trial.[73]

A great variety of laws have been proposed and some few enacted, to curb the press. The following illustrates how extreme such measures may be:

A law was passed in the California legislature denouncing a portrait or caricature of any living person, other than that of an office-holder within the State, without the person's written consent, unless he had been convicted of a crime. Apparently this allows the publication of likenesses of politicians and criminals only. The intent of the law was never made clear, as the newspapers disregarded it as a plain interference with the freedom of the press. The same State proposed a statute requiring the responsible writer's name to every article libellous on its face.[74]

MILITARY AND EXECUTIVE CENSORSHIP OF THE PRESS

The military arm of our government has naturally had but small opportunity to censor or suppress publications. It has, however, on several occasions exercised these functions after the declaration of "martial law." In a miners' strike in Colorado there was a repetition of Civil War methods:

September 29, 190., the militia arrested the working-force of the Victor "Record." . . . The specific charge was based on the statement in the paper that one of the members of one of the military companies was an ex-convict. A detail of 25 infantrymen and 20 cavalrymen marched to the printing office and arrested the editor, George E. Keyner, and four employees, and took them to the bull pen. Under orders from Gov. Peabody the five men . . . were turned over to the sheriff on the evening of September 30. (They were later charged with criminal libel).

On the night of December 4, Maj. H. A. Naylor called at the *Daily Victor Record* and informed its editor and proprietor that a censorship had been placed upon the columns of the *Record*. Editor Keyner was told that he must not publish anything but ordinary news matter, and was compelled to show Major Naylor proofs of the editorial matter which he had already written for the next morning's paper. The leading editorial was produced and the officer told the editor he must not publish it. He forbade the editor to print the official statements of the Miner's Union.[75]

Articles criticizing the militia or State administration were forbidden. The office was attacked by a mob and wrecked.[76]

In West Virginia, in the strike of 1912-1913, the military power arrested C. H. Boswell, editor of the *Labor Argus,* and held him incommunicado. Fred Merrick, a second Socialist editor who came from the *Pittsburgh Justice* to fill Boswell's place, was thrown into prison by the Governor's orders, and the paper confiscated. The house of the editor of the *Socialist and Labor Star,* one Thompson, was searched for the mailing-list of his paper, his stock damaged, and the office department locked up.

> "In Idaho . . . many striking miners were herded in outrageously unsanitary bull-pens by the militia of the State. An editor who foolishly believed the Constitution of Idaho to be of some importance propounded some questions in his paper, calculated to show that this conduct of the militia was in violation of the law. For asking these questions . . . he was also arrested and placed in the bull-pen with the others.

FREEDOM IN THE ISLAND COLONIES

The Federal military power has had little opportunity to interfere with freedom of the press save in our colonial possessions. . . . It seems to have taken advantage of this opportunity on occasion.

> In our military control of the Philippine Islands we find executive authorities arresting an American editor for republishing our own Declaration of Independence . . . with the excuse that it would tend to incite the Filipinos to insurrection.

In Porto Rico, we find an American editor is subjected to some seventy or more arrests, and finally in practical effect banished from the island as the one condition on which he could escape what might prove life imprisonment . . . for publishing what he believed to be true concerning some carpet-bag officials appointed by the President.

In the years since 1917, not covered by this study, the violations of civil liberty in the colonies have been more frequent.

THE LAWS AGAINST ANARCHISTS

The development of the laws against anarchists is an important chapter in the history of liberty. These extreme libertarians have had rather less liberty than anybody else. They present a paradox, for although they do not believe in government, they appeal to the constitutional guarantees of government for protection in the agitation of their views. Their opposition to all government, together with the fact that some few of them have both preached and practiced violence, has caused them to be regarded especially as people outside the pale. Ignorance of their philosophy has led to the confusion of anarchists with other radical groups, such as the Socialists and communists, so that they have suffered from the views of others, and others have suffered from being identified with them.

For clearness we must distinguish the native-born anarchist from the alien, and the philosophical or Christian anarchist from the advocate of the violent overthrow of governments. The native anarchist has existed since the Utopians of the early 19th century, but his doctrines had not been regarded as dangerous, nor had he suffered suppression until after the influx of foreign-born anarchists from Germany and Russia, who fled to this country from 1848 on. They were at first received as exiled republicans from despotic monarchies in Europe coming to a land of political asylum as so many previous rebels against ancient tyrannies had come. As a guest the anarchist was not expected to preach or act against the United States—where it was believed none of the evils he had attacked at home could exist. But as the industrial conflict grew harsher in this country from the Civil War on, these alien agitators and their American followers began to preach their doctrines, not against foreign despots, but against American capitalists and public officials. This could not be endured, so the tradition of free political asylum was slowly abandoned for restrictive laws, federal and state, that would exclude alien anarchists and curb those already here. It is true that most of those who have suffered have been aliens, but they have suffered primarily for their opinions and so are of interest to the libertarian.

ORIGIN OF THE ANARCHY EXCLUSION ACT

In 1888, probably as a result of the Haymarket bomb incident in Chicago,[77] resolution 1291 in the House provided for "the removal of dangerous aliens from the United States."[78] The act failed of passage. The vague term "dangerous alien" marks the beginning of the long struggle to define the person to be excluded. In 1889 Senate Bill 453 made it unlawful for "an avowed anarchist or nihilist or one who is personally hostile to the principles of the Constitution of the United States or to the form of Government," to enter the country. The bill was violently attacked in hearings and failed. In 1890-1893 two investigations of the problem prove the continued interest.[79] Yet in the Immigration Act of 1891 this proviso was included: "Nothing in this act shall be construed to apply to or exclude persons convicted of political offenses, even though they may be designated as felony or crime . . . by the courts of their native land." This reveals still a strong sentiment in favor of the tradition of political asylum.[80]

In 1894, probably as a result of the assassination of President Carnot of France, bills were introduced in both Houses to punish anarchy or attempts on the lives of United States executives, and to regulate the admission to the country of undesirable agitators.   A further attempt was made to define anarchism.   The Hill bill, drawn by Secretary John G. Carlisle, under Cleveland and approved by Richard Olney, Secretary of State, passed the Senate and was side-tracked in the House only by the single objection of a New York Representative.[81]   The old idea still persisted, however, for in 1898 the United States declined to send a representative to an international conference of secret service agents to European governments held to solve the problem presented by anarchists.   (Mr. Roosevelt did suggest later making "criminal anarchy an international crime," whatever that may be.) But the assassination of President McKinley in 1901 by an avowed anarchist renewed the agitation.   On December 16, Senator Vest enquired as to a possible amendment to the Constitution to suppress anarchy.   In 1903 Congress passed an immigration law with this provision[82]:

> Section 38: . . . That no person who disbelieves in or who is opposed to all organized government, or who is a member of or affiliated with any organization entertaining and teaching such disbelief in or opposition to all organized government, or who advocates or teaches the duty, necessity or propriety of the unlawful assault or killing of any officer or officers, either of specific individuals or of officers generally, of the government of the United States, or of any other organized government, because of his or their official character, shall be permitted to enter the United States . . . also provided that polygamists, anarchists, or persons who believe in or advocate the overthrow by force or violence of the government of the United States or of all government or of all forms of law, or the assassination of public officials, shall be excluded from the United States. . . . Persons who have been convicted of offenses purely political, not involving moral turpitude are excepted. . . .
>
> An Act to Regulate the Admission of Aliens,
> *United States Compiled Statutes*, 1903, 170.

The debate on this bill brought out a lingering defence of the tradition of political asylum, Senator Hoar declaring that there were in the world governments that he for one would overthrow by force and violence.[83]   The test of the law came the year of its passage.   John Turner, an English subject and organizer for a labor union in England, came to New York to deliver lectures and also prepare articles on trade conditions for *The Grocer,* a London publication. On October 19, 1903, the Secretary of Commerce and Labor issued a warrant for his arrest and deportation.   On October 23, Turner addressed a mass meeting at the Murray Hill Lyceum on "Trade Unionism and the General Strike."   He was arrested and searched.   Extracts from his speech and from literature found on him were produced against him next day when a board of special enquiry was convened.   He had no witnesses nor means of procuring any; he had no counsel, for the act makes no provision for procuring counsel. His trial was secret.   He was not asked to define the word "anarchy."   There was no evidence that Turner had ever advocated the things prohibited by the act.[84]   The Board ordered Turner's deportation; an appeal to the Secretary of Commerce was dismissed.   A writ of habeas corpus was sued out in the Circuit Court at New York City.   The judge refused to intervene, holding the act constitutional.   On appeal the United States Supreme Court decided likewise:

DEPORTATION IS DUE PROCESS OF LAW

Congress has power to exclude aliens and to prescribe conditions on which they may enter the United States; to establish regulations for deporting aliens who have illegally entered, and to commit the enforcement of such conditions and regulations to executive officers. . . . This does not deprive any person of liberty without due process of law. . . . The act of 1903 does not violate the Federal Constitution nor are its powers as to alien anarchists unconstitutional.   Since both Board and Secretary have found for his deportation on evidence, his exclusion or deportation will not be reviewed on the facts. . . .

If the word "anarchist" should be interpreted as including aliens whose anarchistic views are professed as those of political philosophers, innocent of evil intent, it would follow that Congress was of the opinion that the tendency of the general exploitation of such views is so dangerous to the public weal that aliens who hold and advocate them would be undesirable additions to our population whether permanently or temporarily, whether many or few. . . .

United States ex rel Turner versus Williams
194 *United States Reports* 279.

In the last paragraph the Supreme Court establishes the doctrine of "constructive anarchy" by basing its decision on the "dangerous tendency" of the exploitation of these views, "however innocent of evil intent." The rule is first made and with general approval against the advocates of violence; next it is invoked against those philosophers who do not believe in governments lest they incite others to violence; last it is stretched to include any one who seeks to change the form of government by whatsoever means, economic or political.[85] The application of these doctrines to exclude anarchist publications from the mails is discussed above under "Freedom of the Press."

Deportations of anarchists were unusual until after 1919, a period which is not here covered. That of Maxim Gorki, Russian novelist, political radical and social philosopher, was achieved under another provision of the immigration laws, covering exclusions for moral reasons. Gorki entered the country, but was forced to withdraw on account of a public clamor against his relations to a woman who by American interpretations was not his legal wife.

An interesting example of the official attitude toward anarchists was the sentence in 1908 of William Buwalda of San Francisco, a private in the United States Engineers, to five years imprisonment in a military prison for attending a public meeting under anarchist auspices and shaking hands with the speaker after the lecture.

General Funston asserts that Buwalda's action was "a great military offense, infinitely worse than desertion . . . a serious crime, equal to treason. The first duty of an enlisted man is unquestioning obedience and loyalty to the government to which he has sworn allegiance; it makes no difference whether he approves of that government or not." . . . It is quite true that the meeting had been arranged by anarchists. Had Socialists issued the call there would have been no objection. General Funston says: "I would not have the slightest hesitancy about attending a Socialist meeting myself." [86]

THE STATES VERSUS THE ANARCHISTS

The States have denied the anarchists liberty to advocate their views, generally under police-power laws such as those against unlawful assembly and inciting to crime. New York led the way, having enjoyed more experience with anarchists than less cosmopolitan communities. Johann Most and Emma Goldman, the two most pursued of all anarchists in America, were convicted under such laws. The trials of Herr Most which began in England (7 Q. B. Division 244) opened in New York City after a meeting held on November 12, 1887, the day of the hanging of the Chicago anarchists. It was suppressed, and Most and a few of his followers stole away and opened another. He was arrested and tried for inciting to violence, though his threats were made in open meeting and the only persons endangered, if any, were hundreds of miles away. The charge was brought under the Penal Statutes (3, section 451) for the punishment of three or more persons who attempt or threaten any act tending toward a breach of the peace. Again on September 7, 1901, Most was arrested for reprinting in his weekly, *Freiheit*, apparently by mere co-incidence on the day President McKinley was shot, an article by one Carl Hanzen, written fifty years before. The Court of Special Sessions convicted the defendant of misdemeanor.[87]

The decision was based on "breach of the peace" and the "abuse of free speech."

THE NEW YORK CRIMINAL ANARCHY LAW

As a result of the excitement after President McKinley's assassination, New York in 1902 put on the statute books a criminal anarchy law. An abstract follows, given so fully because this law was the progenitor of many similar laws enacted by more than thirty states during and after the World War.

Section 468.   a. Criminal anarchy is the doctrine that organized government should be overthrown by force or violence or the assassination of the executive head or any of the executive officers of the government, or by any unlawful means.

b. . . . whoever by word of mouth or writing advocates, advises, or teaches the duty of criminal anarchy . . . prints, publishes, edits, or issues or knowingly circulates, sells, destributes or publicly displays any book, paper, document or written or printed matter in any form containing or advocating, etc. . . . organizes or becomes a member or voluntarily assembles with any society, group, or assembly of persons to teach or advocate such doctrines . . . is guilty of a felony and punishable by imprisonment for not more than ten years, or by a fine of not more than $5,000.00 or both.

d. Whenever two or more persons assemble for the purpose of advocating or teaching the doctrines of criminal anarchy . . . such assembly is unlawful and every person voluntarily participating therein by his presence, aid, or instigation, is guilty of a felony, and punishable (as in section b).

e. The owner, agent, superintendent, janitor, caretaker, or occupant of any place, building or room who wilfully and knowingly permits therein any assemblage of persons prohibited by section 468 . . . is guilty of a misdemeanor and punishable by not more than two years imprisonment, or by a fine of not more than $2,000, or both.[88]

WHAT HAPPENED TO ANARCHISTS

The following list, with no pretensions to completeness, notes some of the violations of civil rights of anarchists in the decade 1906-1916:

1906—February. Philadelphia. Meeting in honor of Johann Most's sixtieth birthday forcibly broken up by the police.

—October 27. New York. Three speakers at an Anarchist meeting arrested and put under bail.

—October 30. New York. Protest meeting against the preceding action was broken up by the police, and women clubbed.

1907—September. General Brigham, police commissioner of New York City, prohibited the Central Federated Labor Union from displaying red flags.

—November 11. New York Mass-meeting in commemoration of the Chicago Anarchists broken up by the police.

1908—January. Washington, D. C. Major Sylvester, chief of police, tried to prevent Emma Goldman from speaking in the capital of the nation. He cancelled the license of the hall in which the meeting was to be held, and later issued a "temporary license" so the rights of the hall-owner to free renting might be protected.

—Meeting in Philadelphia broken up.

—Chicago. Hall refused for anarchist meeting.

1909—May 23. New York. Meeting of anarchists in Lexington Hall broken up by police, with clubbing and arrests. They tried to intimidate the hall-keeper.

—June 8. East Orange, N. J. An address on the Drama by Emma Goldman scheduled for a Forum meeting was forbidden by the police, and official pressure forced the refusal of English's Hall, which had been rented, and the return of the deposit on the rental. Under the leadership of Alden Freeman, the meeting was held in a private barn before 1,000 people. Later the Orange

Chapter of the Sons of the Revolution asked for
Freeman's resignation.

January 14. San Francisco. Emma Goldman
was arrested to prevent her speaking. This same
year she was arrested in Philadelphia and tried to
secure a decision on her rights in the courts.[89]

1913—April 4 and 11. New York. Disturbances in
Union Square.

—April 13. Los Angeles. Lucy Parsons, widow of
Albert Parsons, one of the Chicago anarchists
hung in Chicago in 1887, and George Markstall
were arrested for selling literature without a license
(an account of the famous Anarchists' trial).
At the police station the matron made Mrs. Parsons strip for searching and tried to pull off her
husband's ring.

The police point of view toward anarchists is curtly put
by a famous policeman, Robert A. Pinkerton:

In New York the police have carried on relentless warfare against the "Reds." They have gone even to the
length of "illegally suppressing" their meetings. On one
occasion I remember when a lot of anarchistic sentiments
were being shouted from a speaker's stand in Union
Square, the police without warrant descended upon the
meeting and broke it up. This was reprehensible from
the standpoint of the stickler for social and political
rights; but there are certain conditions that cannot be
dealt with from the ordinary point-of-view, and anarchy
is one of them.[90] These people should all be marked and
kept under constant surveillance, and on the slightest
excuse be made harmless.

WOMEN AND CIVIL RIGHTS

We have seen but little reason to consider the civil rights
of women as women. Women were protected as men were
by the Bills of Rights and could assemble, speak, print, and
secure as freely the protections of law. Indeed they did things

more freely, for since they could exert little physical force and had no vote, men were not afraid of them, and could exercise a sentimental chivalry, even if they denied justice to the "inferior sex."

It is true the Constitution is a charter for a man's state (hence the Nineteenth Amendment), and excluded any mention of woman as also of God. It gave her no political rights, and by silence acquiesced in her "chattel status." This lack of political power and her economic dependence were the real restraints upon women. Moreover, social tradition and religious sentiments were effectual bars to her freedom. We do not therefore attempt any record of her economic or political status, disfranchisement, religious *tabus,* or the hypocrisies of the composite chivalric and Pauline doctrines as to women.

There is one field, however, in which women *have* suffered as women; from a bitter and relentless sex discrimination, in the use of the police power against prostitution. The treatment of prostitutes has been one long record of invaded liberties. Search and seizure without warrant, illegal arrests and detentions, deportations without legal authority, enforced migrations by entire groups, the use of the male *agent provocateur,* even tarring and feathering, beating, and rail riding at the hands of mobs—these are but a few of the persecutions that have marked the treatment of this evil. This persecution of so-called "outlaws" has been so conventional that there is not even any record of their sufferings. We cannot even offer a list of cases for we have found only here and there a hint like the following:

June, 1869. The Mayor of Pittsburgh has ordered the arrest of every woman found on the streets alone after 9 o'clock in the evening, the consequence of which is that some respectable ladies have seen the inside of the lock-up.

As advocates of radical causes women have suffered along with men. Perhaps the longest tale is among women-workers, whether as units in industry, as strikers, or as propagandists. "Mother Jones" suffered repeated invasions of her rights;

leaders like Elizabeth Gurley Flynn went to jail for agitation; Emma Goldman, the anarchist, was made a greater propagandist because of what she suffered from the police.[91]

There was no sex distinction in these cases. The women suffered what the men suffered.

In preaching certain moral reforms, women have also suffered, especially for abolition and temperance. This summary indicates how women advocates were treated between 1830 and 1880.

The mobbing of Garrison in Boston took place at a women's meeting. Women were mobbed in Philadelphia, and Pennsylvania Hall burned while they were holding both abolition and temperance meetings. One of the speakers declared the slaves they defended were freer than they themselves.[92] At the New York Convention, women were mobbed. The force of their faith was proven by Lucretia Mott, who being a Quaker, refused to call the police to use force to suppress the mob.[93] On a speaking trip of women from Buffalo to Albany a succession of mobs broke up the meetings, or the women were prevented even from securing halls. Finally, the Mayor of Albany boldly preserved order, and gave the crusading women a testimonial. The Mayor of Boston broke up a meeting.[94] In one city where they had secured a concert-hall for a public fair, their flag was torn down, and the high constable ejected them and their property into the street.[95] They were practically denied the right of petition when Congress refused to consider petitions for the abolition of slavery.[96] How women were interfered with in education has been told in the case of Prudence Crandall, and that of the "smelling committee.[97]

We note also the refusal of certain civil rights to women. The restrictions are as old as 1884, when females were excluded from the New Haven grammar school.[98] The right to follow an occupation that requires a special license was long denied in many states. Mrs. Myra Bradwell, editor of the Chicago *Legal News*, fully qualified as a lawyer, was refused admission to the Illinois Bar by the Supreme Court on the ground that "she would not be bound by the obligation necessary between client and attorney by reason of the disability imposed by her married condition." The United States Supreme Court sustained the refusal on the ground that the Fourteenth Amendment did not guarantee the right to practice law as a privilege of citizens of the United States. This was the first appeal in the United States based on the Fourteenth Amendment.[99] Similar struggles for the right to practice medicine and even to enter professional schools are now happily all old stories.

THE WOMAN'S SUFFRAGE MOVEMENT

The suffrage movement naturally tested both the civil rights and the civil liberties of women. Under the first came the actual attempts by women to vote, and the result should at least be noted here:

> On November 5, 1872, Miss Susan B. Anthony and other women appeared at the polls in New York State, and were finally allowed to vote in the presidential election. They were prosecuted under the federal "Enforcement Act"—a measure primarily intended for political use in the Southern States then under "reconstruction." This act made it an offence against the United States for persons not having the right to vote to cast a ballot for candidates for the House of Representatives. The suffragists claimed that their trial was unfair and that they had been denied the right to trial by jury, because the judge had instructed the jury to bring in a verdict of guilty. Miss Anthony was fined $100. The inspectors who had accepted the votes were jailed, but almost immediately released by presidential pardon.[100]

Before the appearance of the so-called "militants" among the suffragists the violations of civil liberty had been irritating but not serious. Meetings were broken up by disorder and hooliganism which went unpunished by the police. Both hooligan and policeman merely reflected the current sentiment of

ridicule.   Such incidents as this necessarily accompany any
new movement:

> Susan B. Anthony went to Southern Oregon in 1879
> and while sojourning in Jacksonville, she was assailed
> with a shower of eggs, since known as "Jackson argu-
> ments" in that section, and she was also burned in effigy
> on a principal street after the sun went down.[101]

By 1913 the increasing political power of the women of
the country through their votes in many States, and the wide-
spread endorsement of their demand for federal action, had
brought them into conflict with the police power.   The struggle centered in Washington, D. C.   The first failure to police
protection was when the Capital police and military allowed
hoodlums to mob and almost break up a parade of suffragists
on March 3, 1913, the day preceding Mr. Wilson's first
inauguration.   The Inauguration Parade was perfectly policed.
    Thereafter the "militants"—members of the Congressional
Union for Equal Suffrage, later the Woman's Party—pressed
for the passage of a constitutional amendment granting equal
suffrage, and sought to secure the President's endorsement and
political aid by direct petition and interview.   When these
failed, they stationed a picket of some half dozen women at
the White House gates with suffrage banners, (January 10,
1917).   June 20 and 21 some rioting and flag-snatching
occurred over a banner on which was blazoned the statement
of Elihu Root, one of the American mission to Russia, that
the United States enjoyed equal suffrage.   Meanwhile the
United States had entered the World War, and the popular
psychology had been worked into the belief that this chal-
lenging of our democracy was disloyal and unpatriotic, and
should be abandoned until the return of peace.
    The authorities, unintelligent and overwrought by the pre-
valent war hysteria, undertook the police suppression of this
dangerous movement and arrested six women on June 24, and
tried them in the police Court of the District of Columbia
on the technical charge of "obstructing traffic,"—an ancient

ally of suppression. The defense claimed their right to picket, citing their five months' immunity from arrest, and charged that it was the arrest not the picketing that produced obstruction of traffic. They were found guilty of violating the police ordinance and the act of Congress, fined $25 each or the choice of three days in the District jail. They chose jail.

On July 4, thirteen women were arrested for disorderly conduct,—due to the resistance of one woman when spectators seized from her copies of *The Suffragist* she had been selling for weeks. Eleven women served three days in jail. July 14, sixteen women were arrested and given sixty days in the District Workhouse at Occoquan, Virginia, for obtsructing traffic. They claimed to be political prisoners, but suffered treatment which they regarded as calculated indignity. After three days they were pardoned by the President without explanation. August 14, 15, and 18, a banner addressed to "Kaiser Wilson" produced serious riot, that at Cameron House, suffragette headquarters, being thus described:

> Miss Lucy Burns stood on the threshold with a banner in her hand. Three sailors in uniform sprang on her, dragged her to the curb and tore the banner to bits. . . . Others brought a ladder . . . climbed to the second balcony and tore down the "Kaiser Wilson' banner, the American flag, and the Woman's Party flag. One sailor struck Miss Georgiana Sturgis. . . . The mob had been assembled for over an hour. Shortly before five o'clock a bullet was fired through one of the windows . . . passing about 18 inches over the head of Mrs. Ella Dean. . . . The police reserves cleared the street about quarter to five. . . .[102]

The value of flags and other property destroyed during this week according to the women was $1,440. The total police action was the arrest of six women on technical charges.

The arrests continued from week to week, but we note only the high spots. September 4, twelve women were given sixty days, and some were placed in solitary confinement for protesting against conditions in Occoquan workhouse. By October 15, four women were given the maximum sentence of six months as an alternative of a $25 fine. On October 20, Alice Paul, the leader of this movement, and Dr. Caroline Spencer, were recalled under suspended sentences and given six months with one additional month. Miss Paul went on a hunger strike, was removed to the District jail, at one time was confined in the psychopathic ward as a test of her sanity, and was forcibly fed for 21 days and then released in very weak physical condition. The next group were sent to Occoquan (except one). They struck at their treatment and the refusal to consider them political prisoners. No one could see them, not even their lawyer. Sixteen refused food, some for ten days. Lucy Burns, a leader, was handcuffed to the bars of her cell. Their attorney had to secure a writ of habeas corpus from the United States Judge Waddill, Eastern District of Virginia, on the ground that they were illegally incarcerated in Occoquan workhouse when they had been sentenced to the District jail. The writ originally returnable November 28, was dated ahead to the twenty-third for fear the hunger strike might produce serious consequences. At the hearing it was admitted that the only basis for the transfer of the women was "a verbal order made five or six years ago." Judge Waddill in summing up said:

> The locking up of thirty human beings is an unusual
> sort of thing and judicial officers ought to be required
> to stop long enough to see whether some prisoners ought
> to go and some not; whether some might not be killed
> by going; or whether they should go, dead or alive. This
> class of prisoners and this number of prisoners should
> have been given special consideration. You ought to
> lawfully lock them up instead of unlawfully lock them
> up—if they are to be locked up. . . . The petitioners
> are, therefore, one and all, in the workhouse without
> semblance of authority or legal process of any kind . . .
> they will accordingly be remanded to the Washington
> jail.

All thirty were returned to the district jail from which

they were liberated four days later on the order of the sentencing judge, A. R. Mullowny, who refused to give a reason for his summary order.[103]

In the summer of 1918 the arrests were resumed. August 6, forty-eight women were arrested for trying to speak from the base of a statue in a park opposite the White House. Some were arrested before they had spoken. They were charged with assembling in a public park without a permit. After a postponement by the government this was changed to a charge of violating a section of the Peace and Order Act which provides against loud and boisterous talking, comment on passers-by and indecent or profane language. Others were charged with climbing on a monument. Twenty-six women were sent to a man's workhouse, abandoned as unfit for habitation, where all but two hunger-struck. They were released after five days. The suffrage amendment was considered in the Senate on September 26, when President Wilson urged the measure because he "wanted a spiritual instrument." In the debate Senator Cummins of Iowa said:

> I do not believe these women committed any crime, and while I have not particle of sympathy with the manner in which they conducted their campaign, I think their arrest and imprisonment, and the treatment they received while in confinement are a disgrace to the civilized world and much more a disgrace to the United States which assumes to lead the civilized world in humane endeavor.

In December and January, 1919, the militants burned President Wilson's books and speeches with ceremonies and kept fires burning in Lafayette Park. Eleven were brought to trial and fined $5 or given five days for starting bonfires between sunset and sunrise. This was reported in the Paris press.

When President Wilson landed at Boston from Europe, in February, the local suffragists made a demonstration and several were arrested for "loitering"; three on Boston Common. They were sent to the House of Detention with sentences for eight days. An anonymous person paid their fines so they were released. The final demonstration was before the Metropolitan Opera House in New York where the President was making a speech. The suffrage pickets were roughed by the police and crowd, and five arrested charged with "disorderly conduct" but later released. (See *Jailed for Freedom* by Doris Stevens.) Meanwhile in the election of 1918 the suffragists claimed to have defeated five out of seven Democratic Senators in western states. The Congress went Republican. This evidence of power brought not only freedom of speech and assembly but the suffrage amendment itself which was passed by the House on May 21, by 304 to 89, and by the Senate on June 4, by 66 to 30. The reversal from police persecution to constitutional recognition is a startling proof that those who have power enjoy liberty.

FREEDOM OF TEACHING

Freedom of teaching is not a civil liberty. No constitutional guarantee protects either teacher or student. The concern of the constitutions of some States with education is to guarantee that schools be provided by the community, with length of terms, language to be used, and compulsory attendance, specified in several instances.[104] But in its elements teaching is a combined exercise of the rights of free assemblage, free speech, and free press. It is the source of all true progress in social liberty however much politics may try to obscure the point that all freedom in government should be to quicken the process of education in large masses of people. Therefore, freedom of teaching in the large sense, includes freedom for the pulpit and for the arts, including the drama.

Freedom of teaching means, technically, that the individual teacher, or the faculty, or teaching group, shall be free to teach as their consciences see the truth without dictation from the State authority or private boards, through their economic control of positions and advancement. The problem of university control is not within the province of civil liberty[105] but the importance and increasing acuteness since 1885 of the old and familiar struggle for academic freedom in American colleges and universities urges a brief list of cases. They will be found to be connected with the other issues of industrial and social freedom.

The struggle began early in this country, with the disciplining of the first president of the first College, Henry Dunster, of Harvard,[106] who displayed an independence rare in later university presidents.

There was an amusing paradox during the Revolution when the Tory President of King's College, now Columbia University, having been vanquished in a debate by young Alexander Hamilton, was disciplined by the patriot students and townspeople. The intolerance toward Quaker teachers at this time has been described. (See page 8.) It is probable that cases occurred before the Civil War involving religious orthodoxy though there is little record of such events. The failure to reappoint a professor (as this was the method of discipline) did not secure general notice. The cases arising out of anti-slavery agitation have been noted. (Page 120.)

Since the Civil War, the cases fall into three groups: the theological (1859-1890); the economic-political (1885-1900); and the social (1897-1917).[107] To these must be added the War cases (1917-1918). This extended list of dismissals of teachers for their dissent from the popular view of the World War is not here covered.

The theological cases simply continued the old dispute between science and religion, the *casus belli* at this time being the doctrine of evolution.[108] For example, in the seventies Professor Winchell was forced out of Vanderbilt University for a difference of view on theology. In 1884, Dr. James Woodrow, professor of Natural Science and Revealed Religion in the Presbyterian Seminary of South Carolina, was forced to resign for advocating in his classes the doctrine of evolution. The University of South Carolina gave this relative of the future President of the United States a chair in science.[109] At Princeton in the eighties arose a controvesry over the orthodoxy of the celebrated president, Dr. James McCosh; and a little later, Professor Charles Toy of the chair of Semitic languages in the Louisville Theological Seminary, was forced to withdraw from that institution. He accepted a chair at Harvard.

The marked increase of cases since about 1890, especially in the departments of economics and government, coincides with our vast industrial expansion, the struggle between labor and capital, and the replacing on University boards of control of the representatives of religion with the representatives of the state or of great wealth. Men began to differ not on eternity, but on society, and were punished as of old lest they contaminate the young. The new importance of the social sciences with their research into actual present conditions, and the presentation of their statistical revelations on the evils of our industrial system, revelations that could not be blotted out by political manipulation, aroused certain vested interests to the need for weeding out and silencing these intellectual war-plots. University extension and extra-mural labors had brought the teacher into touch with vital problems in the community life. He had to speak out—and then, to fight for freedom. He had to resist too the stifling effects on himself, his ideas, and his teaching, of the munificent gifts to universities from men of vast wealth and power. There follows a brief list of type cases. It does not pretend to be exhaustive; nor does it pretend to decide the disputed details in each case, whether for example the word "dismissed" means that a teacher was forced to resign, or simply dropped from the next year's teaching staff. No final judgment on the facts is offered.

In 1893 George D. Herron was dismissed from Iowa College on account of his radical views on marriage. He was a Socialist and it has been held that his political views were urged against him. His views were also brought into the record when in 1919 President Wilson appointed him to a War commission. In 1895, Professor E. W. Bemis, associate professor of economics and sociology was dropped from the faculty of the University of Chicago, because he opposed the granting of franchises to certain public utility corporations, and for criticizing the railroads during the Pullman strike of 1894. In 1896, President E. Benjamin Andrews of Brown University expressed views on the money question then agitating the nation, and was severely criticized. He withdrew as president in 1899. In 1900 Edward A. Ross, professor of sociology, was forced to resign from Leland Stanford University because he had expressed economic opinions not approved of by the widow of Senator Leland Stanford, founder of the University. President David Starr Jordan found himself in the embarrassing necessity of disciplining Professor Ross, though he denied that economic questions governed the action.[110] In 1911 Professor E. M. Banks was dismissed from the University of Florida for writing an article in *The Indepent* on the Civil War. In the same year, Arthur W. Calhoun, of the department of history and economics, was dismissed from the Florida State College for his views on Socialism. (See *The Independent*, August, 1911.) In 1915 Professor Calhoun was dismissed from Maryville College, Kentucky, and in 1918, he was refused reappointment at Clark University because he had refused to sign an enforced loyalty pledge. In 1912-1913, Dr. John M. Mecklin resigned from the Department of Philosophy in Lafayette College under pressure for a failure in orthodoxy. This case was investigated by joint Committees of the American Philosophical and the American Psychological Societies of which Dr. Mecklin was a member. He was vindicated by the report.[111] This same year Willard C. Fisher was suspended from Wesleyan College, Connecticut, ostensibly for a humorous remark in an address suggesting that the churches be closed for a while so that people might find out their usefulness to religion. The deeper animus was probably against Professor Fisher's activities in public affairs. In 1914, Dr. Scott Nearing, instructor in economics in the Wharton School of Finance at the University of Pennsylvania, was denied promotion on account of his statistical enquiries into local and state corporate and public service enterprises. Dr. Clyde King was also disciplined by

Pennsylvania.[112]   About the same time, Dr. Joseph K. Hart, sociologist, was forced out of the University of Washington because the authorities believed his extension lectures implied an interest in politics.

In 1914 as a result of the lengthening list of teachers who had been disciplined for their opinions, and as a result of the joint action of the American Political Science Society, the Sociological Society, and the Economics Association in investigating the case of Professor Willard Fisher, and because of similar action in other cases by the Philosophical and Psychological Societies, there was organized the American Association of University Professors.   Its chief function has been to define and protect by investigation and report the rights of teachers in our institutions.   The formation of such a union was one of many signs in the United States just prior to 1917 of a wide-spread feeling that we were enjoying much less liberty than our traditions were supposed to guarantee. The reader is invited to study the authoritative reports of this Association for evidence as to the suppression of academic freedom.   Less authoritative, but not less informative, is *The Goose Step* by Upton Sinclair.

These cases reveal no denial of any constitutional right. The courts can rarely be invoked even on the contractual questions involved since the status of the professional contract assumed in most cases permits easy and swift severance of relations.   The offending teacher is simply disposed of; rarely, by immediate and conclusive action after the offense, but generally by indirect and dilatory action in order to prevent any clear issue of academic freedom.   Publicity is avoided by granting the teacher a year's leave without pay, during which time he is supposed to resign; or pressure is brought to make him resign at the term end.   The economic weapon is usually the simplest— simply failure to advance the salary or rank of an offender, or simply failure to reappoint him.   In most cases there is a combination of economic and social pressure to prevent the exercise of a special gift for making a living in a profession of limited opportunities, and to injure his professional reputation and prestige. The worst danger here as elsewhere is intimidation. Fear keeps many teachers, none too bold at best, from voicing what they know to be true about the society that surrounds them, or the history they are supposed to interpret. Most of them are not fighters. They are experts on information, with a desire to be let alone in their work. So when their opinions are disapproved, their position and experience are not such as can resist intimidation. The young scholar learns early he can succeed best by silence. There is little academic freedom in the sense of the right to teach without institutional coercion or censorship of personal faiths.

In religion and in pure science freedom of belief has been won. Teachers can hold any faith or none, and adopt what physics and cosmology they wish though it is wise not to announce one's atheism from the roofs. The schools are at least neutral. But in other fields there is little freedom enough,—for teaching new economic or social philosophies, for discussion of sex, for disseminating what may be called internationalized history, or for radical ideas of anarchism or spiritism. The recent legislation against teaching the doctrine of evolution does not fall within our period.

In one department of science, medicine, there has been a constant struggle against both religious and social pressure. Even in 1727 in Boston, we were having a dispute about inoculation which still flourishes in the anti-vaccinationist. The issue as to who is to have control over a man's body, himself or society, is very confusing. But generally it is being decided in favor of society, which protects itself against the danger to public health arising from a failure to conform. The right to resist state vaccination is not held as a civil liberty. Even such a personal matter as the prevention of conception is held to be within the police power of the state. The opponents of dissection, of vivisection, or of cremation get no sympathy —these things serve the state. Yet there are methods of social amelioration against which instinct and prejudice draws a line, e. g., the sterilization of the human unfit. As to euthanasia witness the outburst against Dr. Osler's jocular proposal for killing off persons of a certain age, and the storm over a Chicago doctor's refusal to operate to save the life of a hopelessly crippled infant.   In practical medicine, there have been continued efforts to prevent treatment by Christian Science, faith healing, spiritism, etc.   These fall more directly into questions of religious freedom.[113]

The most serious danger to liberty is in the modern conception of public education.   Here we are having compulsory education by the state in the ideas the state prescribes.   These ideas are composed of the demand of the popular mind, plus the interjected ideas of economic powers, who through many processes exercise a considerable influence on education.   Education is censored by the press and the electorate with the design of standardizing the commonplace, and leaving no room for the radical, the experimenter, or the creator.

The public school and compulsory education can be made the foundation of a servile state.   Both teachers and students will learn the traditional history, support the established government, conform to all the conventions, until the schools become machines for the production of conventional patriots with no ideals of liberty and no desire for it.

The control is exercised through public or private boards acting on teaching and teachers.   The content and method of teaching are prescribed with certain factors such as flag saluting and sometimes religious observances.   But the latter has been largely eliminated, through judicial decision.   The question of saluting the American flag has arisen in case of Socialists who did not want their children taught nationalistic patriotism.   The use of a prescribed language makes for more perfect conformity.   Alien groups have tried to preserve the rights to their own tongues, but almost universally without success.

Of course children can attend private schools.   But the state through its superior power is rapidly extending its monopoly of all primary and secondary education.   Moreover there is an increasing tendency to punish those who teach doctrines disapproved by the established government. The school that advocated a radical change in such a form and openly announced that it had taught children this creed would find itself sooner or later prosecuted for sedition, anarchy, or immorality. Moreover, the source of all teachers, private as well as public has come under control. The university does not produce the radical teacher.

CHAPTER VIII

THE DEFENSE OF LIBERTY

THE LIBERTARIANS

CERTAIN aspects of civil liberty in the decade before 1917 are worth noting in conclusion. These include: First, the efforts of certain unpopular minorities struggling for liberty to limit the liberty of other minorities; second, the increased interest in the whole problem of civil liberty; third, the rise of individual libertarians and of organizations devoted to the protection of liberty within the State.

Before 1917 and the common need for many minority groups to resist the war discipline, there was a surprising lack of solidarity among the minority groups themselves. Instead of uniting to defend the principle of liberty, certain elements attacked one another or worked so independently that they gave but little mutual aid. There was small recognition of the need of freedom of thought for everybody. The doctrinaires fought among themselves instead of against common oppression. This was particularly true of the Socialists who sought to prevent the Anarchists from hatching eggs in their nest. For example:

On the occasion of the recent Haywood meeting at the Grand Central Palace (New York City), some members of the Socialist arrangement committee attempted to prevent our comrades from distributing the leaflet, "To the Unemployed and Homeless," issued by the Anarchist Federation. When persuasions and threats proved futile, the Socialists called the police, insisting especially on the arrest of a young woman who was very active in distributing the leaflets. The police did not appear anxious to

325

make the arrests, but when the Socialists insisted, finally the hand of the law forced some of our comrades to leave the hall. This is not a solitary example. Such incidents have been but too frequent.[1]

On the occasion of the May Day celebration this year at Union Square (New York City), the secretary of the Socialist party happened to discover a wagon from which members of the I. W. W. were addressing the audience. He forthwith called in the police to keep the I. W. W. from speaking in the Square.[2]

The Socialists are declared by the Anarchists to have asked the Washington, D. C., police to stop Emma Goldman from speaking. The lack of solidarity extended even to their own members. Theodore Schroeder declares that when a Colorado Socialist was arrested on an alleged charge of obscenity, but in reality for organizing, Socialists generally refused to help fight the charge as it would prove embarrassing. A Pittsburgh Socialist local refused to hear a syndicalist lecturer, and many of the more liberal members resigned as a protest. We may go outside our time-period to record another instance. At the Socialist national convention in Chicago after the World War, the ruling faction had a minority of radical "left-wingers" excluded by the "capitalistic police." Max Eastman, editor of the radical periodical, *The Liberator* wrote: "Barney Berlin, for twenty-five years a worker in the Socialist movement, presented what seems to me the only justification for the Executive Committee that there is. He reminded the convention of historical instances in which legal and constitutional forms and formulas have been violated in the interest of a deeper principle. . . . "I glory in their spunk in having saved the party. . . . Necessity knows no law! . . . is a maxim that lives in the heart of every live man."

Victor Berger, once Mayor of Milwaukee, added a comment of suggestive character: "We in Milwaukee would have done it a good deal better than Germer did, *because we have our own police.*"

The thesis of power remains the same; the Socialist will use it to stop the liberty of others. It is very discouraging to the libertarian to discover that men who had personally just been defending their very lives from governmental prosecution would use for justification of their own oppressive acts the ancient excuse that "necessity knows no law."

But such evidences of oppressive instincts among common claimants of civil liberty are sporadic. The true note of the period is an increased interest in and a vigorous defense of civil liberty. There has been a growing sense that we had too complacently accepted liberty as an inheritance, won by our forefathers, and somehow mysteriously embodied in the parchment of constitutions. This new interest in civil liberty arose partly out of a new realization of its essential value in our complex industrial age; partly out of the common experiences of the social reformers; partly because of the increased number of cases in which liberty was sacrificed to the interests of powerful conservative groups. Something had to be done to resist stifling encroachments and to extend the bounds of liberty for new classes and purposes.

Signs of this restless feeling have been the renewed attention paid to civil liberty by lawyers and their journals, the inclusion of new guarantees in State constitutions (*vide* Oklahoma's 1908), the organization of the Free Speech League and similar local organizations in California and elsewhere; the activities of various defense leagues of Socialists, I. W. W.'s and other labor bodies; the devotion of an entire annual meeting of the American Sociological Society to the problem of "Freedom of Discussion," the formation of the American Association of University Professors for the investigation of academic freedom, university control, et cetera; and finally, the scrutiny of the facts about freedom of speech and assemblage by the Federal Industrial Relations Commission of 1915. The last named body put a point to the whole uneasy feeling by the following recommendation:

With full recognition of the gravity of the suggestion, it seems necessary to urge the Commission to make the following recommendations:

I. That Congress forthwith initiate an amendment to
the Constitution providing in specific terms for the protection of the personal rights of every person in the
United States from encroachment by the Federal and State
governments, and by private individuals, associations, and
corporations. The principal rights which should be thus
specifically protected by the powers of the federal government are the privilege of the writ of habeas corpus,
the right to trial by jury, to free speech, to peaceable
assembly, to keep and bear arms, to be free from unreasonable searches and seizures, to speedy public trial, to
freedom from excessive bail, and cruel and unusual punishments.[8]

Here is a pathetic faith in the paper guarantees,—to re-
assert rights that had already been guaranteed in the Bill of
Rights and by the Fourteenth Amendment. The amendment
really needed was in the spirit of the people.

The third sign of the times was the appearance of pure
libertarians—men and women who defended the principles of
liberty for use by all people, yet without any special axe to
grind themselves. These are rare folks even among the social
reformers, who on the whole think they have the right pre-
scription for society and who hate therefore to see their plans
upset by misguided persons with other plans. They are as sure
of their social panaceas as was the Church in the Middle Ages.
The minority which comes into power persecutes for its faith's
sake as once it died for it . . . indeed the fact that some died
for it proves it true, they figure.

The organizations which have represented the libertarian
view have been the Free Speech League; the Legal First Aid
Society, and the American Civil Liberties Union (formerly
the National Civil Liberties Bureau). The first was a pioneer
in fighting cases from 1905 to 1915 and insisting upon the
value to society of freedom of speech and press. It was,
however, largely made up of philosophical anarchists and
interested itself chiefly in freedom of expression for anarchistic and sex ideas. Its publications and protests aroused

a new interest in liberty, and the organization served as a rallying center. It has now ceased to function.

The two other societies grew out of the needs of the World War, and are beyond our scope. The legal aid group was especially for the help of conscientious objectors in the eastern states during the war period. The American Civil Liberties Union is the first nation-wide organization to enlist the general public in the common cause of protecting all liberties. The Union has done heroic work, both during the War and since. It is made up of Quakers, labor leaders, radicals, liberals and even some conservatives. It functions best in the interest of labor and where economic issues furnish the bases of a struggle. It offers to any person or any group whose liberties have been restricted, an agency of information, and legal advice and financial aid. It is interested in general liberty as opposed to that of liberty for any particular group. This is an encouraging sign that some day men will realize the inward significance of the struggle for social freedom in a democracy.

Men must learn that liberty can be won only through action —and when won it must be shared. They must realize that restraint on any minority, no matter how obnoxious, injures everyone as it establishes a principle which may in time be used against those now in power. Some day men will realize that it is not a mere phrase—that highest ideal of liberty— to be willing to die that other men may have the right to teach what you believe to be false and dangerous.

REFERENCE NOTES

NOTES TO CHAPTER I

1 (Page 2). C. A. Duniway, *Freedom of the Press in Massachusetts,* p. 131.

2 (Page 2). W. G. Sumner, *Alexander Hamilton,* quoted in J. E. Cutler, *Lynch Law,* pp. 59, 61, 71 ff. The violence is also treated in A. P. Peabody, "Boston Mobs Before the Revolution," *Atlantic Monthly,* September, 1888; A. M. Simons, *Social Forces in American History,* p. 12, and bibliography; and John Fiske, *Critical Period of American History.* It is fair to American liberty ideals to add that some of the resistance at Boston was due to a fear that religious liberty might be curtailed "by an evident design of the English ministry to send a bishop to America." See C. H. Van Tyne, *Loyalists in the American Revolution,* p. 109.

3 (Page 7). Lorenzo Sabine, *Loyalists of the American Revolution,* Introduction and chap. ix, pp. 75-83; Egerton Ryerson, *Loyalists of America,* chap. xxxiv, with abstracts of the proscription laws; Justin Winsor, *Narrative History of America,* Vol. VII, article by the Rev. G. E. Ellis, and bibliography; A. C. Flick, *Loyalism in New York;* J. B. McMaster, *History of the United States,* I, 106-128; James H. Stark, *Loyalists of Massachusetts,* pp. 54, 55.

4 (Page 8). Van Tyne, *Loyalists,* pp. 207-215; Isaac Sharpless, *Quakers in the Revolution,* chap. viii, pp. 172 ff. on "Quaker Sufferings."

5 (Page 10). Most of these disloyalty charges must have been largely groundless for when Howe's British army in turn passed through this same region, it seized provisions and supplies from the Quaker farms and subjected the owners to indignities. Sharpless estimates the position of the Friends thus: "There were a few radical Tories; a much larger number of radical friends of the Revolution; the rest were quiet sympathizers with the Revolution." The persecutions here and in the Southern States were the first cause of the emigration of Friends to Ohio and Indiana. Later, the blight of slavery in the South accelerated this by thousands. The chief treason of the Quakers was that they were well off. Washington expressed this practical view: "They are a harmlesss, peaceable and industrious people who will produce meat and bread, and if they will not sell it to us, we can take it as we need it." For a story of the Virginia case see Thomas Gilpin, *Exiles in Virginia.*

6 (Page 10). For similar reasons Shay's Rebellion (1787-1788) is not studied here. The status of a rebel is not one on which to rest evidence of lost liberty; moreover, both factions were guilty. The privilege of the writ of habeas corpus was suspended, freedom of the press restricted, private persons deported, and liberty generally depended on who had the power. See Minot, *Shay's Rebellion,* pp. 24, 36, 51, and elsewhere.

7 (Page 11). Richard Hildreth, *History of the United States,* IV, 30.

8 (Page 13). Marshall speaks of "general principles which are common to our free institutions, having force superior to legislation." 6 Cranch 87. Kent declares "the right of self-defense in these cases is founded on the

Law of Nature, and is not and cannot be superseded by the laws of society." *Commentaries,* II, 16. See Roscoe Pound, "Scope and Purpose of Sociological Jurisprudence," *Harvard Law Review,* XXIV, and XXV, p. 593 ff. from which the above ideas are condensed; also, C. J. Tiedeman, *Limitations on the Police Power;* and Hughes, *Datum Posts of Jurisprudence.* Pound declares: "Few juristic theories have been more barren than the 18th Century natural law of American judges in the 19th Century." *Op. cit.,* p. 611.

9 (Page 14). "The potency of the common law was that it was viewed as a kind of practical offspring of the unwritten 'law of nature' and as of the most popular character." Dean Pound denies this. "We formerly held the Common Law superior to legislation because it was customary and rested on the consent of the governed. To-day we recognize that the so-called custom is a custom of judicial decision, not a custom of popular action."

10 (Page 15). Thomas Wharton, *State Trials of the United States,* p. 196. The principle of common law jurisdiction was finally denied in 1812. See page 34 of text.

11 (Page 16). John R. Commons and others, *History of Labor in the United States,* I, chap. v, and p. 504; McMaster, *History,* III, 153, 512; C. A. Beard, *Economic Interpretation of the Constitution.* For the legal facts see Reeves, *History of English Law,* II, 390; Commons and Andrews, *Principles of Labor Legislation,* chap. iii, and pp. 91-106, with bibliography; E. Freund, *Police Power,* sections 325, 331; Stephens, *History of the Common Law,* III, 203; Carson, *Criminal Conspiracies,* p. 150.

12 (Page 18). John R. Commons, *Documentary History of American Industrial Society,* III, 383, 385.

13 (Page 18). Thatcher, *Criminal Cases,* p. 609; Metcalf, *Reports,* IV, chap. iii; *American Decisions,* XXXVIII, 346. See also People *v.* Fisher, *American Decisions,* XXVIII, 501; Commons, *History of Labour,* I, 504; *Documentary History,* IV, 162, 261; Robert Hoxie, *History of Unions,* p. 88 ff.

14 (Page 19). Stephens, *Digest of Criminal Law* (6th ed.) sections 96, 97, 98. He also declares seditious libel to be: "The intentional publication, without lawful excuse or justification, of written blame of any public man, or of the law, or of any institution established by the law." *History of the Criminal Law,* II, 353.

15 (Page 19). Zechariah Chafee, Jr., "Freedom of Speech in War Time," *Harvard Law Review,* XXXII, Number 8, p. 946 (later enlarged in the book, *Freedom of Speech*), is a brilliant analysis of this field. See also J. M. Schofield, "Freedom of the Press," in *Proceedings of the American Sociological Society,* IX, 70, 78 ff., and Patterson, *Liberty of the Press,* p. 82.

16 (Page 20). The beginning of an attempt to extend the test from "no censorship" to a discrimination between "liberty" and "license" failed. "The effectual freedom of the press must continue to depend upon the liberality of officers of the government and the independence of juries, or in the last analysis on the support of public opinion." C. A. Duniway, *Freedom of the Press in Massachusetts,* p. 141.

17 (Page 21). Hannis Taylor, *Origins of the Constitution,* p. 305.

18 (Page 22). T. W. Wilson, *History of the American People,* III, 153.

19 (Page 25). *Report of the American Historical Association* (1912), pp. 115-126.

20 (Page 26). For details of the various cases see McLaughlin, *Life of Lyon;* Hildreth, *History,* II, 248 and 367; F. T. Hill, *Decisive Battles of*

the Law, pp. 1-27; Francis Wharton, *State Trials of the United States,* pp. 333 (on Lyon), 659 (on Cooper), 684 (on Haswell), 688 (on Callender), 323 (general facts), 322 other libel trials, including Cobbett's and Judge McKenna's definition of libel (1797). See Federal cases, 8,646, 14,704, 14,865, 15,834. Hildreth, *History,* IV, 298; V, 247,365. For the Impeachment of Judge Chase, see *Annals of Congress,* 8th congress, 2d session: 195, 201 ff. and p. 2,093 for abstract of the first Senate bill. *Annals of Congress,* year 1811, 1st session contains results of an investigation into the matters here noted. Joseph Story, *Commentaries,* III, 164-167, and section 158, note, contains interesting views.

21 (Page 28). See also letter to Mason, Oct. 11, 1798; *Correspondence,* III, 402; Randall, *Life of Jefferson,* II, 417. Cf. Jefferson's denial of the right of Federal grand jury to discipline free correspondence between citizens in 1797, Hildreth, *History,* II, 160.

22 (Page 29). *American State Papers,* Miscellaneous, I, 181.

23 (Page 29). Hildreth, *History,* V, 297, 350.

24 (Page 30). *Kentucky Resolutions,* sections 3 and 6.

25 (Page 31). St. George Tucker, *Blackstone's Commentaries,* I, part 2, appendix G, on "The Right of Conscience and Freedom of Speech and of the Press." See also the *Report to the Virginia House of Delegates,* January 11, 1800.

26 (Page 31). The French also made use of sedition charges. "The most frequent and most notorious use of the Bastile was to imprison those writers who attacked the government or persons in power. It was this which made it so hated as an emblem of despotism and caused its capture and demolition at the time of the Revolution." Encyclopedia Brittanica (11th ed.) article on "Bastille." We may be thankful that we have never imported that further doctrine of the English law which forbade reflections upon any sovereign! "To publish injurious charges against a foreign prince or ruler was also held punishable as a public offense, because tending to embroil the two nations, and to disturb the peace of the world." Cooley, *Constitutional Limitations,* p. 525; *English State Trials,* XXVII, 627; May, *Constitutional History of England,* II, chap. ix. For discussions of the problem of sedition see, Bikle, "The Jurisdiction of the United States over Seditious Libel," *University of Pennsylvania Law Review,* January, 1902, L, 1-25; Chafee, *Freedom of Speech;* W. S. Schofield, "Freedom of the Press," in *Proceedings of the American Sociological Society,* Vol. IX; article by Alexander Johnston in *Lalor's Encyclopedia,* p. 56; Bishop, *Criminal Law,* Vol. I; I Wheat. 215 and 8 Peters 658.

27 (Page 34). For charge in full see Cooley, pp. 530-531, note.

28 (Page 35). F. J. Stimson, *Federal and State Constitutions.*

29 (Page 37). Stimson, *Federal and State Constitutions,* p. 145, gives the State provisions. The "greater the truth, greater the libel" fallacy endured in England until Lord Campbell's Acts, 1843 (statute 6 and 7 Victoria, chap. xcvi). It will be recalled that the United States Sedition Act of 1798 provided for the truth as a defense, and decision on the libel by the jury. For the Croswell Case, see Johnson's Cases, III, 337, 394, and VII, 264; J. T. Morse, *Life of Hamilton,* II, 324; Hildreth, *History,* II, 592; V, 518. Cf. Woodfall's Case (1770), *State Trials of England,* XX, 870; May, *Constitutional History,* II, 114; Cooley, *Limitations,* p. 569.

30 (Page 37). C. A. Duniway, *Freedom of the Press in Massachusetts,* pp. 159, 160. By 1827 the common law doctrines of libel had not been abrogated, but these had been modified to such a degree that the rights of authors . . . were secured though at the same time they were not released from responsibility for their acts."

31 (Page 38).   Vidal et al. v. Girard, 2 Howard 127.

32 (Page 40).   Updegraph v. the Commonwealth, 11 Seargeant and Rowles, 394. See *Debates of the New York Constitutional Convention of 1821*, p. 463.

33 (Page 41).   Theodore Schroeder, *Constitutional Free Speech Defined*, chap. vii. See also Kneeland, *Review of Trial; Speech in His Own Defense; Review of the Prosecution by a Cosmopolite*; 20 Pickwick 206, and 37 Massachusetts, 206; 151, Mass. Reports 154.

34 (Page 41).   Schroeder, *op. cit.*, p. 162, quoting Dane, *Abridgment of American Law*, VI, 667.   Other cases of similar nature are recorded in Muzzy v. Wilkins (New Hampshire, 1803), I Smith; Hale v. Everett, 53 New Hampshire, 9; State v. Chandler, 2 Harrington 553; Johnson v. Barclay, I Harrington 1; in re Bell, City Hall Records (N. Y.) 38.   See also Booth v. Ryecroft, 3 Wisconsin Reports 183, and Bishop, *Criminal Law*, I, section 497; II, sections 74-81.   The modern case of Moore will be found in Chapter VIII below.   It reversed the Ruggles decision.

35 (Page 43).   This case also opened the question as to when a picture is merely lewd and when a work of art.   See the discussion in Theodore Schroeder's works.

36 (Page 44).   Schofield, *op. cit.*, pp. 78, 114.

37 (Page 44).   Annals of Congress, January 24, 1807; Hildreth, *History*, II, 625; Thomas Benton, *Abridgment of Debates;* 4 Cranch 469; Jefferson, *Works*, V, Letter to Colvin, Sept. 20, 1810.   For other cases defining the jurisdiction of Federal and State courts over the writ, see: ex parte Bollman, 4 Cranch 75; 35 Statutes at Large, chap. 321, 1088; U. S. v. Insurgents, 2 Dallas 335; Hepburn v. Ellzey, 2 Cranch 445; ex parte Kearney, 7 Wharton 38; ex parte Tobias Watkins, 3 Peters 192; ex parte Dorr, 3 Howard 103.

38 (Page 48).   For main facts see Parton, *Life of Andrew Jackson*, II, chap. xxiii.   Also John Slidell (representative from Louisiana) in address to the House, December 29, 1843, on the bill to refund the fine.

NOTES TO CHAPTER II

1 (Page 50).   J. B. McMaster, *The Acquisition of the Rights of Man in America*, p. 32.   This valuable effort to overthrow the popular fallacy that absolute equality existed in American States, immediately after July 4, 1776, has strangely been limited to five hundred privately printed copies.   For the Personal Liberty Acts see A. B. Hart, *History by Contemporaries*, IV, 88, 89, 93; and J. C. Hurd, *The Law of Freedom and Bondage*.

2 (Page 51).   H. H. Bancroft, *Popular Tribunals*, Vols. XXXVII and XXXVIII, of his *Works*, and Cutler, *Lynch Law*, will give the student of extra-legal popular justice, the genesis, methods, and history of these movements.

3. (Page 52).   Sharpless, *History of Quakers in Pennsylvania*, II, chap. iii.   Cutler, *Lynch Law*, also records an attack on a small-pox hospital.

4 (Page 53).   *Niles' Weekly Register*, II, 373, 405, "Report of the Committee of the Council and Ten Citizens."

5 (Page 54).   Hildreth, *History of the United States*, V, 327.

6 (Page 54).   *Niles' Weekly Register*, III, 96, 112, 176.

7 (Page 54).   For other details see *The Aurora* (Philadelphia), August 11, giving the testimony before the Mayor's committee; *True American*, August 18-19; *Annals of Congress*, Vol. III, Papers Relative to the Recent Riots at Baltimore; John T. Morse, *Memoir of Henry Lee*; J. B. McMaster, *History of the United States*, III, 548.

8 (Page 55).   J. R. Crandall, *The Morgan Episode*; J. B. Hammond, *History of Political Parties in New York*, II, 237-239, and chap. xxxviii;

Alfred Creigh, *Masonry and Anti-Masonry in Pennsylvania since 1792;* McMaster, *History,* V, 108-120; Alexander Johnston, "Anti-Masonry" in *Lalor's Encyclopedia.*

9 (Page 56). Henri Brown, *Narrative of the Anti-Masonic Excitement,* records most of the above incidents.

10 (Page 56). Stimson, *Constitutions;* and McMaster, *Acquisition of Rights,* pp. 86-87.

11 (Page 56). Two evangels of the Perfectionists were ridden on rails by the people of Colerain, Massachusetts, for liberties with their female disciples in 1835. See *Niles' Weekly Register,* December 5. Note also McMaster, *Acquisition of Rights,* pp. 90, 96.

12 (Page 58). Justin Winsor, *Memorial History of Boston,* III, 521.

13 (Page 59). Public opinion finally forced the passage, March 16, 1839, by the Massachusetts legislature, of an act making the community responsible for damages suffered under such circumstances. Since the measure was not retroactive, the Ursulines got no damages. It may be noted that laws similar to the above now exist on other statute books, and some State Constitutions even provided for the responsibility of counties and sheriffs for lynchings. But such laws are apparently honored only in the breach, and it can be safely said that never at any time anywhere in the United States has there been a real effort to punish the perpetrators of such mob violence, or to provide damages to the victims for the arson and theft which go with violence. The popular mob has too much political power!

14 (Page 60). H. J. Desmond, *The Know-Nothing Party,* p. 130.

15 (Page 61). Such instinctive hooliganism is quite different from such an incident as the "Hannah Corcoran riot" in Boston in 1853, so-called from the conventional rumors that the girl had disappeared through Catholic machinations. The Reverend Thomas F. Caldicott, of the First Baptist Church, prayed and preached to arouse the feelings of his auditors. Finally hand-bills were distributed inviting the "Friends of Liberty" to assemble in front of the Catholic Church on Richmond street. But the Mayor got out the forces, read the riot act, and finally dispersed the mob. Here rowdyism is also better than the cold-blooded refusal to let a priest visit Catholic immigrants stricken with ship-fever, and detained on Deer Island and in the Poor House.

16 (Page 61). Dubose, *Life of Yancey,* p. 291.

17 (Page 61). N. S. Shaler, *History of Kentucky,* p. 219. Most of the above facts on these events were taken from that interesting book, *The Know-Nothing Party,* by Humphrey Joseph Desmond. The author's name suggests a reason for bias toward the Catholic Irish, but the facts seem honestly recorded.

18 (Page 61). George W. Julian, *Political Recollections,* p. 142.

19 (Page 62). L. F. Schmeckbier, *History of the Know-Nothing Party in Maryland,* p. 39.

20 (Page 62). *Ibid.,* p. 102.

21 (Page 62). *Ibid.,* pp. 74-87.

22 (Page 62). Hinton R. Helper's economic analysis of the effects of slavery on labor in the South, written by a Carolinian, was violently hated by the Democrats for its arguments in favor of abolition. See Schmeckbier, *op. cit.,* p. 105.

23 (Page 63). Von Holst, *Constitutional History of the United States,* V, 188.

24 (Page 63). *The Baltimore Sun,* April 22, 1861, cited by Schmeckbier, p. 53.

25 (Page 64). Donahue *v.* Richards, 38 Maine Reports 376 (52 Am. State Reports 444).

26 (Page 64). Schmeckbier, *op. cit.*

27 (Page 64). Desmond, *op. cit.,* pp. 39-40.

28 (Page 65). See *infra,* chapter VII.

29 (Page 66). Joseph Smith, *History of the Church of Jesus Christ of the Latter Day Saints,* I, 242.

30 (Page 67). W. A. Linn, *Story of the Mormons,* p. 134.

31 (Page 68). Smith, *History of the Church,* I, 312.

32 (Page 68). Smith, *op. cit.,* pp. 312, 327.

33 (Page 69). Smith, *op. cit.,* I, 334.

34 (Page 71). Smith, *History of the Church,* II, chaps. iii, xi, xii, xiv-xvi; Linn, *Story of the Mormons,* chaps. v, vi, vii, ix; J. P. Greene, *Facts Relating to the Mormon Expulsion from Missouri,* Cincinnati, 1839; Missouri General Assembly, *Documents in Connection with the Mormon Disturbances;* McMaster, *History,* VI, 249, 454-458.

35 (Page 72). *St. Louis Globe-Democrat,* October 6, 1887. See also Smith, *History,* II, chap. xiii. About forty Mormons were killed in the campaign, but only one citizen, with fifteen badly wounded. General Clark addressed the Mormons thus: "If I am called here again, you need not expect mercy, but extermination, for I am determined the Governor's order shall be executed. . . . And, O, if I could invoke the great spirit, the unknown God to deliver you from those fetters of fanaticism with which you are bound. I would advise you to scatter abroad, lest you excite the jealousies of the people, and subject yourselves to the same calamities." The "jealousies of the people" is an accurate word for the cause.

36 (Page 73). Brigham Roberts, *Rise and Fall of Nauvoo,* p. 248.

37 (Page 75). *The Philadelphia National Gazette,* quoted in the *Free Enquirer,* September 23, 1829.

38 (Page 75). *Mechanics Free Press* (Philadelphia).

39 (Page 75). *The Liberator* (1834), p. 195. For violence in labor and political disputes see McMaster, *History,* VI, 86, 96, 224-7, 367, and *Acquisition of Rights,* pp. 54-60; Commons, *History of Labor,* I, 390, 415-418.

40 (Page 75). The luxuriant labor press—75 to 100 publications were started, including two dailies—seems to have suffered no interference, nor were the labor parties oppressed in any way. The Loco-foco riots in New York City (1835 and 1837) were just examples of the general inter-party courtesies which characterized the period.

41 (Page 76). It is interesting to note a similar freedom in England where Knowlton's book was reprinted, and for forty years ran through several editions. But in the seventies, there as here, a spirit of moral censorship arose. In 1876 Charles Watts had to plead guilty and withdraw the book; and when in 1877, Annie Besant and Charles Bradlaugh republished the volume they suffered prosecution on moral grounds by the Crown.

42 (Page 77). *New York Courier and Enquirer,* March 15, 1834.

43 (Page 79). William Goodell, *The Rights and Wrongs of Rhode Island,* p. 13.

44 (Page 80). Section 1 of the law provided that those who served as moderators or clerks of illegal town meetings and elections should be fined a thousand dollars and imprisoned six months; Section 2, that any person signifying that he would accept any executive, legislative, judicial, or ministerial office through such pretended elections, or becoming a candidate therefore would be adjudged guilty of a high crime and misdemeanor.

45 (Page 81). Goodell, *op. cit.*, pp. 27, 38, *et seq.*

46 (Page 81). A. M. Mowry, *The Dorr War*, p. 227, says: "The Charter government is censurable, not only for the exceedingly large number of arrests, but for the indiscriminate character, the methods of making them, and the treatment of the prisoners."

47 (Page 81). Mowry, *op. cit.*, pp. 227, 229.

48 (Page 82). A Rhode Islander, *Might and Right*, pp. 305, 310.

49 (Page 82). Goodell, *op. cit.*, pp. 76, 79.

50 (Page 83). Letter of April 11.

51 (Page 83). See 3 Howard's Reports.

NOTES TO CHAPTER III

1 (Page 85). Alice D. Adams, *The Neglected Period of Anti-Slavery.*

2 (Page 85). William Birney, *Life of James G. Birney*, p. 228.

3 (Page 86). *American Commonwealth*, I, 393.

4 (Page 86). Harriet Martineau, *The Martyr Age in the United States*, p. 11.

5 (Page 87). See Cutler, *op. cit.*, pp. 92-102 for account of hanging of twenty-six men for alleged gambling in Mississippi; *Liberator*, I, 180, and IV, 153, 168.

6 (Page 88). Harriet Martineau, *The Martyr Age of the United States*, p. 17. See the *Liberator*, V, 156, for Dresser's statement, and a full list of the trial committee. Oliver Johnson, *Garrison and His Times*, XI, XII, XIII, 180-220.

7 (Page 88). Cutler, *Lynch Law*, p. 102.

8 (Page 88). Oliver Johnson, *Garrison and His Times.*

9 (Page 89). Henry Wilson, *Rise and Fall of the Slave Power*, II, 667.

10 (Page 89). Adams, *Neglected Period of Anti-Slavery*, p. 112.

11 (Page 89). Adams, *op. cit.*, pp. 23, 60; Goodell, *Slavery and Anti-Slavery*, p. 434.

12 (Page 89). E. Von Holst, *Constitutional History*, III, 121, discusses the State laws on matter exciting the slaves.

13 (Page 89). Virginia Code (1849), chap. cxc., 8, section 22.

14 (Page 90). Oliver Johnson, *Garrison and His Times*, p. 217.

15 (Page 90). Johnson, *op. cit.*, p. 179.

16 (Page 91). Compare with the later successful use of extradition to bring labor leaders from one State to another for trial for their opinions. See chap. vii below.

17 (Page 91). Bowen, *Arthur Tappan*, p. 13.

18 (Page 91). E. Von Holst, *Constitutional History*, III, 110.

19 (Page 92). Von Holst, *Constitutional History*, III, 114.

20 (Page 92). William Goodell, *Slavery and Anti-Slavery*, p. 440.

21 (Page 93). *Life of James G. Birney*, pp. 222-227. The substitution of "money-power" for "slave-power" makes the above description precisely fit certain modern conditions.

22 (Page 93). Von Holst given an interesting reason for the persecutions. "The radical character of abolitionism was in the most flagrant contradiction with the Anglo-Saxon spirit of conservatism. This spirit instinctively recoiled from a creed which rejected on principle any attempt toward the

adoption of a middle course. . . . It felt itself all the more severely wounded when the prophets and judges had to a certain extent divested themselves of their nationality." *Constitutional History*, III, 104.

23 (Page 94). Birney, *op. cit.*, pp. 250-251.

24 (Page 96). *Proceedings of the Anniversary Meeting* (Boston, 1855), Account of the Mob by Garrison. Theodore Lyman, 3rd, *Papers Relating to the Garrison Mob* (Cambridge, 1870), presents the Mayor's defense, pp. 14-24. Wendell Phillips said that Mayor Lyman, in private conference, had urged the Abolitionists to discontinue their meeting, while professing his earnest determination to protect them at any cost. They consented to do nothing to excite the public, but would hold meetings enough to assert their right to meet. Francis Jackson later offered his home to the ladies, for a meeting-place, in a stirring letter: "One house at least shall be consecrated to the preservation of the right to speak. And if, in defense of this sacred privilege which man did not give me, and shall not (if I can help it) take from me, this roof and these walls shall be levelled to the earth—let them fall, if they must. They cannot crumble in a better cause. They will appear of very little value to me after their owner shall have been whipped into silence."

25 (Page 96). C. W. Bowen, *Arthur and Lewis Tappan*, p. 6; Johnson, *Life of Garrison*.

26 (Page 97). Bowen, *op. cit.*, p. 10.

27 (Page 97). F. G. Fontaine, *History of American Abolitionism.*

28 (Page 97). Henry Wilson, *Rise and Fall of the Slave Power*, pp. 279, 557.

29 (Page 98). Samuel J. May, *Recollections*, p. 163.

30 (Page 98). Von Holst, *Constitutional History*, III, 103; *Niles' Register*, XLIX, 146-149.

31 (Page 98). Anthony and Harper, *History of Woman's Suffrage*, I, 285.

32 (Page 98). J. J. Chapman, *William Lloyd Garrison*, p. 199. Wendell Phillips was later invited to speak in Plymouth Church, Brooklyn, with the pastor on the platform to vindicate free speech, and the city authorities protecting the meeting. See Johnson, *Garrison and His Times*, p. 381.

33 (Page 99). *The History of Pennsylvania Hall* by the Managers of the Pennsylvania Association.

34 (Page 100). *History of Pennsylvania Hall.*

35 (Page 100). William Goodell, *Slavery and Anti-Slavery*, p. 436.

36 (Page 101). Johnson, *Garrison and His Times*, pp. 32-38.

37 (Page 101). Birney, *Life of James G. Birney;* see *The Liberator* for other cases.

38 (Page 101). Wilson, *Rise and Fall*, II, 670.

39 (Page 104). James G. Birney, *Narrative of the Late Riotous Proceedings Against the Liberty of the Press.*

40 (Page 105). Cutler, *op. cit.*, p. 109; *Niles' Register*, June 4, 1836, L, 234; *Liberator*, May 14, 1836, VI, 79, 83.

41 (Page 107). A monument has been dedicated to the "martyred" Lovejoy on the site of occurrence.

42 (Page 107). The above facts are mostly condensed from the *Memoir of the Reverend Elijah P. Lovejoy*, by Joseph and Owen Lovejoy, with Introduction by John Quincy Adams.

43 (Page 107). Henry Tanner, *Martyrdom of Lovejoy*, p. 168; Edward Beecher, *Riots at Alton.*

44 (Page 108).   William Goodell, *Slavery and Anti-Slavery*, p. 442; J. C. Lovejoy, *Memoir of the Martyr Torrey.*

45 (Page 108).   Wilson, *Rise and Fall of the Slave Power*, p. 632.

46 (Page 108).   *Ibid.*, p. 633.

47 (Page 109).   *The Charleston Courier*, July 31, 1835.

48 (Page 110).   Birney, *Life of James G. Birney*, p. 189.

49 (Page 110).   *Niles' Register*, Sept. 5, 1835.

50 (Page 111).   Gales, *Register of Debates*, XII, 704, 753.

51 (Page 111).   John C. Calhoun, *Works*, V, 191 ff.; Senate Documents, 118, 24th Congress, second session.

52 (Page 111).   *Register of Debates*, XII, part 2, 1,374, 1,675.

53 (Page 112).   Wilson, *Rise and Fall of the Slave Power*, II, 670; McPherson, *History of the Rebellion*, p. 191.

54 (Page 112).   Edward McPherson, *History of the Rebellion*, p. 192.

55 (Page 113).   C. L. Vallandigham, *Speeches*, p. 225, note.

56 (Page 114).   Von Holst, *Constitutional History*, II, 116, 121-130; *Niles' Register*, XLVIII, 448; Birney, *op. cit.*, p. 192, note.

57 (Page 114).   *Annals of Congress*, Vol. I; Elliot, *Debates*, IV, 407, ff. Hildreth, IV, 177, 386.

58 (Page 115).   Hildreth, *History*, IV, 386; Benton, *Abridgment of Debates*, and *Thirty Years' View*, I, chap. cxxxv, and II, 22, 33, 36, 37; Sharpless, *Quakers in the Revolution*, p. 237; Lalor, *Encyclopedia*, III, 167-173.

59 (Page 115).   *Register of Debates*, XII, 28.   For further details of the gag-rule see *Ibid.*, XIII, 269, 271; Von Holst, *Constitutional History*, II, 235, 251, 272 *et passim;* Benton, *Debates in Congress*, I, 201, 207; XII, 705; XIII, 24, 266, 566, 702; XIV, 289; *Niles' Register*, LXI, 350.   On petition, see Joseph Story, *Commentaries*, II, section 1894.   *Congressional Globe*, 27th Congress, second session, February 5, 1842, pp. 208, 215, and Wilson, *Rise and Fall of the Slave Power.*   For the House Rules see Asher W. Hinds, *Precedents and Rules of the House of Representatives.*

60 (Page 116).   Massachusetts Assembly, 1837, *Senate Document 84;* Von Holst, *op. cit.*, II. 284.

61 (Page 117).   Wilson, *Rise and Fall of the Slave Power*, II, 478-495.

62 (Page 118).   H. V. Ames (editor), *State Documents on Federal Relations*, VI, 54.

63 (Page 118).   Oliver Johnson, *Garrison and His Times*, p. 123.

64 (Page 118).   *The Patriot*, Concord, New Hampshire.

65 (Page 119).   Samuel J. May, *Recollections.*

66 (Page 119).   *The Liberator* (Boston), September 27 and October 11, 1834, gives the arguments on the constitutionality of the "black law."

67 (Page 120).   Johnson, *op. cit.*

68 (Page 120).   Wilson, *Rise and Fall of Slave Power*, II, 667.

69 (Page 120).   Johnson, *Garrison*, p. 142. .

70 (Page 120).   Birney, *Life of James G. Birney*, p. 145.

71 (Page 121).   James Sprunt Historical Publications, X, Number 1, 1910, *Benjamin Sherwood Hedrick.*

72 (Page 122).   Fifty-one of them published a Defence—an admirable statement of the right of student bodies to freedom of research and discussion. It is in the *Liberator*, I, 178, Boston, January 10, 1835.

73 (Page 123). E. Crosby, *Garrison, Non-Resistant,* p. 21.

74 (Page 123). C. W. Bowen, *Arthur Tappan,* p. 13.

75 (Page 123). *The Liberator,* August 15, 1835, p. 3.

76 (Page 123). May, *Recollections,* p. 127.

77 (Page 123). The student may find much data in: Phillips, *The Conquest of Kansas;* Charles Robinson, *The Kansas Conflict;* E. L. Thayer, *The Kansas Crusade;* L. D. Bailey, *Border Ruffians in Kansas;* L. W. Spring, *Kansas, Prelude to War for the Union;* House Reports, 647, 36th Congress, 1st Session, *The Corode Investigation;* W. E. Conelley, *Quantrill and the Border Wars;* W. P. Tomlinson, *Kansas in 1858.*

78 (Page 124). *New York Times,* January 25, March 25, July 10, and August 6, 9, 12, 14, 1862. Phillips declared he would never take the oath of allegiance while the Constitution permitted slavery.

NOTES TO CHAPTER IV

1 (Page 129). Abraham Lincoln, *Works,* II, Letter to Mr. Hodges.

2 (Page 130). It is to be noted that the clause on the writ occurs in the section wherein are enumerated the powers of Congress.

3 (Page 131). For the bitterness of the opposition, especially by the Democrats, see the newspapers, July-December, 1861, and *Debates in Congress and Senate,* December 16, 1861, and April 29, 1862.

4 (Page 131). Lincoln, *Works,* II.

5 (Page 131) McPherson, *History of the Rebellion,* p. 154.

6 (Page 132). Lincoln, *Works.*

7 (Page 133). 12 Statutes at Large, 755, c. 81.

8 (Page 133). Alexander Johnston, in *Lalor's Encyclopedia.*

9 (Page 134). Rhodes, *History,* IV, 230-231, note. He compares this with imprisonments in England during the Napoleonic Wars: "From April to December, 1798 . . .70 or 80 persons had been apprehended, but not brought to trial. . . . In December only a few still remained in prison. From May, 1799, to February, 1800, but three men had been arrested; yet it was a subject of indignant remonstrance by two lords . . . that twenty-nine persons were immured in jail still without being brought to trial."

10 (Page 134). Marshall, *American Bastile,* introduction, p. xxxii.

11 (Page 135). Rhodes, *History,* IV, 234.

12 (Page 135). Bryce, *American Commonwealth,* I, 61.

13 (Page 136). Roger Taney, *Reports,* Ex parte Merryman. See McPherson, *History of the Rebellion,* VIII, 154 for the facts.

14 (Page 136). *Official Records,* series 2, II, 20, "An Opinion on the President's Power of Arrest."

15 (Page 136). See *The Public Record of Horatio Seymour,* pp. 94-100, 121, 254. For Curtin's action see *The Philadelphia Enquirer,* Feb. 13, 1863. The violent pamphlet warfare was led by Horace Binney, Mr. Lincoln's chief apologist. McPherson's History gives the views of Binney and Parsons. See also B. R. Curtis, *Life and Writings,* II, 306; and a volume of pamphlets on both sides in the New York Public Library.

16 (Page 137). *Official Records,* series I, XXIII, part 2.

17 (Page 137). McCabe, *Life of Horatio Seymour,* pp. 135-150 gives the "Albany Resolutions" by the Democratic Party of New York, and Letter to Erastus Corning, *et al.;* Lincoln's Letter of Defense to Erastus Corning,

and the Albany Democrats is in *Works*, II, 360. Raymond, *Lincoln*, p. 378;
Hart, *History by Contemporaries*, IV, 402, and Guide to Readings, sec. 213-
214. Appendix, *Congressional Globe*, 37th Congress, 3rd session, pp. 53-59.
See Vallandigham's Speech in Congress, Jan. 14, 1863.

18 (Page 137). J. F. Rhodes, *History*, IV, 245-252.

19 (Page 138). James L. Vallandigham, *Memoir of C. L. Vallandigham*,
supplement, p. 63.

20 (Page 138). Clement L. Vallandigham, *Speeches*, p. 505.

21 (Page 139). Vallandigham, *op. cit.*, Nicolay and Hay, *Lincoln*, VII,
chap. xii.

22 (Page 139). Lincoln, *Works*, II, 342.

23 (Page 139). I Wallace 243.

24 (Page 140). C. L. Vallandigham, *Speeches*, p. 472.

25 (Page 141). Account reprinted from *The Philadelphia Enquirer*.

26 (Page 143). Ex parte Milligan, 4 Wallace 2. See Marshall, *American
Bastile*, pp. 71-91 for his imprisonment; James A. Garfield, *Works*,
I, 143 for argument to the court; Ben Pittman, *Trials for Treason at
Indianapolis*, story of the trial.

27 (Page 144). Frank Moore, *Rebellion Records*, I, 78, 123, 190: II,
460. See also McPherson, *Political History*; Marshall, *American Bastile*.
The Philadelphia incident is in the *New York Times*, April 16, 1861.

28 (Page 144). See note 27.

29 (Page 144). Moore, *Rebellion Records*, III, 3, quoting the *New Haven
Palladium*.

30 (Page 145). *Ibid.*, p. 4.

31 (Page 145). The New York *Tribune*, August 20, 1861, p. 5.

32 (Page 145). The New York *Tribune*, August 31, 1861.

33 (Page 146). Nicolay and Hay, *Life of Lincoln*, VI, 334; McPherson,
History of the Rebellion, pp. 522, 546; Fleming, *Documentary History of
Reconstruction*, II, 221, *et seq.*

34 (Page 146). *Report of the Judge Advocate General*, April 30, 1864.

35 (Page 147). Lincoln, *Works*, II, 290; Nicolay and Hay, *Life of
Lincoln*, VI, 334.

36 (Page 147). *Orders of the War Department*, November 30, 1863;
Lincoln, *Works*, pp. 480, 481, 491, 521.

37 (Page 149). Marshall, *American Bastile*, p. 119.

38 (Page 149). Moore, *Rebellion Records*, III, 5, prints an account
from the *New Haven Palladium*.

39 (Page 149). Moore, *Rebellion Records*, II, 490, reprint from the
Boston *Journal*.

40 (Page 150). Moore, *Rebellion Records*, II, 531.

41 (Page 150). McPherson, *History of Rebellion*, p. 188.

42 (Page 150). *Official Records*, series 2, II, 936-956.

43 (Page 151). Marshall, *American Bastile*, p. 111.

44 (Page 151). Here he includes the arguments by Amos Kendall, 1835,
and the Attorney-General, 1857, justifying the non-delivery of "incendiary"
Abolitionist mail. See above pp. 109, 112.

45 (Page 152). E. McPherson, *Political History*, p. 189.

46 (Page 153). *Congressional Globe*, 37th Congress, 1st session.

47 (Page 153). Record Book, State Department, reported in *Official Records,* series 2, II, 771.

48 (Page 154). New York *Tribune,* September 4 and 9, 1861.

49 (Page 154). Official Record, *loc. cit.,* pp. 802-804.

50 (Page 155). New York *Tribune,* July 17, 1861.

51 (Page 156). Rhodes, *History,* IV, 253; Horace Greeley, *The American Conflict.*

52 (Page 158). McCabe, *Life of H. Seymour,* pp. 177-178; see also *Public Record of H. Seymour,* pp. 218-220.

53 (Page 158). Fleming, *Documentary History of Reconstruction,* I, 441.

54 (Page 159). *Ibid.,* p. 441.

55 (Page 159). For conscription in the Revolutionary War see chapter I. In 1812 it arose in minor technical questions as to the right of the States to conscript, on the powers of State versus National armies, and respecting the status of members of the militia. See Houston Moore, 5 Wheaton 1; Martin *v.* Mott, 12 Wheaton 19; Luther *v.* Borden, 7 Howard 1.

56 (Page 159). See Knoedler *v.* Lane, 45 Pennsylvania State Reports, 238, for long arguments, and a very full opinion by the judge. For similar decisions upholding the law in the Confederacy see R. P. Brooks, *Conscription in the Southern States,* and cases—34 Georgia 27; 39 Alabama 254; 26 Texas 386.

57 (Page 159). 12 Statutes at Large 731.

58 (Page 160). J. A. Marshall, *The American Bastile,* pp. 303-316 presents one side of these incidents.

59 (Page 160). Fite, *Social Conditions during the Civil War,* p. 189.

60 (Page 160). Herman Schluter, *Lincoln, Labor, and Slavery* (a Socialist interpretation) declares: "The cause of the draft riots in New York was exclusively social. It arose from the fact that the propertied class with all the force of its economic and political prestige, attempted to unload the blood tax . . . from its own shoulders onto those of the working class." Chap. iv, p. 203. For facts on the New York Riots see Col. James B. Fry, *New York and Conscription,* 1863; James D. McCabe, *Life of H. Seymour,* and *Public Record of H. Seymour;* S. F. Headley, *The Great Draft Riots,* p. 149, *et seq.;* A. B. Hart, *History by Contemporaries,* IV, 376; Rhodes, *History,* IV, 321, 328; Nicolay and Hay, *Lincoln,* VII, chaps. i and ii; Anna Dickensen, "The New York Riots," *Harper's Magazine,* January, 1867. *The Congressional Globe,* and New York City newspapers of the period.

61 (Page 161). Fite, *op. cit.,* p. 192.

62 (Page 162). Fernando G. Cartland, *Southern Heroes,* p. 131.

63 (Page 162). 13 Statutes at Large 6.

64 (Page 162). Lincoln, *Works,* II, 243, 573.

65 (Page 163). Other records are: Ethan Foster, *The Conscript Quakers* (privately printed, the Riverside Press, 1883); Allen Thomas, *History of the Quakers.*

66 (Page 164). Cyrus Pringle, *The Record of a Quaker Conscience,* edited by Rufus Jones.

67 (Page 164). Cartland, *op. cit.,* Introduction by Benjamin Trueblood, p. xxvii.

68 (Page 165). Cartland, *Southern Heroes,* pp. 191-193.

69 (Page 165).   Cartland, *op. cit.*, chap. ix, and p. 200.

70 (Page 166).   Cartland, *op. cit.*, chap. ix, and p. 200.

71 (Page 166).   J. R. Commons, *et al.*, *History of Labor in the United States*, II, 23.

72 (Page 167).   Schluter, *Lincoln, Labor, and Slavery*, p. 214.

73 (Page 168).   Schluter, *op. cit.*, p. 216.

NOTES TO CHAPTER V.

1 (Page 170).   S. Humphrey, *The Indian Dispossessed;* Francis E. Leupp, *The Indian and His Problem;* James McLoughlin, *My Friend, the Indian;* Helen Hunt Jackson, *A Century of Dishonor.* The publications of the Indian Rights Association (Philadelphia) contains many facts, especially on the swindling of the Indian out of his property.

2 (Page 170).   *Report of the United States Commission to President Grant,* 1869.

3 (Page 171).   Helen Hunt Jackson, *A Century of Dishonor,* p. 337.

4 (Page 171).   Bishop Whipple, Introduction to *A Century of Dishonor,* p. vi.

5 (Page 171).   *The Present Situation in Indian Affairs,* Indian Rights Association (1912), p. 10.

6 (Page 173).   George W. Williams, *History of the Negro Race in America,* I, 144-170.

7 (Page 173).   J. B. McMaster, *Acquisition of the Rights of Man,* p. 32.

8 (Page 174).   Brawley, *op. cit.*, p. 23. See also Hart, *History by Contemporaries,* III, 600 ff.; IV, 88, 89, 93, on Personal Liberty Acts. Thayer, *Constitutional Cases,* Vol. I, gives cases testing Negro rights. J. C. Hurd, *The Law of Freedom and Bondage,* 2 vols., gives a digest and discussion of laws on race and slave distinctions before 1858.

9 (Page 174).   Von Holst, Constitutional History, II, 96.

10 (Page 175).   Cutler, *Lynch Law,* p. 124. This gives data on negro crimes and illegal punishments in 1830-1850, and 1850-1860. Nat Turner led a plot to murder the white population of Tidewater, Virginia, in 1837, which was disclosed by another negro accomplice, and about 100 negroes slain. See *Niles' Register* XLI, and Message of Governor Floyd, December 6, 1831. Cf. the Vesey Riots, South Carolina, 1822. See also Winfield H. Collins, *The Truth About Lynching in the South,* pp. 21-23.

11 (Page 175).   Gilbert T. Stephenson, *Race Distinctions in American Law,* pp. 7, 8; Thayer, *Constitutional Cases,* I, 473, and chap. iv, 475, 550, etc.

12 (Page 176).   *The Civil Rights Cases,* 109 United States Reports 3.

13 (Page 176).   Hannis Taylor, *Origins of the American Constitution,* chap. ix gives a good discussion of the meaning of these three amendments.

14 (Page 176).   *The Slaughter House Cases,* 16 Wallace 36, 125; and William D. Guthrie, *Lectures on the Fourteenth Amendment,* p. 2.

15 (Page 177).   Guthrie, *op. cit.*

16 (Page 178).   Walter L. Fleming, *Documentary History of Reconstruction,* I, 243. See also pages 273, 341 for specimens of the laws; and G. S. Merriam, *The Negro and the Nation,* chap. xxx for a resumé of the laws; G. T. Stephenson, *Race Distinctions,* for reasons for the enactment of the codes.

17 (Page 179).   John W. Burgess, *Reconstruction and the Constitution.*

18 (Page 179).   Stephenson, *op. cit.*, p. 107, declares the purposes of this

amendment were: (1), to make the Bill of Rights binding on the States; (2), to give validity to the Civil Rights Bill of 1866; (3), to declare who were citizens of the United States. It was successful only in the last aim.

19 (Page 179). Committee of the House of Representatives, 42nd Congress, 2nd session (1871-1872), *Report on the Affairs of the Late Insurrectionary States*, 14 vols. of which several are devoted to the Ku Klux Klan. Other data is in *Documentary History of Reconstruction*, II, chap. xii; Hart, *History by Contemporaries*, IV, 495; Cutler, *Lynch Law*, pp. 138-139, 147, 151. Picturesque accounts are, Lester and Wilson, *Ku Klux Klan*, and J. M. Beard, *K. K. K. Sketches*.

20 (Page 179). Fleming, *op. cit.*

21 (Page 180). General Philip H. Sheridan, *Report of the Military Commander to President Grant*, 1875.

22 (Page 181). Senate Reports, 44th Congress, Executive Document, No. 2, I, 271.

23 (Page 182). *Loc. cit.*, pp. 22, 23.

24 (Page 182). *Congressional Record*, December 18, 1879, X, pt. 1, pp. 155-170 gives evidence of this partisanship.

25 (Page 182). Henry Windom and Henry W. Blair, Senate Reports, No. 693, pts. 2 and 3, 46th Congress, 1st and 2nd sessions (1879-1880). The minority report directly contradicted these conclusions.

26 (Page 183). Cutler, *Lynch Law*, pp. 226, 276. George Holt, "Lynching and Mobs," *American Journal of Social Science*, November, 1894, p. 67; A. E. Pillsbury, "A Federal Remedy for Lynching," *Harvard Law Review*, XV. 707; *Report of the Negro Society*, 1911-1912; *Bill Against Lynching*, Senate Number 1117, 57th Congress, 1st session; House Judiciary Committee of the 65th Congress, 2nd session, *Hearing on a Bill to Protect Citizens Against Lynching*.

27 (Page 184). *Op. cit.*, p. 265; see chap. vii, "*Developments and Excuses for Lynch Law.*"

28 (Page 184). *Thirty Years of Lynching in the United States*, p. 29, published by the National Association for the Advancement of Colored People. Cases of 43 whites and 138 Negroes have been omitted because the data could not be verified. The record of the Chicago *Tribune* covers also: 1885, —78 cases; 1886, —71; 1887, —80; 1888, —95. These two groups added to the list give a grand total of 3,729 cases from 1885 to 1919. This pamphlet includes the date, place, name and alleged crime in its 3,224 cases, and details of 100 typical cases. Cutler's *Lynch Law*, chap. vi, presents similar data; and Winfield H. Collins, *The Truth About Lynching and the Negro in the South*, p. 21 ff., gives facts on lynching before 1860, the small number of cases during the Civil War, and a small record (1866-1868) which does not agree with facts above.

29 (Page 186). *The Crisis*, December, 1911.

30 (Page 186). *The Crisis*, December, 1911.

31 (Page 187). *The St. Louis Post-Dispatch*, special correspondence.

32 (Page 188). *The Crisis*, September, 1918, p. 222, *The Work of a Mob*, report of the Association for the Advancement of Colored People.

33 (Page 188). Cutler, *Lynch Law*.

34 (Page 188). *The Crisis*, August, 1911.

35 (Page 189). *Thirty Years of Lynching*, condensing North Carolina newspapers.

36 (Page 189). Martha Gruening and W. E. B. DuBois, *The Massacre*

of East St. Louis, p. 1. United States Congress, *Report of the Rules Committee on the Riot at East St. Louis.*

37 (Page 190). Ray Stannard Baker, *Following the Colour Line,* p. 15.

38 (Page 191). Laws of Georgia, 1905, p. 166. Stephenson, *Race Distinctions,* pp. 144, 145.

39 (Page 192). *The Crisis,* January, 1918, pp. 6, 7.

40 (Page 192). *The News and Observer,* Raleigh, N. C., August 19, 1906.

41 (Page 192). **Baker,** *op. cit.,* p. 126.

42 (Page 192). *Ibid.,* p. 152.

43 (Page 193). **Baker,** *op. cit.,* pp. 79-80; A. J. Stone, *Studies of the American Negro;* Booker T. Washington, *Up from Slavery,* and *The Story of the Negro.*

44 (Page 193). Cutler, *Lynch Law,* p. 229.

45 (Page 194). Baker, *op. cit.,* p. 160.

46 (Page 194). Baker, *op. cit., p.* 257.

47 (Page 195). New York *Tribune,* August 23, 1919.

48 (Page 196). Article I, section 8, clause 4; article II, section 11.

49 (Page 196). E. A. Ross, *Social Control.*

50 (Page 197). *House Executive Documents,* No. 2, p. 113. 32nd Congress, 1st session; and Resolution of Congress, March 3, 1853.

51 (Page 197). *Foreign Relations,* 1891, pp. 665, 713. See also Henry Cabot Lodge,, "Lynch Law and Restricted Immigration," *North American Review,* 1891, p. 602; E. W. Haffcutt, "International Liability for Mob Injuries," *Annals of the American Academy of Political Science,* II, 69. A list of such cases is in John Bassett Moore, *Digest of International Law,* VI, 812, 840, 843, and 848. See *Foreign Relations,* XXII (1899) for President McKinley's statement in his annual message, December 5, 1899.

52 (Page 197). The details and an account of this problem are given in Charles R. Watson, "Need of Federal Legislation in Cases of Lynching," *Yale Law Journal,* XXV, 573. Page 576 gives other cases of Italians.

53 (Page 197). *Thirty Years of Lynching* gives an idea of the record. See also Executive Reports, December 19, 1906, Anti-Spanish Riots by Secretary Metcalfe.

54 (Page 198). Mary R. Coolidge, *Chinese Immigration,* is the most valuable book of facts. See also *Report to the Legislature of California,* app. 3 (1862, 2nd session); Hittell, *History of California,* Vol. III; H. H. Bancroft, *Works,* Vol. XXXVII.

55 (Page 198). Prescott F. Hall, *Immigration,* pp. 207-208; Lucille Eaves, *Labor Legislation in California;* George F. Seward, *Chinese Immigration.*

56 (Page 199). Coolidge, *op. cit.*

57 (Page 199). *Statement and Brief on Chinese Question* before the Committee on Foreign Relations (1876), Senate Report No. 689, app.

58 (Page 199). James Bryce, *American Commonwealth,* II, 372; Hittell, *History of California,* IV, 595; H. H. Bancroft, *Works,* XXXVII, 662. Cf Constitution of California, 1878, Article 19.

59 (Page 199). Bancroft, *Works,* Vol. XXXV; Coolidge, *op. cit.,* p. 265; Hittell, History, Vol. IV.

60 (Page 200). Condensed from various sources. See *United States Foreign Relations* (1881), China, p. 320.

61 (Page 200). Their rights had previously been defined and protected

by the Burlingame Treaty, 16 Statutes at Large 740; and the Treaty of 1880 (22 Statutes at Large 827).

62 (Page 200). People versus Hall, 4 California Reports 399.

63 (Page 202). See *How the United States Treaty with China is Observed in California,* by Friends of International Right and Justice, for a complete account.

64 (Page 202). Ho Ah Kow versus Matthew Nunan, 5 Sawyer Reports 622.

65 (Page 203). B. S. Brooks, *Brief before Congressional Committee,* Appendix.

66 (Page 203). Senate Report 689, 44th Congress, 2nd session, p. 433.

67 (Page 203). Sidney L. Gulick, *American Democracy and Asiatic Citizen*ship, p. 37. On the Exclusion Acts see Hall, *Immigration,* chap. xv, 327 ff. and Chinese Exclusion Cases, 130 United States Reports, 581.

68 (Page 204). *United States Foreign Relations,* 1886, China, pp. 166-168.

69 (Page 206). This pamphlet contains many facts on the economic issues. Other information may be obtained in John Bassett Moore, *Digest of International Law,* VI, 820, 826-835; and Congressional Documents, 1885, numbers 2368, 2460, p. 109.

70 (Page 206). Mrs. S. L. Baldwin, *Must the Chinese Go?* pp. 35-36.

71 (Page 207). Judgment on Chinese was finally vested in the Secretary of the Treasury, Act of August 18, 1894 (28 Statutes at Large, c. 301, p. 390).

72 (Page 208). John W. Foster, "The Chinese Boycott," *Atlantic Monthly,* January, 1906, p. 122.

73 (Page 208). *Op. cit.,* p. 48.

74 (Page 208). Ex Parte Chin Loy You, 223 Federal Reporter 833.

75 (Page 208). This chapter, of course, does not attempt to cover the late manifestations of anti-Japanese sentiment—the decision by the United States Supreme Court that Japanese cannot become citizens because they are not members of the "white race," and the exclusion of Japanese altogether from the country by the Immigration law of 1924.

76 (Page 209). Gilbert T. Stephenson, *Race Distinctions in American Law,* p. 160.

77 (Page 209). Report of Secretary Metcalfe. (December 19, 1906).

78 (Page 209). For the international principles involved see A. S. Hershey, *Japanese School Question and the Treaty Making Power; Congressional Record,* December 12, 1906, speech by Rayner in the Senate; American Society of International Law, *Proceedings,* first annual meeting, April, 1907; S. L. Gulick, *American Democracy and Asiatic Citizenship,* and *American Japanese Problem; Japanese Immigrant Cases,* 189 United States 86. *Political Science Review,* I, 393, 510; Charles Butler, *Treaty Making Power.*

NOTES FOR CHAPTER VI

1 (Page 211). The purely legal struggles of labor, and the progress of labor legislation with respect to picketing, boycotts, combinations, and so orth are not treated in this study, save as injunctions may affect civil berty, and as illegal arrests may deny legal rights such as peaceful picketig. Labor and the law may be studied in J. R. Commons, *Trade Unionism nd Labor Problems;* Commons and Andrews, *Principles of Labor Legislaon;* G. G. Groat, *Attitudes of the Courts to Labor Cases,* Columbia Studies, LII; Harry W. Laidler, *Boycotts and the Labor Struggle;* F. J. Stimson,

Handbook of the Labor Laws in the U. S. Massachusetts Department of Labor, *History of Important Labor Cases*, Bulls. 70, 190; E. E. Witte, *The Courts in Labor Disputes*, Annual reports of the U. S. Bureau of Labor Statistics; *Decisions of the Courts on Labor*, Library of Congress, *References on Boycotts and injunctions.*

2 (Page 211). The story of labor itself, from the organization of the first national union of importance, The Brotherhood of the Locomotive Engineers (August 17, 1863), through the Knights of Labor, The Farmers' Alliance, The American Federation of Labor, down to the Industrial Workers of the World, can be studied in Commons, *et al., History of Labor in the U. S.*, II, *passim.*; R. F. Hoxie, *Trade Unions in the U. S.*; C. D. Wright, *Battles of Labor;* T. V. Powderly, *Thirty Years of Labor;* James C. Sylvis, *Life of William Sylvis;* Helen Marot, *American Labor Unions;* Morris Hillquit, *History of Socialism in the U. S.*

3 (Page 212). F. P. Dewees, *Molly Maguires;* Rhodes, "Molly Maguires," *American Historical Review*, XV, 547; Commons, *History of Labor*, II, 181-185; Allan Pinkerton, *Molly Maguires and the Detectives.*

4 (Page 212). E. W. Martin, *History of the Great Riots;* C. D. Wright, *Industrial Evolution*, pp. 201-301; Ohio Bureau of Labor, *First Annual Report;* Allan Pinkerton, *Strikers, Communists and Tramps.*

5 (Page 213). Robert Hunter, *Violence and the Labor Movement*, studies the use of violence by labor and by employers, anarchy (chap. vi, "Johann Most in America") and syndicalism (x. "The Newest Anarchism"). Chap. xi, "The Oldest Anarchy," is a statement of the use of violence against both workers and government that includes many violations of civil liberty since 1886, with a good bibliography.

6 (Page 213). Samuel H. Hays, Attorney-General of Idaho, Report on the Insurrection in Shoshone County.

7 (Page 213). See record in *United States v. Louis Salla,* Idaho Circuit Court of Appeals.

8 (Page 214). O. P. Briggs, *A Policy of Lawlessness,* a Partial Record of Riot, Assault, Murder, Coercion and Intimidation in Strikes of the Iron Molders' Union, 1904-1907. See account of Strike at St. Paul Foundry Co., May, 1908. For the other side see International Molders' Union of America, *History of Conspiracy to Defeat Striking Molders.*

9 (Page 215). Carrol D. Wright, *Labor Troubles in Colorado*, p. 149.

10 (Page 215). United States Bureau of Labor, *Bulletin 139*, pp. 43-44. For other details see Charles E. Russell, *These Shifting Scenes;* F. Dell, "On Dynamite," *New Review.*

11 (Page 216). Methods of American Private Detective Agencies, Appleton's Magazine, VIII, 444, October, 1906. See House Reports 2447, 52nd Congress, 2nd session, *Employment of Pinkerton Detectives;* House Miscellaneous Documents, Number 335, 52nd Congress, 1st session.

12 (Page 218). United States Bureau of Labor Statistics, *Bulletin 139*, p. 69.

13 (Page 218). United States Bureau of Labor, *Report on Strike at South Bethlehem, Penn.*, pp. 40-41.

14 (Page 218). J. A. Maurer, *Constabulary in Pennsylvania;* C. D. Wright, *Labor Troubles in Colorado.*

15 (Page 218). Industrial Commission of 1901, *Testimony of Geo. J. Thompson*, VII, 719.

16 (Page 219). *Confessions and Autobiography of Harry Orchard*, 1907; C. D. Wright, *Labor Troubles in Colorado*, pp. 169-191, gives a "frame-up" and fake confession; A. W. Ricker, *Spies in the Labor Unions*, covers the

same points; Morris Friedman, *The Pinkerton Labor Spy*, gives an intimate picture of such spies with quotations from reports purporting to have been made by Pinkerton operatives, as members of miners' unions in Cripple Creek, Colorado, and even as union officers.

17 (Page 219). Charles P. Neill, *The Strike at Lawrence*, Senate Document No. 870, 62nd Congress, 2nd session. In this case a later prosecution of the officers of the woolen mills was undertaken but without convincing results.

18 (Page 221). Wright, *op. cit.*, pp. 152-159 (condensed).

19 (Page 222). *International Socialist Review.*

20 (Page 222). A fuller discussion of this problem with cases is given in chapter VIII.

21 (Page 222). John Swinton, *Appeal to the Legislature*, Albany, March 24, 1874; Hillquit, *History of Socialism*, p. 200. Similar events took place in Chicago.

22 (Page 224). *International Socialist Review*, December, 1909; March, 1910.

23 (Page 226). Harris Weinstock, *Report on the Disturbances in San Diego* (condensed).

24 (Page 226). C. P. Neill, *Report on the Lawrence Strike*, Letter of Strike Committee.

25 (Page 226). The Right of Free Speech at Lawrence and Legal Aspects of the Lawrence Strike, *The Survey*, March 9, 1912, p. 509.

26 (Page 228). *Report*, p. 55. See Neill, *Report*, pp. 59-62 for tables of arrests.

27 (Page 228). John W. Brown, *Constitutional Government Overthrown*, p. 56.

28 (Page 230). Statement of the facts in the dissenting opinion of Justice McKenna in Pettibone *v.* G. Nicholls, 203 U. S. Reports 192.

29 (Page 230). In re Moyer, 12 Idaho Reports 250; in re Pettibone 12 Id. 264; see 118 Am. State Reports 214. See Hyatt *v.* Corkran, 188 U. S. 691.

30 (Page 231). Pettibone *v.* Nicholls, 203 U. S. Reports 192.

31 (Page 231). Pettibone *v.* Nicholls, 203 U. S. Reports 192.

32 (Page 233). All the above are from the *Hearings on House Resolution No. 6*, May 29, 1911.

33 (Page 234). *Hearings Before a Congressional Committee*, House Document No. 671, 62nd Congress, 2nd session, pp. 177, 304.

34 (Page 235). Report of the Agent for the Massachusetts Society for the Prevention of Cruelty to Children, *The Survey*, April 6, 1912, p. 71.

35 (Page 235). James P. Heaton, "Legal Aspects of the Lawrence Strike," *The Survey*, July 6, 1912, pp. 508-509. The general facts of this strike will be found in C. P. Neill, *Report on the Strike of Textile Workers, in Lawrence, Mass.*, Senate Document No. 870, 62nd Congress, 2nd session. November 1, 1913. In the copper strike in Michigan children were sent away without interference.

36 (Page 235). *International Socialist Review*, June, 1913, p. 850.

37 (Page 237). *Mother Earth*, VIII, 145.

38 (Page 239). Henry W. Ballantine, "Martial Law," *Columbia Law Review*, XII, 529-534. See also Resolution 31, House Military Committee, 56th Congress, 1st session; "Military Law in Colorado," *Army and Navy Journal*. For the whole problem see Winthrop, *Military Law and Prece-*

dents, Century Digest, XXXIV, secs. 6, 44; *Century Digest of Constitutional Law,* X, sec. 133; *Annotated* Cases, 1914-C, 1-56; Ex parte Merryman, *Taney's Reports 246;* U. S. *v.* Jackson, *Thayer's Cases,* II, 2354; Johnson *v.* Duncan, *et al.,* 3 Martin 530 (Louisiana 1815); Ex parte Moore, 64 North Carolina 80; James A. Garfield, *Works* (edited by Hinsdale), on Whiskey Rebellion, p. 143; Milligan Case, p. 162.

39 (Page 238). Commission on Industrial Relations, 1915, *Manley Report,* I, 49, 50, 57, 58.

40 (Page 238). Frank *v.* Smith (1911), Kentucky Reports.

41 (Page 239). Job Harriman, *The Class War in Idaho.*

42 (Page 240). Job Harriman, *The Class War in Idaho,* p. 25.

43 (Page 241). Samuel Hays, *Report to the Governor by the Attorney-General.*

44 (Page 241). In re Boyle, 6 Idaho 609; 96 American State Reports 286.

45 (Page 242). Carroll D. Wright, *Labor Disturbances in the State of Colorado* (1880-1904) with Correspondence, Senate Document 122, 58th Congress, 3rd session, p. 78.

46 (Page 242). See B. M. Rastall, *Labor History of the Cripple Creek District,* Univ. of Wisconsin Bull., p. 198.

47 (Page 243). Wright, *op. cit.,* p. 181-186.

48 (Page 243). Wright, *ibid.,* p. 216.

49 (Page 244). Wright, *op. cit.,* chap. xxv, 229-246, on Moyer Habeas Corpus Case.

50 (Page 244). In re Moyer, 35 Colo. Reports 159; 117 Am. State Reports.

51 (Page 244). Moyer *v.* Peabody, *et al.,* 148 Federal Reporter 870.

52 (Page 244). 212 United States Reports 78.

53 (Page 245). W. H. Glasscock (Governor), *General Orders,* Number 23.

54 (Page 246). State ex rel. Nance *v.* Brown, Dec. 19th, 1912, 71 West Va., 519.

55 (Page 247). In re Jones, *et al.,* 71 West Virginia Reports 567.

56 (Page 247). John Brown, *Constitutional Government Overthrown;* Report and Testimony of the West Virginia Mining Commission, appointed by Gov. Glasscock, Aug. 28, 1912; Senate Report 37, 63rd Congress, 2nd session, *Conditions in Paint Creek;* "Civil War in West Virginia," *The Survey,* April 5, 1913; "Sweet Land of Liberty," *Everybody's,* May, 1913.

57 (Page 248). Henry W. Ballantine, "Martial Law," *Columbia Law Review,* XII, 529-534. See also Resolution 31, House Military Committee, 59th Congress, 1st session; "Military Law in Colorado," *Army and Navy Journal.* For the whole problem see Winthrop, *Military Law and Precedence; Century Digest,* XXXIV, sections 6, 44; *Century Digest of Constitutional Law,* X sec. 133; *Annotated Cases,* 1914-C, 1-56; Ex parte Merryman, *Taney's Reports* 246; U. S. *v.* Jackson, *Thayer's Cases* II, 2354; Johnson *v.* Duncan, *et al.,* 3 Martin 530 (Louisiana, 1815); Ex parte Moore, 64 North Carolina 80; James A. Garfield, *Works* (edited by Hinsdale) on Whiskey Rebellion, p. 143; Milligan Case, p. 162; H. J. Hershey, *The Power and Authority of the Governor and Militia in Domestic Disturbances* (a partisan brief to the U. S. Commission on Industrial Relations, 1915); Francis Lieber, "Document 79 of War Dept.," *North American Review,* November, 1896.

58 (Page 248). John Swinton, *Striking for Life,* p. 98. Compare with

the refusal of the government to support postal rights in the South (1836), or to send troops into Missouri during the Mormon persecutions, or in 1904 to answer the appeal of Governor Peabody of Colorado for troops to suppress strikers, and the threat of troops against the Dorr government (1842), and the use against Coeur d'Alenes strikers (1899).

59 (Page 249). Grover Cleveland, *The Government and the Chicago Strike* gives the federal case; Swinton, *Striking for Life,* p. 445 ff., presents the labor view of this controversy. It may be noted that what may be called neutral evidence, *The Report on the Strike of 1894,* by the special United States Strike Commission, seems to show that there was no violence during the Pullman strike proper and very little at Chicago until the arrival of the troops. The Superintendent of the mails at Chicago declared that the mails were never delayed over twenty-four hours. Testimony brought out that much violence was provoked by agents of the railroads, or drunken marshals.

60 (Page 250). Commission of Industrial Relations, 1915, *Principal Report,* p. 52. See Commons, *Trade Unions and Labor Problems;* Hoxie, *Trade Unions,* pp. 234-235; Stimson, *The American Constitution,* pp. 48, 51, 65. Protests against government by injunction had become so strong that evidence was gathered in *Report and Hearings on Conspiracies and Injunctions,* by Judiciary Committee (1900), and in *Hearings of the Industrial Commission* (1901), VII, 610, 1035, and index.

61 (Page 251). Grover Cleveland, *The Government in the Chicago Strike,* p. 13. See Swinton, *Striking for Life;* and E. V. Debs, *The Federal Government and the Chicago Strike,* for the labor viewpoint. United States Strike Commission, *Report and Testimony on the Chicago Strike,* Senate Document Number 7, 53rd Congress, 3rd session, gives official data. W. F. Burns, *The Pullman Boycott, and* W. H. Cowardine, *The Pullman Strike,* are picturesque accounts of events.

62 (Page 253). The injunction can be read in full in U. S. *v.* Debs, *et al.,* 64 Federal Reporter 724-726.

63 (Page 253). Federal Reporter 724.

64 (Page 253). 158 United States Reports 564.

65 (Page 254). 62 Federal Reporter 828 gives Judge Grosscup's charge to the Grand Jury which returned the indictment; 65 Fed. 4, p. 210, his refusal to quash the indictment.

66 (Page 254). *Report of Commission,* I, 44, and V, 10, 771.

67 (Page 255). Hillquit, *History of Socialism,* p. 237, gives a proclamation of the Anarchists.

68 (Page 255). See also C. D. Wright, *Industrial Evolution,* p. 246; Powderly, *Thirty Years of Labor,* p. 81, and appendix which gives the platform of the Socialists (anarchists) of that day; F. T. Hill, *Decisive Battles of the Law* is a story of the trial, and Frank Harris, *The Bomb,* is a novel about these events. A legal view is in Joseph E. Gary, "Chicago Anarchists," *Century Magazine* for April, 1893.

69 (Page 256). John P. Altgeld, *Live Questions,* II, 34-46, "Reasons for Pardoning Fielden, *et al.*"

70 (Page 256). People *v.* Spies, *et al.,* 122 Illinois Reports 1-267.

71 (Page 256). 126 Federal Reports 253; 194 United States Reports 279.

72 (Page 258). John P. Altgeld, *Live Questions,* II, pp. 142 ff., "Reasons for pardoning Fielden, *et al.*"

73 (Page 259). See above Chapter V, p. 176, for statement on value of the 14th amendment. See President Taft's opinion in commuting the sentence of Warren. The case was Warren *v.* United States, 183 Fed. 718.

NOTES FOR CHAPTER VII

1 (Page 264). Frank J. Goodnow, *The American Conception of Liberty*, p. 21.

2 (Page 264). E. Freund, *Police Power*, pp. 9-11.

3 (Page 268). *Police Power*, p. 11.

4 (Page 268). C. G. Tiedemann, *Limitations on Police Power* (2 vols.), contains a discussion of these points.

5 (Page 268). *Loc. cit.*

6 (Page 269). Brunk *v.* Stratton, 176 New York Reports 150, decision by Justice Cullen of the Court of Appeals.

7 (Page 269). United States *v.* Moore, 104 Federal Reporter 78. The case arose over words published by Moore in' *The Blue Grass Blade*. The opinion of the court is in *The Truthseeker Annual* (1895). See also Theodore Schroeder, *Constitutional Freedom of Speech Defined and Defended*, chap. vi. For Chancellor Kent's opinion in the Ruggles case see above pp. 38-39, and Schroeder, *op. cit.*

8 (Page 269). Schroeder, *op. cit.*, is based on this case. See also *The Outlook*, CXV, 96-97.

9 (Page 270). See above chap. II for school question in Know-Knothing period.

10 (Page 270). Both major parties did the same thing in 1924. The present chapter does not consider the revival of the Ku Klux Klan, or modern anti-Semitism.

11 (Page 270). S. H. Cobb, *The Rise of Religious Liberty in America*, pp. 522-3.

12 (Page 271). People *v.* Pierson, 176 New York Reports 201.

13 (Page 271). For the text see MacDonald, *Selected Statutes* (1861-1898), p. 42.

14 (Page 272). United States *v.* Reynolds, 98 United States Reports 145.

15 (Page 272). United States Reports, 1-40.

16 (Page 273). John Nicholson, *The Tennessee Massacre*, p. 6.

17 (Page 273). See Clifford P. Smith, *Christian Science and Legislation*, (*passim*); Alfred Farlow, *The Relation of the Government to the Practice of Christian Science;* Peter V. Ross, "Metaphysical Treatment of Disease," *Yale Law Journal*, XXIV, No. 1, Nov., 1914; John D. Work, *The Public Health Service*, speech in United States Senate, January 5, 1915; Wm. A. Purrington, "Manslaughter, Christian Science and the Law," *Medical Record*, November 26, 1898. The basic English case against a parent for a failure to call in a doctor for a sick child is Regina *v.* Wagstaff, 10 *Cox Criminal Cases* 531.

18 (Page 274). *Proceedings*, Vol. IX. This volume will repay careful study. It lists many cases. See also above for freedom of speech and assemblage with respect to labor movements.

19 (Page 274). *Ibid.*, p. 4-5. The present volume is evidence that Professor Ross is inaccurate when he declares these rights were "established so long ago." They have never been established in fact.

20 (Page 275). Industrial Relations Commission, 1915, Principal Report, pp. 98 to 100, under "Policing Industry." See the testimony of Gilbert Roe, II, p. 10,471; Theodore Schroeder, p. 10,841; Samuel Gompers, p. 10,853; S. S. Gregory, p. 10,535; Harris Weinstock, p. 10,573; W. D. Haywood, p. 10,572. See Schroeder, *Free Speech for Radicals*, pp. 8, 100, *et seq. Case and Comment*, XXII, p. 455.

21 (Page 275). E. Freund, *Police Power*, sec. 165; see A. V. Dicey, *The Law of the Constitution*, chaps. vi and vii, and note v. He notes the basic English cases; Reg. *v.* Carlile, 6 C. and 'P. 628; Reg. *v.* Burns, 16 Cox C. C. 335; Reg. *v.* Ernest Jones, 6 State Trials (n. s.) 783, and Reg. *v.* Fussell, ditto, 723.

22 (Page 276). Proceedings, p. 16. Per contra, we must note the historic devotion of the Boston Common to public meetings; the establishment in Cleveland Civic Center of three formal stone pulpits, the inspiration of Mayor Tom Johnson; and the sensible liberality displayed by Col. Arthur Wood as Police Commissioner of New York City.

23 (Page 276). John Graham Brooks says, *op. cit.*, "I was in two company-owned towns in Colorado. . . . The school-houses (owned by the companies) could no more have been secured for free assemblages at that time than the Catholic Church could have been hired for an A. P. A. dance."

24 (Page 276). The complex legal aspects may be studied in the following cases: Gibbons *v.* Ogden, 9 Wheat, 211; U. S. *v.* Cruikshank, 92 U. S. 542 (see p. 552 for opinion on Bill of Rights amendments and list of other cases); Boyd *v.* U. S., 116 U. S. 616; Davis *v.* Massachusetts, 167 U. S. 43; State *v.* Hunter, 106 North Carolina 796; Fitts *v.* Atlanta, 121 Georgia 567; Commonwealth *v.* Abrans, 156 Massachusetts 57; Love *v.* Thalan, 128 Michigan 545; Citizens Bank *v.* Board of Assessors, 54 Federal 73; African Church *v.* City of New Orleans, 15 Louisiana 441; Daley *v.* Superior Court, 112 California 97; People *v.* Wallace, 85 App. Division, N. Y. 170; People *v.* Judson, 11 Daly (N. Y.) 83; People *v.* Tylkoff, 212 New York 197; Vanarsdale *v.* Laverty, 69 Pennsylvania 103.

25 (Page 278). Dr. Kate Baldwin, of Philadelphia, introduced a bill in the Pennsylvania legislature to legalize the birth control movement. The general crusade against the idea has subsided, and it has become in many places almost respectable.

26 (Page 279). Nations cannot agree on this question. In England, since 1900, the principle has been that the government has nothing to do with the guidance of public opinion, and that the sole duty of the state is to punish libels of all kinds. But in France and other Continental nations, it is held the right *and duty* of the state to guide the literature of the country. A. V. Dicey, *The Law of the Constitution*, chap. vi, "Right to Freedom of Discussion," quoting Dalloz, *Repertoire*, XXXVI. An Englishman lists these four principal conditions upon which freedom of discussion reposes: (1) a common faith in the rationality of the individual citizen; (2) a sense of external and internal security; (3) a conviction that discussion of any given subject cannot in the last resort be suppressed; (4) that the state must be the final arbiter of discussion for the sake of law and order. E. S. P. Hayes, *The Case for Liberty*, p. 59.

27 (Page 279). See chapter III. This refusal of equal service was justified by Attorney-General Cushing: "Congress does not assert its right to carry into a State, matter which the State regards as seditious or objectionable." 8 Cushing's Opinions 489.

28 (Page 280). Louis F. Post, editor of *The Public*, described the process: "The coterie would at first carefully limit the censorship to . . . matter most intensely offensive to public morals. A vast majority of the people, their thoughts centered upon offenses against morality and drawn away from offenses against liberty, would cordially approve the innovation. The courts, keen to see that a decision in favor of a minor offender would make a precedent, favorable to the repulsive class, would prefer making a precedent against liberty in the guise of a precedent for morality. . . . The censorship would then be extended to less offensive matter." "Our Advancing Postal Censorship," in *The Public*, VIII, 290-291.

29 (Page 281). In the principal lottery case the Court held: "The freedom of communication is not abridged, unless Congress is absolutely destitute of any discretion as to what shall or shall not be carried in the mails and compelled arbitrarily to assist in the dissemination of matters condemned by its judgment through the governmental agencies it controls." In re Rapier, 143 U. S. 110. See Clearing House v. Coyne, 194, U. S. 108.

30 (Page 281). "Nor can the department undertake to state what would or would not be mailable in advance of the matter being actually presented for transmission in the mails." Letter to the publishers of *The Public*, VIII, 819. The regular instructions to subordinates read: "The postmaster shall not give opinions to the public."

31 (Page 283). Louis F. Post, "Our Despotic Postal Censorship," *The Public*, VIII, 815.

32 (Page 283). *Report, with Hearings, on the Second Postal Rates*, by a Committee of Congress (1906-1907). Some 98 per cent of 4,652 weeklies, 999 per cent of 103 dailies, and 97 per cent of 186 monthlies, favored the right of court review. See pages 27, 32, 164, 495, and 676 for points in this connection.

33 (Page 283). Ex parte Jackson, 96 U. S. 733; Boyd v. United States, 116 U. S. 616; Arbitary Searches and Seizures, *The Greenbag*, XVIII, 273 (1906). Francis Leiber has some fine words on private correspondence in his *Civil Liberty and Self-Government*, chap. ix, 90-94.

34 (Page 283). In re Wahl, 42 Fed. Rep. 822 (May 12, 1890); 56 U. S. 604; 162 U. S. 420. Freund, *Police Power*, sec. 48 covers secrecy of letters and telephone messages.

35 (Page 284). Hoover v. McChesney, 81 Fed. Rep. 472.

36 (Page 284). It is possible that fraud orders may be inspired by special interests against those whose financial methods they disapprove. A fraud ban against the use of the second-class mails was issued against one E. G. Lewis, and his People's Bank, of St. Louis, Mo., based on the alleged financial condition of his bank. Later investigation failed to prove that the alleged condition had existed. It was charged that more orthodox financiers had instigated the suppressive action to rid themselves of a dangerous competitor for the people's savings. See Louis F. Post, "The Growing Power of Our Postal Censorship," *The Public*, VIII, 420; *Statement of the Postmaster General to the Press*, July 9, 1905; *House Reports*, No. 1601, 62nd Congress, 3rd session; Lewis v. Morgan, 229 U. S 288; United States Bank v. Henry J. Gilson, et al. (Opinion by Judge Smith McPherson, United States District Court, Eastern Missouri.)

37 (Page 284). Chapter III gives early cases of such prosecutions.

38 (Page 284). 17 Statutes at Large 599, c. cclvii, revising section 148 of the postal regulations. Congress has previously passed a less precise and embracing law (March 3, 1865), which was enlarged to include obscene matter on the outside of envelopes, June 8, 1872. The facts about the Comstock Law are noteworthy. "The history of the statute . . . is by no means creditable. It was one of the 200 acts passed as pendents to the Omnibus Bill by the corrupt Congress, notorious for the Credit Mobilier and Back Pay legislation, under the suspension of the rules during the last minutes before 12 o'clock P. M., and was signed with the same indecorous haste by the President who was sick in bed, and did not read them." C. L. James, *An Appeal to the Women of America* (pamphlet), p. 7, note. H. L. Mencken in the article "Puritanism as a Literary Force in *A Book of Prefaces*, p. 258, writes: "All opposition, if only the opposition of inquiry was overborne in the usual manner. That is to say, every Congressman who presumed to ask what it was all about, or to point out ob-

vious defects in the bill, was disposed of by the insinuation, or even the direct charge, that he was a convert defender of obscene books, and by inference, of the carnal recreations described in them." U. S. Criminal Code, pp. 211-212-245.

39 (Page 285). Now sections 1141, 1142, 1143 of the Penal Laws of New York. See Charles Gallaudet Trumbull, *Anthony Comstock, Fighter*, p. 157, for statistics of cases prosecuted by Comstock until his death (1915). See also Mencken, *op. cit.*, p. 258 ff.

40 (Page 285). *Report of the Trial of E. H. Heywood;* Boston *Globe*, Jan. 9, 1878.

41 (Page 285). 24 Federal Cases 14,571; 16 Blatch, 338; 30 N. Y. Supplement 361.

42 (Page 286). U. S. *v.* Harman, 45 Federal Reporter 414, affirmed in 50 Federal Reporter 921. See *The Kansas Fight for a Free Press* (pamphlet) by the Lucifer Publishing Co., Valley Falls, Kan., which reprinted the four offending articles, and *Arguments in Support of the Demurrer to the Indictment of M. Harman*, E. C. Walker and George Harman, by G. C. Clemens and David Overmeyer.

43 (Page 286). Louis Post, articles cited above, *The Public*, August 12, and October 12, 1905; March 6, 1906.

44 (Page 288). U. S. *v.* Bennett, 16 Blatchford, 368-9.

45 (Page 288). *Idem*, 362; People *v.* Muller, 96 N. Y. 411; U. S. *v.* Clark, 38 Fed. Rep. 734.

46 (Page 288). U. S. *v.* Heywood, see U. S. *v.* Bennett, supra.

47 (Page 288). U. S. *v.* Slenker, 32 Fed. Rep. 693; People *v.* Muller (see above) Anti-Vice Motion Picture Co. *v.* Bell, in *New York Law Journal*, September 22, 1916; Sociological Research Film Corporation *v.* City of New York, 83 Misc. 815; Steele *v.* Bannon, 7 L. R. C. L. series 267; U. S. *v.* Means, 42 Fed. Rep. 605, etc.

48 (Page 289). *Birth Control Review*, December, 1918. For prosecutions under various local ordinances see section on Freedom of Speech and Assemblage, page 277. The history of this movement in conflict with repressive opinion can be followed in Victor Robinson, *Pioneers of Birth Control*.

49 (Page 289). Margaret Sanger, *The Suppressed Obscene Articles* (pamphlet) contains the text of the three articles, "The Prevention of Conception," "Open Discussion," and "The Birth Control League."

50 (Page 290). Hobart Coomer *v.* U. S., 213 Fed. Reporter 1. The brief for Coomer presented to the Circuit Court by Theodore Schroeder contains some interesting points on the constitutionality of the prosecution.

51 (Page 291). United States *v.* Fred Warren (not reported in the digests).

52 (Page 291). For Taft's opinion see *Report of Federal Relations Commission of 1915*, p. 47; the case is Warren *v.* U. S., 183 Federal Reporter 718. The court repeated the old philosophy of the censorship: "The unrestricted use of the mails is not one of the fundamental rights guaranteed by the constitution. . . . Liberty and freedom of speech do not mean the unrestrained right to do or say what one pleases at all times and under all circumstances. . . . The idea of government implies some restraint in the interest of the general welfare, gradually enlarged . . . designed to exclude from the mails that which tends to debauch the morals of the people or despoil them of their property."

53 (Page 291). B. O. Flower, *Story of the Menace Trial*, pp. 19-29.

54 (Page 292). United States *v.* Bernarr Macfadden, 165 Federal 51.

55 (Page 292). Manifesto of Magon, *et al., Mother Earth,* II, 548.

56 (Page 293). Senate Document 426, 60th Congress, 1st Session.

57 (Page 293). See Lindsay Rogers, "Federal Interference with Freedom of the Press," *23 Yale Law Journal* (May, 1914); the *New York Sun,* March 24, 1908; cf. *27 Harvard Law Review* (November, 1913).

58 (Page 294). 25 Statutes at Large, 1129, chap. 321, sec. 211. See *Mother Earth,* III, 64; and 36 U. S. Statutes at Large, part 1, 1339, for the inclusion of arson in this legislative catch-all.

59 (Page 294). Whitman replied: "Yours of the 21st received with the curious list (I suppose of course from the district attorney) of "suggestions," lines, pages, pieces, etc., to be expunged. The list, whole and several, is rejected by me, and will not be thought of under any circumstances."

60 (Page 294). See Mencken, *A Book of Prefaces,* p. 270 ff. and an article by Channing Pollock in the *Bulletin of the Author's League,* March, 1917.

61 (Page 295). The case of the People *v.* August Muller, *96 New York Reports 408,* in which Muller was indicted, October, 1884, under section 317 of the Penal Code, of New York, for showing obscene pictures exemplifies the difficulty of defining the obscene, and the difference in view between the artist and the mass mind.

62 (Page 296). *United States Compiled Statutes,* 1916, p. 6389. The implication as to the possible morality (and perhaps competitive quality) of the foreign-born pictures is not without humor.

63 (Page 296). Mutual Film Co. *v.* Ohio Industrial Commission, *236 United States Reports* 230; Mutual Film Co. *v.* Hodges, 236 United States Reports 247.

64 (Page 296). Frolich and Schwartz, *The Law of Motion Pictures,* p. 383, *et passim.*

65 (Page 296). T. Schroeder, *Free Speech for Radicals,* p. 7.

66 (Page 297). 35 Colorado Reports 253.

67 (Page 297). Patterson *v.* United States, 205 United States Reports 464.

68 (Page 297). Henry Schofield, "Freedom of the Press," p. 114, in *Proceedings of the American Sociological Association,* 1914.

69 (Page 297). *Mother Earth,* Vol. VIII.

70 (Page 298). Cutler, *Lynch Law,* p. 229.

71 (Page 298). *The International Socialist Review,* July, 1910.

72 (Page 298). John Graham Brooks, *Proceedings of American Sociological Society,* IX, 16.

73 (Page 298). Federal Commission on Industrial Relations, 1915, *Report,* I, 55; *International Socialist Review,* June, 1913, p. 853.

74 (Page 299). Henry P. Brown, "Liberty of the Press," *American Law Review,* May-June, 1900.

75 (Page 300). Carroll D. Wright, *Labor Trouble in Colorado,* p. 187.

76 (Page 300). Wright, *op. cit.,* p. 261; Rastall, *Labor History of the Cripple Creek District.*

77 (Page 302). See above chap. VII.

78 (Page 302). Compare with the provision of a similar sort in the Alien Act (1798), above chap. II.

79 (Page 302). House Report 3492, by a Select Committee of the Two Houses; Senate Report 2333, by the Senate Committee on Immigration, February 22, 1893, 52nd Congress, 2nd session.

80 (Page 302). Edgar Lee Masters, *Brief in Turner's Case*, p. ii; *Compiled Statutes*, 1901, p. 1224.

81 (Page 303). *Congressional Record*, August 17, 1894, House Report 3472.

82 (Page 303). The outburst against anarchy was very intolerant. See James M. Black, "The Suppression of Anarchy," *American Law Review*, XXXVI, 190, and address to the New York State Bar Association, 1902; "The Prevention of Presidential Assassination," *North American Review*, No. 541, p. 173; Gen. Lew Wallace wanted to change the constitutional definition of treason "and for the suppression of such acts Congress shall have the power to do whatever it may judge requisite."

83 (Page 304). Congressional Record, XXXVI, part 1, p. 44.

84 (Page 304). See Edgar Lee Masters and Clarence Darrow, *Brief for Turner*, pp. 97-99, before the United States Supreme Court. This presents valuable statements on the principles of civil liberty involved in the anarchist exclusion act.

85 (Page 305). For the general right of the United States to expel persons dangerous to the State, see Fong Ting v. United States, 149 U. S. 698, and Teun v. Davis, 100 U. S. 257. The principle that an executive order from the immigration commissioner is final, constitutes due process of law, and will not be reviewed by the courts, had been declared after the Immigration Act of 1891 in Nishimura Ekiu v. United States, 142 U. S. 657.

86 (Page 306). *New York World*, July 19, 1908, letter by Emma Goldman. See the *New York Evening Post*, June 30, 1908, statement by Gen. Funston.

87 (Page 306). 126 New York Reports 108; 171 New York Reports 423.

88 (Page 307). See also T. Schroeder, *The Criminal Anarchy Law*, on suppressing the advocacy of crime, Publications of the Free Speech League, N. Y., 1907.

89 (Page 309). Goldman v. Reyburn, et al., 28 Pennsylvania District Reports 883. See *Proceedings of the Sociological Society*, quoted supra, p. 44.

90 (Page 309). "Detective Surveillance of Anarchists," *The North American Review*, CLXXIII, 615 (No. 540, Nov., 1901).

91 (Page 311). *Federal Commission on Industrial Relations*, 1915, testimony of Crystal Eastman on "The Political and Industrial Status of Women," II, 10,782.

92 (Page 311). Susan B. Anthony, *History of Woman's Suffrage in the United States*, I, 326, 329, 341; McMaster, *History of the United States*, VI, 490.

93 (Page 311). Anthony, *op. cit.*, I, 546, 571; 467-468.

94 (Page 311). McMaster, *op. cit.*, p. 284.

95 (Page 311). Anthony, *op. cit.*, p. 343.

96 (Page 311). Anthony, *op. cit.*, p. 338.

97 (Page 311). See above chaps. II and III; and McMaster, *op. cit.*, VI, 78. The files of *The Lily*, edited in New York by Amelia Bloomer, are interesting evidence.

98 (Page 311). E. A. Hecker, *History of Women's Rights*, p. 168;

McMaster, *History*, I, 125. The end is not yet here as is shown by the present agitation for a 20th Amendment to the Constitution, guaranteeing the privileges and immunities of men throughout the United States.

99 (Page 312). Bradwell *v.* Illinois, 16 Wallace's Reports 130; see Anthony, *op. cit.*, II, 601-626. In re Lockwood, 154 U. S. Reports 116 declares that the Virginia Supreme Court had a right to interpret the statute regulating admission to the bar, against women.

100 (Page 312). Anthony, *op. cit.*, II, 627. In Missouri Mrs. Minor sued an officer of election for refusing to accept her vote. In 1875, in this case, the United States Supreme Court decided that the Fourteenth Amendment did not confer the right of suffrage on all the citizens of the United States as one of their privileges and immunities.

101 (Page 313). Anthony, *op. cit.*, III, 446, 775.

102 (Page 314). *The Suffragist*, August 18, 1917.

103 (Page 316). *The Suffragist*, December 1, 1917.

104 (Page 317). F. J. Stimson, *Law of State and Federal Constitutions.*

105 (Page 317). See J. McKeen Cattell, *University Control;* Evans Clarke, *University Government* (unpublished).

106 (Page 318). See L. R. Whipple, *Our Ancient Liberties,* under religious liberties.

107 (Page 318). U. G. Weatherly, "Freedom of Teaching in the United States," *Sociological Society's Proceedings,* IX, 144-146; and *Ibid,* "Reasonable Restrictions Upon the Scholar's Freedom" by Henry S. Pritchett.

108 (Page 318). See Andrew D. White, *The Warfare of Science and Religion* (2 vols.).

109 (Page 318). White, *op. cit.*, I, 70-88, 313, and bibliography.

110 (Page 320). See *Report of the American Economic Association,* IX, 166.

111 (Page 320). *Proceedings of the American Psychological Society,* 1914.

112 (Page 321). See *Publications,* American Association of University Professors, II, No. 3, part 2; and Lightner Witmer, *The Nearing Case.*

113 (Page 323). See p. 273, *supra.*

FOOTNOTES FOR CHAPTER VIII

1 (Page 326). *Mother Earth*, III, 123.

2 (Page 326). *Ibid.*, June, 1913.

3 (Page 328). *The Manly Report*, recommendations I, *61.*

INDEX

A

Abolitionists, attempted extraditions of—91-92; deportations, 90; in Dorr War, 92; economic and social pressure against, 122-123; laws opposing, 89, 93; mob violence, 86-89, 94-100; postal censorship of, 109-114; problems in North, 93, in South, 85-92; purposes of, 84-85; suppression of free press and speech, 94-109; persecution of teachers sympathetic to, 118-122.

Academic freedom, see Teachers.

Adams, Abijah, prosecuted under Sedition Act—26.

Adams, John, Federalists under—20-23; prosecutions of Alien Act under, 24-25.

Adams, John Quincy, on Lovejoy—104; on right of petition, 115.

Adams, Thomas, charged with seditious libel—26.

Alarm, The, censored for anarchistic tendencies—297.

Algerine Laws, as affecting civil liberty—80-81.

Alien Act, provisions of—21-23; prosecutions under, 24-25; constitutionality of, 30; see Sedition Act.

Aliens, see Chinese, Japanese, Jews, Mexicans.

Allentown *Democrat and Republican,* attacked by mob—148.

American Civil Liberties Union—329.

Anarchists, Chicago—255-257; history of, 301; laws against, 301-305; New York Criminal Anarchy Law, 307; Obscenity Statute used against press of, 292; records, 308-309; State opposition to, 308-309.

Andrews, E. Benjamin, criticized for opinions—320.

Anthony, Susan B., in suffrage fight—312-313.

Anti-Federalists, violence against—11.

Appeal to Reason, suppressed under Obscenity Statute—290.

Art Students League, raided under Obscenity Statute—295.

Assemblage, freedom of, economic radicals denied—74-75; injunction against, 254; labor denied, 15-18, 217, 222; laws in South against, 89; ordinances against, 274-276;

Providence resolution, 79; under Know-Nothing Party, 61-63; violations in Civil War, 144-146; violation in Rhode Island, 11.

Aurora, prosecuted for seditious libel—20.

Avery, prosecuted for blasphemy—41.

B

Bache, Benjamin F., prosecuted for seditious libel—20.

Baltimore *Evening Transcript,* military suppression of—158.

Baltimore riots—52-54, 62-63.

Bangor, Maine, *Democrat,* barred from mails—151.

Banks, Prof. E. M., dropped from university for opinions—320.

Bassett, George Spencer, in faculty fight on negro question—194.

Bemis, Prof. E. W., dropped from university for opinions—319.

Bennett, D. M., prosecuted under Comstock law—285.

Bill of Rights, in American Revolution—3; interpretation, 12-14; proclaimed, 11-12.

Birney, James G., mob violence against—93, 101-103; rejected by college authorities for opinions, 120.

Birth control, arrests of agitators for—76, 277-278; federal action against, 288-289; opposition to, 262-263.

Blackstone, defines freedom of press—18.

Blanding, freedom of press case against—37.

Blasphemy, defined—19; prosecutions, 38-41, 269.

Boswell, C. H., arrested under military rule—300.

Boycotts, against authors—2.

Bridgeport *Advertiser and Farmer,* mobbed—149.

Broad Street riot against Irish—60.

Brooklyn *Eagle,* mailing privileges denied—151.

Brown, David, arrested for sedition—27-28.

Brown, John, used violence in abolitionist cause—84.

359

INDEX

Bruce, Eli, discriminated against because a Mason—56.

Bunker Hill, Idaho, labor insurrection—213.

Burke, John D., prosecuted under Alien and Sedition Acts—24.

Burns, Lucy, in suffrage fight—314-315.

Burnside, General, activities against civil liberty—136, 139, 155-156.

Burr, Aaron, writ of habeas corpus denied to—44.

Buwalda, William, imprisoned for shaking hands with anarchist—305.

Byrne, Ethel, arrested for imparting information on birth control—277.

C

Cable, George W., forced from South for attitude on negro—194.

Caldwell, J. B., prosecuted under Obscenity Statute—286.

Calhoun, Arthur W., dropped from faculty for opinions—320.

Callender, James Thompson, tried under Sedition Act—26.

Camp Chase, political prisoners at—140.

Catholics, convents violated—58-59; discriminations against, 270; election riots, 61; Know-Nothing party against, 57; persecution in schools, 63-64.

Censorship, of art—294-295; California law on, 299; literary, 294; under local police powers, 297; military and executive, 299-300; of morals, 284; of moving pictures, 295; of press, 285-296; State resolutions on, 113. See Postal Censorship, Obscenity Statute, Press.

Channing, Dr. William Ellery, protest against persecution of abolitionists—107.

Chase, Justice, opinions on Sedition Act prosecutions—25-27.

Chicago *Times*, suppressed—155.

Chinese, discriminations against—197-8; education of, 203; illegal arrests, 207-208; laws restricting, 200; mob violence against, 199, 203-206; Tacoma deportation, 206; Wyoming massacre, 205.

Christian Observer, government seizure of—150.

Christian Scientists, interference with rights of—273.

Cincinnati *Enquirer*, military suppression of—158.

Civil War, significance of—126, violation of civil liberties in, 127.

Clairvoyance, ordinances against—274.

Clapp, freedom of press case against—37.

Clay, Cassius, anti-abolitionist violence against—109.

Colleges, intolerance in—145.

Collette, Victor, prosecuted under Alien and Sedition Acts—24.

Colorado, against labor—241-3; federal troops against labor in, 248.

Columbus, Ohio, *Crisis*, destroyed by military—148.

Committees, of Correspondence and Safety, activities—7, formation, 7; local, powers of, 6-7.

Common Law, as part of constitutions—14; blasphemy prosecutions, 38-41; and freedom of press, 18; minority parties prosecuted at, 20; obscene publications and, 42-44; seditious libel in relation to, 34-37; of strikes, 15-18.

Comstock, Anthony, activities of—285, 287-288.

Connecticut *Courant*, prosecuted for seditious libel—34.

Conscientious objectors, resistance of—160-166. See Quakers, Dunkards.

Constitution, censorship forbidden by—20; interpretations of, 12-14; on rights of aliens, 196; State, failure to protect minority parties, 10; suspension during war, 129; violence over, 10-11.

Coomer, Hobart, prosecuted under Obscenity Statute—290.

Cooper, Myles, mob attack on—4.

Cox, Yancey, resisted the draft—166.

Crandall, Prudence, anti-abolitionist violence against—119.

Crandall, Dr. Reuben, prosecuted for abolitionist opinions—90.

Criminal conspiracy—15. See Labor.

Croswell, seditious libel case—36.

Cumberland *Alleghanian*, destroyed by mob—148.

D

Daily Victor Record, suppressed—299.

Debs, Eugene, imprisoned for disobedience to injunction—251-253.

Democrats, persecutions of, and by—62-63.

Dennie, Joseph, judge decides no verbal treason in case of—32-34.

Dorr, Thomas Wilson, elected governor—79; in Dorr government, 80-83.

Dorr War, history of origin—78; results of, 83; violations of civil liberty during, 81.

Dred Scott Decision, affecting negro—175.

Dreiser, Theodore, literary censorship of—294.

Dresser, Amos, persecuted as abolition agent—87-88.

Dunkards, in American Revolution—5; in Civil War, 165.

Dunster, Henry, disciplined for teachings—318.